ADVANCE PRAISE FOR

Elsie Ripley Clapp
(1879–1965)

"*Elsie Ripley Clapp (1879–1965): Her Life and the Community School* by Sam F. Stack, Jr. offers us an illuminating entrance not only into Clapp's life, work, and thought but also into a period of educational transition that is frequently studied but often misunderstood. We are indebted to him for his balanced and thorough research as well as his telling the story of Clapp's work, especially her emphasis on community and schooling. No doubt his research will become the standard work on her for decades to come and serve as a model for writing an educational biography."

Douglas J. Simpson, Professor and Helen DeVitt Jones Chair,
College of Education, Texas Tech University

Elsie Ripley Clapp
(1879–1965)

Alan R. Sadovnik and Susan F. Semel
General Editors

Vol. 42

PETER LANG
New York • Washington, D.C./Baltimore • Bern
Frankfurt am Main • Berlin • Brussels • Vienna • Oxford

SAM F. STACK, JR.

Elsie Ripley Clapp (1879–1965)

HER LIFE AND THE COMMUNITY SCHOOL

PETER LANG
New York • Washington, D.C./Baltimore • Bern
Frankfurt am Main • Berlin • Brussels • Vienna • Oxford

Library of Congress Cataloging-in-Publication Data
Stack, Sam F.
Elsie Ripley Clapp (1879—1965): her life
and the community school / Sam F. Stack, Jr.
p. cm. — (History of schools and schooling; v. 42)
Includes bibliographical references and index.
1. Clapp, Elsie Ripley. 2. Educators—United States—Biography.
3. Women educators—United States—Biography.
4. Community schools—United States—History—20th century.
I. Title. II. Series.
LA2317.C49 370'.92—dc21   2003011134
ISBN 0-8204-6842-8
ISSN 1089-0678

Bibliographic information published by **Die Deutsche Bibliothek**.
Die Deutsche Bibliothek lists this publication in the "Deutsche
Nationalbibliografie"; detailed bibliographic data is available
on the Internet at http://dnb.ddb.de/.

Cover design by Sophie Boorsch Appel
Cover photo of Elsie Ripley Clapp reprinted by permission,
courtesy of Barbara Ripley Myers Rahn

The paper in this book meets the guidelines for permanence and durability
of the Committee on Production Guidelines for Book Longevity
of the Council of Library Resources.

© 2004 Peter Lang Publishing, Inc., New York
275 Seventh Avenue, 28th Floor, New York, NY 10001
www.peterlangusa.com

All rights reserved.
Reprint or reproduction, even partially, in all forms such as microfilm,
xerography, microfiche, microcard, and offset strictly prohibited.

Printed in the United States of America

*To Mom and Dad,
who built
community through
love and compassion*

Contents

List of Illustrations ix

Acknowledgments xi

Introduction: Elsie Ripley Clapp (1879–1965)
   Her Life and the Community School 1

Chapter One: Hicks Street, Brooklyn Heights 7

Chapter Two: Growing Up: Adolescence 23

Chapter Three: Vassar College (1899–1903) 39

Chapter Four: Barnard and Columbia:
   The Beginning Teacher 55

Chapter Five: Elsie Ripley Clapp and John Dewey (1907–1912)
   Student and Teacher 77

Chapter Six: Learning by Living 89

Chapter Seven: Business, War, and Growing Confidence 111

Chapter Eight: The City and Country School 125

Chapter Nine: The Rosemary Junior School, 1924–1929:
   Greenwich, Connecticut 139

Chapter Ten: Ballard, Kentucky 1929–1934 163

Chapter Eleven: The Arthurdale Community School (1934–1936) 187

Chapter Twelve: The Later Years 211

Chapter Thirteen: Epilogue 235

Illustrations 241

Notes 251

Index 305

Illustrations

Figure 1. William Gamwell Clapp in 1879, the year of Elsie's birth 241

Figure 2. Elsie posing with her chinchilla muff 242

Figure 3. Elsie and her younger sister Marjorie 243

Figure 4. Elsie, her mother Sarah Louise Ripley Clapp, Marjorie and Lawrence Circa 1897 244

Figure 5. A nine-year-old Elsie posing with flowers 245

Figure 6. Elsie as a young girl 246

Figure 7. Elsie in her later teens 247

Figure 8. Elsie in her basketball letter sweater from Vassar 248

Figure 9. Elsie as a young woman ready to begin her career as a teacher 249

Acknowledgments

Special acknowledgment goes to Barbara and Sheldon Rahn, who provided access to Elsie's memoirs, photographs, and correspondence. They were always willing to answer my questions and provided gracious hospitality when I visited them. They read and commented on the manuscript, making sure personal information about Elsie was correct. The project would not have been possible without their assistance. I owe them my deepest gratitude for helping me gain a glimpse of a woman who contributed her life to progressive education.

I wish to thank Susan Semel and Alan Sadovnik for giving me the opportunity to work with them over the years as we all sought to better understand progressive education. We all hope our historical studies will give insight into current practice.

This project was supported by fellowship grants 1535 and 3024 from the West Virginia Humanities Council. I also received financial support from a West Virginia University Faculty Senate Research Grant and a small grant from the College of Human Resources and Education, West Virginia University.

I would like to acknowledge the assistance of the Center for Dewey Studies and the staff in Special Collections, Morris Library, Southern Illinois University. The registrars from Vassar and Barnard College provided information on Elsie's courses. The archivists at the National Archives in College Park, the University of Illinois, and Teachers College also provided important information about possible sources. The interlibrary loan department from West Virginia University provided invaluable assistance in locating secondary source materials. I would also like to acknowledge Arthurdale Heritage Inc. who allowed access to their materials through their museum and archives in Arthurdale, West Virginia.

Grateful acknowledgment is hereby made to copyright holders for permission to use the following copyrighted material:

Barbara and Sheldon Rahn, 2004. Elsie Ripley Clapp Memoirs (1879–1965), Elsie Ripley Clapp correspondence, and photographs of Elsie Clapp and family.

Katherine Salzmann, Manuscript Curator, Elsie Ripley Clapp Papers, Special Collections Research Center, Southern Illinois University, Carbondale.

Harold Forbes, "Arthurdale Homestead Project," A & M 2178, West Virginia Regional History Collection, West Virginia University Libraries.

Nancy Roosevelt Ireland, Eleanor Roosevelt Papers, Franklin Delano Roosevelt Library, Hyde Park, New York.

Finally I want to express my appreciation to my family, my wife Linda, daughters Katie and Ashley, and son Sam. Thanks for your patience when Dad needed to be left alone to write.

Introduction

Elsie Ripley Clapp (1879–1965) Her Life and the Community School*

Anyone who has ever approached writing a biography knows how daunting a task it is. Samuel Johnson, the English essayist and lexicographer, described biography as a type of narrative writing "that which is most eagerly read and most easily applied to the purpose of life." No species of writing, he believed, was "more worthy of cultivation than biography, none can be more delightful or more useful, none can more certainly enchain the heart by irresistible interest, or more widely diffuse instruction to every diversity of condition."[1] Ralph Waldo Emerson suggested that "There is properly no history: only biography."[2]

My personal interest in biography began as a child when I read with pleasure and delight the rather superficial stories of military heroes and athletes. Like most biographers I have an interest in studying people, what makes us think and act the way we do, what makes us tick. Reading biography helped me as a child better understand myself, the first step in relating and developing empathy toward others. George Herbert Mead argues in *Mind, Self, and Society* that you and I locate the self as the object of others. Mead goes so far as to see history itself as a series of biographies. The reflective self is a dialogue between the subject "I" and the social object "me," and, if pushed far enough, this forms the early foundation for community. Jack Campbell believes that studying the life of another is something human beings do to make sense of the world. In making sense of this world the subject "I" acts on the world and the world acts back—a type of transaction/interaction of the subject "I" and the social object "me." John Dewey referred to this type of transaction/interaction as experience and believed it took place best in the context of democratic community.[3] This was a central thread of progressive education.

Like that of many education historians, my interest in progressive education was stirred by reading Lawrence Cremin's *Transformation of the School* during graduate school. I began my study of progressive education by investigating community schools and writing a dissertation on the Parker School District in the textile community of Greenville, South Carolina, 1924–1951. The Parker School District, composed of numerous textile mill villages, adopted the philosophy of progressive education. The school district saw itself as the center of community life, and it was, but it sacrificed preparation for living in a democratic society for training students for work in the textile industry. One of the central goals in this work is to better understand the progressive notion of school and community and its relationship to democratic society. Relying on Cremin, I believe no clear definition of progressive education exists. It took many forms and interpretations.

Elsie Ripley Clapp (1879–1965) believed she understood Dewey's concept of democratic community and attempted to apply it through developing what she termed the "socially functioning community school." On several occasions she clearly articulated that her work was an expression of his ideas, but that is only one component of her work. This application of Dewey's theory does not make her the "dutiful daughter," but Elsie often contacted Dewey for advice, and he was more than a professional mentor for her, he was her friend.[4] A biographical study of Elsie Ripley Clapp provides the student of progressive education an excellent means to better understand the nature of the democratic community school. It is for this reason Elsie began to collect her own papers and those she had saved from Dewey. She wanted her work to be explored and understood.

Within the last two decades, Elsie Clapp's contributions to progressive education have been increasingly explored, largely in dissertations. Thomas Hutchenson writes that Clapp's plan for the Arthurdale School "serves as a manifesto for community education, stressing lifelong learning, the acknowledgment of the fundamental importance of trusting and encouraging people's own initiative and resourcefulness, diversity and individual talent, and a curriculum based on the special needs of the community."[5] Catherine Surdovel describes Elsie's work at the Ballard School in Kentucky as an excellent example of community education. She writes, "The loyal spirit that was generated in the hearts of its students and parents created outstanding community participation."[6] Using a postmodern approach, Diana Moyer suggests that studying the life of Elsie Clapp points out the problems of binary opposition, such as the use by educational historians of the categories "child centered" and "social reconstructionist." The use of such categories by progressive historians has created more confusion than clarification. People are rarely so easily bracketed. Moyer argues and is correct in claiming that Elsie fits in neither category. Moyer writes, "Clapp's practice like that of many progressive educators, exceeded the boundaries of the philosophical divisions that existed within progressive education."[7]

In her work *Pragmatism and Feminism*, Charlene Siegfried considers Elsie one of the lost women pragmatists "who exposed the deleterious effects of the artificial boundaries that isolated the school from its environing community." Siegfried further expresses her belief that the women pragmatists took Dewey "one step further by adopting the radical position that scholars ought to be or become members of communities plagued by the problems their theories are

INTRODUCTION

supposed to solve." When logistically possible, Elsie insisted her teachers live in and become active participants in their community. In further describing these women pragmatists, and most definitely Elsie Clapp, Siegfried writes, "They uniquely integrated their professional and personal lives, deliberately putting themselves in experimental situations for the purpose of answering their own needs along with those of others. Their experiments were experiments in community living as well as in community problem solving."[8]

Biographers and historians need access to primary and secondary materials. Primary materials can give us a better view of the human experience in a very personal way. In Elsie's case I was able to locate her autobiographical notes, which she wrote in the late 1950s, and other significant correspondence near the end of her career. With the aid of notes from the Clapp collection at Southern Illinois University, interviews with people who worked with her and with her family, plus her newly discovered correspondence, I believe we can gain an understanding of what she perceived to be her most important contribution to progressive education, the socially functioning community school. Through the use of primary and secondary materials I hope to make some sense of her life, not just what she did professionally but who she was. I have attempted to describe the epiphanies in her life, using her voice as much as possible. I will discuss her growing self-esteem, her perception of her appearance, her professional and personal relationships, the 1890s depression which devastated her family's finances, her health problems and her links to progressive education and what she perceived as her role as an educator.

By the time Elsie wrote her memoirs, the Progressive Education Association was no more and the journal to which she had contributed and then edited had also met its demise. I believe Elsie wrote her notes because she desired to express herself and to explain herself. In composing her autobiographic notes, Elsie is attempting to reach out and appeal to the reader saying, "this is who I am and I want you to know me."

Elsie wrote to articulate why she chose to spend her professional life applying the ideas of John Dewey in building the community school. She was trying to make sense of "the reality" of her life in writing.[9] She was also writing to make a genealogical record for her family, but it was for her contributions to progressive education that she wanted to be remembered.[10] Unfortunately, Elsie never finished writing her memoirs, and her writing stops just prior to one of her most important contributions in progressive education—her work at the Ballard Memorial School in Louisville, Kentucky. Why did she stop writing? We do not know. It is impossible to know whether the work was simply lost or whether she just stopped writing. If she did make a decision to stop writing, she may have perceived that her work, *Community Schools in Action* (1939) and *The Use of Resources in Education* (1952), were the keys to understanding her and her work and there was no need to further explain them or herself.[11] Fortunately I was able to locate personal correspondence just prior to the publication of her last work.

A biographical study of Elsie Ripley Clapp can give us insight into one of the best-known and respected women in progressive education circles. It is important for the voices of women like Elsie to be heard in order to grasp a sense of their struggles and their experiences. Women like Elsie took the ideas of progressive education to the front lines and put them into practice. Barbara Finkelstein writes that by studying the lives of women we can gain insight into how people transform lived experiences in human relations. Within this context, she asks us to pay attention to the "educationally highborn women" who can help "reveal the processes by which people transform lived experience into new human relationships, power hierarchies, status definitions, educational arrangements and civic influences...."[12] "For female progeny of the educationally highborn," Finkelstein explains, "biographical stories disclose privilege and restraint, educational riches and political and economic properties. For these young women, the family defined, organized, managed—indeed constituted—the first community within which they acquired the rudiments of learning and the adornments of language."[13] Elsie clearly fits the definition of the "educationally highborn." Writing about the use of biography and private voice, Janet Miller emphasizes that biography can provide for us a means to understand how historical, cultural, economic, social forces influence the lives of teachers. She believes biography "can provide insight into how educators, influenced by particular historical moments and contexts, constructed versions of themselves as educators."[14] Norman Denzin suggests that the primary obligation of the biographer is to the subject, yet at the same time I wish to make a significant contribution to what we know and understand about education through allowing her to share her experiences. The biography, the story of a life, can help us better grasp the human side of education, a process where we learn to reflect, imagine, critique, and understand. I hope through the historical method of biography to capture this sense of Elsie Ripley Clapp although I realize there will never be a perfect picture of her.

Good educational biography is a testimony to the dignity of the human being, the dreams, the sacrifices, and the hopes of the individual. According to Kathleen Weiler, the last twenty years have seen a strong impetus to acknowledge "the lives and world of women teachers."[15] While this is true, much more needs to be done to address those educators like Elsie Clapp who worked beyond the traditional boundaries and limits of progressive education. Elsie Clapp brought progressive education to two rural public schools in Appalachia, in Kentucky and West Virginia, states still racked by economic hardship. Elsie could be described as a "practical visionary," a woman, "driven by an imaginative mission, using education as a field of endeavor to improve society in many and various ways."[16] She was never the political revolutionary, nor was she a radical feminist although she knew many and worked with some. Elsie's life does need to be studied, not simply because through extensive research she has "been found," but because her life and her work can serve to illustrate many of the contemporary issues surrounding education in a democratic society, our triumphs and our failures. Following the advice of Ivor Goodson, I have tried to tell Elsie's story cognizant of the social, economic, and political forces that influenced her personal existence and her pedagogy but also aware that we may need to scrutinize and critique her view of the community school.

Why educational biography? For me, educational biography serves a purpose. In my own philosophical bias as a critical pragmatist, I see biography as a means to an end and then to further means. Through studying the lives of educators, we can get a glimpse into the social microcosm of the classroom. We can learn about human relations, gender, class, ethnicity, resistance, and curriculum. For Elsie this includes her personal struggle to resist the hegemony of the "cult of domesticity," the role of the Victorian woman. We can gain insight into the power of social, political, and economic forces and how they affect individual lives, communities, and thus education.[17]

I make no claims in trying to write Elsie's story from the view of an objective, dispassionate observer. We make far too many mistakes in trying to explain or predict human behavior. I am attracted to her because of her attempt to put into practice the idea of community, which I believe can enhance our understanding of democracy and the school's role in our society. Her point of view as a practitioner is vital to keep in mind. At times I like her immensely, but at times she seems the insensitive, spoiled brat of her youth and elitist Brooklyn Heights upbringing. In retrospect, at times Elsie saw herself this way. She critiques her own insensitivity. I hope the reader will find Elsie's story informative, illuminating, and entertaining, but I do also hope the reader will engage her in a dialogue to better understand not just what she did but who she was and why she dedicated her life to developing the community school. Elsie believed that education, like life, is a process of learning through our daily experiences. This best takes in community. For Elsie Ripley Clapp, that process of learning, engaging the experience of the learner best took place where the school was the center of community life. What follows is her story.

Chapter One

Hicks Street, Brooklyn Heights

Elsie Ripley Clapp was born on November 13, 1879, in Brooklyn Heights, New York. Brooklyn Heights faced the waterfront and attracted people who did not wish to live in Manhattan. Now a historic district, the location and architectural styles attracted prominent residents in the 1870s and 1880s. Residents included Washington Roebling, who oversaw the construction of the Brooklyn Bridge, and later the well-known minister Henry Ward Beecher. The growth of Brooklyn Heights was further stimulated by the Fulton Ferry Terminal, which eventually provided reliable service in commuting to New York City. Seeing a lucrative investment, Brooklyn Heights developers began to build row houses that varied in design. The architectural styles of the individual homes reflected the wealth of the owners and the popular styles of the period. By the time of Elsie Clapp's birth, the Heights was known for its affluence and prosperity. Prosperity led to significant developments in religious, social, and educational organizations. The prosperity of the Brooklyn Heights residents led to further investment in the community, the most outstanding examples being churches, e.g., Grace Church, a Gothic revival structure built in 1847 on Hicks Street. Elsie was familiar with this and other architectural landmarks of the day and they fascinated her.

Elsie's childhood years in Brooklyn Heights centered around the family, the neighborhood and homes of her relatives, cousins, and grandparents. All were within easy walking distance. Her home at 176 Hicks Street was located on the far southern end. In her autobiographical notes, Elsie described this world in amazing detail, giving a brief history of Brooklyn Heights. "In the 1600s, Brooklyn Heights was inhabited by Carnesie Indians who gradually drifted away as Dutch settlers on Manhattan bought their land. In the 1700s the Hill, covered with hickory, oaks and walnut trees, sloped down to a beach on which a few Dutch houses stood flanked by cabbages and tulip beds. Toward the end of the century it had become an area of orchards, rough pastureland and sandy stretches where pigs, cows, and horses roamed. By the end of the War of 1812 Clover Hill was occupied by a group of farmers who sold their fruits and vegetables in Manhattan. It was in 1841, the year that the city of Breuekelen received its charter, that my Grandfather George Clinton Ripley and his bride, Hannah Bass Penniman, came to Brooklyn Heights to live."[1] The family had moved from Boston on November 24, 1841.

As a young child, Elsie Clapp spent much of her time in the home of her maternal grandparents, the Ripleys who lived at 164 Hicks Street. One can easily visualize her grandparents' home through her description. Elsie fondly recalled the "shape of the mantle shelf over the fireplace... the plate glass front windows covered with stiff white lace curtains." From the windows she watched the people passing by, "grocery boys delivery basket on arms, darting in and out of areaways and the lamplighter who came along at dusk to put his long torch to the corner glass lamp." "They were out in the world where I longed to be," Elsie wrote, "but during my childhood I felt destined forever to be someone who just looked on at life passing by." These feelings of insecurity would diminish some as Elsie entered high school, yet as a young woman she constantly searched for self-identity, to break out of the traditional gender role and rigid boundaries of the late nineteenth century Victorian woman.[2]

Family life at 164 Hicks Street centered in the back parlor, a room dominated by a marble fireplace and a tall walnut bookcase. Folding doors opened into the front parlor, closed during the winter months to conserve heat. In the comfort of the back parlor, Grandfather Ripley, with his "snow white hair," read aloud one of the Psalms from a thin leather-covered book. "He read these well," Elsie recalled, "and at the time I thought the language gorgeous. Then each person rose and knelt by the side of his chair for a silent prayer. In the winter months, Grandfather would sit reading his paper, feet outstretched over the register while Grandmother sewed or knitted; we children made popcorn over the grate fire."[3] "In the center of the room," Elsie noted, "was a round table where Grandmother sewed or knitted and on it a wrought-iron lamp with a white alabaster shade, each of its eight sides embossed with scenes that glowed in the light. When the servants went up to bed they stopped in to leave a dish of fruit and a knife with which Grandmother would peel an apple, cutting it into thin cross-sections, while we waited with our mouths open."[4] Elsie recalled her grandfather spent much time at a large "table covered with green baize at which he did a great deal of writing." "All children personalize their surroundings," Elsie wrote years later. "In any case, a child's memories of the world he lives in, so important to him are especially vivid. It is a small world no taller than himself, filled with his experience and the things he sees, touches, hears and smells." Although Elsie had made numerous trips to Hicks Street as an adult, she recalled certain characteristics of her childhood with incredible detail. Her childhood interest in architecture remained with her for life.[5]

Like many houses in Brooklyn Heights, 164 Hicks Street had "a stoop or high flight of front steps, flanked on either side by ornamental railings. At the top of these steps were heavy double doors which could be closed in bad weather. Between them and the house door, the upper half of which had central and side panels of glass frosted in an elaborate design, was a vestibule paved in

CHAPTER ONE 9

black and white marble squares where we children played marbles and jack stones by the hour." In the elite and class-defined world of Brooklyn Heights, delivery boys and servants did not enter through the front door but through the basement area. The basement area at 164 Hicks Street included a dining room, baking room, kitchen, and pantry. On Saturday mornings, Grandmother Ripley "wearing a big apron over her black silk dress and her spectacles pushed up into the square of lace she wore on her head, baked pies, cakes and cookies." "Squeezed in among the barrels of flour that lined the little room," Elsie wrote, "we children watched all that went on, and of course enjoyed the scrapings." The dining room was "furnished with an oval mahogany table and a sideboard over which hung a picture of Mary, Queen of Scots." In the kitchen Elsie remembered a built-in stove and a table covered with a red-checkered cloth where the servants worked and entertained friends. The servants lived in the third floor attic, where Elsie recalled seeing boxes of seashells they had brought from Ireland and also rosaries hanging by the mirror.[6] Writing years later, Elsie remembered one of the Irish servants of her grandparents, Mary Rooney. According to Elsie the servants were "loyal, cheerful and kindly, they identified themselves with the lives of the families in which they worked; to this day they are held in loving remembrance." In reality, Elsie's world was quite different from the world of her Irish nurses. Prior to 1920, domestic service was the dominant occupation for Irish women. Most were uneducated and housework was the only work often made available to them. Domestic service meant "long hours, heavy work, lack of freedom and isolation."[7] Elsie did not rely on her memory alone in her description of the Irish. In retrospect, this is an interesting statement for her to make given her liberal, although never radical, politics in later years. How could the Irish servants actually identify with the families they served? Due to prejudice and stereotypes, Irish women in this era had little choice but to work as servants or domestics, and it is unfortunate we cannot hear the voice of Mary Rooney.[8]

One of Elsie's favorite spots at her grandparents' home was the garden under the careful and nurturing guidance of Grandmother Ripley. "The soil of Brooklyn Heights where farms had once flourished was still rich," Elsie noted, trees lined the streets, magnolias grew in side gardens and in their back yards people raised flowers and flowering shrubs, even berries, grapes and fruit trees. In the large backyard of 164 Hicks Street flowerbeds surrounded a central grassplot, separated by paved walks. On these Anna Ripley and I used to jump rope and play hopscotch; in midmorning when Mary Rooney called us we went to sit on the bench under the house awning and have sponge cake and lemonade."[9] "Grandmother Ripley's garden was a lovely spot," Elsie fondly recalled, " and beautifully cared for." Professionally manicured, the garden contained rosebushes, lilies of the valley, scarlet salvia bushes, geraniums, petunias, and pansies. "Rosebushes filled one whole side of the garden," Elsie described, "and the other held white and lavender lilies, bleeding heart and fuchsia. The garden was ours," Elsie remembered, "but though we sometimes took a leaf of sweet geraniums or lemon verbena to crush and smell, we picked the flowers only at Grandmother's request. I still remember the joy of plunging one's hand among the leaves to gather lilies of the valley, Grandmother's favorite flower."[10]

Due to age, Grandmother Ripley rarely left the house at 164 Hicks Street other than to take a carriage ride usually with a relative to pick flowers, or go to church. "Sometimes I went too," Elsie recalled, "perched on a little seat facing them, dressed in black silk mantillas and carrying tiny ruffled parasols, they both wore black bonnets that tied under the chin."[11] Born in 1812, Elsie's grandmother was in her seventies when Elsie was young and was nearly deaf. Elsie enjoyed reading to her from the newspaper and from a devotional guide titled *Daily Thoughts for Daily Living* which Grandmother Ripley kept on her bedside table. Deeply interested in religion, Grandmother Ripley prized visits from her local pastor, Charles Cuthbert Hall of the First Presbyterian Church, and expressed her joy to young Elsie when Pastor Hall convinced her it was not necessary to believe in infant damnation, a Calvinist doctrine that had always bothered her.

As a young girl, Elsie spent much time with her grandmother in the sewing room, just off the bedroom. While her grandmother knitted, Elsie sometimes held a skein of yarn while her grandmother wound the knitting ball. Sometimes she played with the box of buttons while her grandmother told stories where and how the various sets of buttons had been used. Once Elsie spilled a bottle of glue on the carpet and recorded her Grandmother's response. "All Grandmother said as she got down on her knees to clean up the mess was, accidents will happen in the best regulated families. I have always remembered this instance of her tolerance and kindness." Apparently this tolerance and affection spread beyond the family, and as a young child Elsie was astonished at all the people who came to call on her Grandmother Ripley, not only friends and relatives, but also "old Irish servants who came in their best bonnet and shawl to pay respects to Mrs. Ripley."[12] Elsie had great respect for her Grandmother Ripley, confided in her, sought her advice and saw her as a friend. As a young girl Elsie did not seek this kind of solace from her mother or her father.[13]

Young Elsie Clapp also deeply admired and loved her maternal grandfather, George Clinton Ripley. Named for New York's Governor Clinton, Elsie described her grandfather as an "able and trusted officer of the Home Life Insurance Company whom many considered austere, even forbidding [but] was—as we children knew—above all else companionable." With nostalgia Elsie wrote, "I was entirely content reading with him by the fire in the back parlor—he in his armchair with the paper and I stretched out on the rug beside him, poring over Audubon's bird book or an illustrated copy of Stanley's *Darkest Africa*. Usually silent, he listened to us by the hour. As I grew older, I began to realize Grandfather's force and quality and gradually began to know more about his interests. Despite his reputed Puritanism, he loved music."[14]

Grandfather Ripley loved music as much as he loved reading, helping the First Presbyterian Church obtain an organ and making music a more vital part of the church service. He served on the Board of Directors and helped establish the Philharmonic Society of Brooklyn. He also served as president of the Long Island Historical Society and its museum. Elsie recalled the exuberance she experienced as a child poking among the varied and unsorted articles in the Museum and "the thrill of finding stuck away in a dark corner, a framed copy of the Declaration of Independence…. Sitting on the floor, the better to read its faded writing," Elsie recalled, "I copied in pencil on a school pad the entire document and with the wish to share my latest treasure, gave it to my mother." Elsie attempted to impress and receive praise from her mother, something she greatly desired, throughout her childhood. She did not record her mother's response.[15]

Elsie Clapp's deep love for American history was inspired by her grandfather as she listened to discussions in the parlor between men of note invited to her grandfather's home. Grandfather Ripley shared with Elsie his involvement with the Underground Railroad and his support of antislavery. When his local pastor refused to read the Emancipation Proclamation in 1863 from the pulpit, Grandfather Ripley read it "from start to finish" from the steps of the church, his audience consisting of a few grocery boys and a few passers-by who stopped to listen.[16] When Elsie and her family moved into Grandfather Ripley's home following the family's economic misfortune in the 1890s depression, Elsie cared for him. She remembered he "was restless, apt to wonder away in search of Grandmother and his lost youth. We were still companionable and he told me stories of his early experiences and of his courtship with Grandmother."[17] George Clinton Ripley passed away in October 1895, at the age of eighty-three, but his influence on young Elsie remained for a lifetime. He showed her a quiet, compassionate demeanor, yet at the same time he showered generosity on the church, community, servants, and other family members he cared for. Through him, young Elsie gained an appreciation for the past, becoming a student of history, which later served her well in her challenge to traditional pedagogy and subject matter and in her own attempts to help students gain a sense of the past to better understand themselves. Grandfather Ripley opened a new world for a young woman who often felt isolated and trapped in the traditional female role of the Victorian era coupled with her affluent lifestyle. Elsie Clapp saw in her maternal grandparents wisdom, kindness, and understanding.

Their home was a place where children could feel safe; it was stable and a place to enjoy. This was her true home, not that of her parents.[18]

Elsie's love of history was further stimulated by her mother's sister, Mary Churchill Ripley, who lived next door at 178 Hicks Street. "I wish I knew how to convey the kind of person Auntie was," Elsie fondly wrote, "for in my childhood and during later years she was a source of stimulation." Auntie, as Elsie called her, would regularly come in the afternoons to play with her and her younger siblings, Marjorie and Lawrence. Marjorie was born in 1884 and Lawrence in 1886. Auntie drew elaborate charts detailing important events in history. Elsie explained: "With her we made History Paper Dolls, representing the English Kings and Queens and their children. But of all the things she did with us the one I best recall was her of drawing charts of civilizations—great concentric circles drawn on sheets of paper in which were entered events from earliest times to the present. To these charts, or to Auntie rather, I owe in part at least my enduring interests in history."[19] Grandmother Ripley and Auntie were two women young Elsie seemed to love and respect, yet she seemed most attracted to the active lifestyle of Grandfather Ripley and her father, William Gamwell Clapp, as she listened frequently to parlor discussions of politics and the news of the day.[20]

Elsie's father, William Gamwell Clapp, was born on March 15, 1853, and was the oldest son in his family. He attended Lehigh College in Bethlehem, Pennsylvania, but left college early to help his father, George Moseley Clapp, in the Washington Iron Works. George Moseley Clapp, Elsie's paternal grandfather, was general manager of the iron works and had asked his son to take the position of bookkeeper because the former bookkeeper had escaped with the firm's money. The foundry was located at Newburgh-on-the-Hudson. Over the years according to Elsie, the iron works had manufactured machinery for sawmills, oil wells, and steam engines and during the Civil War built two monitors for the government. A monitor was a generic term for a warship on which one or two guns rotated on a turret. The vessels were iron plated to avoid penetration by enemy cannon and were the prototypes of modern warships. According to Elsie, one of the monitors constructed by the Washington Iron Works, the *Sunapee*, was sunk in the Battle of Mobile.[21] Elsie remembered her grandfather Clapp as a "cheerful and genial man, hospitable and generous and deeply loved in his home. He loved music and played the organ." "Grandfather Clapp, a big brown man," Elsie noted, " had a way of wrinkling up his nose and shifting his eyes until his glasses, which he wore on a ribbon, fell off, a trick I found very engaging." Elsie described Grandmother Clapp as having a "cameo-cut face and her air of serenity very beautiful; nothing seemed to ruffle her, yet she was warm and responsive." "The family it seemed to me," Elsie wrote, "were always singing as a group, in duets or trios. Father, I thought, must miss that at our house."[22]

CHAPTER ONE

Elsie described her father much as she described Grandfather Ripley. "Memories of my father are among the happiest of my childhood," she recalled, "he radiated a sense of well being and was full of fun, and we loved to be with him. I can still remember the eagerness with which we listened for his key in the door at night. He had a gift... of making you feel that something special happened when he came into a room." Others enjoyed his gaiety and his charm. He was a great favorite with Grandmother Ripley, and he and Auntie shared many jokes. Elsie's father was popular and had a large circle of friends. Well read, his library contained copies of Gibbon, Prescott, Thackeray, Milton, and Dickens. This early exposure to literary classics stimulated Elsie's love of history, music, literature, and the arts. Elsie's father and mother were gifted musicians, her father an excellent vocalist and her mother a pianist. "One of my early memories," Elsie noted, "is Father sitting on my bed and singing to me while I endured the miseries of a homemade mustard plaster."[23]

Sarah Louise Ripley, Elsie's mother, was a gifted musician and had honed her skills at Vassar where she had participated in at least four piano concerts. Elsie occasionally attended the Brooklyn Philharmonic with her mother. "She brought along the score of the symphony," Elsie recollected, "and later discussed the conductor's interpretation of the work. I have since appreciated the training she gave me in analyzing the symphony's structure, in identifying its themes and noting their recurrence and variations which has so much increased my understanding of symphonic music."[24] Elsie sought to emulate her mother's skills at the piano to no avail. "I remember spending weary hours at the piano practicing to a metronome and Mother's voice calling down from upstairs at the slightest mistake. Herself a gifted pianist... she had little tolerance of the fumbling efforts of a young beginner so, though she ardently desired that I learn to play—a desire I shared—her impatience soon disheartened me and my efforts ceased." Elsie Clapp sought her mother's love and admiration, yet as a child she never seemed good enough, either in appearance or in her musicianship.[25] Sarah Ripley Clapp exemplified what Barbara Welter describes as the nineteenth century "cult of true womanhood." Welter grounds the "cult of true womanhood" in four virtues: piety, purity, submissiveness, and domesticity. From Elsie's description of her mother, it is clear that submissiveness and domesticity are issues. Within the "cult of womanhood," a woman's identity was directly connected to the goals and aspirations of her husband and only within the institution of marriage. The ideal nineteenth century woman concerned herself with charity, running an efficient household, bearing and taking care of children, and mastering needlework in all its varied forms. She was also to have an affinity for flowers, fancy adornment, and good taste. The stability of the family and the society depended on her acceptance of these traditional hegemonic cultural norms. While she notes many of these characteristics in her mother, Elsie rejects the majority of them even as they attempt to dominate her in her own search for identity.[26]

Elsie's relationship with her mother was strained, and Elsie rejected many of her mother's values defining gender role. Writing in retrospect, Elsie claimed that as a child she did not like her mother very much. She described her mother as "imperious and insistent, with a quick temper and a sharp tongue, and she and I got on none too well. In general, I spent my time with my cousins the Ripleys and at Grandmother Ripley's and actually saw little of her. As a child I never forgave her for not being a regular mother; never once that I remember did she dress or undress me, or do any of the little things for me that the mothers of most children did. And I was a disappointment to her: I was homely; I hated social functions, and we shared few interests." Once her mother spanked her. Elsie remembers having said to her mother, "You've no right to touch me. I'll never speak to you again." Elsie maintains she kept this promise "for many weeks. After this episode Mother reasoned with me—a pretty discouraging business, I imagine—for at the end I would say, 'No, I am not sorry'."[27]

Nevertheless, Elsie considered her mother very attractive and wished to look like her. "Mother seemed to me to be a kind of fairy princess," Elsie noted. To make her nose more pointed, like her mother's, young Elsie sometimes slept with a clothespin attached to her nose. "My nose, I thought, studying my reflection in the mirror, was the main problem," she recalled, "something could be done about that."[28] Compared to her younger sister Marjorie, Elsie was considered the ugly duckling. This was clearly pointed out to her when one of the Irish servants remarked, "You ain't near as goodlookin' as your sister, are you? But, there, they do say as how the ugliest come out all right in the end."[29] Seeking immediate assurance that she was not ugly, Elsie sought out her mother, who told her that regardless of appearance she possessed other virtues. "Her assurance that I possessed other virtues did not console me at all," Elsie recalled. "Although, like everyone, I admired my sister with her golden-brown hair, high color and hazel eyes, I had never considered my own looks."[30] Her mother's response only reinforced Elsie's concern about her appearance and her perceived homeliness. Throughout her life, Elsie Clapp never saw herself as pretty and was more of a tomboy, more active than passive, not the Victorian image of the ideal young lady. Even as an adult Elsie was self-conscious about her appearance and was rather camera shy. Elsie remembered one picture of herself, "a fat little girl in a plush coat with a chinchilla muff." Elsie saw her mother as spoiled, a process that began in her mother's childhood but was exacerbated by her father's lavish gifts. These gifts included expensive laces, combs, fans, and jewels. "Each year," Elsie recollected, "Father brought her linen sheets and pillowcases, tablecloths and napkins all embroidered by the nuns in Ireland, jewels from Tiffany's in Paris, and from Liberty's in London the silks which she so prized."³¹ In reality, family photographs from the era show that Elsie looked much like her mother. They shared many interests and characteristics, some of which Elsie would nurture and others she would discard.

Regardless of their differences, Elsie felt her mother's influence. "I can see that she made a strong impression on me," Elsie wrote, "and succeeded in getting me to adopt—her idea of poise—meeting any and all happenings imperturbably—and her code of reticence—no talk about one's own or the family's affairs and no discussion whatsoever about the affairs of others."³² As an adult Elsie did become closer to her mother, even becoming friends with her, yet as an older child Elsie sensed an arrogance and lack of significance in the lifestyle of her mother and her friends. Elsie, her mother, and Grandmother Ripley often spent time together on shopping trips to New York. On a typical shopping day they traveled on the Wall Street ferry up to the shopping district on West 23rd Street where Stern's, McCreery's, and Altman's were located. They made an occasional trip to Tiffany's or lunched at the St. Denis Hotel, which, Elsie noted, was "famous for its Vienna rolls and for its coffee or chocolate topped with whipped cream after which we caught fascinating glimpses of other people's so-different lives through the windows of the houses we passed."³³ "The Wall Street ferry trip home was always fun," Elsie recalled, "in winter we would watch the chunks of ice floating in the River and jamming up against the piles as the boat came into its slip and was secured through ropes by turning a great master's wheel by hand."³⁴

Elsie lived at 176 Hicks Street until the age of fifteen when her family moved in with her maternal grandparents as a result of her father's losses during the Panic of 1893. Architecturally, the house was similar to her own home. Elsie's first home consisted of several floors, the nursery being on the third floor which Elsie remembered best and where she spent time with Mollie, her live-in Irish nurse. Elsie described her daily routine. "My memories of life there include bathing at a built-in washstand and Mollie's sternness about ears and teeth, dressing in the mornings before a coal-grate fire, throwing down pennies to the German Band in the street below or to the Organ man and his little monkey. And I still recall the inflexible rule that all toys be picked up before our nursery supper was brought up—a supper of brown bread, milk, and applesauce which we ate at a low table in front of the coal fire."³⁵

The first floor at 176 Hicks Street contained two large rooms, the back parlor being used as a dining room with oak furniture, a long sideboard, a square dining room table and dark blue upholstered chairs. The room was surrounded by photographs of famous paintings and photographs Elsie's father had brought back from his travels in Europe. The front parlor contained bookcases by the fireplace and Elsie's mother's piano, on which stood a vase of roses and a jar filled with the violets Elsie's father provided each week. Straight yellow-rose curtains, her mother's favorite color, hung over the window-seat boxes which held her mother's sheet music. Elsie's bedroom was on the third floor, and guests who spent the night also stayed on the third floor in a large guest bedroom. Elsie recalled a close friend of her mother, Auntie May Nelson, who often came to stay. "When she was there," Elsie recalled, "Mother who was usually dignified and somewhat aloof changed beyond recognition; she and Auntie May would lie on the bed and eat candy and giggle—'just like two girls,' I said in disgust."[36]

Sunday was a favorite day for Elsie as a young girl and she remembered it as family day. Following breakfast, the family attended services at the First Presbyterian Church. The service had little appeal to a child so she watched the soloists in the choir or amused herself by reading the hymnal. Sunday dinner followed church with the occasional culinary delights of "roast beef, currant jelly and brown potatoes, romaine lettuce salad with crackers and cheese and spinach with a hard-boiled egg on top... followed by coffee for the grown-ups and for everyone ice cream from Maresi's—vanilla bisque covered with raspberry ice." Supper was often Welsh rabbit or lobster.[37]

Elsie sometimes spent Sunday afternoons walking with her father, a time she cherished as they traveled down Clinton or Henry Street to South Brooklyn. Sundays were a time for family while during the week much of the daily childcare was handled by hired nurses as was typical in families of status and wealth. During the week, Elsie, her sister Marjorie, and brother Lawrence often took afternoon walks with their nurse, Mollie, who was responsible for their daily care. During the day, the streets were full of excitement, bustling with noise and activity. One of Elsie's and Lawrence's favorite places was the firehouse on Pierrepont Street. She described the potential for excitement: "There if we were lucky enough to be present when the first alarm sounded, we saw the firemen sliding down the greased pole get into their suits and helmets while the white fire-horses were backed into the traces, and then watched the Engine, beginning to steam, shoot out the door, with the men clinging to it."[38] Their most frequent destination was the Lookout on Montague Hill. From this perch, they could see cable cars, the ferry house, tugboats, the Brooklyn Bridge, and even the Statue of Liberty. "Through these visits to the Lookout and walks over Brooklyn Bridge," Elsie noted, " the river and its life were a part of my life in childhood. In bed at night at 176 Hicks Street, two blocks away, I would go to sleep listening for the deep note of a steamship as it left its Pier and turned toward the narrows and the Lower Harbor, or for the bleat of the Fog Horn when the mists rolled in from the sea."[39] Using her imagination, Elsie saw her future as a tugboat captain.

CHAPTER ONE

Across the street from 176 Hicks Street were the Love Lane Livery Stables "whose red faced long-skirted green coated drivers took us back and forth to and from dancing school and parties." Gardens along the way were also popular stopping places for Elsie and her siblings. "Strange little gardens they were," Elsie recalled, "luxuriously green with a fountain in the center where birds bathed in a series of stone basins; they were entered through a gate in the iron fence separating them from the sidewalk."[40] Being the eldest, Elsie was often bored walking along with her younger siblings and other children. Mollie, her nurse, often stopped to talk with other nurses and children who were out walking. Elsie's favorite activities near home included rolling hoops, roller-skating, and riding velocipedes, and Elsie soon had the freedom to travel around the block by herself, "down Pierrepont to Willow Street, along Willow to Clark, back to Hicks Street on Clark, or the other way."[41] On one of her excursions she stopped by the church to speak with Pastor Hall of the First Presbyterian Church. Elsie had been troubled by the theological doctrine of the Trinity, which she did not understand. Elsie described the incident. "I remember leaning my hoop up against the church wall and climbing up to Mr. Hall's study to thrash out the matter with him. However busy he might have been, I never knew he had other things to attend to. Perched on his high windowsill I went into it thoroughly with him and finally we agreed to disagree. Looking back, I appreciate his kindness and patience in dealing at length with a child's doubts and queries." Pastor Hall most likely sensed that Elsie was no typical child, somewhat precocious, bright, and inquisitive. He was also a close friend of the family which strongly supported his church.[42] Elsie held great respect for Charles Cuthbert Hall her entire life. "The qualities he possessed of spiritual strength and human understanding," Elsie wrote, "and the dignity and beauty of the services attracted an increasing number of people and during my childhood and early girlhood the First Presbyterian Church was a prime facet in the lives of many Heights families." Hall eventually resigned his position to become president of Union Theological Seminary in New York. Elsie always considered her home church to be the First Presbyterian Church.[43]

Due to the heat and humidity in the city during the summer, well-to-do families on the Heights, including Elsie and her family, often spent summers in the countryside or in Europe. "Like most of the families on the Heights," Elsie noted, "we spent the summer in the country. When I was very small we stayed in Easthampton and Southampton, but my memories of these places are confined to some windmills and rolling downs covered with heather." Many summers were spent in Westhampton or at the Howell House with cousins and family, both close enough for her father to come and join the family for the weekend and both near the ocean.

Elsie described a typical summer: "A great deal of our time was spent beside the Hotel tennis courts, watching the older boys and girls and speculating endlessly about their love affairs, over which we kept a close watch. A high cedar tree grew at the jut of the hotel, its upper branches just opposite our rooms which opened on the second story piazza where much of the courting went on nights. Inside our rooms was too far away to hear what was said satisfactorily."[44]

One summer Elsie and her family spent time at a working farm in Monticello in New York State. This rural area introduced Elsie and her cousins to a new environment and to "new pleasures—wading in brooks, making cornstalk dolls, and playing in the barn, tumbling in the hay mow and sliding down the feed chutes." Another summer was spent in the Adirondacks near Lake Honendaga, where her father owned a few acres of land and a place where Elsie camped out with relatives and friends. She fondly recalled spending this time with her father, "going off with him and the guides, learning how to walk a rough trail, paddle the canoes across the waterways and help carry them across the portages between. Father enjoyed fishing for trout in the mountain streams and wanted me to learn the art. I never became a first-rate caster, but I was able to contribute to the mess of fish for supper, which were broiled, wrapped in leaves, over the open fire. Best of all I liked being off with Father, he was an ideal companion for a child, sunny, even-tempered and full of fun." Elsie rarely mentions her mother on these summer excursions, but one cannot imagine her mother or many other girls taking part in these activities in this time of being prim and proper.[45]

As a child, one of Elsie's favorite activities was playing with her paper dolls, which she kept in a scrapbook designed like a house. "Members of our doll families were kept in a catalogue or bulletin whose pages, each headed with a name, contained pictures cut from magazines showing the mother in street dress, the mother in evening dress; the father in business suit, in dress suit, etc., and each child in both everyday and Sunday clothes. In our scrapbook house our doll families lived a continuous and to us interesting life, visiting back and forth and doing all the things our own families did."[46]

One summer at Lake Honendaga in the Adirondacks, Elsie spent some time camping with her father at their open-face log cabin with an outdoor fireplace. "Occasionally we spent the night over at our camp," Elsie recalled, "the wide bunks filled with freshly-cut balsam boughs made a comfortable bed, and I would lie listening to the loon's heart-breaking cry and watching the flames leap up as father or one the guides threw fresh logs on the fire. One awoke to a breakfast of flapjacks, which the guides used to toss in the air and catch on the griddle—a skill we children greatly admired and tried, unsuccessfully to emulate."[47]

CHAPTER ONE

In 1890, when Elsie reached eleven years of age, her father decided to take the entire family abroad for his annual business trip. Being a stockbroker, he had clients in England and Scotland and Elsie was thrilled at the opportunity. She wrote, "We sailed on the Steamship *Germanic* of the White Star Line, and the high point of the voyage for us was an iceberg we met. I well remember the odd compartments in the English train in which we traveled north all day through fields of daisies." The Clapp family began their stay in Edinburgh, Scotland, where each morning Mollie carried the children to Edinburgh Castle to watch the changing of the Guard. "Leaning over the ramparts of the back of the Parade Ground," Elsie noted, "I could see far below old houses in narrow streets and one morning I climbed the wall and scrambled down the steep slope to investigate. Of this enterprise I remember my being brought back to the hotel by a policeman with a patent leather strap under his chin and my family's surprising relief."[48]

Following the stay in Scotland, the family traveled to South Kensington, London. Elsie spent some time at the South Kensington Museum and became acquainted with the curator as he told stories of the past and valuable treasures of the museum. "Mother and Father led a gay social life," Elsie explained, "riding horseback in Rotten Row in Hyde Park and, in the long summer twilight, driving off in a hansom cab to join their English friends at some party where Mother was to be presented at court. I remember going with her to have her dress fitted; it had to be a special kind of dress and she had to wear a tiara of three feathers in her hair. I also watched someone teach her how to make a low curtsy and back out of the room without tripping over the train of her gown. These solemn preparations both intrigued and disgusted me."[49] Once again we see Elsie spurning what she perceived her mother's superficial and frivolous lifestyle where women were seen as no more than objects or things of beauty. Perhaps young Elsie, on the eve of adolescence, realized she could never be a part of this world and in many ways did not desire to be. She did not comprehend at this time in her life why her mother behaved in such a way, and yet was repulsed by the artificiality of it all. Elsie wanted something more, what she thought was a life of substance and meaning, a life much like that lived by her father and Grandfather Ripley.[50] Elsie deeply loved and respected her father and sought a more sympathetic and emotional relationship with him, but due to rigid gender roles, the relationship was more of companionship than sympathetic confidant. Elsie did not feel she could speak to him about becoming a woman. However, she did find a sympathetic confidant in Grandmother Ripley. It was Grandmother Ripley who shared Elsie's deepest secrets, and her death left a void in Elsie's life just as she was beginning to better understand herself. Prior to her teenage years, Grandmother Ripley and her father, William Gamwell Clapp, were the most significant others in her life.

Elsie resisted and fought against the shallowness of the Victorian woman, who, as Blanche Cooke describes, "was above all, deprived of the capacity for free thought and independence. A simple and compliant figure, she ran from ambition and refused the trappings of power." Elsie rejected the submissiveness and the domesticity associated with the Victorian image of true womanhood. As an adult, she saw no reason why one's identity had to be found through marriage or through motherhood. She noted and praised her mother's artistic gifts and talents, but these seemed neglected and superficial, her mother playing a role rather than really being herself and living her own life. Elsie Clapp was beginning to fashion herself into a young woman, not a simple and compliant person by far, but one of great complexity, with a growing compassion and a willingness to challenge the status quo. Up to this point, Elsie had led a privileged, protected, sheltered existence. She did not comprehend that other people lived differently.[51]

Elsie was growing into a more mature young woman, coming of age during the 1890s, a decade of great economic and social change for her family. Even under these circumstances, she continued to live a sheltered existence. Elsie was among a generation of middle- and upper-class women who attempted to sort through the "rigid stereotyping of behavioral norms, tightly bounded by gender, race and class."[52] As she matured she was becoming a more acute observer of the social, political, and economic forces that had so influenced her own life but had rarely paid attention to how her existence influenced the lives of others. Nevertheless, these limited reflections began her process of deconstructing the "cult of womanhood." This is evident as Elsie struggled to form her own values and conception of self. Her understanding of community, a concept so important to her philosophy of life and education in later years, was virtually nonexistent. It existed only through the personal relationships with family and close friends. Elsie preferred to fashion her own world rather than let the world fashion her, yet there was a soft side to Elsie not revealed on the surface. This soft side was related to a lack of confidence that would haunt her for much of her life. In her early teens her protected world would come crashing down and change her life forever. Elsie felt isolated as a child and in reality she was. Her existence was defined by the tight boundaries of the Victorian era. These boundaries in her own life confined her in a world of rigid class, ethnic and gender distinctions. Her protected world was far from the norm and she did not see how her own existence was based on the oppression of others. To define herself she had to break through these rigid boundaries.

In discussing the notion of self, Elsie's later mentor, John Dewey, suggested the self is not fixed, but in the process of making. "In the self we find inconsistency and disharmony... a person can be sympathetically attentive in one situation and harshly arrogant in another." These characteristics describe Elsie Ripley Clapp well at this point in her life.[53]

Chapter Two

Growing Up: Adolescence

Following the trip to England and Scotland, Elsie turned twelve years old, and her life entered a new phase. In Elsie's world, she had passed a milestone and was now considered an adult. She had gained a conventional rite of passage. "After this trip abroad my childhood was somehow over," she declared, "I was 12 that fall [1891] and ate dinner downstairs with my Father and Mother, and they began to include me in their activities, taking me riding in the Park and, when we went down to Lakewood, New Jersey, or to Storm-King-on-the-Hudson for the Christmas holidays, the three of us went skating and ice-boating together."[1] These activities were augmented by William Gamwell Clapp's memberships in numerous clubs. His success and wealth made these accessible, and he was also an accomplished equestrian and oarsman. When the maids had the evening off, Elsie vividly remembered going to the Hamilton Club to dine with other Heights families where the waiters "seemed to know everybody and everybody's business."[2]

Since Elsie's father belonged to an equestrian club, she also rode. Riding gave her a sense of freedom and allowed her to spend more time "outdoors on the doctor's orders." Elsie began to experience health problems in early adolescence, some of which would plague her all her life, yet these often seemed related to stress and in her own attempt to find self. Regardless, Elsie continued to participate in activities with her father and mother. She had been riding about two years with her mother and father when the Hamilton Club's riding master approached her father. Elsie described the encounter and wrote, "Father learned from a new Riding Master at the Club, a military man, that I had a poor seat and put me forthwith under his instruction. It was a strenuous course: I learned to ride without a saddle and to trot, pace, canter and finally jump, without reins." Proper women rode sidesaddle in that era, and Elsie recalled how handsome her mother looked in her dark habit and silk hat. Sarah Ripley Clapp had ridden since she was a student at Vassar and was in young Elsie's mind still a fairy princess.[3]

Shortly following the family's return from Europe, Elsie began to attend a "small private school run by a friend" of her mother's. Apparently this was Elsie's first exposure to a formal educational setting. "It must have been a poor school," Elsie recalled, "for before I was thirteen I had finished its curriculum. Aside from gaining some familiarity with French and discovering ways to get answers to arithmetic problems, I learned nothing I can recall. I had always been interested in the photographs of churches and cathedrals among those my Father brought back each year from abroad, and after our own trip to England and Scotland, I developed a special interest in Gothic architecture; using every book I could find I made countless drawings of groined arches, flying buttresses and rose-windows."[4] Much like her friend and colleague, Lucy Sprague Mitchell, Elsie believed her real early education took place through family interaction and extensive reading in the libraries of their fathers. "The real education I received in childhood," Elsie explained, "came through familiarity with the libraries of my Father and Grandfather and association with the older members of my family and exposure to their interests—Auntie's enveloping interest in history, Mother's music and Grandfather's Symphony concerts. To this our trip abroad must be added and probably also the Dancing class I attended with the other children on the Heights." Elsie attended dance class with her friend and future progressive education colleague, Jessie Stanton. Under the patient direction of a Mr. Dodworth, who always wore a "full dress suit," Elsie learned the waltz, polka, the schottische, and how to enter and leave a room. She later wrote, "It sounds absurd, but I became a good and confident dancer." Elsie was not simply learning to dance but how to become a woman within the boundaries of her social class and status. Elsie believed dance gave her a sense of poise and always felt herself an accomplished dancer. "But the extraordinary fact remains that until I entered high school," she noted, "I had little schooling that amounted to anything."[5]

Although still not close to her mother emotionally, Elsie shared her mother's fascination for fashion. Elsie noted her mother's displeasure when a tailor made someone else a dress too similar to her own. "And I have a vivid memory of the tailor on Livingston Street," Elsie wrote, "where Mother and I went to have our riding habits made. We rode sidesaddle then of course, and the long skirts of our habits had to be fitted and adjusted to us as we sat on the saddle set up in his back room. I took great pride in my vests and ties, in my derby from Knox the Hatter, in my shining riding boots and in the silver tipped riding crop Father had given me."[6]

Elsie's mother and grandmother were excellent seamstresses, a skill expected in the Victorian woman, and Elsie consciously observed their skill. "At that time the making of dresses was arduous," Elsie explained, "waists were boned at every seam, as were collars; the long full skirts had stiffening eight to ten inches from the bottom, and their edges which swept the ground were protected by a wide piece of binding. When I was small I was entrusted only to cut out the edging which trimmed underclothes and pull bastings."[7] Elsie's description of the sewing process as arduous, further gives insight into the confining world of "the cult of womanhood" of the late nineteenth century. Even

CHAPTER TWO

sociocultural boundaries of confinement and bondage found themselves expressed in fashion and clearly defined one by class and status.

During the summer of 1893, when she was fourteen years of age, Elsie's family rented a small cottage near the Oneck House in Westhampton, New York. She recalled this summer as a time of maturation and with a sense of humor wrote, "I was, I remember, undergoing an adolescent attack of romanticism during which I dressed every afternoon, put a rose in my braids and left the rest to fate. Mother was unexpectedly understanding and made no comment at all on what certainly odd behavior, but treated it as natural—as perhaps it was—and patiently showed me how to put up my hair."[8] Elsie channeled this energy to her interest in horses and over the past two years had become a fairly accomplished equestrienne. Her father owned two horses, "a sensitive high bred roan" and a "sturdy English cob." "It was my job to exercise them," she explained, "and I jumped them both. The riding master taught me a great deal about handling horses and about exhibition riding in which I took great interest. In fact, I recall now with some amusement, that my greatest disappointment that year was my parents' refusal to let me ride tandem... ride one horse while driving another." Elsie exhibited her riding skills in horse shows, but during one weekly horse show, the girth of the saddle loosened and the horse fell. In spite of the long riding habit she was wearing, Elsie was able to jump clear. "Father, I remember, fearful lest I lose my nerve," Elsie recalled, "insisted that I finish the Show on his horse, Prince."[9]

Elsie's closest friends were the children of relatives or the children of her parents' friends. Elsie was coming of age, and many of her friends were being given "coming out" parties by their wealthy parents. Three of her closest friends during these days were Florence Field, Louise Murray, and Laura Hubbard. Elsie described Laura Hubbard as "a vivacious and resourceful girl, who, with less money than the rest of us, yet held the position of leader in our little group. Her father was, I remember, a naval officer and perhaps it was travel and more varied social experiences that gave her poise and independence; certainly she already knew how to entertain and I recall many gay boy-and-girl parties at her home."[10] Laura, Louise, and Florence were from families in the same social class, and Elsie lived the life of a girl from a family of wealth and status. "My father, a maid, one of the Love Lane coachmen, or a District Messenger boy escorted me to and from even a supper at another girl's home. It was, I think in 1894, that I began to attend Junior Assemblies and go about socially," Elsie recalled. "I had ceased to worry about my lack of good looks, for I had made the intoxicating discovery that popularity did not depend wholly upon them. Unexpectedly, I had many beaux among the boys I knew as well as the less orthodox but more interesting boys I met at parties... I had no favorites, but I enjoyed their attentiveness and especially liked having my Dance

Card filled before parties began. Cotillions even for the younger set were quite elaborate, and my room was filled with the favors one received at the end of each figure."[11] The fancy parties and cotillions were a mask of things to come as Elsie's family situation changed due to economic forces.

Elsie was entering adolescence, and only in retrospect did she begin to understand the deep complexity of her family's changing situation in the 1890s. She wrote, "The fact was that during the first fourteen years of my life (1879–1893), the country, occupied with its internal expansion was increasingly prosperous, and I as a younger member of a well-known and well-to-do family enjoyed privileges and prerogatives of which I was quite unaware." Grandfather Ripley had done well in the insurance business as president of the Home Life Insurance Company and following retirement remained in a consulting role. William Gamwell Clapp, Elsie's father, owned a brokerage firm. "My Father's brokerage firm with an office at 37 Wall Street," she explained, "dealt in stocks and bonds and through these years had been increasingly successful. He and his partner, John French, were I knew interested in street-railways in Duluth, and he handled also investments for various English and Scotch clients—a business that took him abroad for part of each year. In our Hicks Street houses we lived the well-ordered conventional life of well-to-do people in that locality."[12] William Clapp's investments up to the 1880s had been sound and had made him a wealthy man.[13]

In spite of her upbringing, Elsie realized her world contained certain restrictions, yet it was sometime later in life she fully realized and appraised them. In retrospect she described her life as lacking spontaneity. "Growing up in this world, there was nothing impromptu, meals, walks with Mollie and the children, dancing school, even parties, all came at regular and appointed times." Elsie's family lived according to what she called a "Rich Man's Code of Simplicity," meaning that it was in bad taste to have a butler, but one could have as many maids as desired or affordable. Dinners and receptions were often catered with flowers provided by a preferred florist. "We lived unostentatiously perhaps," she explained, "but luxuriously. Certainly the comforts and service we enjoyed, the dinners and parties at the house, Mother's linen, china and silverware, her clothes and jewels, the houses and Father's many clubs, our trip to England and Scotland and the way we lived over there spelled money. At the time I took these things for granted and never thought about them. Now that the children were older and I was going out more, it seemed perfectly natural that Mollie, who had been our nurse, should attend to keeping my clothes in order. I remember one wintry afternoon stepping into the street all dressed to go to some reception feeling I owned the world."[14] Writing her memoirs years later, Elsie seemed embarrassed by the superficiality of her lifestyle, a lifestyle of ritual to confirm status and social role. While she criticizes the frivolous lifestyle of her mother, Elsie was part of this world built on the service and sacrifice of others. This false sense of security and stability became evident soon during the economic downturn of the early 1890s.

Elsie Clapp's naive confidence was soon shattered, but even in her confidence, she sensed a confinement, a lack of openness to her privileged world although she did not fully understand it. The fragility of her affluent existence came to the forefront in the 1890s with one of the worst economic depressions in U.S. history. "I now know that the Panic of 1893 was marked by a business depression which," Elsie noted, "becoming increasingly severe, lasted until 1898. In it many business firms (like my father's) which dealt in stocks and bonds failed. I still remember what a shock it was to learn that the father of some girls I knew had committed suicide. No one, surely no one we knew, I felt would do such a thing like that. This reaction and my complete unawareness of the strain and anxiety my father must have been going through seems now to me incredible. It was, I think due not only to my ignorance of economic conditions, but also the way in which I was brought up."[15] Elsie believed it very important to convey this understanding to her reader and wrote, "I have not succeeded in depicting the life I lived if I have not conveyed an impregnable sense of security and the assumption that the life we led was the kind people like ourselves always led."[16]

Elsie refers to the depression of the 1890s as the Panic of 1893, and at fourteen years old, it changed her life forever. Economic historian Michel Beaud refers to the later nineteenth century as the second period of capitalism, an era characterized by new technology and industrial techniques, affirmation of the workers' movements, concentration of capital and a new wave of colonization and imperialism. By 1884, the railroad industry, in which Elsie's father had heavily invested, had experienced a crisis, leading to slower construction of lines, lower stock prices, and some bank failures. This gradually improved and the United States experienced some growth before 1893. However, by 1894, railroad companies once again saw their profits fall. Beaud writes, "The stock exchange prices for railroad securities collapsed and 491 banks failed. The depression grew worse in 1894 with more unemployment and an effort to reduce wages."[17] The Depression of 1893 had hit many in the South and the farm belt in the late 1880s, largely in cotton and agricultural businesses. This depression hit Wall Street and the East Coast in 1893 and was part of a worldwide economic crisis. Twenty-five percent of the railroads went bankrupt, and this hurt Elsie's father. Industry was also challenged by growing labor unrest. Two of the more famous labor disputes during this era were the Homestead strike at the Carnegie Steel Works near Pittsburgh and the Pullman strike outside of Chicago.[18]

Responding to great personal loss and the economic misfortunes of the Depression of 1893, Elsie's family moved in with her maternal grandparents, the Ripleys. The horses were sold and William Clapp had to give up most of his exclusive clubs, yet in spite of this economic misfortune, Elsie's life seemed to change little. "I was sorry to have to sell the horses and sorry that Father had to give up most of his clubs, but the tenor of our life seemed to me little changed," Elsie recalled. "At once we joined a bicycle club near Prospect Park, where we kept our wheels, and he and I did a good deal of bicycling together, I clad in costume of divided skirt, shirtwaist and coat in which I dressed at the Club." Elsie's parents attempted to mask the reality of their economic situation. Her siblings Marjorie and Lawrence had to face the difficulties of a growing complexity within the family while Elsie was heavily involved in school activities. There was a significant life change on the horizon because Elsie was getting ready to enter high school, an experience that stimulated her intellectually and socially but, most importantly, exposed her to a small extent to people outside her social class. Elsie began her formal educational studies at the Packer Collegiate Institute.

Prior to admission to Packer she interviewed with Packer President Truman Backus who served as President from 1883 to 1908.[19] Elsie described her new experience and wrote, "The fact, I suppose, was that I was just entering a new world of high school which already was re-channeling my interests. For the first time I came into contact with people outside the family and social groups in which I had grown up. The most challenging of these people was Dr. Bachus [Backus], a big shaggy man who asked me many questions I could not answer about what I had studied."[20] Backus, concerned with Elsie's responses turned to Elsie's mother and said, "it's all right... we can teach her something."[21] Elsie described her mother's reaction to Backus' statement. "Mother who had, of course, been dismayed and chagrined by the display of ignorance in my interview with Dr. Bachus, did not discuss the matter with me, but I felt her insistence that I do well in my work at Packer."[22]

The Packer Collegiate Institute had originated in 1844 as the Brooklyn Female Academy. Two years after its founding, Dr. William B. Sprague of the Albany Institute delivered the following speech dedicating the first building at the Brooklyn Female Academy and articulated his conception of ideal womanhood. "Providence was designated to her, her appropriate sphere, and though it be a retired, quiet, and if you please in some respects a humble sphere, it is a glorious sphere, notwithstanding—glorious because heaven has crowned it with the means of honorable usefulness... I do not disparage but honor her, when I say that her throne is in the nursery, and beside the cradle... think it not hardship, ladies, that public opinion excuses you from appearing in the arena of political conflict, or from saying at the ballot box who shall be our rulers, or from standing further as God's commissioned ambassadors to treat a dying world."[23] Some fifty years later Elsie and many of her generation, including friends and colleagues, had rejected Sprague's archaic ideal of womanhood, but they understood well the oppression this attitude conveyed as they continually struggled against it.

Four years after its founding the Brooklyn Female Academy was destroyed by fire. It was rebuilt through the generous financial support of Mrs. Harriet L. Packer.[24] With a gift of $65,000.00, Mrs. Packer sought to erect an institution for girls to be instructed "in the higher branches of literature."[25] Mrs. Packer further desired to broaden the horizons of young women often too restricted by the Victorian "cult of womanhood." Mrs. Packer thought wealthy young girls like Elsie ought to learn the virtues of self-control and discipline. Packer historian Marjorie Nickerson believes Packer inspired "her girls with a sense of proportion, a sense of the stability of the human spirit."[26] She wrote, "The aim of Packer has always been to develop fine character and efficient intelligence in its students. An "efficient intelligence" implies that Packer has not been only a school for the intellectual aristocracy, although it has done well by some members of it, but that it recognizes that a woman, whether a self-proclaimed intellectual or not, wishes and needs to be intelligent, and efficiently so."[27] Nickerson describes Packer's philosophy as one of progressive conservatism, progressive in the sense of "of what is best in time and environment."[28] This attitude of progressive conservatism was described by Nickerson as still containing the narrow conception of "the cult of womanhood." According to Nickerson, during Elsie's era at Packer the ideal woman was "still considered by the unenlightened majority to be a vine, graceful, and pleasing, but not so clinging as formerly, and she was supposed to have some capacity to grow by herself and to support some of her own weight. Her mind was still considered popularly to be inferior to that of men, but she was more and more required to be able to use what mind she had... women were expected to take some interest in national and international affairs and in the welfare of the community."[29] This notion of progressive conservatism is important to keep in mind as we attempt to understand Elsie's thoughts, particularly her later work in progressive education and the role of the community school. Progressive conservatism will define her own version of progressivism in a moderate sense, but it also conveys how difficult it was to challenge patrilineal attitudes in society and academe.

Elsie attended Packer during one of its most productive periods, largely due to the able leadership of Dr. Truman J. Backus. Backus favored the humanities, specifically English literature, but also strengthened the instruction of science during his tenure. He added geology, physiology, and zoology to the curriculum, and Packer was considered well equipped to provide this instruction. Science instruction was considered by many to be beyond the mental capacity of young women, but Backus disagreed. During Elsie's era, there were two curriculum tracks, the classical and mathematical. Elsie chose the classical and studied classical Latin and Greek. She also studied drawing and gymnastics, which took the form of dance and art. Packer was clearly a college prep institution for girls, with many of the girls continuing their education at Vassar, Barnard, Wellesley, Mt. Holyoke, and Bryn Mawr.[30]

During Elsie's high school years, Brooklyn had a population of at least a million and was best known for its arts and sports, generally horse racing and yachting. Elsie held an interest in art and sports. Like Elsie, most of the girls at Packer came from the Brooklyn Heights area. Marjorie Nickerson, Packer Institute historian, noted the styles of the typical Brooklyn home of the era, notably similar to Elsie's own descriptions. "The rooms had noble proportions; the furniture was massive but dignified, the pictures large and plentiful but good and well-framed, the ornaments greater in number than in a modern room of equally good tastes, but beautiful and well arranged, the piano inlaid with mother-of-pearl, the tables large and polished, the chairs comfortable, the library lined with finely chosen and finely bound books; the whole effect was one of leisure, culture, charm and gracious living." This was clearly the world of Elsie Clapp.[31]

Prior to entering high school at the Packer Collegiate Institute, Elsie had begun artwork under Miss Eleanor Coleman, the art teacher at Packer. Elsie's parents had sensed she held an interest in art and had furnished her an art studio in their home. Elsie continued her artwork throughout her life, but never felt herself an accomplished artist, perhaps more due to lack of self-esteem than actual talent. "Nevertheless, the work I did at Packer with Miss Coleman opened my eyes to the fact that, gifted or not," Elsie explained, "one worked, and worked hard and long to attain even fair results." Taking an interest in Elsie, Eleanor Coleman asked her about future plans. What was she going to do with her life? "I do not know what I am going to do," Elsie responded, "play around for a few years and then come out, I pose." Concerned about this cursory response, Coleman arranged to see Elsie's mother. Miss Coleman believed it absurd that a young girl of fourteen should be finished with formal education. Convinced by Miss Coleman's argument, Elsie's mother went to see the head of Packer, Dr. Backus, about entering Packer as a student in the fall.[32]

Upon entering the Packer Collegiate Institute, a disappointed and surprised Elsie was placed in the Third Academic, which corresponded to the eighth grade, two years below her age level. "Chagrined, I set about doing two years in one," Elsie explained, "taking both a Beginner's and a First Year Latin Class. Fortunately, I had the same teacher in both and, with her help, I got hold of the rudiments of Latin Grammar and acquired a reasonably large

CHAPTER TWO

beginner's Latin vocabulary. By the second semester I was able to drop the Beginner's class and joined instead a Second Year Class, which was reading Cicero's *Orations* while continuing the work in Julius Caesar. It was not easy, for doing my daily assignment I constantly found myself ignorant of some basic fact. I understood that I strove so hard because part at least of what I learned I should by rights have known, but even so I was astonished to discover that the results of all my efforts was no more, and hardly as much as, was expected."[33] Elsie realized that her lack of formal education put her at a disadvantage when placed in the rigorous classical/liberal arts environment at Packer. For a year or so Elsie read background material to give class material more meaning and to catch up with the other students. This required of Elsie a mature self-discipline and dedication, traits she had not strongly exhibited up to this point in her life.

Due to her family's economic situation Elsie attended Packer on a scholarship.[34] Although Elsie emphasizes the drastic change in her family's economic situation in her memoirs, during the summer of 1895 she continued to live the life of the wealthy. Elsie was vacationing with her family near Newport, Rhode Island, and often attended gala summer parties and dances with girls in her social set. According to one social reporter these events included the "promise of an unusual array of youth and beauty."[35] On July 2, 1895, Elsie attended an elaborate dinner in honor of the English Legation. "It was an affair that hardly will be surpassed," a social columnist reported, "in the brilliancy of the season. The table decorations were of maiden hair ferns and American Beauty roses."[36] A few days later Elsie attended another function, a small dinner party for six guests given by Mrs. Alva Vanderbilt. Later that summer Elsie gave a luncheon coupled with a sailing party on a yacht decorated in "red roses in great profusion."[37] In retrospect, upon writing her memoirs, Elsie had the benefit of looking back and carefully weighing the decline of her family's fortunes. In 1895 at the age of sixteen she lived the social life of the upper class and was educated with them at Packer. In retrospect, writing her memoirs, Elsie seemed embarrassed by this affluent and superficial behavior.

Elsie considered the Packer Collegiate Institute an unusually good school, and the teachers were exceptionally able. She studied Latin with Laura Giese and George Whicher. Elsie described her Latin experience with Giese. "Translating Caesar was relatively simple, but Laura Giese, the scholar with who I read Cicero's *Orations* demanded a close and fair rendering of Cicero's thought and meaning and moreover, such a knowledge of human history as would give point and face to his allusions. So perforce, I got up Roman history on the side."[38] Elsie also studied Latin with another teacher and "gentle scholar," George M. Whicher, "who somehow elicited from his students unprecedented efforts." Whicher was considered to be an excellent humanities teacher, whose expertise focused on the classics and poetry. He published some poetry in the

New York Herald Tribune and served as a reviewer for the paper. Whicher is described by Packer alumni as "young, whimsically humorous, scholarly, vivid," who "won friends on every side... a gifted, a stimulating and imaginative teacher."[39] Elsie gave credit to Clara Crampton for stimulating her knowledge and interest in math. Clara Crampton taught Elsie geometry at Packer, and it was from her that Elsie gained her first understanding of mathematics and logic.[40]

In English Elsie studied under Kate Morgan Ward, whom she described as "a merry person, with a quick wit who was not only well informed but scholarly." Kate Ward held a Bachelor of Arts from Wellesley and had studied in Berlin, Paris, and Oxford. When Ward arrived in 1895 at Packer she began to organize the individual English teachers into a department. A Packer student described her as "a little dynamo of energy... and many of her students were spellbound by her teaching... she had a great spiritual pull plus worth and humanity... and responded quickly and with supreme tact to the exuberance of youth."[41] Ward was further described as a socialist, not on the extreme left but certainly not the norm at Packer, as Nickerson describes, "where the great majority of parents, students, teachers and trustees were rather on the conservative side in politics."[42] Perhaps it was Kate Ward who first exposed Elsie to socialist thought through her stimulating discussions in economics and sociology. A year after Kate Ward's arrival, Packer students expressed interest and joined the College Settlement, an organization of college students interested in settlement work.

Elsie's parents were pleased with her progress at Packer; most certainly her mother was. "She was I know, both pleased and relieved when it slowly became apparent that I had a mind," Elsie wrote, "and she took pride in the fact that I was attempting to use it. I recall also Father's pleasure in what I was getting from my studies. He had a good mind and we began to share our literary enthusiasms, and for the first time, he discussed with me his own intellectual interests."[43] The Packer experience was good for Elsie, not because it challenged her intellectually but also extended her socially. Elsie wrote, "Packer was challenging to me intellectually, it was equally so socially. The first year when I found myself in large classes with girls I did not know who were personally distasteful to me, I was wretched." Eventually skipping the ninth grade, Elsie found school life much more comfortable when placed with girls her own age in First Academic or tenth grade. "I found myself," she wrote, "in a group nearer my own age who were exceptionally able. These girls, most of whom I would not otherwise have known were, I discovered, my equals or superiors in general intelligence." Elsie's universe was slowly becoming more open from the secluded world of Hicks Street. At Packer, Elsie came in contact with Irish Catholics who were not her maids, but her peers. She also gained experience with diversity and social class difference, although she still had much to learn.[44] "Plunged into the hearty and democratic world of Packer," Elsie wrote, "I was, one would suppose, out-in-the-world where I had longed to be. But I, myself never thought of Packer as the world—it was school. I did, however realize that my life now had in it new people and new interests."[45]

While a student at Packer, Elsie most enjoyed her studies in Latin and English, an interest explored further through her graduate work at Columbia University and as an educator. She experienced an excellent liberal arts/classical academic program at the Packer Collegiate Institute, one that prepared her well for higher education. Yet, typical of most high school students, Elsie claimed it was the social experience, the true friends at Packer, that really mattered to her most. "They did not know or care who or what, my family was or where or how we lived," Elsie wrote. "When I was stuffy they ragged me, ridiculed any pretension of any kind that reared its head, brought out in me a hitherto unexpected quality of deviltry, stood by and backed me up at need. It was my first experience of this kind of comradeship, and I never wearied of this association on the basis of shared work and living."[46] In a narrow sense, Elsie was beginning to learn about community.

Lilian Main, Lucy Burns, and Amy Dunlap were Elsie's closest friends at Packer. Lilian's father was a mechanic and lived in an area of Brooklyn unknown to Elsie. Elsie described each of them. "Lilian herself had greater fineness and integrity and more all-around ability than I would ever possess. She was a born leader and remained the Class President after we graduated, revered and adored always by all the girls in their class to the very end." Amy Dunlap was Irish and pretty and "though quick witted… was not intellectual; she got by on a combination of good looks, natural shrewdness and an easy adaptability, and was not above bluffing, although disarmingly frank when caught." Elsie described Lucy as a "well-to-do" Irish Catholic. "Her father was a successful banker, her mother placid and philosophical, her eight brothers and sisters good-looking, vagarious and bright, their priest a familiar family friend. I have never known anyone like them. Tall, awkward, swift and lazy, with flowing red hair, an inward mind, and a sunny and lovable disposition, Lucy was in all ways a law unto herself. She worked when she felt like it, but always made the outstanding class contribution. She took part in all plays, fumbling her lines during rehearsals, but when the play was produced, giving a perfect characterization, extemporizing lines if she did not remember them."[47] Lilian, Lucy, and Elsie attended Vassar together, while Amy became the registrar for the Packer Institute. Eventually receiving a degree from New York University and earning a Master's at Columbia in 1916, Amy returned to Packer to teach sociology and economics. She continued in that position until her death in 1940.[48] Plunged into the more diverse world, although still elite and restrictive, of

Packer, Elsie Clapp finally felt that she was experiencing the world, the "world in which she longed to be."[49]

During the summer of 1896, Elsie and her family again rented a cottage on Bellport, Long Island. Elsie continued to attend gala summer functions in accordance with her social status.[50] Now seventeen years old, Elsie described herself as a lusty, tempestuous, and doctrinaire young person who like most late adolescents was becoming bored with her parents' activities, even though three years earlier she had been thrilled by their increased attention. She described this personal turbulence. "I found the trips back and forth across the Bay in Mr. Crane's big sailboat which my parents enjoyed extremely boring and I detested the pen-and-ink drawing lesson I took with a mediocre artist and his amorous assistant."[51] Like many adolescents, Elsie was restless. Lured by the promise of a sailboat from her father as soon as she could swim a mile, she spent much of her time in the water trying to reach that goal. She expended some of this restless energy walking around Bellport. On one of her walks she observed a woman beating a small child with a stick. Not hesitating, Elsie opened the gate, took the stick from the woman and hit her with it, telling her that if she heard the child ever cry again, she would tell the world what the woman had done. Elsie told her family about the experience that evening when she returned home. "Father pointed out to me that it was none of my business and said that if she complained he would not defend me." In an indignant moral tone Elsie responded, "That's all right, I'm not the one who needs defense. But you won't hear anything, and if she ever beats that child again I shall do just the same thing. I kept a sharp look out, but heard nothing more; she was, I knew, afraid of me."[52]

Elsie described another such incident on the New York subway in trying to make sense of this period of restlessness in her memoirs. Elsie had given up her seat to an elderly woman carrying a large basket. As soon as Elsie stood up, a small elegantly dressed man slipped into the seat. Elsie reached down, grabbed him by the collar, and yanked him up. Frightened, the man scuttled away, and to Elsie's surprise and embarrassment, the car cheered.[53] Her description of yet another confrontation provides additional insight into her growing restlessness, independence, and temperament: "One morning sitting at a desk by a window opening on the piazza, I overheard by chance the conversation of some women who were calling on Mother. They were talking about a girl who had gone abroad with a chaperoned group and was later found to be pregnant. Their remarks were a mixture of smug prudery and a ghoulish relish of salacious details; when they left Mother, disturbed, tried to apologize for them."[54] Elsie did not accept her mother's defense of her friends and replied, "It makes no difference; they were horrid and I shall never speak to them again." She never did. Although the same women vacationed in the same summer colony

CHAPTER TWO 35

year after year, Elsie did not know how her mother excused or explained her silent behavior toward the women. "Just let them ask me why," Elsie responded to her mother, "And I shall tell them. Whatever that girl did, it could not have been as bad as what they said about her. And they are old, too."[55]

Even though Elsie was becoming more influenced by her peers and growing sets of friends, Grandmother Ripley still held a special place in her life. Since the families now lived together, this relationship had time to mature. Elsie was secretive to a point and confided only in her grandmother. Elsie described their relationship. "My memories of life at home in 1897–1898 center about Grandmother who had been my companion and confidant ever since I entered Packer in 1895. Except for one time when she had a quinsy throat when I was a small child, I do not ever remember Grandmother being ill. But now she was confined... to her room and moved about it with difficulty, using a cane and small chair on coasters. Because of my carrying voice she could hear me without her phone and I read to her daily; she was I remember, very much absorbed in the news about the Spanish American War which was declared in April."[56] Part of the summer of 1898 the family spent in Brooklyn, but due to the intense heat in August, Elsie's father took them to Shelter Island. Elsie continued her gala social engagements, attending on August 9 a dinner and cotillion given in honor of the daughter of F.O. French.[57]

On September 4, 1898, Grandmother Ripley passed away while the family was still on summer vacation. Elsie was deeply touched by the loss of her grandmother and wrote, "During those experiences in High School Grandmother Ripley was my special friend and confidant. No one knew as much about me or my school interests; ever since we had moved into 164, I always went to her room to see her when I first came home from school. I cannot now recall her wise and witty comments on the tales I poured into her ear, but sympathetic as she was she saw into a situation and pricked any boasting and pretense. I was lucky to have such a confidant, and I knew it—even then."[58] The house at 164 Hicks Street was never the same without Grandmother Ripley. In an era in which expression of personal feelings and emotions was undermined by Victorian stoicism, Elsie had lost the one adult she could confide in. As an adolescent and teenager seeking to find herself in the midst of personal economic and social change, Elsie needed someone to communicate her innermost concerns. Elsie immersed herself in her schoolwork. She had lost a dear friend and no one could take her place.[59] "Work at school continued unabated," Elsie recalled. "Without any ulterior purpose I and my cronies, Lucy Burns and Amy Dunlap, pursued those subjects we especially enjoyed—English and Latin. After a full history of English literature with Kate Morgan Ward, we took her Nineteenth Century Prose and Poetry. In Latin we spent a second year with Mr. Whicher on Horace, reading his *Satires* and *Epistles*. Then with a new member of the staff,

Linda Shaw King, who was an excellent Latin Scholar, we read Livy and Plautus and Sallust."[60] The final summer before graduating from Packer, Elsie and her family returned to Newport.

In her final year at Packer, Elsie and her close friends Lilian and Lucy had decided to go to Vassar College in Poughkeepsie, New York. Elsie's mother had attended Vassar, but Elsie does not mention this as a factor in her decision. Due to the academic rigor at Packer, Elsie and her friends sought to enter Vassar as sophomores. They were able to consider such a possibility because of their extensive studies in Latin and English. Making the decision to go to college was not so easy for Elsie for several reasons. "I was considerably surprised," Elsie recalled, "to learn that Father and Mother did not know whether or not they could send me. It was arranged finally that I was to have the Watkins-Elting Scholarship just established by Mattie Elting, a family friend of Aunt Bessie and Aunt Edith Clapp."[61] While a student at Packer, Elsie had continued her work in the Packer art studio under the direction of Eleanor Coleman. Elsie admired and respected Eleanor Coleman for her lack of pretense and other personal qualities. Elsie described Coleman as a "small, quiet person, with a code and quality and effort and a fortitude and stamina unknown to me, who placed art above everything. She openly ridiculed pretension of any kind and was entirely unimpressed by my family's social position. And in the face of her working standards and her ideals, my ideas and indulgent life did seem a bit absurd. As a teacher she was exacting and thorough; challenged, I worked hard and long." Through her art studies, Elsie began to look at her own life more closely. Eleanor Coleman challenged Elsie and made her work for praise. Years later and with a sense of pride Elsie wrote, "It was months before anything I produced met with her approval." Even as an adult, Elsie continued her interest in art and although she did not feel herself gifted yet worked hard at her interest, later studying and making enough progress to work with well-known artist/sculptor William Zorach.[62]

Elsie believed her decision to go to college and not to the Arts Students League disappointed Eleanor Coleman, whom she greatly respected. Elsie wrote, "I had to break the news to Eleanor Coleman that I was not going to the Arts Students League but to College. I had the feeling that I had somehow let her down—not personally perhaps, but the ideal embodied in her work and standards. She was however, a realist with a dry humor; I was aware that she understood me and the situation very well. At any rate she took it philosophically, albeit with some misgivings, for I think she had no particular confidence in my intellectual ability and attributed my decision to my youth and friends."[63] Eleanor Coleman probably never understood the influence she had on Elsie. Years later, Elsie wrote, "I have so often wished that she knew how profoundly the work I did with her, brief though it was, influenced my own attitude toward art and art work. I would want to tell her, too, that though I missed the discipline and inspiration of work at the Arts Students League, art and beauty have through the years been as strong and pervasive factors in my life as my interests in intellectual work and in teaching; indeed at times, they have permeated both." This beginning work in art served as the foundation for curriculum integration and innovation in the arts and humanities throughout the progressive education programs at the Rosemary Junior School in Connecticut, the Ballard School in Kentucky, and the Arthurdale School, the best documented examples of Elsie's educational career. As will be discussed in later chapters, Elsie Clapp saw art as an expressive tool to teach children about themselves and their culture. This form of self-realization was essential in the building of democratic community and a centerpiece of her later progressive pedagogy.[64]

In February 1899, Elsie and a few friends took examinations at Vassar to exempt several courses first and second semesters. Elsie described the event. "The college authorities told us frankly that they had made the examination hard. To their chagrin, however, all three of us passed it with marks above 95, and shortly afterward the head of Vassar's Latin Department, Dr. Moore came down to Packer and visited our Latin class with Linda King to find out how it was that three of her students could do this." Elsie attributed her success to Linda King and George Whicher. She also told Dr. Moore of her own lack of preparation and how hard she had worked to grasp Latin syntax and vocabulary. Following the examinations at Vassar to exempt courses came Class Day at the Packer Institute. Elsie had spent four years of her life at Packer, from 1895 to 1899. Now twenty years old and class historian, she began to prepare a speech for class day. "My family, I remember," Elsie noted, "were horrified by my lack of concern, but actually there was no need to worry. We had been a singing class and I had arranged to have my talk illustrated with class songs. Lucy Burns with her true soprano and Jane Hoagland with her fine sonorous alto could be counted on to come in at the right time. With their help the speech, without previous rehearsal, went off in fine style and showed me what could be done with an audience on occasion. Retrospectively, I wonder how I dared take the risk; at the time I reveled in it. And truth to tell, after the examination we had just taken at Vassar, not even a Class Day Speech seemed very serious or important. I have a vague memory of Commencement Exercises, tinged with the excitement, triumph and shared happiness which may be the hallmark of high-school commencements."[65]

Elsie spent the summer of 1899 in Mantoloking, New Jersey, just below Bayhead, on the Jersey coast. Elsie described the area. "Built on a narrow strip of sand between Barnegat Bay and the Atlantic Ocean, Mantoloking at that time consisted of a group of thirty or forty houses, a store and post office combined a Clubhouse and dock."[66] Gone were the summers abroad or the exclusive retreats due to her father's economic losses during the 1890s depression. It was the summer before college and Elsie Clapp, now twenty years old, remembered this summer as a time of peace and happiness. "There were Saturday night dances at the clubhouse," she recalled, "which were approached by way of a long board laid over a marshy spot, often first pushing off the community cow... moonlight sails and picnics and learning to sail."[67] "Everyone at Mantoloking was interested in sailing and in the hard fought weekly races... so Marjorie and I—growing more companionable as the years between us somehow became less—were in demand as crew in the races; sometimes if there was a girl's class, we sailed ourselves."[68]

Elsie was preparing for another phase in her life. After the period of economic unrest and the devastation it had on her family, she began to see the fragility of her protected world, yet through these trials she began to define herself, her own identity, not the contrived and controlled Victorian ideal of womanhood Elsie saw in her mother and at times in herself. Elsie refused to accept many aspects of the "cult of womanhood" that defined so many women of her generation. This is seen in her growing independence and her rejection of her mother's lifestyle. Her father's economic misfortune opened up her social world, at least to a small extent. Elsie had found friends who could be trusted from different worlds and backgrounds. She was gradually becoming closer to her mother and had developed a maturing relationship with her sister Marjorie, her brother Lawrence and close friends. These growing relationships helped Elsie deal with the loss of her beloved Grandmother Ripley. Elsie had become a bright, sensitive, compassionate, independent, and at times temperamental and arrogant young woman getting ready to go off to college.

The Packer experience, although elitist, exposed Elsie to some diversity in culture and class. It challenged her false sense of pride and prejudice in her own social status and pushed her to compete, not just on her own terms. Elsie was searching to find herself. This attempt at self-realization and understanding was made more difficult by her father's economic misfortune during the depression of the 1890s, but it also opened doors, ever so slightly. Elsie did not fully grasp at the time that her parents were living a false existence, pretending in most cases to live as they always had, but she did realize her life had changed. Elsie's growing interest in art and her admiration and respect for Eleanor Coleman are crucial in understanding Elsie's quest for self-identity. For Elsie, art became a means of expression in a real sense, and presented a challenge to the pretentious world she was beginning to see all around her. Preparing for Vassar, Elsie was beginning a new journey that led her to the profession of teaching, a profession in transition, but one in which she eventually dedicated herself wholeheartedly.

Chapter Three

Vassar College (1899–1903)

Elsie and friends were soon off to Vassar College in Poughkeepsie, New York. Founded in 1861 by brewer Matthew Vassar, Vassar was established as an exclusive girls' school to prepare girls to the same degree as boys in higher education. Several decades after its founding Professor James Orton described Vassar in an essay titled, "What the College Aims to Do," published in a Boston paper. "In the first place," Orton wrote, "it should be understood that Vassar is neither a seminary nor a university, but a college. It aims to give a liberal education as distinguished from an elementary or professional one....The Vassar course of study, while projected with special reference to the sex, is hard and deep, and thorough enough for the average young man....The students are not treated as possible candidates for teaching or marriage; but we aim to enlarge and ennoble woman's sphere, by strengthening and refining her faculties."[1]

Elsie was disappointed with her freshman experience at Vassar due to her excellent preparation at the Packer Collegiate Institute. "The first year (1899–1900) at Vassar was disappointing to me—in the work, at least," Elsie recalled. "For most of the courses we had were not up to the level of those we had at Packer. These included French, History with a pedestrian young professor, a course in the history of English literature which for me was a repetition, and also a course in Latin I found so boring that I never prepared the translation so that I could at least have the excitement of reading at sight."[2]

Elsie did enjoy taking several junior-level classes in nineteenth century literature under Laura Wylie, "the able and witty Head of the English Department." Laura Wylie, a former Packer teacher, was one of Elsie's most respected and admired teachers. Wylie's former Packer students described her as "eager, vivid, brilliant, yet disciplined, reflective, amused and tolerant."[3] Wylie held a Ph.D. from Yale and was one of the first women to be admitted to graduate studies at Yale. Wylie provided for Elsie and her students a model of excellent teaching. One student wrote, "Seated at her desk, an alert, dark figure, noble and beautiful, always leaning forward a little, her great brown eyes flashing from one to another of the girl faces before her... (she made) her classes vibrant with interest, enthusiasm, amusement, and sometimes consternation."[4]

Elsie was also impressed by "an Englishwoman," Florence Keyes, who taught a course on the Textual Criticism of Shakespeare and described her: "Miss Keyes' scorn for unsubstantiated statements, her relentless probing for facts, her contempt for ignorance about history and the basic facts of language, as well as her standards of work and scholarship which was far ahead of any we had so far encountered, introduced us to a new and more mature intellectual world." Elsie found in Keyes the intellectual challenge she needed. Keyes had surprised Elsie when she returned one of Elsie's papers with the notation "words, words, words." Elsie took this critique to heart.[5] "Stung by this comment," Elsie wrote, "I was determined to try to get down to rock bottom and for the following semesters chose for myself a course which included Anglo-Saxon, English Composition, Latin and Greek, Astronomy and Geology, with history of Art and psychology."[6]

Elsie entered Vassar with her good friend Lucy Burns, and they lived off-campus in a cottage "kept by an acid Mrs. Whitlock." Living off-campus was due more to late registration rather than choice, but the arrangement proved fruitful. The Whitlock group, as Elsie referred to the girls in the cottage, also included Crystal Eastman. Living off campus resulted in some missed campus activities, but Elsie and Lucy did not mind missing Chapel Sundays. "We (Lucy and Elsie) were not required, living as we did off campus, to attend Chapel Sundays," Elsie explained, "and the day dragged, so we used to spend the day in a cross-country walk, roaming the Dutchess County hills singing and when we got hungry stopping to beg milk and some cookies or gingerbread."[7] Being athletically inclined, Elsie played field hockey, basketball, and participated in track, where she broke the record for the broad jump. This was long before the era of women's intercollegiate sports and athletics were intramural in nature. One spring evening, Elsie and her off-campus roommates decided to hold a baseball game at midnight. Elsie described the experience. "When spring came we got up a baseball team more renowned for zeal than skill and decided to hold a midnight game. We all went to bed early and arranged to have the colored cook call us at the stroke of midnight; sleepy and unenthusiastic, we did manage to play a couple of innings and get back to bed without waking Mrs. Whitlock, our landlady. Word of this exploit must have leaked out however," Elsie explained, "for to our surprise we found ourselves in disgrace. When on campus we moved in a climate of disapproval, and members of the faculty cut us dead when we met them. Finally the Dean, still called the Lady Principal, summoned us to her office. When we lined up before her all she said was 'and such big girls too,' which was smart—and smarted."[8]

Elsie was allowed to go home on most weekends although this was not typical for most Vassar students. Elsie's mother had made special arrangements with the Vassar authorities. "They, like the holidays," Elsie noted, "were filled with the gaieties of my old social set—afternoon teas and receptions, dinners, and dances."[9] One Christmas Elsie invited a Vassar friend, Theo Hadley, to spend the holiday with her family and Elsie described her. "She was a tall blond girl of Norwegian ancestry, and, more recently German parentage who was unusually mature and self-reliant. My family, like her classmates, found her unusually likable, father especially. She had brought her violin with her, and I remember her playing silhouetted against the lighted Christmas tree. And I recall, too, how shocked she was at the soft life I led and the way I was spoiled and my food preferences catered to."[10]

Even as a young woman in college, Elsie still felt her mother's dominance. When Elsie made the decision to go to Vassar and not the Arts Students League, she promised her mother that she would "come out" as expected of young ladies of her social class. Elsie recalled the event. "The reception mother gave for me was a ghastly affair. All her friends must have rallied around, for no girl I knew had a larger reception, more flowers, or more formal attention." Elsie sensed this was a desperate attempt by her mother to restore the past, something they could not afford. "It meant a great deal to her; to me it meant nothing at all, and I felt guilty about that, but I returned to College and was soon immersed in life there." As the eldest child, Elsie left home first and felt guilty that she was not home to help her family. On the surface, her mother and father put up a good front, but Elsie believed Marjorie and Lawrence were under a great deal of pressure living and making sacrifices she did not have to make. This psychological anguish may be the cause of Elsie's early health crises. Being away at Vassar made her feel guilty, but it also removed her from the tense situation at home.[11]

Back at Vassar, Elsie spent much of her first year in the library, which seemed a haven compared to the classes she described as dull and boring. Elsie described her sanctuary. "The Library was even then unusually good, and we were permitted to go among the stacks. At the front of the great end—windows overlooking the Driveway—was a low seat where I used to read, books heaped at my feet… classes may be dull," she mused, "but at least I have this library."[12] Through books, Elsie extended her horizons and expressed her excitement in reading for the first time Francis Bacon's *Advancement of Learning* and discovering that "precious essayist," Alice Meynell. Elsie was most attracted to the humanities and had some problems with advanced algebra. She flunked the final exam, turning in a blank piece of paper. Elsie blamed her failure on the teacher, a Miss Gentry, who noisily cleaned out her desk during the exam. "I found myself paralyzed by the noise," Elsie explained, which was "always disagreeable to me. As I could not on my scholarship afford any but high marks, I got one of my former teachers, Miss Crampton of Packer, to coach me so that I might be ready to take another examination, which it is my impression that Vassar allowed her to give me for apparently I had turned in a blank paper. We worked, I remember, in Grandfather Ripley's Extension; I recall too, the relief of being taught by Miss Crampton who had the gift of making mathematics understood by students."[13]

Elsie chose an excellent tutor. A graduate of Packer, class of 1890, Clara Crampton became head of the Packer math department in 1892, and she was considered to be one of the best Packer teachers. She had an "unusually quick mind and great enthusiasms; merry and joyous, she made mathematics fascinating to some of her students and clear to all of them. She was simple, friendly and perfectly fair."[14] With Crampton's help Elsie improved her math grade. She understood losing the scholarship meant leaving Vassar.

Following her first year at Vassar, Elsie and her family once again spent the summer of 1900 at Mantoloking, New Jersey. Activities that summer included berry picking "up the Matedeconk River," which usually included more uninvited chiggers than berries. Small boat sailing and races dominated most of the activities, although this summer Elsie had a suitor, Moffat Myers. One evening, following a moonlight sail, Moffat offered Elsie a hand to the dock. Showing her independence, Elsie rebuked Moffat's gesture and in the moonlight darkness immediately found herself in the water by the dock. "When Moffat gallantly dived in after me," Elsie explained, "I was for some obscure reason furious, gave him my cloak to hold and climbed in over the stern." Both were embarrassed by the accident but apparently unseen by the spectators due to the darkness. Elsie and Moffat again set sail. Upon returning to shore, Elsie found the blue flowered design of her dress imprinted upon her body. "For another week or so I had to forego my morning swim and endure the nonfunny remarks from the whole summer community. Moffat of course especially enjoyed my predicament."[15] The rest of the summer Elsie was known affectionately as the tattooed sailor.

Following summer vacation, Elsie and Lucy Burns returned to Vassar where they shared a two-bedroom dorm room on campus. They now felt more a part of the Vassar experience. Lucy and Elsie were strengthening their relationship and Elsie enjoyed Lucy's "lovable disposition, her brilliance of mind and her erratic habits of life and work." This relationship was important to Elsie, because it "not only conditioned our life and made it exciting and unpredictable, but because it became in time a kind of legend."[16] Being exciting and unpredictable, Lucy was quite a change from Elsie's routine and rigid upbringing. "Lucy's abilities and attainments were unquestioned," explained Elsie. "Lucy excelled at Shakespeare and as a linguist did work of distinction in science and economics, was a memorable actor in college Plays, and served on the College Debating Team." Lucy always enjoyed a good debate. A born debater, she made brilliant expositions and effectively demolished her opponents' rebuttals. Lucy helped form the student government at Vassar and according to Elsie helped develop its constitution and by-laws. Elsie and Lucy were also active in drama and participated in the college play, *The Intruder*. Along with this interest in drama, Elsie continued her intramural activities in field hockey and basket-

CHAPTER THREE 43

ball.[17] "When Lucy was interested in her studies," Elsie noted, "she worked prodigiously by any standard; when bored, she loafed without conscience." Lucy had a certain charisma and drew people to her. This popularity resulted in a crowded dorm room and frequent intellectual arguments and discussions. Elsie thought of Lucy as a revelation. "She would lay aside all activities and engagements for a dish of talk and then, having spent the night in discussion would curl up in a patch of sunshine on the floor and sleep the morning through. One of Lucy's practices was used as the signal for a party; she had a habit of marking her place in the book she was reading by one of the clean new bills her banker father sent her. It was understood that when found they were to be used for a group treat of ice cream and chocolate cake."[18]

In November of her second year, Elsie began to experience abdominal pain. Unable to diagnose her condition, the college doctors advised her to get outside as much as possible. Taking their advice, Elsie sometimes walked the hills around the Vassar campus alone, against Vassar rules. Cross-country walks were to occur only in groups of three. One November afternoon Elsie decided to walk to a hill village about five miles from campus. On her way back to campus she decided to travel through the village of Arlington, what she described as a "scrubby Italian village" at the corner where the trolley from Poughkeepsie turned into the road leading to the College's main entrance gate. Elsie described the incident. "At this hour in November it was getting dark. Just after I passed through a small hamlet on this back road I heard a scuffling in the leaves behind me and caught a glimpse over my shoulder of a burly Italian; suddenly I realized, somewhat incredulously, that he was following at my heels. He kept so close that at the time I felt his breath on the back of my neck."[19] Rather than turn and run to the nearest house, Elsie decided to trudge on and hoped she looked big enough and tough enough in her basketball letter sweater. "My best bet it seemed," Elsie recalled, "lay in striding boldly on; I was a big youngster and, in my heavy class basketball team sweater knew I must look bigger. The few vehicles that passed were filled with men obviously just from the pub who eyed me curiously and though I scanned each one closely I could see no possible helper, so the man and I walked on."[20] Frightened, Elsie knew she was in a bad situation. Finally reaching Arlington and the edge of the campus grounds, the man drew back and Elsie climbed the fence. "I said nothing about my experience," Elsie explained, "for I had broken one of the few College rules and knew that I might lose my off-campus privileges. I did, however, tell a boy I knew and he provided me with a pistol and told me how to use it. I also took no more long cross-country walks alone."[21] Luckily Elsie made it back in time for dinner that evening.

Later in the fall of that year, Elsie's family moved to Germantown, Pennsylvania, where her father had a new position. Grandfather and Grandmother

Ripley were now deceased, and the house at 164 Hicks Street had been sold. Going home to Germantown during the Christmas holidays was disconcerting. Elsie was deeply distressed by her family's move to Germantown, perhaps seeing it as a clear indication her world actually had changed. "So when I went home at Christmas time," Elsie observed, "I found all the familiar furniture and furnishings in a strange stone house whose windows looked upon an unfamiliar suburban world."[22] Once again she began to suffer abdominal pain. The local Germantown doctor treated her with ice packs, and Elsie spent Christmas day in bed. "It was for me a comfortless vacation," Elsie noted, "I hated Germantown on sight, and I specifically disliked a pale young man and his wife who seemed to be continually at the house. They were ordinary, and I could not understand why Mother and Father tolerated them." Finally the Germantown doctor diagnosed chronic appendicitis, and Elsie tried to persuade the doctor to operate. "He did not favor an operation, favoring the policy of freezing out the inflammation. Christmas Day I spent in bed with an ice bag. In lieu of dinner Lawrence presented me with cheery mottoes."[23] Elsie believed the doctor was afraid to perform the operation and that he was incompetent and she despised him. Frustrated and angry at what she perceived as the doctor's incompetence, Elsie returned to Vassar for the spring semester.

Back at school but still suffering from bouts of abdominal pain and unable to eat, Elsie subsisted on a diet of soft-boiled eggs. "I got up only for classes and spent the rest of the day on the bed," Elsie recalled, "even during the absorbing discussions going on in our sitting room. In spite of this restriction, I got a good deal of work done—enough at least to convince myself that I was on the right track in pursuing my self-imposed task of tackling languages." Although ill, Elsie immersed herself in her studies.[24] "I did get my teeth into Anglo-Saxon and liked it," Elsie noted, "and I enjoyed taking Fast Greek under Abby Leach, the head of the Department of Greek and Latin, who taught us by the inductive method. For the class, which was an able group, after being lost for the first six weeks, woke to the fact that they had mastered the rudiments and were able to read simple Greek with some ease."[25]

Near the end of the spring semester, Moffat Myers invited Elsie to the senior dance at Columbia University. "I found an evening dress and accepted at once. I stayed overnight at the Myers' house on 70th Street... to be sure, I danced through the evening with a painful stitch in my side, but the fun was worth it."[26] However, upon her return to Vassar, Elsie experienced such pain that she had to go the College infirmary. Realizing the danger of the situation, the Vassar doctors called Elsie's family. The family, along with the Germantown doctor, met Elsie in Philadelphia where the surgery was performed to remove the appendix in a private hospital that evening. Elsie believed she barely survived the operation and was appalled when her Germantown doctor came to the hospital to see her. Shocked by his appearance Elsie remembered he "apologized abjectly. Remembering the avoidable pain of the past months, I said nothing at all."[27] Following some complications, Elsie returned to Germantown in an ambulance. "As the family story has it," Elsie recalled, "I, who could not even turn over in bed, was found one night curled up at the foot yelling for help because a bat had gotten into the room. That summer we had a scourge of caterpillars, and during my convalescence I used to lie on a steamer chair under the heavy trees on the lawn helplessly watching them descend on me. At night Marjorie and Lawrence would go around tossing out the intruders that entered by the vines encircling every window."[28]

Elsie's only consolation that summer was traveling around the countryside with the same Germantown doctor who had refused to operate on her. The doctor seemed embarrassed by his behavior and was trying to make it up to Elsie by taking her on these fresh-air rides. Another consolation "in that dreary summer" was the half-hour a day Elsie was allowed to read at the nearby Quaker Library, where she became acquainted with Greek drama. Elsie's recuperation proved beneficial in one aspect. While recuperating she became much closer to Marjorie and Lawrence. "The years between us somehow dwindled," she wrote, "and we became friends and companions. My congeniality with Lawrence and our enjoyment of each other's minds dates, I know, from that summer. Legend has it that once, when I had been moved downstairs and carefully established on a couch in the hall with Lawrence to watch me, we were found hours later violently arguing. Both of us complained bitterly when I was put back to bed, saying that we had not yet settled the first point under discussion. As I got stronger I used to go up to Lawrence's room on the third floor and look over with him his collection of Class Books and pictures."[29] Lawrence and Marjorie adjusted to Germantown better than Elsie. During Elsie's recuperation Lawrence was in the tenth grade and had received honors at the Germantown Boys School, a school he liked. Marjorie attended the Stevens School in Germantown.

The move to Germantown clearly brought home to Elsie the fact that the life she knew so well on Hicks Street was gone forever. "The pale young man I disliked had been given Father's job," Elsie wrote with dismay. "It seemed that Father was gotten down here just to organize the work and train the young man. Father was bitter about it, as well he might be. He was that summer a white and shaken person. Would I, Mother would ask, go for a walk with him? I would and did gladly, although our walks were silent ones. Father never said much about himself, but we used to be close friends, and I was startled to find that now we seemed to be too far apart to communicate with each other. It worried me, for he was tortured I knew, though by what I did not know."[30] Elsie knew their close friendship had been damaged beyond repair. The depression of 1893 had changed the Clapp family, although Elsie's mother and father continued to pretend to move among the affluent and live as they always had. Elsie knew she attended the Packer Collegiate Institute on scholarships and also was given an Elting Scholarship to attend Vassar. Yet the coming-out parties, the holidays, and the summer outings confused Elsie at the time as to the seriousness of the family situation. "My parents never discussed financial matters with me," Elsie recalled, "and my father at no time spoke of his anxieties and pressures. However, I blamed myself for being so immersed in high school and then in College that I had lost touch with him and, accepting things as they came, failed to see and appreciate their cost, and now, at this last reserve, I had somehow failed someone who always had been remarkably kind and generous, and I was not at home when the family sold the house and moved to Germantown. Marjorie, because she had helped Mother dismantle 164 and resettle in Germantown, had a better knowledge of the state of affairs and could better realize the tragedy of the loss of the Germantown position, father's best hope since 1893."[31] Throughout her memoirs Elsie expresses guilt in being so self-absorbed and perhaps even a spoiled brat during these difficult times for her family.

Following a summer of recuperation Elsie prepared to return to Vassar. She feared some dire circumstance or fate might keep her in Germantown. Her concern did not diminish until she climbed aboard the train to begin the trek back to Vassar. Elsie's father traveled with her as far as New York City with the hope of a new job prospect. Elsie was beginning her third year at Vassar with hope, optimism, and yet deep concern for her father and the family situation. Soon after Elsie's departure from Germantown, the family moved back to New York, settling on Madison Avenue below 26th Street.

Elsie's third year at Vassar (1901–1902) was punctuated by continued health problems. Despite the surgery, she still suffered from abdominal pain. The Vassar College doctors suggested rest, but Elsie found it difficult to attend classes and envied the healthy girls able to attend on a regular basis. Elsie described her difficulty. "The classes I missed by these futile attempts to recuperate I made up by passing off by examination extra Latin I had taken at Packer Institute," she wrote. "That year at Vassar my courses consisted of English, Greek, German Latin Prose, and Psychology—this time taken with a young man named Bawden from Chicago University who taught Biological Psychology, which was found much more interesting than the theological brand taken the first year with President Taylor."[32] This new psychology excited Elsie, and she absorbed much, applying the theory later in her practice.[33] The new psychology challenged the traditional idealist and realist view of mind as separate from the environment. William James viewed the mind as active and discrete. This more biological view of mind, also addressed by George Herbert Mead, "focused on the total organism adjusting to an environment, and treated mental processes as foundations of the interactions between the two."[34] John Dewey and James were trying to move psychology and even philosophy into a more scientific framework and a less theological one. A decade earlier James had produced his landmark *Principles of Psychology* in 1890. For James the active nature of the mind helped us understand the reality of the environment. However, this active nature not only received and sorted the information but for James held the key to "transforming the environment."[35] James stated, "The knower is an actor, and co-efficient of the truth on one side, whilst on the other he registers the truth which he helps to create."[36] James' view presented a challenge to knowledge as static; knowledge was now a tool to fashion the world according to the needs and desires of humankind. This was an obvious challenge to the traditional teacher/text approach to knowing in the formal setting of the school that was viewed by Dewey as antithetical to democracy and for James antithetical to mind.[37]

Excited by her studies but still suffering from pain, Elsie occasionally had the opportunity to go to New York for the weekend as her family resided in a boarding house on Lower Madison Avenue. During spring break of her third year, Elsie's Aunt Edith took her to a physician who believed her recent bouts with abdominal pain were caused by scar tissue. According to Elsie, the doctor softened the adhesions with electrical treatment, and the treatment helped the pain subside. Summer vacation that year was again spent in Mantoloking, New Jersey. Elsie described the summer. "As usual, we all found companions; Lawrence went with Stuart Myers and sometimes, Jim; they sailed, and loafed around. It was, I think, that year that Stuart and Lawrence took it upon themselves to watch over a fool minister who, knowing nothing about sailing, would on a free reef day take out his whole passel of small children; fussing and fuming, the boys would follow in one of our boats until they had seen the minister with his kids safe back in port."[38] Elsie, Lawrence, and Marjorie spent time with the Myers family. Sailing, weekly boat races, and dances were the center of activity. For Elsie, this summer was a very memorable one but not a good one due to the growing tension in her family. "Father was nervous and uneasy," Elsie recalled, "and often made trips to New York to see about some business prospect, each time departing hopefully and returning disappointed. Then one night, aroused by some noise, I got up and saw father, white and shaken, coming upstairs with a lamp—and suddenly I knew that he was drinking. Mother's tradition and code required that she admit nothing derogatory. I gave her every chance to tell me and finally questioned her directly, but she put aside any questions as impertinent and ridiculous. After that however, life for me was different, days filled with the usual summer gaieties, and nights when I lay awake till dawn when things seemed to quiet down. Of course we caught

Mother's unexpressed fear that people would know this. And, of course, I helped as I could—playing golf with Father and walking with him miles up the beach. Finally the summer came to an end, and with a sense of relief—and guilt—I returned to College."[39]

Once again, returning to Vassar brought a sense of relief, and Elsie began to immediately rectify her lack of credits due to her frequent illness-induced absences. In trying to remedy the situation, Elsie wrote a letter to a group of faculty assigned to deal with curriculum issues. It took the form of a petition.

Petition to the Faculty of Vassar College by Elsie Ripley Clapp
I entered college in the fall of 1899 as sophomore on the Watkins-Elting Scholarship. During the first semester of the following year of 1900-1901 I had appendicitis attacks, with an operation in May, and resulting illness during the greater part of last year, 1901-1902. The frequent enforced absences from college during these two years have prevented me from completing 13 out of 17 courses taken during that period. Four courses are completed and credited; 13 are just unfinished - 7 of them lacking only three weeks.

The full number of hours for the three years' work is 88. The number of hours to my credit as finished is 66, leaving 22 hours due. I have taken 36 hours in class almost to the end of the semester; 14 of these hours can be offered as ready now (soon); these are Psychology, which I have taken twice almost to the end of the course; Astronomy A which lacks only a few hours of observation work. And 9 hours which can be offered within 5-6 weeks (i.e. Freshman French, 6 hours, and Art B, 3 hours. The 14 hours ready now (soon) and the 9 hours ready in six weeks, together make up the 22 hours still lacking from the required total of 88 hours.

I held the Watkins-Elting scholarship on entrance for three years. In 1901 it was extended for me to four years, and expires in June, 1903. I depend on this scholarship to finish my college course. I am therefore anxious to complete my incomplete courses and finish the work during this year.

The committee requested Elsie meet with President Taylor, whom Elsie remembered as "pleasant, but bewildered."[40] To her dismay Elsie was not aided or assisted by any member of the faculty. Elsie never forgot this. "In later years, when the Vassar faculty used to tell me how highly they regarded my work," Elsie recalled, "I remembered [their lack of support] somewhat grimly."[41] From a faculty member's perspective perhaps it was not fully clear how Elsie wished to make up the twenty-two hours. She seemed most concerned with the loss of the scholarship that allowed her to attend Vassar. She asked the faculty to allow her to finish the courses before June 1903 when the scholarship expired. This confusion may have led to President Taylor's involvement. The lack of faculty response and support surprised Elsie and hurt her deeply. Because she did not have enough credits, she did not graduate with her class. Elsie made up most of the incompletes but lost her scholarship, which eventually forced her to leave Vassar.

During this time [school year 1902–1903], Elsie's family still lived on Madison Avenue, and Marjorie was working with cousins Florence and Anna Ripley

CHAPTER THREE 49

in a leather studio in New York. Elsie does not record whether Marjorie had to work to help support the family, nor does Elsie discuss any financial assistance received from her grandparents or the Ripley estate. Nevertheless, the loss of the Watkins-Elting scholarship meant Elsie had to find another means to finance her education. One of her mother's friends, Mrs. Alfred T. White, helped to a great extent, and Elsie recalled that she "remembered us with her usual lavish generosity."[42] Still feeling guilty about the family situation, Elsie decided to finance her own education and began to sell dinnerware at school. Elsie had learned about the dinnerware from Amy Dunlap, her friend and former classmate at the Packer Collegiate Institute and now the Packer registrar. Elsie felt she could no longer burden her family so she packed her bags and traveled to Trenton, New Jersey, to visit the factory where the dinnerware was made. Elsie became an official salesperson of Beleekware.[43] Her first order of twenty dollars was shipped to her at Vassar. "I was of course, frightened at my own temerity, but on return to college I took some brown wrapping paper and made and addressed individual notices to the entire student body. To my astonishment a large number of people came and bought the plates, tea-sets, and tankards I had ordered so that I was able not only to pay for the first shipment but also to order more. It proved to be a moderate though steady source of income throughout the year." The ability to help pay for her own education decreased Elsie's anxiety about the family situation, but did not alleviate it.[44]

Since Elsie did not have enough hours to graduate with her class, she had to take a second senior year with the Vassar class of 1903. Unfortunately, she still missed classes due to illness. Friends brought class lecture notes to her and checked out required library books. Elsie had a small tuition scholarship but "earned all money for clothes, books, and incidentals by cataloguing a large collection of photographs for the Greek Department, by tutoring beginners in Latin, by selling the Beleekware, and making cocoa for Room Parties....When I was not able physically to do these things some member of my crowd did them for me. When I was ill, Clara Frederick, one of the group who had a warm comfortable single on the second floor in Main, swapped rooms with me, saw to my affairs and took care of me to boot. As far as companionship went, this was one of the best years in college. During the day we each went our own way but every evening we gathered around nine in the suite occupied by Eleanor Carey and her roommates for tea and talk. I took great pleasure in these nightly gatherings when my spirits were low. Maude Peiper, another Whitlock group member who had become a distinguished pianist, used to take me into the old chapel and play to me by the hour. She and I were always astonished to find when we came to leave that big hall was filled with listeners."[45]

Elsie relied on her friends for help with her classes but also for companionship. Close friends and frequent participants were Maude Peiper, Marion Blitz,

Margaret Judson, and Crystal Eastman. Elsie made special note of Marion, Margaret, and Crystal. "Marion was a young Jewish girl and with the exception of Lucy Burns," Elsie noted, "the most brilliant conversationalist I ever knew, who made Sunday afternoons memorable with good talk. In appearance Marion was almost repulsive—ugly and grossly fat. One day I remember, she told me she realized this and had decided that both for her race and herself she must be acceptable for other reasons." Perhaps Marion reminded Elsie of herself, and Elsie might have found Marion's resolution acceptable. Like Marion, Elsie never considered herself physically attractive, not like her mother and sister Marjorie. Elsie also sought acceptance through other means.[46]

Margaret Judson was the daughter of the pastor of the Washington Square Judson Memorial Church in New York, a church known for its community work and parish house. Elsie thought of Margaret as a "friendly and generous person with a flair for literature and an interest in education." One evening Elsie and Margaret stayed up all might following their first reading of John Dewey's *My Pedagogic Creed*. Neither could believe such a school could actually exist. Dewey first published *My Pedagogic Creed* in the *School Journal* in 1897. Written in terms of belief statements, Dewey attempted in *My Pedagogic Creed* to explain his views on education, the school, subject matter, method, and social progress. Dewey defined the role of the teacher, not simply a trainer but more of an artist paying attention to feeling and emotion and investing that into proper social growth. Based on his brief experience at the Dewey Lab School at the University of Chicago, Dewey was beginning to challenge traditional education and the "dullness, formalism, and routine of which failed to provide the proper environment for helping a child gain the power of judgement." The child in Dewey's Lab School was seen as an "active, dynamic being with impulses, interests and activities of his own."[47] Based in the new psychology, teaching was not viewed as a means of filling the mind up or drawing it out. Building upon Peirce and James, Dewey suggested ideas were tied to activity, and they came to us through interaction with and within the environment. Dewey called this interaction experience. The mind, our ideas and ideals were related to social life and experiences in the real world. Dewey biographer Dykhuizen writes, "It follows that the school must be organized along social rather than individual lines, that children must be given opportunity to engage in group activities centering in some interest and challenge their abilities. Through the free give and take of such shared experiences, the child's mind escapes the narrow confines of its private life, entering into the larger life of his followers where it finds the stimulus and sustenance necessary for highest and fullest development."[48] John Dewey referred to this type of school environment as a miniature community, a means to prepare for social life, to engage it, and ideally prepare the participatory democratic citizen. The formal school separated the intellectual from the moral, and for Dewey this was a threat to democratic society. In the future Dewey would have enormous influence on Elsie Clapp and her philosophy of education although at this point she could only compare it with her own experiences in the classical/liberal/traditional education Dewey challenged. Elsie will eventually embody much of Dewey's thought in forming her conception of the community school.[49]

One of Elsie's most influential friends from the Class of 1903 was Crystal Eastman, the sister of Max Eastman, whom Elsie would meet in graduate school at Columbia. Elsie and Lucy had met Crystal Eastman when they had lived off campus in the same boarding house, Whitlock Cottage, their first year at Vassar. Elsie made note of her admiration of Crystal. "Of all my 1903 friends the most interesting to me was Crystal Eastman, whom Lucy and I had known well the first year at Whitlock Cottage. She was then a big, beautiful child—naive and unspoiled. There was always a special kind of bond between Crystal and Lucy; both were, in different ways, children of nature in Rousseau's sense, and quite different from the rest of us conventional and inhibited people." Crystal's father was in charge of the pastoral work of Dr. Thomas Beecher's Church in Elmira, New York. Elsie described Crystal's father. "I remember Mr. Eastman, tall, lean, and brown, with straight hair like an Indian, coming in late and tired and sitting down contentedly to a bowl of bread and milk for supper."[50] However it was Crystal's mother, Anis Ford Eastman, who impressed Elsie most. Elsie remembered Crystal's mother as engaging and enlightening who often stood in the pulpit for her frail and ailing husband. "Mrs. Eastman… made pies and cakes in the kitchen, delivered Commencement addresses and in between time worked on her Sunday sermon and talked to us," Elsie recalled. In his work, *Heroes I Have Known*, Max Eastman included a description of his mother. He wrote, "Anis Ford Eastman was brave—possessed in full measure the courage of her convictions—but her bravery was so mingled with gentleness, delicate considerateness, and was so unpretentious that this characteristic did not always appear upon the surface. She was hotly intolerant of sham and consoling sophistries. At the same time she was most tolerant of honest differences.…Withal she was extraordinary tactful, far beyond mere adroitness and finesse."[51] Crystal informed Elsie that regardless of how busy her mother was, she always found time to talk to them, often under the trees talking and reading with her and Max. Anis Eastman fascinated Elsie. Here was a woman involved, making a difference in the world and refusing to be bound by Victorian tradition and conviction. In Anis Eastman, for the first time in her life, beyond some of her teachers and Mary Churchill Ripley, Elsie saw a professional woman, a mother who was intellectually engaging, active and took the time to communicate on a personal level—all traits she missed in her own mother.[52]

The Vassar years were an important time in Elsie's life, but looking back on the years, she viewed the college experience as difficult and discouraging. "For three of the four years I was there I felt guilty about the Scholarship I held and for some time I had a recurrent nightmare about being able to get my college work finished. However looking back, I am amazed not that I accomplished so little, but that under the circumstances, I got done as much as I did... the necessity of earning the money I needed I did not mind at all, but I felt guilty not to be taking my share of responsibility at home, at the same time feeling quite bereft to have no one in the family present at my class Day." Her family's absence deeply hurt Elsie. She had been voted a member of the class of 1903 and had located a dress to wear but could not afford the bouquet. She was greatly relieved when her good friend Margaret Judson gave her one as a graduation present. Unable to graduate with the Class of 1903 due to lack of credits, Elsie watched from the gallery as her friends participated in the ceremony. A mother of a student asked Elsie about her future plans. "I was, I said," Elsie responded, "going at once into teaching as I did not have enough funds to come back. She opened an absurdly small silver mesh bag crammed with bills and thrust these into my hand." Elsie refused the offer but never forgot this example of generosity.[53] Up to this point in her life Elsie had not given a career much thought. She seemed to view college as an experience to prepare her for womanhood although she did not relish what that meant in Victorian terms. There were few career options open to women at the time, but Elsie had been exposed to some excellent teachers and women who were successful, and she respected their work. This group of professional women included Laura Wylie, Clara Crampton, Eleanor Coleman, Anis Ford Eastman, and Florence Keyes. Although she did not realize it at the time, she would become part of a group of professional women teachers who would attempt to shake the American school from its traditional moorings, greatly influenced by the philosophy of her future mentor John Dewey.[54]

The Vassar years for Elsie Clapp proved beneficial in expanding her social and intellectual horizons. "However, it must be acknowledged that in spite of these trials and tribulations," she wrote in retrospect, "I enjoyed my College friends and had the comfort in the sense of belonging to a large and enduring fellowship." Elsie came to understand the importance of belonging and fellowship and applied her personal understanding of this sort of community into the pedagogical principles she later adopted. "Moreover at College I gained an enlargement of mental horizons, experience on a more mature level of independent work and a glimpse, of what research was."[55] College gave Elsie a place where she felt she belonged, a type of community, and it is unfortunate she suffered health problems, perhaps brought on by the stress and concern about her family's situation. She learned to rely on herself—and her friends

CHAPTER THREE

when she needed them. She immersed herself in her studies. The work in Greek, English, geology, and biological psychology stimulated Elsie intellectually and provided an excellent foundation for finalizing her degree at Barnard College and pursuing graduate studies at Columbia University. Not finishing Vassar may have been a godsend for Elsie as it opened up opportunities and relationships she might never have experienced. The Barnard and Columbia campuses and the exposure to graduate work in philosophy opened up a new world for Elsie.

The summer of 1903 was again spent at Mantoloking, New Jersey, and Elsie remembered this summer well. Now a mature twenty-four, Elsie began to see the world from a different perspective and wrote, "Somewhat tardily, it began to dawn on me that summers here were for the benefit of us children, for there was little or anything here to interest Mother or Father. They did not enjoy the small open boat racing we found so enthralling, usually they did not share in an ocean bathing, and they were occasional observers, not participants in the Saturday club races and dances."[56] Elsie now saw her parents as lonely and isolated. "With this realization," she noted, "I threw myself in the effort to entertain father, playing golf mornings on a disreputable sand course, and in the evenings having some of my group at the house, or at least being there myself." Marjorie and Lawrence were still there, but others had moved on. Elsie's former suitor Moffat Myers was now working, and Elsie was again entering a new stage in her life, one that she would become best known for. Before leaving Vassar Elsie had obtained a teaching position at the Brooklyn Heights Seminary. Elsie Clapp was going to become a teacher, more for practical reasons at this point than intellectual ones.[57]

Chapter Four

Barnard and Columbia: The Beginning Teacher

Before Elsie had finished the spring semester at Vassar, she had obtained a teaching position at the Brooklyn Heights Seminary under the direction of family friend Ellen Yale Stevens. Alonzo Gray had established the school in 1851, and upon his death in 1860 the school came under the direction of Charles E. West. West "pioneered a college preparatory curriculum for girls that included math and science previously considered strictly male courses."[1] Henry Stiles in his *History of Brooklyn* referred to the Brooklyn Heights Seminary as a distinguished institution "instilling the confidence and support of an enlightened community."[2] Elsie described her position. "The position for which I was to receive the munificent salary of $500, was Teacher of English in the High School and School Secretary. For the secretarial work I had no preparations other that the work I had done at Vassar for the Greek Department...."[3] Borrowing a typewriter from friends, Elsie spent the summer prior to the opening of the fall term honing her secretarial skills and devising her own form of shorthand. Not willing to financially burden her family, she found lodging at a boarding house between Clinton and Court Streets. The boarding house was under the direction of a Mrs. Langthorne. "She herself opened the door when I went there," Elsie recalled, " and I liked her at once. For the next four years I leased her attic room heated by an oil stove from which I could look down into Packer garden."[4] Elsie still felt a sense of guilt that Marjorie and Lawrence fully "bore the burden of the home situation." "Retrospectively, it is hard to see why I did not at least share this with her (Marjorie)," Elsie noted, "but at the time it was assumed that after leaving College supporting myself by teaching was my job, and the teaching available was in Brooklyn. But I have always been ashamed that she had these cares during her girlhood, the period I had spent at Packer with no home responsibilities." Lawrence was studying at Columbia University in the School of Mines but due to a "lack of maturity" soon left Columbia to seek practical experience with his uncle, Arthur Dwight, a mining engineer in Mexico.[5]

Elsie was thrilled when increased enrollment at the Brooklyn Heights Seminary forced her to make a decision between secretarial work and teaching. "Given my choice," Elsie wrote, "I naturally chose teaching which I found I liked enormously; my students were the kind of girls I had grown up with on the Heights, and I did well with them. Although what I taught them about language and literature was what I had myself learned in high school and college, I worked hard at the job and began to gain confidence." For the first time in a long time Elsie felt healthy and worked diligently to build her expertise and confidence as a teacher.[6] Through her work at Brooklyn Heights Seminary, Elsie came into contact with Florence Greer, a math teacher and assistant principal at Brooklyn Heights, who introduced her to faculty at the Pratt Institute. The Pratt Institute, founded by Brooklyn industrialist Charlie Pratt, was designed to train artisans, designers, technicians, and teachers. It began granting degrees in 1887 with a curriculum designed for both men and women.[7] "It was my first real contact with professional women," Elsie excitedly wrote, "and I was fascinated with their life and interests."[8]

While teaching at the Brooklyn Heights Seminary, Elsie sought to complete her bachelor's degree, but she knew it was impossible without some form of financial assistance. She found a savior in her uncle by marriage, William Chickering. "He was born in Pittsfield, Massachusetts," Elsie noted, "but after he married Aunt Carrie, they moved to California where he became a member of a law firm." Elsie's father had put his sister Carrie through Vassar. A prominent criminal lawyer in California, Chickering had always been kind to Elsie and her family. Uncle Will, as Elsie called him, offered to pay for a year of schooling so she could complete her bachelor's degree and Elsie readily accepted. "He cared a great deal about the family, and whenever he made one of his flying trips East, he took the trouble to see us all and to give us a good time. He enjoyed especially taking Grandmother Clapp to some gay show and watching her laugh."[9] Elsie accompanied Uncle Will on several trips that included Skowhegan, Maine; Chicago, and southern Pennsylvania. On the Chicago train trip Elsie remembered her uncle placing on her lap a copy of Jane Addams' *Hull House*, which she no doubt read with interest. Elsie described the popularity of Will Chickering during the trip. "To me it seemed that he knew everyone on the train; he was, of course California's most prominent criminal lawyer and had scores of friends and acquaintances. He talked to me, young as I was, as to another adult and what talk—opinions and ideas illustrated by his own experiences and punctuated with classical quotations. He encouraged me to talk too, and I found myself telling him all I knew and felt and thought."[10] On one of these trips, Chickering also introduced Elsie to the "coal slums" of Pennsylvania. She had no idea at the time that one of her most important educational contributions would be working with and teaching the children of coal-mining families displaced by the Depression.[11] Will Chickering was more than Elsie's benefactor. Chickering had always treated Elsie with kindness and talked to her as an equal, and Elsie felt she could confide in him, particularly about her father. Elsie's father was still drinking, but according to Uncle Will,

CHAPTER FOUR

Elsie's father had remained faithful to his wife and had not dishonored the family. Elsie seemed relieved by Uncle Will's frankness and understanding of the situation. He thought Elsie worried too much and tried to comfort her about the family situation. Following this discussion Chickering asked Elsie, "What did you pay for that dress? How much salary do you get?" He was appalled when Elsie revealed the "munificent salary" she received as a teacher. He responded, "Why I get many, many times that for a single case." Uncle Will then turned to Elsie and tossed her a bill, saying, "use this to get yourself some decent clothes."[12]

At the age of twenty-six, Elsie felt too old to return to Vassar to complete her degree, so she began to look into transferring her credits to Barnard College of Columbia University. Founded in 1889, Barnard College viewed its mission to give girls in the New York City area a first-rate higher education. There were growing connections between Barnard and Teachers College to better prepare women for professional work, largely teaching.[13] "After examining my Vassar credits, "Elsie explained, "Barnard informed me that I lacked only 26 points for graduation and suggested that while I was finishing these I also take some graduate courses toward an M.A. During the past years I had come to feel that it was ridiculous to be teaching the history of English Literature without knowing anything about the development of ideas, so I chose to take my work for the M.A. in philosophy. This took some arranging. Later, Columbia departments established what they called 'Exchange Credit Courses,' but at the time the Philosophy Department felt doubtful about accepting as its student anyone who was majoring in English, and the English Department did not like the idea of one of its students taking courses in Philosophy. Finally, however, all the necessary permissions were secured."[14] Elsie was admitted to Barnard College on September 24, 1907, and listed her address as 59 Livingston Street, Brooklyn. Elsie received 100 points of credit from Vassar for previous courses.

While Elsie was completing her education, her family situation appeared to improve. Her father had been hired as a broker for the O'Day Brothers, "and some measure of his old warmth and geniality returned." "As always he said little about himself," Elsie wrote, "so one could only guess how difficult it was for him, and what an achievement this comeback was, really."[15] Lawrence was now back in New York to continue his engineering studies at Columbia. "Lawrence, always a family person," Elsie recalled, "enjoyed being at home and having a place where he could entertain his friends. Marjorie and I tried to have something planned for the weekends, and I used to invite some of the undergraduate girls I knew at the college Dormitory over for supper Sunday night." Elsie believed her mother and father enjoyed these occasions.[16] "It was fun to have Lawrence at home again," Elsie wrote, "and he, I know, enjoyed being with us and enjoyed, too, having his friends welcomed. He had the Clapp gift of making small incidents pleasurable; when he ranged the apartment after work was done in the evening in search of crackers and fruit, somehow it was a signal for everyone to participate." Both Elsie and Marjorie worked to keep weekends lively. Elsie had grown closer to Marjorie and Lawrence and Elsie wrote particularly about her relationship with Lawrence. "Our congeniality, discovered that summer in Germantown," she recalled, "still held. We both discussed our work, of course, often exchanging papers we had written on metallurgy and philosophy for each other's criticism; I can remember feeling inadequate and inexperienced as he talked to me about his personal problems."[17]

Elsie began graduate studies during the 1907 summer session and had saved enough money to pay for the session. To help with the cost of tuition and board, she also served as an assistant to her cousin, Lou Daniel, Dean of Women at Teachers College. During this session Elsie took History of Philosophy with William P. Montague and also a course in Fundamental Problems in Philosophy under F.J.E. Woodbridge. Prior to his appointment at Columbia, Montague had taught at Harvard and Radcliffe. He was among the leaders in the new realist movement in philosophy, professing what he termed animistic materialism, "that every item of human existence could be explained in terms of physics." Woodbridge had studied philosophy at the University of Berlin and was an Aristotlean scholar. He had "worked out a version of Aristoleanism which replaced the Aristotlean categories of matter and form with the newer categories of structure and activity while retaining Aristotle's notion of a natural teleology."[18] Elsie fondly remembered a critique for one of Woodbridge's classes "sitting under the trees on an Island Knoll in the middle of Riverside Drive." In retrospect, Elsie was a bit embarrassed that the critique was on one of Professor Dewey's articles. "The paper, however, impressed Woodbridge," Elsie noted, "and when Uncle Will Chickering went up to the university to see the men with whom I was studying, Woodbridge encouraged him in his plan to give me a year of graduate study."[19] Elsie sent one of her papers to her uncle and he responded: "I enjoyed reading it. It is so many years since Plato, Aristotle, Kant, and the long line of philosophers passed in essay before me that I cannot say the essay was thoroughly digested in one meal. I return it serene in the satisfaction that the professor whose mind runs in the same channel was satisfied. It means a lot to me that your work was well done. No investor likes to have his bank fail."[20] On top of her studies in philosophy, Elsie also enrolled in an English course on Elizabethan Lyric taught by John Erskine, whom she described as young and enthusiastic.[21]

"In 1907–1908 when I began work at the University," Elsie recalled, "I had, thanks to Uncle Will's generosity, no cares or responsibilities about money for books, clothes and incidental expenses and experienced the pleasure of

CHAPTER FOUR 59

new and stimulating work which I now had the health to enjoy. Determined to get some solid accomplishments behind me, I worked hard and the courses I took opened a new world to me mentally."[22] This financial stability allowed Elsie to concentrate on her studies by taking courses in her growing areas of interest; history, philosophy, and philosophy of education. Elsie took the required courses in economics and German, required of all graduate students. She continued her interest in philosophy studying Aristotle with Woodbridge and Plato with Wendel Bush. Bush had studied at Harvard with William James and George Santayana. In describing Bush, Dewey biographer George Dykhuizen wrote, "From James he acquired a penchant for the empirical, scientific, clinical approach to the problems of philosophy; from Santayana he absorbed an interest in the religious and aesthetic aspects of culture."[23]

Elsie also studied at Teachers College, officially chartered on January 12, 1889, thanks to the efforts of Columbia President Barnard, Nicholas Murray Butler, James Earl Russell, and a significant financial contribution by Grace Dodge. Russell led Teachers College from "pedagogical formalism" and sought to build a body of professional knowledge, scholarship, and technical skill.[24] President of Columbia University Nicholas Murray Butler described the progress of Teachers College in 1914 in his annual report. "It has steadily pursued the path marked out for it in the beginning of treating education as a unit resting on philosophical foundations. That foundation has in it elements psychological, elements economic, elements historical, and elements philosophical, in the narrow sense of that word. To each and all of these Teachers College devotes itself impartially, and it presents to the University of which it is a part and to the public a conception and treatment of education that, after all these years, remains unique. The work of Teachers College is a model upon which reformers in education all over the world shape their proposals. It is constantly visited by educators of ranks and distinction from all parts of the world."[25]

Elsie was part of this loose movement to professionalize education, to see it as a subject worthy of study by itself and within the traditional academy. No institution symbolized this movement more than Teachers College. Elsie took courses at Columbia and Teachers College. "I also was a participant in a Practicum in Philosophy of Education held by Professor MacVannel of Teachers College," Elsie explained, "where I came to know my lifelong friend, William H. Kilpatrick. The courses I took with John Dewey Saturday mornings at Teachers College on Social Life and the School Curriculum and Modern Ethical Ideas were a revelation, presenting a conception of education new to me but congenial and surprisingly familiar; everything I knew and experienced supported what Dewey said." Elsie does not elaborate on what she meant by familiarity and up to this point she had limited teaching experience. She was first exposed to Dewey's ideas at Vassar, and now they were beginning to make some sense. Elsie Clapp's relationship with Dewey was just beginning, a beginning that would influence both in theory and practice. For Elsie, her association with American's best-known and respected philosopher would mature intellectually over time as she worked closely with him as a graduate assistant and as she enrolled in his classes.[26]

For Elsie, Dewey's course on Types of Logical Theory "was... the most outstanding experience of the year, attended by a group of distinguished students and some members of the Philosophy Department." Discussion usually followed the lectures. Another stimulating class that Elsie and Florence Greer took was Arthur Lovejoy's course on Kant.[27] Elsie described Lovejoy as a "brusque and shy visiting professor." She claimed she was "bewildered" by his "detailed and earnest expositions of Kant's theories."[28] Florence and Elsie were members of the Philosophy Club as were all graduate students in philosophy. The group, although small, included Edna Orvis, Warner Brown, H.L. Hollingsworth and Max Eastman, Crystal Eastman's brother. Crystal Eastman, Elsie's friend from Vassar, was researching racial composition in the Pittsburgh Steel Mills for the Russell Sage Foundation. Brown and Hollingsworth were assisting James Cattell in his psychology laboratory. Max Eastman would become a well-known poet, critic and essayist and taught psychology and philosophy at Columbia. The group met two nights a week on the top floor of the old library and discussions went on until the librarians cut out the lights. Intellectually, Elsie was most impressed by Max Eastman, at the time serving as an assistant in the philosophy department. "I still recall the talks he gave in the big Philosophy Club," Elsie wrote, "and his ability to land a sentence on its feet in extemporaneous speaking. In appearance, Max, like his father was tall, lean and dark as a young Indian. He was the pride and joy of the Department; not for years, if ever, had it had a student with 'an equally brilliant mind.'"[29]

One of the requirements for the bachelor's degree was the Intellectual History of Western Europe given by James Harvey Robinson. "He insisted,'" Elsie wrote, "that we consider matters of history not only national events and political issues, inventions, discoveries and economic data, but also philosophy, art and literature... Robinson himself was brilliant, undogmatic and full of mischief, expected more of his student than human beings could accomplish, and delighted in provoking us to do our own thinking. In class he often read us something that the 'heretics' of a period, past or present, had said, gave instances to show how little difference at the time the invention of printing made, or matched comments in a current newspaper article with those of the writers in the thirteenth, sixteenth, or seventeenth centuries. I found both his viewpoint and his study-approach stimulating; indeed, they became increasingly directive in my own work and thinking." Elsie found this environment intellectually stimulating, particularly the study of the history of ideas.[30] She

CHAPTER FOUR 61

went on to describe this notable year at Columbia. "Chief among its events was a series of lectures given by heads of Departments; some of these—lecture in Ethics by John Dewey, History by James Harvey Robinson—were much admired and to a lesser extent, Metaphysics by F.J.E. Woodbridge, and Psychology by Woodward."[31]

During her senior year at Barnard, 1907–1908, Elsie took courses in economics, education, German, history and philosophy. She received A's in education, history and philosophy but only managed a C in German. Taking these courses gave Elsie the twenty-six points she needed to graduate, and she matriculated from Barnard with an A.B. degree on May 27, 1908.[32] Elsie received her bachelor's degree in English and graduated with the class of 1908. She had taken numerous graduate credits and now desired to apply them to a master of Arts degree "although the university required a year to lapse between the degrees."[33] Uncle Will had given her enough money to pay for the master's degree, but he strongly advised against further graduate study. Elsie's benefactor could see no reason why someone desiring to teach needed graduate work beyond the master's. He wrote the following note to Elsie:

> I fear you would be less fit to go out into the world, except in a very unusual position, than you are now. I think there is great danger of your getting over-educated and thereby looking at things from the standpoint of a pedant rather than from a practical individual, and thus look over your pupils rather than at them... it is as if I had spent all my life thus far in studying law, and perhaps make a good lecturer upon law but not make my salt as a practical lawyer... my experience is that in the world one is learning every day, and that education is only to fit us to suit the talents nature has given us to the best effect.

In his own version of pragmatism, Chickering implied to Elsie that knowledge outside the realm of experience was not helpful. In his own view law school did not mean much without learning how to practice law and in this sense he was correct. Elsie was certainly more educated than the majority of teachers of her day. However, underneath the surface there seems to be a gender bias posing the question why a woman teacher needed to be educated further. This was not an easy decision for Elsie to make. She was among the first classes of women who had graduated from college. In retrospect Elsie responded to her uncle's concerns: "It is now hard to see why I did not talk this matter over with Uncle Will, whom I both respected and admired. Perhaps I was in love with graduate study and believed that the courses planned would be as rewarding as those I had last year. In any case, I was unable or unwilling to believe that longer graduate study would make me a less capable teacher."[34]

Elsie met the requirements for the master's in philosophy by taking John Dewey's course on Psychological Ethics and writing a thesis under the direction of the philosophy department on Creative Imagination. To help with the costs of her continuing graduate study, Elsie attained a position as an assistant teacher in the upper elementary grades at the Horace Mann School, which paid her a salary of five hundred dollars per year. The Industrial Education Association had originally founded the Horace Mann School in 1884. With the establishment of the New York College for the Training of Teachers, later Teachers College, in 1887, Horace Mann School began its distinguished service. Teachers College historian Lawrence Cremin writes that Teachers College "needed a school for experimentation in curriculum and methods, a place where approved practice could be demonstrated and new theories tested."[35] When Elsie taught at Horace Mann, it was one of the largest private schools in the country. Elsie tutored fifth, sixth and seventh grade children needing remediation. "I enjoyed tutoring the children, "Elsie wrote, "but found that substituting for absent teachers, which during the winters months was more frequent than I had anticipated, often interfered with my own class attendance." Finally after teaching five months at Horace Mann, Elsie became the secretary to the *Journal of Philosophy, Psychology and Scientific Methods* under the direction of F.J.E. Woodbridge. Woodbridge helped Elsie transfer from Horace Mann. "The pay was small—$50.00 a month—but no work I ever did contributed more to my education," Elsie recalled. "Woodbridge himself was reasonable and generous. I worked at a desk in his office, the big Philosophy Room and was free to attend my classes, the only requirement being that I get the work done. Working hours were 9 to 5 Monday thru Friday, and 9 to 12 on Saturdays, which of course threw the bulk of my reading and study into the evenings. However, I managed it; I had enough sense after office hours every day, rain, or shine, to take a walk on Riverside Drive from 116th Street to the Soldier's and Sailor's Monument at 86th Street and back, a distance of three miles. This exercise, followed by a hot bath and dinner, enabled me to tackle my work in the evening. Moreover, work on *The Journal*, though strenuous, was never pressing and was to me intensely interesting."[36] To cover the rest of her tuition and board, Elsie served as a residence scholar at Brooks Hall, Barnard College. Here she supervised some undergraduates, performed some administrative duties, and served as a hostess for university guests.

These new positions gave Elsie the freedom to attend classes and contributed much to her informal education. "It was my job to acknowledge the receipt of all new books and arrange for their review by people whom Woodbridge had chosen," she wrote, "to acknowledge the receipt of all manuscripts and take at Woodbridge's dictation all letters he wished to write, to read all philosophic journals the library had—American, English, French, German, Spanish and Italian—and bring to Woodbridge's attention articles that seemed important." This appeared a daunting task and a strenuous one, but Elsie learned much in the process. From 1910 to 1913, the *Journal of Philosophy, Psychology and Scientific Methods* was under the editorial direction of F.J.E. Woodbridge and Wendell Bush. The typical format of the journal included two or three articles followed by book reviews, new acquisitions and notes and news in philosophy. During Elsie's association with the journal's contributors read like a Who's Who in American philosophy and psychology. A short list of contributors included John Broadus Watson, George Herbert Mead, Boyd Bode, Bertrand Russell, Horace Kallen, Ralph Barton Perry, Max Eastman, Ernest Hocking, William James, James Angell, John Dewey, and James Harvey Robinson. Most contributors were men who dominated both disciplines and the academy at the time. Elsie was breaking this intellectual hegemony even though, at the time, this was not her goal. Elsie enjoyed intellectual pursuits and challenges, and during her tenure with the journal she wrote two book reviews.

Elsie's first review appeared in 1911 when she reviewed Stanley M. Bligh's *The Direction of Desire: Suggestions for the Application of Psychology to Everyday Life*. Rather than study the mind per se, "the province of pure psychology," Bligh sought to move the personality of the individual in a more efficient and positive direction. Elsie applauded Bligh's attempt to integrate the individual within the social context. She did not agree with Bligh's designation of certain personality types as a guide to shaping behavior and found the book difficult to read. But most important she challenged Bligh's view that stability and harmony were "to some extent ethical qualities," when attached to certain types of personalities.[37] Elsie argued what constituted the ethical was found in the implications and consequences of action, not personality types. Character counted more for Elsie than personality traits, and the practical implications of behavior were to be guided by inquiry and testing in the realm of real human experience. Elsie emphasized that psychology or philosophy should be in "the interests of human welfare, suggest lines of action and of inquiry which would test and modify psychological principles and maintain a philosophical consideration of their actual value and function in life."[38] Elsie footnoted Dewey's and Tuft's *Ethics*, emphasizing Section Two titled "Theory of Moral Life" and Dewey's *How We Think* to inform the reader of her influence.

A year later Elsie reviewed Willystine Goodsell's, *The Conflict of Naturalism and Humanism*.[39] Always interested in the history of ideas, Elsie was drawn to this work because of its discussion of humanism and naturalism in education along with Goodsell's attempt to reconcile the two. Goodsell defined materialism as the attempt to explain human life through reference to natural forces which operate through the universe. According to Goodsell, objects, events, and values could be explained by fact or cause and effect claims without reference to supernaturalism. Humanism was defined as the belief that human beings were the source of all values and have the ability and the understanding to give meaning to the world. As Goodsell put it, the universe could be described "through the consciousness of man."[40] Elsie critiqued the work for creating an opposition between naturalism and humanism as defined and treated by Goodsell through her analysis of different historical periods. Elsie believed Goodsell failed to see the changing nature of ideas, shaped by humankind and by changes in social, political, and economic forces. Rather than the conflict of naturalism and humanism, Goodsell's attempt seemed to point more to conceptual confusion. In her pragmatist view, Elsie believed the two were not as dualistic as Goodsell approached them and that Goodsell failed to synthesize the two for a better understanding of "the philosophy and art of education."[41] Elsie agreed with Goodsell's intent to reconcile naturalism and humanism through use of pragmatism, but she did not agree with the method Goodsell chose to do so. Elsie closed her review and stated, "The study wants simple and clear purpose, and the conviction which springs from an integral conception of experience, assuring unity of interest and independence of approach and of activity."[42]

From these reviews it is clear that Elsie had a sense of the pragmatist ethic, that the desire for harmony and stability does not always engender ethical consequences. One's actions needed to be based on the implications and practical consequences. Elsie is on the fringe here of expressing an ethic grounded in sympathetic character. As Dewey suggested in his *Ethics*, "the great need for the moral agent is thus a character which will make him as open, as accessible as possible, to the recognition of the consequences of his behavior."[43] Elsie believed that pragmatism reconciled naturalism and humanism. One could use the method of scientific inquiry, questioning, and reflection to help understand the human condition, but naturalism needed humanism to assign value to these conditions. Dewey suggested and Elsie concurred that "both of them are necessary to make up the whole account of human experience."[44] Educators needed to understand that the dualism of humanism (focus on the mind) and naturalism (focus on matter) needed to be resolved. Elsie's three years with the journal stimulated her intellectual growth as she began to grasp the distinctions between the idealists, realists, and pragmatists. These distinctions formed the later foundation for her own pragmatism, which she attempted to put into practice.

Elsie's work on the journal kept her in the midst of the philosophy department, and she became personally closer to the faculty. "Since I was their student," she wrote, "they would often stop and talk with me, and I listened in on their arguments and discussions. I was privileged, and I knew it; despite the small wages I received."[45] The relations with the English faculty were far more impersonal. Even though Elsie received offers for teaching positions, with substantial increases in salary, she remained at her post with the journal. She vividly described this new stimulating work opening up to her. "At this time the Philosophy Department was housed on the top floor of the Old Library Building, and the larger room which held the Department's Library became a natural gathering place. Often in the late afternoon Professor Simkovitch would stroll in, stretch out in an armchair and talk about his students, many of them revolutionaries who, though younger than I, had lived a lifetime already, always in danger from the Czarist regime and often suffering exile in Siberia."[46] Saturdays were workdays for the journal and for Elsie. With a sense of excitement Elsie recalled Saturday mornings when "William James would blow in from Cambridge, charging the whole room with excitement; members of the philosophy department would gather, and James would pass up and down, talking fast and taking them all on in argument." Elsie made herself "small and listened." James had a way of captivating an audience.[47]

Elsie received her Master of Arts degree in philosophy from Columbia University in June 1909 and participated in the commencement. During that summer she continued her studies with Dewey. "Welcoming the chance to study with Dewey when I was not carrying a heavy work-schedule," Elsie recalled, "I took the course he was giving in Summer Session this year on Logic Applied to the Problems of Teaching." Elsie sought every opportunity to study with Dewey even for non-credit. Following the award of the master's degree, Elsie continued her studies in the fall, taking an English course in Historical English Grammar with Otto Jesperson, an exchange professor from Copenhagen, Denmark. She also took courses in Medieval Literature: Ballad and Epic, Anglo-Saxon Poetry and a seminar on Eighteenth-Century Literature under Professor Trent. Elsie described Trent as a southern gentleman and distinguished scholar on the works of John Milton. "The work I did with him," she recalled, "made a deep impression on me, and I have during the years increasingly appreciated his teaching."[48]

Elsie continued to nurture her interest in philosophy and studied again with Dewey, taking a course on Kant, which, Elsie described "was notable for its clarity and conciseness," and also a course on the Philosophy of Education at Teachers College. Each day becoming closer to Dewey, Elsie wrote about an early interaction. "One day Dr. Dewey appeared in the Philosophy Room with his hands full of papers. Could I he asked find time to help him with these? I could and I did." Dewey's students were confused and some were failing. Apparently Dewey's lectures were not effective which he readily admitted. One of Dewey's best-known students, Sidney Hook, described Dewey's teaching style: "Dewey seemed to me to violate his own pedagogical principles. He made no attempt to motivate or arouse the interest of his audience, to relate problems to their own experiences... he rarely provoked a lively participation and response from students... spoke in a husky monotone... his discourse was far from fluent. There were pauses and sometimes long lapses as he gazed out of the window or above the heads of his audience."[49] Max Eastman also recalled Dewey's teaching style. "He was thinking rather than lecturing, evolving a system of philosophy ex tempore, and taking his time about it. The process was impersonal and rather unrelated to his pupils—until one of them would ask a question. Then those glowing eyes would come down from the ceiling and shine into that pupil and draw out of him and his innocent question intellectual wonders as he never imagined had their seeds in his brain or bosom."[50] It was no wonder Dewey was having problems. Elsie recommended Dewey have a conference with each student following each lecture. "We were both surprised at the difference it made," Elsie recalled.[51]

During the spring semester, Woodbridge suggested Elsie compete for a fellowship that required writing a research proposal. With the deadline closely approaching, Elsie protested, knowing she would have to stay up all night to write it, yet she wrote it and submitted the proposal. "I still remember Woodbridge's pride," she wrote, "when he returned from a faculty meeting reporting that only four Fellowships had been awarded, and of these only one to a woman—myself. No father could have been more pleased." Through her work on the *Journal* and her studies in the philosophy department, Elsie had grown close to Woodbridge. Once after Elsie handed in a late paper and offered what she thought was an adequate explanation, Woodbridge responded, "Remember, it is not the reason why it was handed in late, but the fact that it was, that you and your instructor will remember." "Verbally," Elsie wrote in her memoirs, "Woodbridge was a martinet, but I have never known a kinder or more considerate man."[52]

That summer Elsie assisted Dewey in his course on the Aims and Principles of Education at Teachers College, an assistantship she believed Dewey paid for out of his own pocket. By now Elsie had chosen her dissertation topic on the history of English grammar, a topic choice based on discussion with Dewey and his lectures on the structure and function of language. Professor Thorndike, head of Columbia's English department, approved her daunting dissertation topic.

Thorndike recommended Professor George Krapp serve as Elsie's dissertation advisor because of his expertise in the period with which she was working. With the assistance of Professor Krapp, Elsie composed a list of libraries in New England that might have the early primary source documents she needed. Living on a small stipend from the department and living in "deplorable" YMCAs or with friends, Elsie began her studies in the History of English Grammar. Her research took her to the public libraries of Boston, Worcester, and Hartford and the university libraries of Harvard and Yale. At Harvard, Elsie was assigned a reader's desk, and books were brought across the campus in a wheelbarrow, a method she thought casual considering the age and value of the manuscripts. "At Yale University which, like Harvard, did not then have adequate library facilities," Elsie explained, "I finally found the old books I came to consult piled in heaps on the top floor of a house on a side street in New Haven." Compared to Columbia, Elsie did not feel Harvard or Yale had adequate library facilities.[53]

The school year 1910–1911 marked an important period in her intellectual growth. After numerous courses and years of graduate study she was beginning to formulate her own philosophy of education deeply rooted in American pragmatism. Her studies in psychology and her interactions with and reading of James and Dewey led her to a more scientific understanding of psychology and its relationship to pedagogy. Through a discussion group of philosophy students led by Brown and Hollingsworth, Elsie came into contact with Cattell's work in emotional reaction time. She continued her studies in the philosophy department, taking a course on Logic with Montague, and attended Dewey's lectures on Types of Logical Theory, which she termed revolutionary. Elsie began to see the nature of the human being as biological, psychological, and sociological, exemplifying the pragmatic concept of the integration of mind with body.

Regardless of her interest in Dewey, Elsie sensed he was an outsider with his more traditional philosophical colleagues, and her close association with departmental members gave her insight into their differences. "Since coming to Columbia in 1905," she wrote, "Dewey had been engaged in a polemic with philosophers here and abroad regarding the fixed distinctions between inner and outer, sense and reason, the self and the world." Through her work on the *Journal of Philosophy, Psychology and Scientific Methods*, Elsie was able to follow departmental discussions and the important differences. "Montague was a realist," she noted, "Woodbridge called himself a metaphysical realist, and Dr. Bush was a Platonist; and the solipistic problem which engaged them was how the self, which knows only itself, could have knowledge of other selves and of the world around it. To them, the distinctions against which Dewey inveighed were necessary and inevitable. Although his ideas fascinated them, for members of the Department attended most of his courses, they found it difficult to grasp his conception of the individual-in-the-world, acting upon it and reacting to it, living and learning." Elsie was beginning to grasp Dewey's pragmatic notion of experience as some type of interaction or transaction between an individual and the environment. It was Elsie's work in the philosophy department that stimulated her intellectual growth. She was particularly influenced by Dewey and enrolled in each course he gave. During the year Elsie continued her work on the dissertation, locating some valuable research materials in the library of Teachers College. She also spent some time researching the local collection of George Plimpton, who was associated with the Macmillan

Publishing Company. Weekends, holidays, and spare time were spent at Plimpton's home on Lower Park Avenue in New York in his personal library.[54]

Elsie's work with the *Journal of Philosophy, Psychology and Scientific Methods* went well, which gave her more time to continue her doctoral work in English. She continued her studies in the English department with Professor Lawrence in Medieval Literature, Trent in Eighteenth Century Literature, Thorndike in English Drama to 1642, and Krapp on English Literature of the Sixteenth Century. Elsie described Trent as "an invigorating person to work with, giving you enough direction at the beginning of a term paper so that you did not feel lost, then leaving you to your own devices, and finally considering fully and carefully the results you turn in."[55] Elsie audited a course with Professor Springarm on the History of Literary Criticism in Modern Europe to gain a sense of English literary criticism, but her heart was in philosophy. "Although I was faithful in attending to the requirements of the English course," Elsie wrote, "and found both Trent's and Lawrence's courses interesting, it was in philosophy and in philosophy of education that I experienced stimulation and satisfaction."[56] Elsie studied with Dewey again, taking his course on Philosophy and Education in Their Historic Relations. She described her experiences in that course: "Dewey's prodigious learning and his insight enable him to deal with this material as no one else has done. From it I discovered what it is to really know a writer and realized that the insight that discerns significant relations between educational development and the history of thought is the result of both reflection and wide knowledge and experience."[57]

Always concerned about financing her doctoral study, Elsie still worked as a residence scholar at Brooks Hall, Barnard College. She still received fifty dollars a month for her work on the *Journal* and in the spring of 1910 was awarded the Curtis Fellowship in the Department of English. She also received seventy-five dollars for assisting Dewey in some of his courses at Teachers College. Elsie's friends included graduate students in the English and Philosophy departments. She considered herself a member in good standing among the graduate students in the English department yet seemed most influenced and attracted to those in philosophy. Her close friends in English included Dorothy Brewster; Clark Jordan, "an excellent student from the Midwest whom everyone liked and admired"; Carl van Doren, "then courting Frieda Kirchway among the stacks"; and Blanche Williams, "an ambitious young woman later known for her work on the short story."[58] The most notable of these acquaintances, Carl van Doren, would become an editor and critic, best known for his biography of Benjamin Franklin that won the Pulitzer Prize in 1938.

During the summer session of 1911 Elsie continued to nurture her interest in philosophy and assisted Dewey in two of his courses at Teachers College, Foundations of Method and Social Aspects of the School Curriculum. Preparing for the fall semester of 1911, Dewey gave Elsie outlines of his courses on An Analysis of Experience and Theory of Experience for her comments. "As was his custom," Elsie recalled, "he gave me an outline of the course and asked me to give him my reactions, for it was his belief that such sharing helped his own thinking."[59] She worked with Dewey during the mornings and typically spent the afternoons with her father, often attending professional baseball games, "where she learned the fine points of the game" and familiarized herself with the players' batting averages. Elsie continued her correspondence with Dewey that summer as he spent time on his farm in Long Island. This correspondence usually included concepts he wished to explore in class, responses to Elsie's comments, and summaries of lectures and class discussions. In retrospect, Elsie found her mentor patient, kind, and generous in his willingness to work with her. It is noteworthy that Dewey took this time and most likely believed he too was benefiting professionally from his interaction with Elsie. "Dr. Dewey made this exchange seem natural and a matter of course," Elsie wrote, "but I see now how unusual was the trouble he took to educate his young assistant."[60]

Beginning another school year, 1911–1912, Elsie continued working on her dissertation and taking courses in the English department. She took a course with Thorndike on Nineteenth Century Literature and audited Professor Lawrence's course on Chaucer, but soon her academic goals were disrupted by concerns about her family, and Elsie moved in with her father and mother at the apartment on 142 East 18th Street. Elsie knew Marjorie had been the mainstay in the family, and now the stresses of that responsibility coupled with her work at the leather studio had become too much. Marjorie left New York for her health and mental stability and went to spend time with Lawrence in Silverton, Colorado. Elsie's mother supervised the work at Marjorie's leather shop for a short while but eventually sublet the studio. Elsie described this difficult situation: "Though I had returned to Brooks Hall in October when university classes opened, it was soon evident that being alone and lonely was too much for Mother and Father, so I moved down to 18th Street to stay with them. I believed that I could manage my University work while living at home but found it hard to do the all-out, intensive work needed during those last months of preparation. Father was still with the O'Day Brokerage Firm, and Mother was now working for Mrs. Alfred White's Charities in Brooklyn. Daytimes I could be at the University but in the evenings when they were at home I was too conscious of their need of me to retire into my studies."[61] Elsie found it difficult to keep her intensity in her university studies and balance her responsibilities at home. She had always felt Marjorie and Lawrence had borne much responsibility in the home situation while she was away at school, and now it was her turn. It still seemed the family had not fully come to grips with their losses in the Panic of 1893. During the summer of 1912, Lawrence graduated as a metallurgical engineer from the Columbia University School of Mines. All the family attended the graduation. Following his experience in Mexico, Lawrence had decided to continue his formal studies and had resumed his academic work in February 1908. He excelled in his studies and was near the top of his class, receiving the prestigious Illig Medal and being admitted to the honorary mining society. Following graduation, Lawrence took a position as the superintendent of the Silver Lake Mine and Mills in Colorado, owned by the American Smelting and Refining Company.[62]

Elsie felt more at home at Columbia than with her family. She had matured socially and intellectually, and she felt close to many of her fellow students and a few professors, particularly Dewey and Woodbridge. Constantly struggling for self-esteem, confidence, and experiencing feelings of guilt. Elsie soon received a devastating personal blow. Her confidence in herself and her respect for the English department would be drastically altered as she prepared to take her English preliminaries for the Doctor of Philosophy degree. Elsie's confidence had been bolstered by her excellent grades in the English department and her Curtis Fellowship. Professor Trent had used some of Elsie's papers to exemplify excellent graduate student work, yet, underlying Elsie's confidence was a feeling of insecurity. Elsie described her impressions of this time: "I worked hard in those years and was happy feeling that at long last I was getting some solid work done and was succeeding in it. I have often said that while I was at the University no one ever praised me; that was true." This insecurity was enhanced when Elsie's friend Clark Jordan stood for his oral preliminaries in the English department. "He was the most industrious of us and well prepared," Elsie recalled, "we had no doubt about the outcome and sat about the big English Seminar Room waiting to congratulate him. A crushed boy came back. They had, he said, turned him down." Incensed, Elsie blamed Professor Ayres and believed he failed Jordan because he did not consider him to be a gentleman, and "he [Ayres] had not wished to add to the number of such Ph.D.s."[63] According to Elsie, Ayres had expressed his concern to a colleague. "The group saw red," Elsie recalled with indignation, "for Clark Jordan was we knew, a gentlemen in every sense." Undeterred by the fact that she was herself about to come up, Dorothy Brewster registered a protest. "I did also," Elsie recalled, "though probably less tactfully, for I asked whether the English Department was willing to let Ayres's injudicious and— shall we say—ungentlemanly remark represent it. This incident was as I recall several months before the date of my own examination, but no doubt what I said got back to Ayres and rankled...."[64]

Elsie did not like Ayres and believed she had embarrassed him in front of his class by asking questions he could not answer. She described how Clark Jordan's failure affected her and some of the other graduate students: "I wondered if they realized the disillusioning effect of what had been said and done to the other Ph.D. candidates; I, for one, was jolted out of my innocent regard for the Department and felt cynical about the whole business." Dorothy Brewster's examination went well and she passed. Elsie thought Dorothy by far one of the best students in the graduate English group and richly deserved her success. However, Dorothy's passing her preliminaries did not bolster Elsie's fragile and wavering confidence.

Elsie took the English preliminaries in March 1912, and the experience would affect her for a lifetime. "I went to it without undue perturbation," she wrote, "feeling that I knew these men with whom I had worked and what they would require in which, however, I was quite wrong." Elsie's dissertation advisor, Professor Krapp, began the questioning, asking her to outline the course of language development for the fifteenth, sixteenth, and seventeenth centuries. "Then he asked me to describe in detail each period named," Elsie explained, "which I did not feel prepared to do; I sensed, of course, even in my preoccupation the surprise and shock this plain statement of fact occasioned. Then Trent began questioning me in some detail about the literature of the 18th century; his manner was friendly, and I guessed that he was making an attempt to affront the poor impression I had created."[65] As the examination continued, Elsie was caught off guard when Professor Fletcher asked her to name the author and form of the *Faerie Queen*. Elsie's performance up to this point led some departmental members to believe she was not well prepared for the exam although they all knew her reputation as an excellent student. Elsie believed her stellar reputation led the faculty to unrealistic expectations. The examination continued until Professors Ayres and Lawrence began to argue. The argument soon developed into a heated discussion, and Trent began to argue with Ayres. "I did not gather its import but," Elsie noted, "as it continued and involved the others, I supposed it was concerned with some differences in faculty opinion. Professor Thorndike, who chaired the examination, did not enter into the discussion but also made no attempt to halt it. Once Trent said, 'we have not yet finished examining Miss Clapp. I think we should return to that.' However, they completely ignored him and went on arguing among themselves."[66]

Finally, having heard enough and flabbergasted at the actions of the faculty, Elsie stood up and left the room. Thorndike affirmed her action and told her it was best she wait outside. "When he came out in a few minutes, I was looking out the window," Elsie recalled. "I don't know how to tell you, he said, you don't have to, I answered. He was unhappy and said he hoped I would come up again. I replied that I could not then say finally, of course, but that I thought it very unlikely. As I was going out of the door he said again, I don't understand—our most brilliant pupil—I do, I said and left."[67] The incident frustrated, disgusted, and deeply hurt Elsie. Elsie immediately called her father and he met her at the 18th Street subway station. Angry, hurt, exhausted, and depressed by the situation, Elsie described her feelings: "As for me, the whole experience left me utterly spent; some part of me seemed dead, and I felt nothing and cared less. Mother at once arranged to have me stay with Aunt Edith at her hospital, largely a psychiatric facility, in the Lake Pompton district. There I was promptly put to bed and for days had an uncontrollable chill; within a fortnight, however, I had recovered sufficiently to be out tramping the hills."[68]

Spending several weeks with Aunt Edith provided Elsie a time to rest and relax. Edith challenged Elsie to build on her strengths. "During the weeks I was there Aunt Edith and I had many long talks," Elsie recalled, "chiefly about the hospital and its treatments. At that time she was working with some doctors to restore the nervous balance of women upset in their marital relations." Elsie seemed concerned about a history of mental illness in her father's family and how it might affect her. She recalled the conversation with Edith. "Then she spoke of Father's strengths and abilities, obscured in later years, and the traits that might have betrayed him. She talked also about the Ripleys, their austerity and somewhat ruthless strength. I do not remember exactly what she said about Mother, but I glimpsed for the first time the fact that her demands and her lack of understanding of a nature so different from her own had in a way contributed to Father's difficulties."[69]

"Characteristically, what Aunt Edith said was constructive," Elsie noted. "It was up to me, she said plainly, what I made of these family traits; for I, the child of these two people [Sarah Ripley and William Clapp], had to choose to use the 'the Ripley force and determination and the talents and responsiveness of the Clapps; to temper the Ripley's drive with insight and find for the Clapps's emotional frustrations some creative outlet and expression.'"[70] "From my father I inherited an alert and sensitive intelligence; from my Mother, vigor and executive ability. She [Aunt Edith] said finally that, happily and inevitably, I would be like neither and like both, and added that possibly I might gain what neither had. I am now, many years later, quite sure that what she said did not tell me but wisely left me to find out for myself, was the constructive use of one's traits and tendencies is a never-ending job—to be continued every day one lives. It would, however, be impossible to overestimate the effect of what Aunt Edith told me, for it embodies the sum and substance of my later efforts, however well or ill they have succeeded."[71] Aunt Edith advised Elsie to go on with life and build upon her strengths, and Elsie considered her Aunt Edith a godsend at this point in her life.

While Elsie was recuperating at the hospital in Lake Pompton, her friend Dorothy Brewster met with Professors Thorndike and Trent. Dorothy wrote Elsie a note discussing in detail the events that lead to her failure in the pre-

CHAPTER FOUR

liminaries. According to Dorothy's letter, the faculty had no definite plan for how they intended to examine Elsie. The letter suggested that some of the faculty members were disturbed by Elsie's personality, a little annoyed by her desire to do things in her own way and perhaps sensed a degree of arrogance. Dorothy suggested to Elsie that Professors Trent, Krapp, and Fletcher were supportive of her. Trent believed Elsie may have put off till later important topics related to her dissertation. On a more personal level Dorothy expressed her own feelings: "You are a little responsible for the misinterpretation put upon your work," Dorothy suggested to Elsie, "I don't think you should throw the whole thing over. It has been a matter of misunderstanding between students and Department, and you share that in common with the rest. I think I can suggest ways of dealing with the material for a second examination."[72] Elsie must have been stung by Dorothy's implication that her own actions may have lessened her chances. Apparently, Elsie had given the committee the impression she was not well prepared although Dorothy and Thorndike suggested that it was all just a misunderstanding and that Elsie should try again.[73]

Upon reading the letter, Elsie sought to rationalize how she had angered Thorndike and other members of the English department. Elsie believed Thorndike may have been upset by her decision to take a second minor in philosophy and not in English. As she viewed it, a minor in philosophy only benefited her in her studies in the history of thought. At the time Thorndike offered no objection to the minor in philosophy. As a student in Professor Ayres's History of English Grammar, Elsie had brought up questions in class he could not answer. She believed, in retrospect, that this questioning had offended him. He was also aware of Elsie's comments following Clark Jordan's failed preliminaries. Elsie had no idea how she had offended Professor Lawrence. Elsie's relations with the English department were formal and impersonal, what she termed typical student-professor relations. Her work on the *Journal* with Woodbridge, her tight schedule, and family responsibilities kept her from knowing the members of the English department personally. There is no doubt Elsie's heart was not in English but in philosophy, and she was much closer to the faculty in the philosophy department. If the faculty members in English sensed this allegiance, it might also be a reason for their aggravation with Elsie.

Upon recuperation and return to the city, Elsie went to visit Professors Trent and Thorndike. Thorndike stated his disappointment in the fact that Elsie had not passed the preliminaries and seemed puzzled that the faculty could not get the answers they wished and believed she understood the field. Thorndike suggested Elsie did not know or refused through stubbornness to give the answers the faculty wanted. Elsie did not find her discussion with Thorndike illuminating as far as answering her questions and psychologically preparing her for another preliminary exam. Thorndike suggested Elsie try again and that further preparation was unnecessary. "We had a long, talk, friendly enough, but not very illuminating to me," Elsie explained, "for neither he nor I seemed able to explain why my examination had been such a failure. I, on my part, said I had deemed the preparation I had made adequate but that examination had not found it so, and Thorndike was puzzled, because the examiners it seemed, as he said, were unable to get from you the facts you knew."[74] "Further preparation would be unnecessary," Thorndike suggested, "and in my judgment, unwise. Come up again, with a light heart—Clark will pass Miss Clapp." Thorndike's advice troubled Elsie, particularly his reference to Clark Jordan's earlier failure, but he could try again. Was this some sort of cruel ritual? Elsie wondered what criteria were necessary for passing the preliminaries in English.[75]

The interview with Professor Trent went much better, and he expressed disappointment at Elsie's failure. "He confirmed my impression," Elsie wrote, "that the examination had turned into a faculty fight—touched off by the way he added, you had answered the questions put to you." Elsie asked Trent if there were inadequacies in her preparation, and he suggested there were not. Trent explained. "We all had a very high opinion of you—Krapp and I especially, perhaps we had the highest, for we knew you and your work well—but they all had, and I think there was some feeling of disappointment that you did not do more what they expected. I guess you were too honest. You did not begin to give all you knew on the Nineteenth Century Literature. I told those men at the time that they had succeeded in making a good student make a poor showing." Trent also advised Elsie to retake the preliminary with no extra preparation.[76] Elsie replied to Trent that she was not willing to undergo such an experience again. As Elsie left the meeting Trent replied, "You want the degree. Certainly you must get it."[77]

Unfortunately, neither Thorndike nor Trent helped Elsie understand the reaction of Ayres or Lawrence, a reaction Elsie believed would recur during a second examination. Elsie described her feelings: "I was, of course sick at heart, I felt outraged for I knew I had been baited, a fact which Trent did not deny, but also I knew that I had allowed myself to be routed, and of this I was ashamed." Elsie believed that the examination questions were too closely related to her dissertation topic and should have been addressed during the final defense, not the preliminaries. Her understanding of the situation was not enhanced by her discussion with Thorndike or Trent and that the "antagonism and hostility that had been allowed to interfere" would occur once again. "My only comfort," Elsie noted, "was a note from Dr. Dewey to whom I had communicated the bare facts." Dewey appeared to be stunned by the actions of the English faculty. "I thought I knew University life," he wrote, "but find I have it still to learn. The whole situation eludes me completely so that I cannot react in any intelligent way, so far as advice is concerned... all I can make of it is that they thought you needed a little discipline and that requiring a second examination would give it to you." Dewey further suggested that the philosophy department would give Elsie a degree if she took an examination and wrote a thesis. Even though Elsie had taken numerous hours in philosophy, she did not have enough credits to apply for the doctoral degree in philosophy. According to Elsie, Dewey accepted part of the blame for Elsie's failure. "I have often wondered," he wrote to Elsie, "whether if you had got a more intelligent response from me on the subject of first choice of dissertation of your proposed thesis on creative imagination (a topic which had been my first choice of dissertation subject) if it would have made any difference."[78]

In retrospect Elsie wrote, "I had long realized that philosophy interested me more than English but I believed, and Dewey confirmed this, that my professional work must be as heretofore, in English teaching."[79] Dewey had supported Elsie's work in English and viewed her expertise in literature as a benefit. Prior to the failure in the preliminaries, he had encouraged her to continue her studies in English and suggested to her in a letter, "I should dislike to see you adopt philosophy as a profession, but since there is no danger of that, it is more to the point to say that I cannot read what you have written me or follow the suggestions of your conversation without feeling that you need not worry about the dangers of excess formulations."[80] This letter indicates a lack of understanding by Dewey and even a lack of communication with Elsie. Unfortunately, Elsie accepted Dewey's advice without question and it is clear Dewey failed to perceive her true interest. He did not explain why he preferred Elsie to remain in English instead of philosophy other than the fact Elsie had been an English teacher. Her admiration for him was so great that she accepted his advice without question. Apparently Dewey saw Elsie's primary role as teaching, and graduate study would enhance her abilities in that realm. Elsie was not alone in her feelings of frustration in trying to establish a professional and personal identity. Did she fully understand the realities faced by educated women of the day? According to Joyce Antler in *The Educated Woman and Professionalization*, during the years 1899–1922 the most popular occupation for college-educated women was teaching. Like many educated women of her generation, Elsie was torn between her professional/intellectual interests and the needs of her family. Like other women seeking doctoral degrees at the time, Elsie felt a "lack of encouragement" from male professors with the exception of Dewey and Woodbridge, although they too misunderstood her desires. It was difficult for Elsie to accept some personal responsibility for failing the doctoral comprehensives, but in retrospect she realized this was due to a fragile self-esteem. She simply did not have the courage or fortitude to challenge the all-male English department at Columbia.[81]

Although Elsie was emotionally distraught by the events and suffering from lack of self-esteem, she had triumphed over the "cult of domesticity" in many ways. She certainly felt a responsibility to her family due to the economic situation, but she never envisioned her identity as being found only through traditional marriage and the traditional domestic setting. Elsie was not her mother.[82] The failure to pass the preliminaries and Elsie's refusal to undergo a second examination marked a major turning point in her life. Her confidence was shaken by the experience and she did not formally return to Teachers College until 1921 when she once again assisted Dewey in some of his courses. Under a tough exterior lay a sensitive, less-confident and hurt young woman. Taking the advice of her Aunt Edith, Elsie decided to pull herself together and continue living, learning from the experience, and seeking a creative outlet for her emotional frustration. Elsie did not blame Dewey for her failure and still considered him her primary mentor. She had studied with him over a period of five years, his influence being prominent in the years to come. It is important at this crucial juncture in Elsie's life to discuss what she had learned up to this point, including the influence of Dewey and their close association.

Chapter Five

Elsie Ripley Clapp and John Dewey (1907–1912): Student and Teacher

Elsie Clapp considered John Dewey to be the most important intellectual influence on her life. From 1907 to 1912 she took numerous courses with him, audited others and assisted him with many others.[1] Elsie took extensive notes on many of Dewey's lectures, responded to his course outlines and course summaries, and conversed with him on philosophical and pedagogical issues. Elsie's professional papers include some of Dewey's own notes on lectures, reports of lectures, and accompanying letters to Elsie. Unfortunately, there is much more commentary from Dewey than from Elsie in these papers, but that is expected since she was responding to him and did not duplicate her responses. She kept many of the materials Dewey sent her for comment. At this point we can only examine what ideas she may have been exposed to and follow her career to ascertain her eventual interpretation of these ideas, most notably the conception of community. It is also important to examine Dewey's own ideas during this period. What was he thinking and publishing and what ideas did he expose his students, including Elsie, to in class?[2] By examining these materials we can gain a small glimpse and some understanding of Elsie's philosophy of education on which she later based much of her practice. From 1907 to 1912 Elsie was exposed to Dewey's central ideas about desire, thought, reflection, knowledge, and judgment. All these relate to his concepts of community, democracy, and education—important ideas in her later work. This chapter attempts to understand and explore what ideas Elsie derived from her close interaction with Dewey, his pedagogy and his pragmatism.[3]

Elsie Clapp was first exposed to Dewey's thought during her sophomore year at Vassar when she became familiar with his *Pedagogic Creed* and other works such as *School and Society* (1899), a series of lectures given to the parents of the Dewey Lab School in Chicago.[4] In *School and Society*, Dewey challenged the Lockean notion that the mind was a blank slate and simply needed to be filled with information. Building on a more modern view of mind and certainly influenced by William James' *Principles of Psychology*, Dewey suggested that the child was much like a little philosopher, attempting to make sense of its world through interaction/transaction in the environment, what he termed experience. Dewey believed the child had a natural capacity to activity, desiring and seeking to know and understand its world. The child gained this understanding through four tools: communication, construction, inquiry, and expression. The problem of the traditional school was that it typically ignored the experience of the child and tried to shape and mold a person's experience to subject matter rather than basing subject matter upon experience. This traditional process made education remote and bookish, teacher and text centered, but most crucially it undermined the "native impulses" of communication, construction, inquiry, and expression.[5] These characteristics are embodied through Dewey's early discussions of community. In *School and Society*, Dewey wrote, "A society is a number of people held together because they are working together along common lines, in a common spirit, and with reference to common aims. The common needs and aims demand a growing interchange of thought and growing unity of sympathetic feeling."[6] Dewey believed these native impulses were fundamental traits of the participatory democrat and thus needed to be nurtured in the school setting. These traits will be addressed and documented by Elsie Clapp through her work at the Rosemary Junior School, the Ballard Memorial School, and the Arthurdale School, the most important experiments of her educational career.

Dewey understood the difficulty of moving education into a more progressive direction. "I do not think it is possible," he wrote to Elsie in 1911, "to overstate the degree in which traditional education is dead; the trouble is that we educators having been ourselves educated in it are too dead to bury it and start afresh. Student activities indicate the necessity that mind can be employed only upon the activities of life."[7] Dewey was suggesting to Elsie that teachers needed better professional training, but they also needed to understand what modern psychologists were saying about how we come to know, really how we come to learn. Dewey was trying to re-conceptualize what was meant by learning. In a democratic society this new view of learning took on special meaning and purpose.

During the five years Elsie associated with Dewey, he was beginning to draft and articulate a vision of the role of education in a democratic society, and she played an active role in shaping that vision. Unfortunately, Dewey rarely gave credit to the women who influenced his thinking, but in the Preface to *Democracy and Education*, he gives credit to "Miss Elsie Ripley Clapp for many criticisms and suggestions."[8] One begins to see Elsie's own thought on democracy and education by 1911 largely through her notes and references from courses she took and through assisting Dewey in some of his classes. The majority of materials and correspondence during this period relate to the course on Philosophy and Education in Their Historic Relations. Dewey offered this course from October 4, 1910, through May 18, 1911. As a student in the course, Elsie noted Dewey's discussion of the nature of the good and its relationship to desire. Dewey's reading of Aristotle's *Ethics* led Elsie to believe that the good is not simply desire nor is its end leisure or pleasure. The pursuit of materialism did not equate with the good or the pursuit of happiness.[9] Dewey suggested in a Jeffersonian, but also Aristotlean, sense that the pursuit of happiness was not a material or economic one but an ethical one. He further suggested that while there may be conflict, chaos, confusion, and disorder in democratic society, "there is also the freedom to interact and create conditions for accelerated change."[10] "A progressive society," Elsie noted, "is essentially a democratic society—non-stratified, theoretically and to some extent practically as regards to social intercourse and social stimulation."[11] Predating *Democracy and Education* by several years, Elsie wrote in her class notes, "Education has a practical side and a theoretical one. It has a practical sense and a theory in the sense of how a body of beliefs come to be taken as truth or common sense. Education is a process where people are instilled with what the society feels valuable."[12] In her notes, Elsie commented on the challenge Dewey was bringing to the dualism of man/woman, individual/citizen and society, and the dualistic separation which undermined education and participatory democracy.

Dewey saw dualism in traditional philosophy creating a "hard and fast antithesis between terms which are related." Philosophically, this included for Dewey spirit and matter, mind and body, and logic and psychology. Pedagogically, for Dewey and Elsie Clapp, it also included the relationship between school and community, a dualism Elsie would eventually seek to resolve in her own work linking school and community.[13] These were not fixed distinctions but "relative and working."[14] Trying to pull this together for his students, Dewey posed the following fundamental questions to his class: What is good? What is virtue and can it be taught? What is learning and what is knowledge? By posing these questions to his class, reminiscent of Plato's *Meno*, Dewey attempted to stimulate his students to reflect on the nature of the good society. Like knowledge, democratic society was flexible, changing, and responsive to the needs and experiences of the people. In this type of society knowledge could not be static or remote from human experience; however, traditional education had approached knowing in this fashion as typically memorization and recitation. This practice ignored the new psychology and its view of mind, but it also failed to nurture inquiry, reflection, creativity, and imagination, all traits of the democratic citizen. For Dewey, educators could play a key role in changing this, but philosophers could also assist the transition. A new philosophic approach was necessary.

During the summer of 1911, Elsie again assisted Dewey in two of his courses, Foundations of Method and Social Aspects of the School Curriculum, at Teachers College. Referring to a lecture given on August 15, 1911, Elsie wrote that philosophy "should be a method, not an intellectual insurance policy."[15] What did she or Dewey mean by an intellectual insurance policy? Philosophy as an insurance policy created a false sense of comfort. In response to Dewey's lecture and his thought at the time this new method [pragmatism/experimentalism/instrumentalism] was meant to challenge philosophy as an approach to knowledge and truth that neglected questioning and inquiry and accepted things or facts without thought or reflection. Dewey's pragmatism formed itself through human experience with thought and reflection as "the starting point." He defined experience as an interaction or transaction between the individual and its environment; "a practical matter."[16] Dewey's pragmatism presented a challenge to idealism and realism, but Dewey viewed pragmatism at this time as a mediator between idealism and realism. Attempting to explain his position, he wrote, "In somewhat similar fashion, it [pragmatism] claims to mediate between realistic and idealistic theories of knowledge. It holds to reality, prior to cognitive operations and not constructed by these operations, to which knowing, in order to be successful, must adapt itself. In so far, it is realistic in tendency, and pragmatism is usually recognized to have been an influential factor in calling out the reaction against the Kantian and Neo-Kantian idealism dominant before its first appearance."[17] Characterizing this new approach to knowledge, and relating this to subject matter, Dewey stated knowledge is a living process, itself formulated out of hypothesis, through testing in the realm of human experience. It is not static results or the traditional approach to subject matter traditional education takes.[18]

This was an obvious critique of certain aspects of idealist metaphysics and epistemology, but it also presented a problem for the realist scientific community. In an essay "Science as Subject Matter and as Method," published in 1910, Dewey stated that the scientific method "is not just a method which it has been found profitable to pursue in this or that abstruse subject for purely technical reason. It represents the only method of thinking that has proved fruitful in any subject—that is what we mean when we call it scientific."[19] In linking scientific method to thought Dewey later wrote: "If scientific method departed essentially from the methods of reflection and deliberation employed in the daily affairs of life, education in them would be of comparatively little avail outside of the specialized pursuit of science."[20] Dewey was articulating philosophy as a "scientific habit of mind."[21] No doubt this embodied the traits of communication, inquiry, creativity, construction, and expression and clearly associated thought with living and learning. Thought was a process that worked much like the scientific method.

Continuing to respond to this lecture and building upon the previous thought, Elsie wrote in her notes "that thought is much like the logical sequence of math, a uniform sequence of steps—uniformity which is originally externally dictated as the control of the process."[22] There is a close similarity here with Dewey's own discussion of thought in *How We Think*, first published in 1910. Dewey wrote *How We Think* "out of the conviction that training children and youth in the scientific attitude of mind was the primary goal of education." He described this "scientific attitude of mind" in terms of curiosity, imagination, and experimental inquiry. Dewey discussed thought as occurring much like the scientific method which grounds itself in activity and resolving what he termed a felt difficulty. But thought went beyond just a cognitive state. He linked thought to action. Dewey wrote, "The formation of reflective thought is to transform, a situation in which there is experienced obscurity, doubt, conflict, disturbance of some sort, into a situation that is clear, coherent, settled, harmonious."[23] Sounding much like William James, Dewey defined reflective thought as "active, persistent, and careful consideration of any belief or supposed form of knowledge in light of the grounds that support it, and the further conclusion to which it tends."[24] Pragmatically speaking, thought puts an idea to the test to determine its workability. Thought is characterized by orderliness and a logical sequence of steps. It did not end with "a state of perplexity or doubt or hesitation," but served as the beginning of action, a "research or investigation directed toward bringing to life further facts which serve to corroborate or to nullify the suggested belief."[25] Dewey knew it was educators, teachers like Elsie Clapp, who had the best opportunities to nurture this kind of thought or reflective thinking.

Reviewing Dewey's *How We Think* for the *Journal of Philosophy, Psychology and Scientific Method*, Elsie's friend and colleague Max Eastman wrote, "Thus the feature of this book, as an exposition of the new logic, is, that is what it declares true thought to be. In that respect it is unique. And that is the respect in which its author is eminent among those who are called pragmatists. Therefore I venture to say that this little 'educational book' contains the heart of his philosophy. It contains it, moreover, in a form and language comprehensible to minds uncorrupted by philosophic scholarship."[26] Boyd Bode wrote in *School Review* that *How We Think* was "that rare kind of book in which simplicity is the outcome of seasoned scholarship in diverse fields. Logical, psychological and educational theory are made to contribute to a work which is intelligible to the layman."[27] Written with less philosophical jargon, Dewey wanted *How We Think* to appeal to a broader audience, largely educators, thus opening a more public door to his pragmatism.[28] According to Dewey biographer George Dykhuizen, *How We Think* was one of the best statements of his pragmatism although it was primarily directed to educators interested in what was being termed by many as the "new education."

Shortly before the fall semester of 1911, Dewey and Elsie had been corresponding about courses Dewey was planning to offer on Analysis of Experience and Theories of Experience. In a letter to Elsie dated September 2, 1911,

Dewey expressed his gratitude: "And I have found much enlightenment," he wrote, "in what you have now sent me. So great is my indebtedness, that it makes me apprehensive, not I hope that I am someone as to be reluctant to being under obligation, but that such a generous exploitation of your ideas as is likely to result if and when I publish the outcome, seems to go beyond the limit. At the same time I want to hold you to your word about further communication."[29]

In discussing philosophy as experimental method, Elsie critiqued traditional philosophies. "Idealism and materialism resolve it [philosophic method] into an illusion," she argued, "to the former this life is not a trying, but a trial preliminary to a verdict… to the latter everything was all over when it was begun; there is nothing to try it is all condition, no use to do anything because there is no use to do anything."[30] Dewey soon contributed an extensive definition of experience to the *Cyclopedia of Education*. In the *Cyclopedia*, Dewey defined experience as "essentially a practical matter, i.e. a matter of repeated exercise and of its effects; while it reinterprets practice as action."[31] Experience was associated with trying out, a testing in action, "to undergo, to endure, to suffer… It [experience] is an active process," Dewey wrote, "every organism by its nature tries its active powers upon the world around it… it is deliberate and purposive; it involves a forecast of consequences that may follow and the endeavor to manipulate the means requisite to produce these consequences."[32]

Perhaps using Dewey's own words, Elsie had noted philosophy was a method, a trying out, an experiment. It was not the acceptance of knowledge prior to experience; acceptance without testing in the realm of human existence. Nor was it simply knowledge by the acceptance of scientific fact by definition, for a fact meant nothing until human beings had given it meaning through action or interaction—experience. "Do not call it experience unless the modification of conscious action," Elsie wrote in her notes. "Education is a social process whereby the individual is assisted by others having foresight of consequences. All human experience is social in character and can be explained as an interaction of biological and social factors."[33] In a more communal sense, Dewey defined education as "essentially a moral and social process; it consists in the operation of all the influences, conscious and unconscious, that shape character and give direction to the affections."[34] As life itself indicated, we learned by everyday experience through interaction in the real world. This was a type of continual reconstruction of experience as Dewey conceptualized it. Elsie noted the importance of understanding education as a social process and thus an ethical one. Traditional education sacrificed the social, stressing individuality and competition at the expense of cooperative community and larger democratic society. A more "progressive education" is needed to nurture thought and reflection in an environment of freedom and experimentation—just like everyday living.

Elsie's notes further suggest Dewey's own attempt "to effect a reconciliation of the long opposition of the empirical, the a posteriori, and the rational and a priori," once again attacking the dualism.[35] Dewey went on to describe thought as a "factor of experience," and it is through thought that we act, on and with the environment, and this should occur deliberately. A thought was only a tentative hypothesis, itself being formed through experience. It was subjective, not absolute or objective outside of experience.[36] How did all this relate to Elsie's philosophy of education? An important relation is the pragmatic challenge to the epistemology of idealism and realism, both lodged in American schools and their approach to knowledge or subject matter. Elsie viewed subject matter as a form of accumulated human experience. Her practice at Rosemary, Ballard, and Arthurdale articulates this understanding in the attempt to integrate subject matter. It is further seen in the curriculum as Elsie's progressive colleagues and teachers sought to relate subject matter to the real-life experiences of the children living in Kentucky and West Virginia.

Elsie kept Dewey's lecture notes he sent her on a topic, the Peculiarity of Knowledge, and its relationship to education. Peculiarity in this sense meant something different from the usual or ordinary means of knowing. It also pointed to the distinguishing characteristic of the pragmatic method and its challenge to knowledge as static or absolute. In these notes, Dewey stated that philosophy is the theory of education, yet, "it still has to take place and find duplication; it does apply itself even to the education of the philosopher."[37] Here as in *How We Think*, Dewey characterized thought as reflection, as a sorting out, connecting the past with the future, understanding its meaning and then making judgments based on one's reflection. Dewey descriptively terms this process as discerning, gazing, perceiving, searching, hunting, and understanding. The pursuit of knowledge was an active process. In the lecture notes he stated ignorance is overlooking, slurring, not caring for, inattentiveness, hardheartedness, and unwillingness to learn.[38] In an earlier lecture Dewey had described ignorance as "tragedy, a relentless movement to doom."[39] Trying to make sense of this new approach to knowledge and its relationship to experience Dewey wrote, "The new hope of educational progress lies in the creation of an environment which, while adapted to the pupils' capacities, habits, and purposes, shall provide problems that will evoke and direct thought, on the conceptual function, and that shall organize inquiry into a broad and fruitful view of nature and society."[40] In essence this is Elsie's own view of the community school, an institution designed to create this type of environment. Elsie and Dewey both understood that the traditional school setting did not create this type of environment. It tended to ignore individual capacity, prior experience, and defined purpose for the pupil. It often did not provoke reflection or inquiry and rarely connected its approach to knowledge to the larger society. In Dewey's understanding it did not foster intelligence as active problem solving and transformation. It did foster ignorance, apathy in learning, inattentiveness and carelessness, clear dangers to democratic society. Philosopher Thomas Alexander writes, "The basis of democracy is the community, a localized place where human life is nurtured, where a willingness and power to listen precede any given speaking. Above all a community is a source of ideals."[41]

Elsie's understanding of the community school and education is grounded here. She clearly sought to create an environment that connected school and community. One way to accomplish this was to pay attention to the prior experiences of the children, their history and their culture, helping them to understand their role in the school community but also the community at large. Education was experimental, a type of trying out. However, at this time (1911–1912), for Elsie it is more theoretical than practical. As Elsie understood and Dewey implied, education should not be perceived as strictly an individual or as a social process: it is both. While democratic society championed the freedom of the individual, it did not do so at the expense of the community and society as a whole. But what was the role of the individual in the community of a democratic society?

In what was possibly an unpublished paper titled, "Self and Want," in Elsie's possession, Dewey articulated his concerns about self, desire, want, and the need for the individual to balance this with an emphatic understanding of the consequences of choices.[42] Continuing the thought of the role of the individual in community and the larger society, Elsie transcribed Dewey's notes from a lecture titled, "One and Many." In the lecture, Dewey discussed the danger of atomism, which he defined as equals broken up—"while they may be different they come together and may seem interrelated in each other... atoms are like the democratic individuals."[43] The traditional school focused too much on individual success and competition rather than cooperation. It failed to understand the empathic nature of democratic living, what Dewey termed sympathetic character. Dewey emphasized there is responsibility and liability and sacrifice in the course of human interaction. According to James Campbell, "the successful life of a democratic community requires of the citizens a level of commitment to the common welfare" which precludes "the kind of privations that the individualist perspective advocates." "While Dewey is in agreement with this point, he also seems strongly drawn by the possibility of an ethical argument for adopting a social stance based in obligations of justice. According to this egalitarian approach we have all received unearned benefits from the prior efforts of the human community and this debt must somehow be repaid."[44] Dewey used the settlement worker as an example of one who puts self-interest, the ego, aside for the benefit of the greater community.[45] Our own well-being is based on the well-being of others. The settlement worker served as an excellent example for many progressive women reformers had some background or at least an understanding of settlement work. Dewey suggested that if self or class interest dominates, democracy will find itself at risk.[46] While diversity is a characteristic of democratic society, it should not result in separation or balkanization where communication no longer takes place. The settlement workers in Dewey's view embodied and grasped the "sharing of interests," a cooperative effort to address the problem of existence in a modern industrial society.[47]

In exchanging correspondence and lecture notes with Dewey, Elsie may have stimulated this response.[48] Elsie and Dewey continued to address the concepts of desire and interest during the course Philosophy and Education and Their Historic Relations. From a pedagogical perspective, Dewey linked interest with motive and this related to the desire to know or resolve what he termed a problem or felt difficulty related to his work in *How We Think* and scientific attitude of mind. He viewed interest as an emotional connection to some experience. In paraphrasing Dewey from notes, Elsie wrote: "JD says in some situations the strongest seductive force of desire is fuel to its alliance with interest in coming to know. The edge of desire is sharpened by the sense that the only way to find out is to try and that there are most interesting developments connected with finding out."[49] Experience allowed one to better utilize intelligence, but one needed the freedom to try out, to problem solve. Traditional education ignored or disconnected the interest or emotion through the belief that subject matter operated outside of experience—thus, as Dewey previously suggested, education became remote and bookish; it failed to connect to experience. Ignoring interest failed to stimulate thought and reflection and led to boredom and ignorance rather than intelligence. The goal of the educator was to capture this interest or motivation and bond it to subject matter. Subject matter was nothing more than accumulated human experience. There was no need for it to be remote, static, and impersonal. Intelligence was more than a cognitive state; it was reflective thought in action. For Dewey it was problem solving tied to judgment.[50]

In Elsie's notes on Time and Intelligence, a topic most likely related to the courses on Analysis and Theories of Experience, Dewey defined intelligence as analysis and analysis as resolution. Intelligence is action or effort; it searches and discerns, but it is largely based on experience as we attempt to use our knowledge to make sense of the world. As Elsie had put it, simply, we learn by trying out, by experimenting, by testing. Intelligence was not action without reflection, but what Dewey had called discernment. For Dewey, discernment was guided by judgment, "forming an estimate or valuation after investigation and testing. An intelligent act, guided by judgment, was reached by the "process of reflective inquiry and deliberation."[51] The mere accumulation of brute facts as knowledge did not signify intelligence. Dewey couched knowledge within the concept of wisdom, which was knowing coupled with moral values. One acts on the world and the world acts back, using the experience to enhance a better world for everyone. In all its simplicity, this was the chief goal Dewey held for education in a democratic society.[52]

Dewey sent Elsie a short summary of his lecture notes on December 15, 1911. He suggested in the notes that subject matter was experience and in process, meaning that it (subject matter) is really a culmination of human experiences up to a point in time. Subject matter was not static but constantly in flux and subject to change.[53] "Education is a social process," Dewey wrote to Elsie, "whereby the individual is associated by others having foresight of consequences. All human experience is social in character...."[54] This reinforced the idea of education as a communal effort, at best an interaction among people guided by ethical association. Elsie later wrote, "From a personal point of view, subject matters are men's interests. From a social point of view, they are usable facts that are available. Learning is, of course, always personal, and can be individualistic. But a community school has social ends of some sort in view and arranges its plans and activities and gathers data for these."[55]

Although Elsie wrote this statement in the late 1930s, she believed she was doing what Dewey desired in reforming the American school, emphasizing the school as a tool to restore community life. For Elsie education was social and individual, not an either/or, not one at the expense of the other. As Elsie ended her formal student years at Columbia, she may have desired to write her own book on the analysis of experience. She had collected a folder of fifty-three pages of notes and correspondence with Dewey on the subject, but she never published a manuscript. However, twenty-seven years later, through her book *Community Schools in Action* (1939), she chronicled her own experiences for others to analyze and to utilize. She certainly accepted that human experience was social in nature and that shaped her understanding of the community school. By the time Elsie left Columbia University and Teachers College, with a master's degree in philosophy, she had been exposed to some of America's most innovative thinkers and philosophers, certainly in education. She considered Dewey her most important and influential mentor. Their personal and professional relationship was nurtured during this five-year period. Elsie knew Dewey on a personal and professional level although they always referred to each other as Dr. Dewey and Miss Clapp. Both Dewey and Elsie agreed on the conceptualization of education as signifying "the sum total of processes by means of which a community or social group, whether small or large transmits its acquired power and aims with a view to securing its own continued existence and growth."[56] Dewey's major concern was the continuance of democratic society. This survival depended on a different type of education. This "new education" needed to nurture "scientific attitude of mind" inquiry, expression, imagination, communication, reflection, and critique. This required a new conception of knowledge, formed by vigorous questioning, inquiry, and a trying out in the real world of human existence. Linked to this new knowledge was an emphatic understanding of the role of the individual in society. Individual desire and will had to be balanced with the shared interests of the people to benefit the common good. The new education needed to provide the environment for preparing citizens for participatory democracy.[57]

Elsie was exposed to these basic ideas about democracy and the role of education in a democracy. "Democracy inevitably carries with it increased respect for the individual as an individual," Dewey wrote, "greater opportunity for freedom, independence and initiative in conduct and thought, and correspondingly increased demand for fraternal regard and for self-imposed and voluntarily borne responsibilities."[58] Community is located in fraternal regard, shared interest, and working together for the benefit of the social whole. Since democracy is ethical association, this demands control of individual will and desire for the benefit of the common good.[59] The role of education was to build community by enhancing human interactions to solve the problems of everyday life. It is a type of shared action where the individual works with others to meet common goals. This cooperation enhances their own self-consciousness. As James Campbell states, "emergent selves are social through and through growing within and because their communal life, developing in a situation of shared living."[60] These values might be realized, and this is why Dewey emphasized learning local traditions and custom as part of building community. Elsie embodied this concern, and it is clearly seen through her practices in Kentucky and West Virginia but also through her editorial work for the journal *Progressive Education*. For Dewey it was not mere acceptance of values without question, but inquiry into their current values and how they benefit the community.

Elsie's humanitarian and ethical understanding of democracy and community would soon be tested as she encountered racism, oppression of the working classes, and the bitter fight for women's suffrage. She soon faced the power of capital and self-interest and their ability to undermine the individual freedoms of free speech and association, the foundations of democratic community. Yet, she would also learn about fraternity and solidarity, people working together for the common good, the glue that holds democratic community together. This conception of democracy and the important role of the school in the community became crucial components of her pedagogy in years to come. The years following her departure from Columbia University offered Elsie an opportunity to see ideas in action and how they played out in true pragmatic sense by trying them out, testing them, one individual child at a time.

Chapter Six

Learning by Living

Following the difficult spring of 1912 and her failure to pass the English preliminaries, Elsie left New York and accepted a teaching position in the fall of 1912 as head of the English department at Ashley Hall in Charleston, South Carolina. "I threw myself into the work with my ever-recurring pleasure in teaching," Elsie recalled, "and the girls in my classes, the School and the city of Charleston were a new and to me fascinating experience." Ashley Hall was an elite girls school "housed in one of the city's beautiful mansions" and Elsie "delighted in the proportions of its spacious high ceiling rooms, the hand wrought spiral stairway that seemed to hang without support" and the "formal garden inside the high walls with its live oak hung with moss, banana trees, and tall pampas grass whispering in the night wind." Always in awe of a lovely garden Elsie wrote, "I spent long hours in the garden watching the bees in their hives and plunging my hand deep into the wide violet borders of the flower beds to pick the long-stemmed fragrant blossoms."[1]

Living in a city steeped in history, Elsie nurtured her own interests, exploring the city, peering through the wrought-iron gates and "walking along the brick-paved sidewalks and enjoying the pink and yellow stucco houses that lined them, gazing up at the tall mansions whose galleries overlooked the gardens." Sometimes she traveled to the battery, where she could view Charleston Harbor, where in the distance stood Fort Sumter, the target of Southern rebels in 1861 that began the Civil War. Seeking to learn more about the city, Elsie decided to find the Charleston Socialist Local. One Sunday afternoon she found it in the switchman's railway tower in the railroad yard. "If the men gathered there were amazed by the appearance of a young northern woman," Elsie wrote, "they gallantly concealed it."[2]

Up to this point in her life, Elsie had lived a sheltered life. In Charleston, Elsie's eyes were opened to racism, and she wrote, "Even to a visitor like myself, it was evident that it was the Negroes, and not the whites, who were active and vigorous. What the white man did I do not know; the white women fanned the hot hours away on their screened balconies while colored 'Mammies' brought up their children. The streets, to my surprise seemed filled with quadroons, tall beautiful girls. I found the explanation when, by chance, I crossed the 'Red Light District' and found it crowded with limousines. The subject was of course never mentioned." Elsie did not feel the need to compare her own affluent upbringing under the care of Irish nurses and servants with how the elite of Charleston were bringing up their children.[3] Her understanding of oppression and racism was limited at this point in her life.

Charleston was a new world for Elsie. The boarding students at Ashley Hall generally came from upstate South Carolina and other southern states while the day students were from the Charleston area. "To my northern eyes," Elsie wrote, "the girls in the school looked wan and listless, but they had nimble wits and a kind of intuitive grasp of facts and ideas. A descendent of Cardinal Wolsey, who was in my classes was perhaps the most brilliant; she wrote poetry, drove a high-powered car, and spent every free hour betting all her pocket money at the race tracks." Besides teaching, Elsie coached the girls in basketball and believed this experience gave her some understanding of the character of Southern women.[4]

Entertainment was part of the elite culture of Ashley Hall, so Elsie and the other teachers were occasionally treated with high hospitality. "Some of the things our hosts did to entertain us astonished me. Afternoon tea might be followed by a visit to one of the old churches and graveyard," Elsie recalled. One evening she and other teachers were taken to an elaborate dinner in one of the mansions, where they were lectured some three hours on various battles of the Civil War. Elsie's students did not share this devotion to the past. "The devotion of their elders to bygone days irked the young people," Elsie remarked, "the girls often declared that though their parents might be content to live in the memory of the past, they were not."[4]

Elsie's best friend at Ashley Hall was fellow teacher Elizabeth Gatch, "a Goucher girl of an old southern family which had known bitter poverty since the Civil War." Elsie described Elizabeth as an ardent southerner but praised her northern virtues of work, which for Elsie included being hard headed. Competent and accomplished, Elizabeth taught science and was considered by Elsie to be an excellent teacher and greatly respected by her students. Elizabeth, like Elsie, was a student of history. Elizabeth taught Elsie about Southern history, notably Sherman's 1865 march to the sea, which left a sixty-mile path of destruction through Georgia and South Carolina. Occasionally Elsie and Elizabeth ferried over to the Isle of Palms, a deserted beach at the time. Both would "lie under the palm trees listening to the dry scraping of their leaves and watching the incredibly blue water."[5]

Prior to accepting the position at Ashley Hall, Elsie had taken the New York State exam for a teaching certificate in English. She had accepted the Charleston position on the condition that if a position opened in New York, she would be free to leave and take it. In February 1913 Elsie was informed of her appointment as a substitute English teacher at the Jersey City High School in New Jersey. "Brief as my stay was," she wrote, "I at least had discovered the astonishing fact that South Carolina, and the city of Charleston in particular, was part of these United States."⁶ Upon returning to New York, Elsie moved in with her parents. Marjorie was now married to Jim Myers, and the couple was living in Auburn, New York, where Jim was studying theology. Elsie's mother continued to work for Mrs. Alfred White's Charity Organization in Brooklyn, and her father continued at the O'Day brokerage firm. Elsie was proud of her father's comeback following the Depression of the 1890s, which so devastated his pride and the family finances. She wondered how difficult it must have been for her father although he continued to indulge her mother with gifts and luxuries. Elsie did not understand why her mother and father attempted to mask the situation. Neither ever seriously discussed financial problems with her, Marjorie, or Lawrence. Recalling the situation, Elsie made a resolution: "I could not help but think that their generation's practice of not admitting things to be the way they were had presented a less than constructive way of meeting the situation, and I resolved that this mistake, at least I would not make."⁷ Elsie had great difficulty keeping this resolution.

Elsie began teaching at the Jersey City High School in the spring of 1913. Jersey City was known as "immigrant city." The Jersey City High School was founded in 1872 to train teachers for the city's public schools. By the time of Elsie's arrival, a new addition had been built called "The Industrial and Technical High School." According to Jersey City historian Barbara Petrick, the high school was guided by the philosophy of progressive education, and she described it as a community school. "John Dewey's vision of the public school was an institution which would supplant the communities which industrialization and urbanization had undermined—the family, neighborhood, the church. As the center of community, the school could provide, not theoretical instruction in remote academics, but a practical experience of life in the democratic industrial society."⁸ Like many public schools adopting progressive reform, Jersey City High School lacked Dewey's vision of social and economic reform as crucial to democratic reform. Jersey City was expected to "Americanize" the immigrants and educate them at a reasonable cost. "Applying the corporate methods of specialization and centralization," writes Petrick, "the high school promised to produce orderly citizens for industrial democracy, at the same time it provided low cost academic training for the future professional and business class."⁹ By the time of Elsie's arrival at Jersey City, the technical/industrial emphasis was clearly evident. The school had a foundry, forge, and woodworking, electrical and machine shops. For the girls there were sewing, millinery, and cooking rooms. The woodworking shop provided furniture for the school, and the print shop printed materials for the Board of Education. This description of the high school reminds the student of progressive education of the famed Gary School in Gary, Indiana, but it also has characteristics of Elsie's later work in Kentucky and West Virginia.¹⁰

According to Elsie, the Jersey City High School had five thousand to six thousand students. Elsie taught three English classes with an average of one hundred and twenty students. She enjoyed the experience and described her approach. "After completing the scanty prescribed reading, we were free to do as we pleased, and I used the time for formal debates and forum discussions. I enjoyed the boys, second- and third-generation Americans, though they were a tough bunch. Realizing that the size of the group made class order imperative, I appointed student-government committees and gave them the responsibility of handling any troublemakers. Though a bit surprised, they 'attended to it,' and the debates and forums ran off smoothly and were much enjoyed."[11] "Whatever teaching I did," Elsie explained, "was after school-hours when I had some of the slower students in for individual help; soon they began bringing their friends, and I finally had quite a large class." Elsie soon had the trust of the students, who put on a tough exterior yet, Elsie recalled, "like all adolescents, were full of interests and energy, curious, alert and friendly. Before long they took to dropping in to discuss their personal problems and to seek advice about venereal disease. The Science Head who knew the district and whom they liked and trusted was a help in cases and questions that outdistanced my knowledge and experience."[12] Although serving at the Jersey City High School in a substitute role, Elsie had proven herself a capable instructor and was soon offered a full-time teaching position at the school. However, at the same time Florence Greer, an associate principal at the Brooklyn Heights Seminary, also offered Elsie a position. Elsie readily accepted the Brooklyn Heights position and was appointed a teacher in the English department.

During her short tenure at the Jersey City High School, Elsie became involved with social welfare concerns in the New York City area. She continued this interest at the Brooklyn Heights Seminary and worked with her friend Florence Greer as a member of the Committee on Children in the Paterson Silk Workers Strike Organization. Elsie worked with Margaret Sanger, Jessie Ashley, and William Boyd as part of the Committee on Children. The Committee was under the charge of International Workers of the World leader Elizabeth Gurley Flynn. Well documented by labor historians, the Paterson Silk Workers Strike officially began on February 25, 1913, when six thousand silk workers left their mills.[13] The strike lasted six months and at its peak twenty five thousand workers refused to work. Paterson historian Steve Golin writes, "The Paterson strike began as an attempt by the workers to control the rate of production; significantly, the reduction in hours that weekly became its unifying demand originated not in the legislature but with the workers themselves." Although different shops had different concerns, in most cases they all expressed the following grievances: low wages and long hours, poor working conditions, sanitation, and housing conditions, reductions in piece rates and

CHAPTER SIX

blacklisting those who complained or voiced opinions. The owners of the New Jersey silk industry argued that the silk industry in Pennsylvania created competition problems for them in meeting the strikers' grievances. This is interesting in light of the fact that many of the Paterson silk manufacturers had decentralized their operations in Paterson with annexes in Pennsylvania. The mills in Pennsylvania continued to operate throughout the Paterson strike, ignoring the pleas from the International Workers of the World [hereafter IWW]. The Paterson strikers were assisted by Greenwich Village intellectuals and the IWW fresh from their recent victory in the textile mills of Lawrence, Massachusetts. However, Paterson proved to be a more complex problem in a very different place. Elsie believed the strike in its many facets made a lasting impression on her, therefore it is crucial to detail her activities as part of this significant labor struggle.[14]

Elsie's involvement with the Committee on Children brought her into contact with some of the most radical social reformers of the era. The leaders of the IWW Committee often held their meetings in the apartment of Bill and Margaret Sanger, a couple Elsie described: "Bill, a quiet, thickset man who had worked as an assistant engineer on the Grand Central Station, and Margaret who had been a trained nurse, younger, red haired, and resilient." Elsie also described the IWW leaders of the strike. "Often Bill Haywood, head of the Industrial Workers of the World, who was leading the strike, would drop in and sometimes others—short, swarthy Elizabeth Gurley Flynn, the adored Irish-Italian speaker at all meetings, and genial Carlo Tresca, editor of a radical labor paper, as well as the poet Arturo Giovanniti who had been arrested in the disgraceful strike in Lawrence, Massachusetts, and whose courtroom defense of American democracy was one the of the most eloquent expressions of this country's ideals I have ever read."[15] In his address to the jury on November 23, 1912, in Salem, Massachusetts, Arturo Giovanniti emphasized the goal that led the IWW to come to Lawrence and assist in the strike, the emancipation of the working class. Giovanniti compared the slavery of African Americans to the modern wage slavery of the industrial workers. He argued that the IWW was being attacked and jailed for its tactics rather that what it stood for, its ideals of freeing the working class from the bondage of industrial slavery. "We shall return again to our humble efforts, obscure, humble, unknown, ununderstood—soldiers of this mighty army of the working class of the workers, which out of the shadows and the darkness of the past is striving towards the destined goal which is the emancipation of human kind, which is the establishment of love and brotherhood and justice for every man and every woman in this earth."[16] Elsie found herself in the midst of one the most important labor struggles in American history.

One of the central players in the strike was Bill Haywood, well known for his work in the Lawrence strike. Max Eastman, Elsie's friend and editor of the socialist paper, *The Masses*, described Haywood as having a "Gibraltar like bearing and a voice like velvet" and able to inspire a crowd with his rhetoric and charisma.[17] Another central player, Elizabeth Gurley Flynn, was born into an Irish-nationalist family that exposed her early to socialist thought. She had become known in the union movement and gained national notoriety through her work in the Lawrence strike. "She had the gift of tongues," Elsie noted, "and always urged her fellow-workers to resistance and to courage; however in what she said there was nothing to which the people with whom I had been brought up could take exception as unpatriotic or un-American."[18] Carlo Tresca was the son of a wealthy Italian landowner, who by the age of twenty-two had organized a local branch of the socialist party. To avoid imprisonment in Italy for libeling a public official, he immigrated to the United States in 1904.[19]

Through meetings and some interaction with the strike leaders Elsie also met Jessie Ashley, a socialist lawyer and a member of the Industrial Workers of the World. Ashley, like Elsie had grown up in a "prominent New York family." Ashley supported radical and activist causes such as women's suffrage and was a gracious contributor to socialist causes including the Paterson strike. Ashley served as the secretary of the IWW strike support committee during the Paterson strike and challenged middle-class New Yorkers to learn about the labor movement.[20] Another associate of Elsie's was Gertrude Light, whom she described as "a versatile, well-read and personable young woman who was a New York tenement house inspector, lived in an obscure apartment on the Lower East Side and spent her spare time entertaining at the Cosmopolitan Club on East 40th Street."[21] Two other prominent figures and distant acquaintances of Elsie's during the strike were John Reed and Lincoln Steffens, both passionate believers in the cause of labor. Lincoln Steffens was best known as a muckraker who exposed corruption in business and government. His autobiography appeared in 1931, describing his political views and affiliation with labor and radical causes. John Reed, an American journalist, became known for his coverage of the Russian Revolution and published in 1919 his exploits and observations in *Ten Days That Shook the World*, later documented in the film *Reds*.[22] "Each night," Elsie recalled, "I listened to talk I did not understand about other strikes and about labor's causes. And when I heard Bill Haywood teasing Margaret Sanger because when they were thrown into the jug in some town, she had complained about the rats that ran over them at night, I was completely out of my depth. I used to go to sleep, hoping that by morning I would have digested the facts and ideas I had learned, for the next day brought totally new and astonishing experiences."[23]

CHAPTER SIX

Of all her acquaintances during the strike, Elsie seemed most impressed with Mary Heaton Vorse, who lived in a small brick house on West 12th Street near 5th Avenue. Mary Vorse had grown up and been nurtured in an intellectual environment in Amherst, Massachusetts, where her father was a professor. "Of all the people I met through our work with the children during the strike," Elsie wrote, "Mary Vorse had the most depth and quality. It was, in fact, on the wharf of her place in Provincetown that the group later known as the Provincetown Players put on their first performance… Above everything else Mary Heaton Vorse was and is a gifted writer, an artist with words… I know no one with whom I would rather talk. She resumes naturally her contact with you, whatever the break in time, and her interpretation of a situation is both penetrating and wise."[24]

As a member of the Committee on Children, Elsie visited "the homes of the workers in New York who had offered to take the children of the Paterson workers while they were out on strike, to determine if they would be good and proper places for the children." The Committee on Children was under the direction of Elizabeth Gurley Flynn. Margaret Sanger, Jessie Ashley, and Dolly Sloan reviewed the applications from families that wished to take the children of the strikers. On April 14, Bill Haywood announced that more than a hundred families in New York had volunteered to take care of the children of the Paterson strikers. This was not an easy task and the IWW had difficulty convincing Italian mothers to part with their children. Many feared retaliation from the silk mill owners if they sent they children away. Others wished to care for their own children regardless of the circumstances. The demand for people willing to take children always exceeded the supply of children although Elsie records having difficulty placing her charges at times.[25] There was a concern among the leaders of the strike that hunger might become an issue if the children were not taken out of the city. The manufacturers were determined to fight and argued that the Paterson workers were better paid than those in other silk mills. Accepting the demands of the strikers would lead to financial ruin. The manufacturers and the IWW prepared for a long strike, and it was in these preparations that the leaders discussed sending the children out of the city.[26]

Now becoming aware of the Lower East Side and tenement housing in New York City, Elsie seemed shocked to discover the conditions of the working classes. "I was amazed to discover how poor and crowded were the homes of those who had offered refuge to the children of their fellow-workers. Everyone was eager to be 'approved' by the Committee so that they could help. 'Sure we can take in another child,' the mother would say. 'Can't he sleep across the foot of the children's bed?' Attempting to distinguish the possible and impossible places for the children, I learned criteria not mentioned in textbooks and new conditions that I, in the ignorance of my sheltered life, did not dream existed. I gained too, an admiration of the mothers who in crowded and ill-ventilated rooms worked all day over the stoves and washtub and managed somehow to keep their children cleanly dressed and well cared for—a fact that seemed to me, standing in their midst, incredible."[27] Neither Elsie nor Florence Greer seemed to understand that the evacuation of the children of the Paterson strikers was political and altruistic. The IWW had used a similar tactic during the Lawrence strike, where authorities had tried to stop the mass exodus of the strikers' children, creating chaos. Mary Heaton Vorse described the chaotic event. "A week after the first group of the children of the Lawrence strikers arrived in New York, news was flashed that another group being sent to Philadelphia had been prevented from leaving town by the Lawrence police. There had been a riot at the railway station. Mothers had been clubbed and arrested. Children were actually separated from their parents and sent to the poorhouse. It was one of those senseless exhibitions of police violence common to the labor movement. A roar of indignation came from the workers of America."[28] The riot had aroused sympathy for the strikers in Lawrence, and was considered a clear IWW victory. However, unlike the Lawrence police, the Paterson authorities did not respond to the evacuation of the children. Paterson historian Steve Golin writes, "In Lawrence and Little Falls the authorities had given valuable publicity to the IWW when they tried by violence to prevent the children from leaving the city. The Paterson authorities, having themselves learned something from Lawrence, made no attempt to block their departure."[29] The first eighty-five Paterson children left the city on Labor Day, May 1, 1913, and were placed in homes in New York City. The strike leaders hoped to generate sympathy and, along with sympathy, more relief funds. Not all the children benefited from being sent from home, but in the majority of cases they were given adequate food, clothing, and shelter. On the negative side, some were put to work by the adopting families; others were homesick; some missed the exciting life on the street. Most enjoyed the parade-like atmosphere as they were carried to New York on the backs of decorated trucks.[30]

One of Elsie's most memorable strike experiences occurred during a meeting of the Committee of One Hundred. "It was my good fortune to be present at the first meeting of the Committee of One Hundred, which directed relief for the striker's families. Somehow they had gotten hold of an empty shed, and I watched with interest the assembly of the large committee, which included representatives from silk mills in Astoria, Brooklyn, and workers in New Jersey mills that were also on strike. None of the leaders were present, and I had expected no action but a general milling around with perhaps a speech or two. But in no time at all the shed was divided into an 'office,' a 'committee room,' and a 'meeting hall,' a rough platform erected, boards laid across sawhorses for tables, and some chairs and typewriters appeared as if by magic. In an hour a

CHAPTER SIX

clerical group and committees on fuel and food distribution, children's welfare, meeting, speakers, etc., were busily at work. Messengers came and went. There was no confusion at all; everyone seemed to know exactly what to do and how to do it, and the work went steadily forward. I was impressed by this, my first acquaintance with a large group working cooperatively together. Occasionally someone would pause and looking across the shed flooded with sunshine, say 'Gosh, but it's good to be out in the morning.' I scraped acquaintances with a man and woman from the Astoria mills of whom I was to see a great deal in the months to come, two of the finest and most able people I have ever known. I have often thought of them and their abilities shut up in its silk mills."[31]

Elsie seemed shocked by the ability of these working people to work together in solidarity, in shared interest for the general benefit of the common good. Although uneducated by her standards, they communicated in a way that led to intelligent problem solving. Familiar with John Dewey's theory of democracy by this time, Elsie was seeing it in action applied through the daily affairs of these people as they worked together to solve pressing problems. She continued working with the children. "With the committee approval of our list of New York workers able to take children," Elsie recalled, "we began to bring them in. To the children, I'm sure this trip in trucks gaily decorated with red, white and blue bunting seemed an exciting outing. As there were 60 more children than expected, Florence Greer and I undertook to find lodging for them among our acquaintances. It would we thought, be a new experience for the children, and perhaps create a more favorable and responsible public opinion. In this strike at least the workers had the right on their side," Elsie explained, "for they were striking for more-than-starvation wages for the girls in the mills, and a decrease in the number of looms each man had to tend—a number that could be managed only by the most vigorous youthful employees."[32] Elsie believed working conditions were so bad that the workers had a moral right to strike although the mill owners and *The New York Times* were "as usual propagandizing against the strikers." Elsie began to understand the relationship between capital and the media when some of her reporter acquaintances were fired for reporting strike meetings, with owner editorials characterizing the strikers as villains. "I used to read in the morning papers accounts of a meeting I myself had attended the night before that bore not the slightest resemblance to the facts," Elsie noted, "they were not even objective reporting, but a biased tale designed to prove the strikers villains."[33]

Regardless of the difficulties, Elsie continued to work with Florence Greer trying to find housing for the children of the strikers although the problems were growing and quality placements becoming more difficult. "After we had exhausted the list of our friends, Florence Greer and I turned to college classmates and social acquaintances. Though only a small number took children, without exception all of those we asked sent us money to use for the children. We received gifts of food and clothing from other sources—churches, schools, labor groups, individual workers, etc. It was my job to see that these gifts reached Strike Headquarters, which were, to my surprise, in a saloon on Second Avenue not far from St. Mark's Church-in-the-Bouwerie, furnished—as in Bret Harte's stories—with a brass rail bar, cuspidors, mirrors, paintings, and wing lamps. Needless to say, I had never before been in a saloon; my family would have been horrified, although really I was in good hands and with fine people."[34] For six weeks during the strike, Elsie and Florence ran a school for approximately sixty children, most of Italian descent, on the upper floor of St. Mark's Church. "In all the years before and since," Elsie recalled, "I have never taught children more interesting or with greater natural gifts." One of her favorite students was Emilio, "who had the mind of a scientist," and a nature and temperament that made him a leader although he was illiterate at the time. Emilio and his younger brother Marco attended the school as strikers' children under Elsie's charge. She remembered them with concern and compassion. "With Emilo and Marco we had endless difficulties. They would stay with only what they called 'nice people' and they picked the best. For Emilio and Marco, nice people meant middle and upper middle class. However, the 'nice people' found them too much of a handful, and the boys positively refused to stay at the five-cent house."[35]

One evening Elsie took the boys home to stay with her family when she could not locate housing for them. Marjorie was celebrating her birthday and Elsie wanted to attend the celebration. When Marjorie opened the front door in a white evening dress, the boys thought she was an angel. "They slept soundly in my bed, but when I went in to call them in the morning, I found them all dressed and sitting side by side waiting the next move." Unfortunately Elsie was not successful in finding the boys a place to stay and had no choice but to take them back to their parents. With heartfelt emotion, Elsie wrote, "Having exhausted all my resources for their care, I sadly took them back to Paterson. All the way out in the trolley Emilio talked so convincingly about their beautiful baby and the fine place they lived in that I, who knew most of the children's families and houses, almost believed him. When we arrived and their mother and father stooped through the doorway of the outbuilding they were living in, I saw a baby, still and blue-white, lying in a carton. I was speechless. The parents gave the boys a warm welcome, and nothing could have been finer than their thanks to me for 'all my trouble.' Once around the corner, I leaned up against a tree and wept. Two more mouths to feed, and the baby dying of starvation. I left the money, of course, because, as I told them, Emilio and Marco came back so soon."[36]

CHAPTER SIX

Elsie also fell for a little Italian girl named Francesca whom she described as "strong and beautiful." Part of Elsie's duties at the St. Mark's School was to take the children on field trips. Elsie described several incidents. "One afternoon as we were leaving school, Francesca suddenly clung to the railings around the church and screamed. I was completely ineffective with her. A young workman passing by stopped and spoke to her in Italian, and immediately Francesca stopped clinging and screaming and walked along with us quietly and docilely. Another time when we were crossing the street at the New York entrance to the Brooklyn Bridge, Francesca laid down in the middle of traffic and refused to get up. Remembering some advice the Italian workman had given me, we just walked on and left her, suddenly she was in our midst again."[37] One of Francesca's favorite diversions "was to draw a full tub of water, get into it with all her clothes on and sit in water up to her neck—a practice which required a complete new outfit of clothes."[38] Elsie developed a strong emotional attachment to these children, though as hard as she tried, she realized that she could never be one of them, never truly understand this type of suffering. "Finally it became clear to me," she wrote, "that in spite of our work in the strikers' midst we did not have, and never would acquire, the way of feeling and thinking that was the workers'. I might be greeted as 'Comrade Clapp,' but inevitably I belonged to a different group socially. The best help I could give was to present their cause to people who would listen to me if not to them."[39] Elsie was not part of the Paterson strike because she accepted socialist doctrine but participated because she cared for the children. She accepted the moderate progressive doctrine of educating the middle classes and those in power for social change, not attacking the capitalist system directly and advocating socialism. She shared her comrades' sense of social justice but not their attempt to overthrow capitalist society. She did grasp that a position of dominance made it impossible to truly understand the plight of the oppressed, and she went about reform in her own way as the strike continued.[40]

In an effort to solicit relief funds and extend the message of the strikers to a larger audience, strike workers and leaders held a large gathering on June 7, 1913, in Madison Square Garden. The gathering, known as "the Pageant," was an important turning point in the strike. The Pageant had been the brainchild of Mabel Dodge, whom Bill Haywood trusted. Elsie described her as "the wife of a wealthy businessman, brittle, sophisticated and enigmatic."[41] Elsie claims she did not understand Dodge, but Dodge had the ear of Haywood and John Reed, who would direct the Pageant and wrote the script to be acted out by the strikers. Margaret Sanger's home served as the meeting place for planning, which usually included Haywood, Ashley, Giovanniti, Boyd and Reed. The grand drama was held on June 7, 1913, with approximately 15,000 in attendance, the majority of whom were strikers. Elsie described the event. "The never-to-be-forgotten meeting that spring was staged by the workers themselves in Madison Square Garden—a show where words, songs, pantomimes were directed by the poet Giovanniti. The actors were unrehearsed, but Giovanniti's idea of dramatizing the workers' struggle caught their imagination and the spectacle, which moved along to their singing and Giovanniti's impassioned words, swept the great audience off its feet. It was, I think, the most thrilling dramatic performance I have ever witnessed."[42] Madison Square Garden was all decked out in red, and the production went well and drew publicity and rave reviews from Elsie and drama critics. The following day, a *New York Times* columnist wrote, "The success of the Madison Square venture gives new hope to the agitator, and fresh courage to the strikers. There were no gloomy notes at Haledon today."[43] Approximately 1,029 cast members had taken part and upon their return to Paterson were met by 10,000 supporters, who applauded them along with Flynn, Haywood, and Giovanniti.

Six days after the Pageant sixty-eight strikers were arrested protesting the sentencing of some workers. In a bit of irony, Flynn urged the strikers to bring their children to the strike to serve as pickets. She volunteered to train the children "so that they would know how to do their work when grown."[44] By late June the strike was not going well for the silk workers. While the Pageant had been successful in drawing attention to the plight of the strikers, the strike fund was in the red due to the production costs.[45] There were no funds for the relief of the strikers, and rumors abounded that the IWW leaders had misappropriated the funds although no substantial proof was ever established. Jessie Ashley argued that it "was outrageous to think that there had been dishonesty on the part of strike leaders, unless figures could be produced to show that there had been irregularities."[46] Elizabeth Gurley Flynn, suspicious of Dodge and the Pageant from the start, believed the Pageant was the turning point of the strike in favor of the mill owners. Flynn believed the Pageant took away the focus and removed strikers from the picket lines. Even though it did draw publicity, that was not enough. Paterson historian Anne Tripp accepts Flynn's view and writes, "Heralded as the event which would turn the tide to victory it was instead the beginning of factionalism and defeat."[47]

"The Strike dragged on all spring," Elsie noted. "With considerable awe and admiration I watched the leaders' reckless use of themselves in an all-out effort to bring the Strike to a successful conclusion."[48] Soon after the Pageant, public interest waned in support of the strike, and there was less sympathy for the workers. Elsie believed the owners had grown bold. "Through the newsmen I learned that bombs had been planted by the mill owners under the porches of leading citizens who were sympathetic to the workers," Elsie recalled, "the New York papers carrying accounts of the strikers' violence." By this time Elsie had learned the owners would stop at nothing to defeat the

CHAPTER SIX

workers and with the help of the newspapers blackmailed the workers for planting the bombs.[49] Although Mary Heaton Vorse was not present at the Paterson strike, she does support Elsie's recollection of violence and sabotage. Vorse noted the "unusual intensity and tenacity" of the strike and believed it was due to police brutality. She wrote, "the police systemically assaulted the picket lines, clubbing men and women indiscriminately, and this bred a reciprocal bitterness in the strikers. Then the theory of sabotage loomed large in this strike. The silk workers, in time of stress have always practiced sabotage as have workmen generally, but it had never been openly preached in this country before. When the strike was fifteen weeks old, Haywood made his famous sabotage speech in Cooper Union... it caused his being thrown out of the Central Committee of the socialist party."[50]

The summer offered no relief for the strikers, and Elsie kept working for the strikers' children. "I still had some of the money people had sent me in lieu of taking a child," Elsie wrote, "so once a week I went out to Paterson to see that my orders at the grocery stores for milk and food for the children were being carried out." Elsie usually took a friend on these trips because she "wanted as many people as possible to know conditions at firsthand."[51] Elsie often brought along Dorothy Brewster, her friend from graduate school. Elsie believed this was one way to show the middle class the plight of the striking workers; however, by July 17, 1913, some 6,000 of the workers were back at work. Elsie believed the owners had forged a document of the IWW with Bill Haywood's signature requesting that the strike end and the workers return to work. Elsie was depressed by the defeat and said, "It was my first experience with the letdown after supreme efforts and sacrifice when the struggle has not only been lost but also made futile by trickery and deceit. The excesses with which the leaders sought to compensate their months of work and strain were, however natural, disillusioning."[52] For Elsie, the Paterson strike was characterized by much human tragedy and suffering. The strike ended when the Children's Committee announced the return of the strikers' children on August 1, 1913.[53] Sending the strikers' children to New York and the vicinity did help the strike financially by taking pressure off the relief fund. Approximately 700 children were cared for during the strike. Although the strikers did gain some sympathy when the children left Paterson, it did not have the same effect as in Lawrence.[54]

Elsie believed her participation in the Paterson Silk Workers Strike took her mind off her own problems such as her failure to pass the doctoral preliminaries in English at Columbia. Her problems seemed small compared to the plight of the silk workers and their children for whom she expressed genuine compassion. The Paterson Strike was a learning experience. It opened Elsie's eyes to a class conflict she had never seen before, having been so sheltered by her affluent upbringing. Through her participation in the strike, she saw people dedicated to a just, moral cause who believed that human beings should not be mistreated or oppressed. Elsie was also becoming part of the loose progressive movement that stressed that children needed to be nurtured like plants in a garden. For Elsie education played the major role in creating the proper climate for this type of nurturing. The failure to nurture the child properly could undermine its potential to grow and flower as an adult.[55]

Elsie had learned much about man's inhumanity to man but in a moderate, progressive sense. She was hopeful as to the ability of people to unite and work together in shared interest, a critical characteristic of democratic society and later a vital component of her philosophy of education rooted in the concept of the community school. Elsie continued her interest in social welfare, children's rights, and suffrage while teaching. In the second month of the Paterson strike Elsie had marched in a suffragist parade during the Inaugural parade for President Woodrow Wilson. Estimates of the suffragists, all dressed in white, ranged from 5,000 to 8,000 as they paraded down Pennsylvania Avenue. The marchers had a permit to participate in the parade, but the police failed to protect the women, who were verbally and, and in some cases, physically assaulted by the spectators. Elsie described many of the spectators as "hoodlums who surged out from the sidewalk and forced us to reduce the marching lines to eight abreast... but not a woman faltered. It was the experience of the controlling effect of resolute determination that enabled me I think, to pass unscathed through the rings of drugged dancers."[56] This strike had been organized by the National American Women's Suffragist Association, which had copied the tactics of British suffragists. Members of this organization included Lucy Burns and Crystal Eastman.[57]

During a later textile strike in the area Elsie once again found herself seeking relief and charity for the strikers. Elsie's job was to interview ministers in the city and seek support and charitable aid for the unemployed. Frustrated, Elsie described her role. "Any notion I may have held that churchmen were naturally socially minded was dissipated by the experience; it was incredible how many soft middle-aged men there were among those I interviewed who were embarrassed and disconcerted by my appeal."[58] One local curate had agreed to help several of the unemployed men, but when Florence Greer arrived with several of the men at his church, the curate was nowhere in sight. Florence finally located the man, "a big six footer" cowering behind barrels in the cellar "terrified of the men waiting in the snow outside." Disgusted at the curate's action, Elsie wrote, "As a matter of fact the men were anything but terrifying; some were old and broken, some young and discouraged, all were homeless, hungry and cold. I know for I saw a great deal of them... Living through these experiences with the men," Elsie compassionately recalled, "I saw for myself how unemployment could age a man, and how hunger, cold and hopelessness could steal his confidence and courage—as the soapbox actors rightly said, put him on the scrap heap."⁵⁹ Elsie knew this from her father's experience.

One minister who met the situation head on was Bishop Manning, Rector of Old Trinity Church on Broadway and Wall Street. Bishop Manning greeted the men kindly, and members of his church prepared hot coffee and sandwiches for the unemployed men. Elsie wrote, "The men seemed dazed by their unexpected good fortune, in the morning they left, thanking Dr. Manning for his hospitality and saying that they would like when they got work and were all cleaned up to come to service there." Elsie believed Dr. Manning's actions shamed a number of clergymen for their inaction. The workers also found comfort and solace at St. Mark's Church, where Elsie had previously taught the children of the Paterson Strike. Both liberal leaders and the unemployed at St. Mark's listened to the biblical messages challenging the rich to right social wrongs. Discussion sometimes followed coupled with songs from the *Worker's Songbook*. With a sense of nostalgia Elsie wrote, "It was heartening to hear strains of the old Internationale ring out in these surroundings."⁶⁰

Although extremely busy, Elsie spent what leisure time she had with a liberal drama group composed of earlier members of the Provincetown Players. At the time the group included Gertrude Light, Robert Minor, Lincoln Steffens, Sara Glaspell, George Cooke, and Marion Doolittle. During the spring of 1914, Margaret Sanger asked Elsie to go to court with her to defend her efforts in establishing a birth control clinic. "She wanted," Elsie recalled, "the support of someone who looked supremely responsible."⁶¹ Sanger appeared in court in October 1914 charged by the federal government with violating United States postal codes by mailing her newspaper, the *Woman Rebel*. The paper, which spoke to women's concerns, including birth control, sought to awaken women to social justice issues. It also contained harsh criticism of capitalism. Sanger faced nine counts of violation, which could have resulted in a total of 45 years in prison if convicted. Elsie accompanied Sanger to court in October, and Sanger recalled the incident. "But courage did not entirely desert me. Elsie Clapp, whose ample Grecian figure made her seem a tower of strength, marched up the aisle with me as though she too were to be tried."⁶² At the hearing Sanger requested a longer time to prepare her case but was denied by the judge. Shortly after the hearing Sanger left for Canada because she felt the courts left her no other option.

At the age of thirty-five Elsie was beginning to see the harsh reality of the world far removed from the protected world of Brooklyn Heights and Columbia University. Even prior to leaving Columbia, she had tried to "become more acquainted in the city she had lived all her life." Reading accompanied that understanding. "One summer I subscribed to half a dozen newspapers, including the *Times* and *Tribune*, *The Daily Worker* and *Forward* and the famous sheet of Lafollette, Senior and on a few selected topics clipped and compared items and editorials, and was impressed by the contradictions between them and also by the variations in facts printed in these papers."[63] In an attempt to better understand the economic and political forces that had so much sway on the lives of people, Elsie began her own study of New York City policies and social problems. One day she decided to go to Tammany Hall headquarters on 14th Street to observe a committee meeting. Apparently unnoticed, she sat on a plush chair on the edge of the ballroom. "I listened to the talk of the men gathered around the committee table, pricking up my ears as I heard them dividing up the city's voting districts, arranging for payment of votes and trading groups of repeaters. I got my information all right, and what I heard would have made a real-hot news story. When I told Father about it, he marveled that I was allowed to be there. I looked young and innocent, I suppose, anyway, they paid no attention to me, and sometime later I slipped out unnoticed."[64]

On another occasion Elsie spent time in women's night court and in children's court. She had an acute interest in looking into what she called "white slave traffic" or prostitution and became so knowledgeable that a social service group offered her a job to continue her inquiries. However, Elise had come to the conclusion that the most "potent social instrument was education."[65] Elsie continued to be involved and supportive of worker causes. While picketing in the spring of 1914 with garment worker girls, Elsie was keeping a close lookout for "pluguglies" or strikebreakers hired by the owners to harass the girls. One day a policeman, on the pretense of helping, took one of the girls into a hallway and began to sexually molest her. Suspicious of the policeman's motives, Elsie had followed and quickly ordered the policeman off the girl. "When he grabbed me by the arm," Elsie wrote, " I turned on him with such anger saying 'take your hands off me. Don't you know who I am'." Startled, the policeman backed away. Elsie realized at that point the protected nature of her world, what it was like to be on the other side of the fence, what it meant to be privileged and hold the power to use her social status.[66]

On another occasion, Elsie saw a man exposing himself to a group of children playing on the sidewalk near the Hotel Margaret on Columbia Street. The man had taken one of the children into a dark areaway. Upon noticing Elsie, the man fled. Elsie took the child home. "When I finally found the child's home," she recalled, "and told the mother, she did not believe me and was anything but grateful." At the advice of Florence Greer, Elsie reported the incident to a precinct near the Brooklyn Bridge. "The man at the desk took down the facts and promised increasing policing of those blocks," Elsie noted, "at the same time telling me that it was hopeless to try to locate the man who probably spent one night in one lodging house and the next in another, or on

CHAPTER SIX

a park bench." The policeman informed Elsie of a special unit at Station J that investigated those kinds of crimes, but that the unit was across the bridge. "Don't you be goin' there this time of night, Mam," he advised Elsie. Elsie perceived the warning as official interference and began to search for the special police detail. "I had known vaguely that the district under the Bridge was a tough place, but I was not prepared for the pale strange creatures that came out of the dives and brothels. Twice these people who seemed hardly human formed a closed dancing circle around me, and twice I marched through—the ring of demons, to my relief, opening before me. When I finally reached Station J and reported the case to the head of the special detail, I was cold and shaking. The police sergeant gave me a cup of coffee and asked me how I had reached Station J." Startled by Elsie's audacity, the officer informed her she had just traveled through the city's opium dens. Elsie left the station under the guard of two policemen and on their walk, one said to the other, "See Tim, that's what a real teacher'll do for a kid."[67]

Since her return from Charleston, Elsie had been living with her parents on East 18th Street. Now in her mid-thirties, Elsie had grown to appreciate her father's efforts at a comeback and saw the years of his indulgences as tragic. "I realized, too, that it had not perhaps been solely his fault. I myself had experienced Mother's lack of understanding and the kind of pressure she could bring to bear, and remembering the demands she and the other women on Brooklyn Heights made on their husbands for luxuries and gifts, I could realize how galling it must have been after his business failure, not to be able to meet these."[68] Yet, Elsie also appreciated her mother's effort to support the family. One evening in December 1914, Elsie's father did not return home at his usual time. "We finally ate dinner without him," Elsie wrote, "but were increasingly anxious. Finally I telephoned all the hospitals I knew and then the Police Department. Eventually I found him at an uptown hospital to which, I was told, he had been brought by two gentlemen who said he was taken ill on the subway. Calling cards in his wallet gave his name but not his address. He was unconscious, the hospital told me, but they advised us to come. When we got there about midnight, he was alive but did not know us. We arranged for a private room and a special nurse. The doctor whom we saw said he might remain in this coma for days, but some hours later the hospital called to tell us that Father had died without regaining consciousness."[69] Elsie did not record her feelings or response to her father's death, perhaps, like her parents she could not truly express the devastating loss. As usual, Elsie carried on and took charge of the necessary arrangements for burial.

Elsie made arrangements for the funeral at the First Presbyterian Church in Brooklyn. Lawrence was working as a mining engineer in Colorado, and Marjorie was kept at home taking care of her baby so neither attended the funeral. Pastor Charles Cuthbert Hall directed the service. Following the death of her father, Elsie and her mother leased a small apartment in Irving Place where her mother liked the setting. Eventually, they found and leased a less expensive house on Gramercy Park as Elsie continued her work at the Brooklyn Heights Seminary. Elsie leased the second and third floors while she and her mother lived on the first. The first floor consisted of "a great drawing room, a large bedroom and bath, and another big bedroom built out beyond the rear wall of the house and covering the backyard; the basement included a large and small room, a big kitchen and a furnace room."[70]

Shortly after the death of her father, Elsie began to suffer health problems although she did not link them to her father's death. "I had digestive difficulty and was continually sleepy from auto-intoxication, the doctors said. Nothing I did at school was satisfactory, and for the first time in my life, I had discipline trouble. Miss Greer said that the students had complained of my bad breath, which nearly floored me; I saw a dentist who x-rayed my teeth and crowned two. Though I grimly finished the year, I had lost my confidence and agreed that evidently I could not teach and accepted at a lower salary the position of school secretary." At the time Elsie had her hands full taking care of her mother and most of the household chores. Most of her school salary went to repairing and keeping up the house. Now Elsie's fragile self-esteem and confidence received another blow. She leased rooms for extra income but the rent sometimes went unpaid. Her mother had arthritis and eventually had to discontinue her work at the Brooklyn Charitable Organization. "I was away all day and she was of course lonely," Elsie recalled, "however, we did have some good times together—going to the plays that the Provincetown Players put on in an old theater up in the East 50s and Italian operas given in the old opera house on 14th Street west of Sixth Avenue. The Italians' way of expressing their approval by shouts and huzzahs never ceased to call forth Mother's disapproval."[71]

Losing confidence in her ability to teach and employed as the school secretary at the Brooklyn Heights Seminary, Elsie's health began to worsen. In 1916, she lost sight in her right eye. An examination by an oculist led to the diagnosis of a cataract, which made her secretarial work almost impossible. Working under Florence Greer became more trying by the day. Elsie believed Florence Greer shouldered a heavy role as principal, and though she "had administrative determination and an ability to bend others to her will, she was physically frail." As they were close friends, Elsie sought to protect Florence though at school Florence was "exacting, domineering and just plain disagreeable." Elsie despised the secretarial role and could not do anything right in Florence's eyes. "Miss Greer criticized the way in which I answered the telephone," Elsie recalled, "the way I ran the office and lunchroom, my manner with people, etc., so that I became miserably self-conscious. Life at school was

CHAPTER SIX

for me a kind of refined torture." This stress exhausted Elsie, and she occasionally could not eat, became depressed, and wept openly. Her mother questioned her about her changed behavior, but Elsie was still not able to fully communicate with her mother her innermost feeling and concerns.[72] Writing years later, Elsie found it difficult to believe that she allowed others to treat her so badly. Yet, in retrospect she realized her emotional fragility at the time and her lack of self-confidence. Whenever she considered leaving Brooklyn Heights, some crisis would arise at the school or in Florence Greer's personal life. Regardless of her treatment, Elsie still felt sympathy for Florence Greer and stood by her.[73]

Elsie's role at the Brooklyn Heights Seminary was an extensive one, similar to the contemporary role of an assistant principal but without the pay and status. Besides handling correspondence and the lunchroom, she kept the books and oversaw the maintenance of the school plant. When Elsie brought up the need for a salary increase, she was told the school could not afford to pay her more. Elsie sought other employment but believed the cataract disfigured her appearance. One job interviewer exclaimed, "A job, with that eye, not a chance." Always sensitive to her appearance, she felt that the disfiguring cataract only made her more unattractive. These were difficult times for Elsie. She had failed the preliminaries for the doctoral degree; she had lost her father; she was constantly harassed at work and now had to deal with the cataract that affected her vision, appearance, and self-esteem. Elsie's world was coming apart, and she felt paralyzed by a personal sense of failure. Finally in the summer of 1917, she received some promising news.[74]

Elsie's friend Edith Greer, Florence's sister, had noticed in a medical journal the special work of an eye specialist, Dr. Arnold Knapp. According to Knapp, Elsie's infection had spread through the sinus cavity and into the eye. He suggested that the infected teeth be removed and after the school year he would remove the cataract. One Friday during the school year, a dental surgeon removed all but seven of Elsie's upper teeth and the following week, all but six in the lower jaw. Florence Greer required Elsie to be at work the next week so there was little time for recuperation. Fortunately, Elsie's sister Marjorie came to stay with her and help. In June, Dr. Knapp removed the cataract with no anesthetic and requested Elsie lie completely still for 24 hours. "Long days of loneliness followed. Marjorie was in Pennsylvania and I think mother was with her," Elsie recalled. Once again she was depressed and lonely. The Greers, Edith and Florence, had gone to spend the summer in Maine. A friend, Bessie Moffat brought some flowers from her garden and Elsie greatly enjoyed them—"lemon verbena, rose geraniums and heliotropes, an imaginative gift which gave me so much enjoyment that she often gave them to others."[75]

Mary Churchill Ripley, Elsie's aunt, visited almost every afternoon. An artist and interior decorator, she specialized in oriental rugs, porcelains, and laces. From 1904 to 1906 Mary worked for Tiffany's as a consultant. She had the ability to see through Elsie's tough exterior and often attempted to get Elsie to express her feelings and emotions more openly. She sensed Elsie had a talent for art, but Elsie did not see it at the time, being burdened by the affairs of the family and the Brooklyn Heights Seminary. Three years older than Elsie's mother, Mary Ripley had boundless energy and a zest for life. Elsie saw in her an ideal in her quest for knowledge. Despite failed health Mary published a book titled the *Chinese Rug Book* in 1927. She died in 1929, and Elsie remembered her as a talented, energetic intellectual who, on the surface, was quite the opposite of her mother.

As Elsie recuperated, the news was dominated by the American entry into World War I. Reading was still difficult if not impossible and Elsie longed to read Shakespeare. Finally the time came for the bandages to be removed. "Dr. Knapp took off my dark veils and told me to stop babying myself," Elsie noted. Knapp, perhaps like members of her family, sensed Elsie was feeling sorry for herself.[76] Soon back at school, Elsie took an extra job to cover her expenses and medical bills. Finishing her day at school she often stopped at Child's Restaurant on 42nd Street to get some supper for thirty-five cents. She now worked for a wealthy woman in a lawsuit against a physician who was the head of a professional group of Physicians and Surgeons. Ironically, this same doctor had seen Elsie about her eye condition a few years earlier. Elsie despised the doctor and described her experience with him.

"My experience with this physician, though disagreeable, was fortunately brief. Mother's girlhood friend, Mrs. Alfred White, shared her anxiety about my health and had offered to finance any treatment that proved necessary. When he was giving me a physical examination he made an indecent suggestion. I made no reply but left the office. At Mother's insistence I went to find out about the hospital treatment he advised. As I sat in the waiting room sitting I heard him say something to his nurse, which, together with his remark to me the day before, made me decide to leave without seeing him. Neither Mother nor Mrs. White could understand why I was unwilling to go through with the treatment, and I did not enlighten them." Once again Elsie decided not to reveal her feelings about the incident and kept them to herself. Helping with the secretarial work of the lawsuit justified in Elsie's mind his "rottenness" and gave her some degree of personal justice and resolution. Elsie found some comfort through a visit by her friend, Elizabeth Gatch, whom she had met teaching at Ashley Hall and was now living in New York during the summer of 1917.[77]

Perhaps Elizabeth was a godsend at the time. Elsie was experiencing a difficult time in her life and her insecurity increased. Elsie needed a confidant. She had been sensitive from childhood about her appearance, and the cataract

CHAPTER SIX

only exacerbated this problem. Elsie had lost her father who she greatly admired and cherished despite his problems. Although their relationship had not been the same since the 1890s depression, she still felt a closeness to him she never achieved with her mother. Elsie and her mother were becoming closer, but Elsie still could not reveal her innermost thoughts and feelings to her. During these difficult years, Elise had learned a lot about herself. Her role in the Paterson Silk Workers Strike reinforced her belief in the superficiality of her mother's world and her own world. She was beginning to see the world of the unprotected, the oppressed, and the exploited but in the moderate sense of the progressive tried to educate those around her to action. Elsie had also been educated during these years. Through participation in the Paterson strike, Elsie had seen workers in solidarity, a type of community working together for the overall good. Paterson historian Steve Golin in *The Fragile Bridge* extolled the radical democratic nature of the strike, which he argues drew together the middle-class intellectuals of Greenwich Village and the working class. He believed the Pageant heightened the strikers' own sense of empowerment. Although that strike hurt the IWW, the workers continued through the years that followed in several militant strikes.[77]

For Elsie, the key to reform—be it social, economic, or political—was education. For her it would always be the key. Elsie approached progressive reform by nurturing children and meeting their needs. For Elsie, education was the key to social betterment, and at this point in her life she felt a need to protect the unprotected. She had learned through experience about racism, class conflict and the plight of the working class, political corruption, and sexism. But she had also experienced camaraderie, people working together in shared interest for the benefit of the common good trying to make the world a better place. By 1917, Elsie had formed her conception of community and the role education could play in nurturing it. Soon she had the opportunity to shape her own version of community within a school. Now thirty-eight years old, Elsie continued to grow and mature. She described these difficult years in her memoirs as "learning by living."[78]

Chapter Seven

Business, War, and Growing Confidence

This chapter explores six years in the life of Elsie Clapp, from 1917 to 1923. Elsie spends some time on these events in her memoirs digressing from her own discussion of graduate work and teaching. Why the digression? Writing in the late 1950s, in retrospect, Elsie believed these events were significant in her life and I believe they were. In this chapter Elsie begins to search for her own sense of place. She was still struggling with self-esteem and had lost her father, but through her success in business in Bar Harbor, Maine, and her work with the Red Cross Canteen, her confidence grew. These are also years of forming lifelong friendships, people who supported each other in common endeavors and goals even when they might disagree. During these years Elsie first experiments with progressive pedagogy, renewing her confidence in her ability to teach, but she will continue to suffer from health problems, some due to physical problems, but perhaps related to her growing responsibility to family and friends. While not directly related to the community school, these years are significant in Elsie's life in her own understanding of community from a more personal point of view. This understanding is based on personal relationships and growth she experienced during these years.

Following a difficult year and cataract surgery, Elsie spent the summer of 1917 in Bar Harbor, Maine, most likely because Florence Greer spent her summer there. For centuries Bar Harbor had been the home of the Passamquoddy, a native people. By the time of Elsie's arrival in 1917 the rural village had become a bustling, exclusive summer community for America's wealthy and political elite, who spent their summers in second homes called "cottages," but which could have been more appropriately described as small mansions. According to one Bar Harbor historian, these cottages "were designed essentially for seasonal use, and like the yachts and large pleasure boats that began to dot the harbor they imitated the dimensions of the Gilded Age."[1] Each cottage was large enough to accommodate the families, the staff and the many guests. This list of notables included Charles Eliot, Edsel Ford, John D. Rockefeller Jr., and the Carnegies. Bar Harbor was considered by one writer as "the friendliest and most informal and most open-minded of the fashionable resorts in the United States... the most civilized."[2] Elsie operated a store she named "Another Shop," in which she sold numerous items such as linens and scarves printed by the art teacher at Brooklyn Heights. She lacked startup capital; she had to take many items on consignment. Consignment items included hand-wrought Kalo silverware, broaches, bracelets, and necklaces from a jewelry store on Lower Fifth Avenue. "When preparations were complete," Elsie noted, "I had nineteen dollars and some cents left, part of which I spent on postage for hand-printed announcements I made and mailed to people in the Social Registry of the wealthy Bar Harbor summer colony. Then I opened, and for one month, waited for customers."[3]

Elsie fondly remembered two peculiar customers who came into the store that summer and described them. "One morning a tall, awkward girl and a dowdy middle-aged woman came in, who proved to be Mrs. Carnegie and her daughter. When all accounts were settled at the end of the summer, I found I had $200 clear—which, counting the capital with which I started, was not too bad."[4] Elsie perceived her entry into business as a success.

In April 1917 the United States officially entered World War I. After closing the shop for the summer but still in need of money, Elsie joined the Red Cross Canteen in New York City. In general, the Red Cross Canteen service assisted in the movement of troops to camps and to ports of embarkation. It also took care of transportation emergencies in moving them from point to point. Canteens in the major cities, including New York, often contained lunchrooms, reading rooms, shower stalls, telephone booths, and first-aid stations.[5] Elsie described her decision to join the Canteen as motivated by more than just financial need. "Needing to earn more money and desirous of having a share in the war effort, after the shop was closed in February, I got myself a job with the Red Cross Canteen outfit which had charge of all soldiers and sailors passing through the city on their way to Europe. As it dealt with confidential information regarding the number of troops and naval units, dates and hours of their departures and arrivals, disposition of the wounded, etc., I was accepted for the work only after a minute examination of my personal and family background. Like others connected with the work, I was pledged not to divulge any information I acquired, and had to memorize the telephone numbers and names of the men directing military and naval transportation with whom we were connected."[6] After working the week at Brooklyn Heights, Elsie worked from Saturday noon to Sunday night supervising the canteen headquarters and its many telephones. She believed she had made a real contribution to the war effort.

Elsie continued her business enterprise during the summer of 1918 but had to move her shop to the vicinity of the Bar Harbor hotels and residences. Some of Elsie's customers thought the move would prove disastrous since she was leaving the shopping district, but Elsie proved her critics wrong. "This year I waited two weeks for the first customers," Elsie explained, "but when they came, they came in flocks."[7] The local hotels recommended Elsie's store and this enhanced her business. "One day a buckboard drew up and a young couple came in and bought over two hundred dollars worth of goods," Elsie recalled. "Taking down the name and address to which the things were to be sent, I learned they were Mr. and Mrs. John Rockefeller, Jr. After that they came in and bought the old brass and copper for the new fifty-room house they were building in Bar Harbor. It amused me that, though they bought a great deal each time they came, they always scrutinized each article carefully before purchasing and debated earnestly whether it would cost less to have them sent by freight or express."[8]

That summer Elsie found a friend in Agnes Carpenter, an acquaintance of her Ripley cousins in California. Elsie described her new friend. "Agnes belonged to the old Bar Harbor elite whose names seldom appeared in the papers. She entertained a great deal and brought each house party over to the Shop. Frequently she would take me driving after shop hours in her high dog-cart with a groom up behind. Sometimes she took me calling with her on friends whose cottages, furnished like small museums, were perched high on the mountainside and commanded a view of hills and sea. More often she carried me off to dinner with herself and her mother in their ornate house, and several times I spent the night there, tiptoeing out often after a dawn breakfast to get the Shop ready to open. She was a wholesome and delightful person and gave me the kind of change and companionship I needed."[9] Agnes' acquaintances patronized Another Shop, and this helped Elsie's business succeed.

Elsie became known in the summer community for her taste and attention to detail evident through her selection of merchandise and her creative ways in wrapping gifts. Some of Elsie's most regular customers were employed by the wealthy Bar Harbor summer elite, often chauffeurs who stopped by to pay bills. "Often they would bring me a note from one of my regular wealthy customers asking me to select and send a wedding or a birthday gift. The way the shop wrapped packages had become famous, and I enjoyed doing these gifts up in some unusual way. Later the purchasers would drop in to tell me how much the gift I had selected was liked and thank me for the way it had been wrapped."[10] Elsie enjoyed her work at the shop because she was her own master and knew she was good at the job. While the work was strenuous, a high school girl, who sometimes opened the shop in the mornings, helped her. Elsie usually arrived an hour early to prepare packages for shipping. Nervous about the increased value of her stock, although insured, Elsie kept little cash in the store.

Unfortunately, on top of this schedule, Florence Greer still expected Elsie to provide secretarial work for the Brooklyn Heights Seminary even though Elsie was not on payroll during the summer. "Shop or not... I was still expected to do school secretarial work during the summer. Both years [the summers of 1917 and 1918] Miss Greer required me to come over on Sundays to Southwest Harbor, a two-hour boat trip, to take dictation. I put in my kitchenette shelves for a typewriter and school papers and between customers typed Miss Greer's school letters."[11]

Due to her summer success with the shop and the requests from her exclusive clientele, Elsie opened a small shop on 5th Avenue in New York during the school year. This clientele included the families of J.P. Morgan, John D. Rockefeller, and the Carnegies. "One of these was Mrs. Satterlee, old J.P. Morgan's daughter," Elsie recalled, "an extremely nice and forthright person; a woman who made a hobby of collecting old brass and copper, and a woman whose passion was Chinese coats, the young Rockefeller and Mrs. Rockefeller's sister."[12] Elsie furnished the upper floors of the New York shop with furniture for her Aunt Edith Clapp and rented other rooms to boarders. Many of Elsie's Bar Harbor customers patronized the New York shop, but the business only added to Elsie's anxiety, especially during the school year. Florence Greer made no exceptions for Elsie even though she had encouraged her to continue her business in the city. Elsie gradually found it impossible to continue both jobs. With a note of sadness and relief Elsie wrote about the demise of her business venture. "Fortunately, the sale of the Altman property in February terminated the enterprise. The pleasantest memory I have in connection with it was the Satterlees who came in before Christmas and bought a number of things. After Mrs. Satterlee had left, Mr. Satterlee came back alone. 'My dear,' he said, 'this is too much for you to swing alone. If you need any help, let me know.' Although I did not use his offer, I have never forgotten his unexpected kindness."[13] Once again Elsie spent the summer (1919) in Bar Harbor, Maine. Although she had closed her New York shop, Elsie continued to operate Another Shop during the summer from the studio-bungalow.

The coming school year at Brooklyn Heights offered little promise or hope for Elsie, and her work was constantly "condemned and criticized" by Florence Greer. Yet, her personal success in operating the store over the summers did give Elsie new confidence in her abilities and strengthened her resolve and self-esteem. Elsie had become tough minded. For example, to deflect criticism of her bookkeeping, Elsie had sought the expertise of the treasurer of the Brooklyn Heights School Board, a certified public accountant. She believed this helped her ward off some criticism from Florence Greer. Elsie wanted desperately to teach but was still suffering impaired vision in the right eye even though Dr. Knapp informed her vision in that eye would gradually return. This hope stimulated Elsie to return to her first love, teaching. Florence Greer's criticism of Elsie's teaching hurt but did not deter her will to do what she loved. Elsie continued to search for other teaching employment but could not quit due to the constant repairs needed at her apartment. "Try as I might to get ahead financially, I was not able with the small repairs constantly in need at 9 Gramercy to accumulate enough to forego my regular salary, however small, while I hunted for another job. Moreover, there was always an emergency."[14] Before leaving Maine that summer, Edith Greer had fallen down some stairs and injured her arm and hand. This injury increased Florence Greer's responsibility at home and, in turn, increased Elsie's responsibility at the school. During the winter months, making matters worse, Florence came down with the flu, and Elsie ran the school by day and took care of Florence by night. Elsie believed she could not possibly survive under those circumstances, but the time was not right time for her to leave.[15] Elsie had always felt an enormous responsibility to family and friends.

By the early 1920s there was a growing tension in Elsie's relationship to Florence Greer, which Elsie described as a type of bondage. They had worked together through the Paterson Silk Workers Strike, at Brooklyn Heights Seminary, and usually spent summers in the same locale. However, over the years Elsie had become more distant from Florence and this distance increased due to Florence's shabby treatment of Elsie. They had purchased a car together, but due to repairs needed at 9 Gramercy, Elsie could not pay her half of the car. Florence informed Elsie one Saturday at school that she and her sister had traded the car. "I listened with astonishment," Elsie recalled, "for the car she had used for her purchase was still half mine... I said nothing at all, but I knew as I went out the front door that I was at last free."[16] This economic bondage freed Elsie only to a point, for the chain of personal bondage was more difficult to break. With great difficulty, Elsie made the personal and professional decision to leave the Brooklyn Heights Seminary. "I went over to New York, and all afternoon walked in Riverside Park and finally at supper time from a pay station in a 110th Street restaurant I called Marjorie. She said to take the next train to Poughkeepsie and Jim would meet me at the station. That night and Sunday, Marjorie, Jim and I talked out the situation. Marjorie, bless her, said I was doing the right thing and that they would stand back of me. Early Monday morning I took the milk train into New York and arrived in Brooklyn in time for school."[17] Marjorie and Jim supported Elsie's decision to leave the Brooklyn Heights Seminary in which Elsie had spent over a decade of her life. Financially stressed, Elsie sold the apartment at 9 Gramercy, which relieved her of some anxiety. The Greers wanted Elsie to operate another house, but Elsie was not financially capable of such a venture, although she did try. Elsie asked Marjorie and her husband Jim for the money, but they refused, perhaps realizing she had no need for further fiscal responsibility. Florence and Edith Greer found an apartment on Riverside Drive, and Elsie found a room near Columbia University.[18]

Upon reaching the decision to leave Brooklyn Heights, Elsie immediately registered with a teaching agency, which soon sent her to the Cosmopolitan Club to see the Head of the Girls School of Milton Academy in Milton, Massachusetts. Elsie liked the head of the girls' school, Sara Goodwin. "Upon her invitation I went up to Milton to see the school," Elsie noted, "and a few days later Miss Goodwin wrote offering me the position of Head of their High School English Department." Needing a change and growing in self-confidence and self-esteem, Elsie accepted the job. As might be expected, Florence Greer was not pleased and Elsie recalled the difficult situation. "When the matter was settled, I told Miss Greer that I was leaving. She used all the arguments that heretofore would have moved me," Elsie remembered, "my incompetence and my inability to teach, my loyalty to her and to the school. It was curious—something had snapped—and nothing she said made any difference at all. I knew however, that I must give no ground for reprisals, so I said merely, that I was sorry but had decided to leave."[19] Florence did not believe Elsie had the courage to step out on her own, but Elsie was boosted by a new wave of self-confidence and the moral support of her family. Elsie left Brooklyn Heights in 1921 as a mature woman who wished to continue her first love, teaching, on her own terms. Her success in operating the summer store in Bar Harbor forced her to rely on herself. Although it was stressful she seemed to enjoy the experience although it was tempered by her responsibility to Florence Greer and the school. Elsie did not feel Florence treated her with the respect she deserved. Elsie had showed she had taste and business savvy, evident through her many affluent clients. The Red Cross experience further boosted her self-esteem when she showed she could be given enormous responsibility and carry it through. This newfound confidence gave Elsie the courage to challenge Florence Greer and the emotional hold she had on her. Florence Greer knew full well Elsie's lack of confidence and seemed to be able to manipulate it to her interest. Finally, Elsie mustered the courage to leave Brooklyn Heights following the school term in 1921 to begin a new stage of her life.

Needing employment and a change, Elsie worked during the summer of 1921 for her cousin Lou Daniel, dean of women at Barnard College. Elsie also dropped by to see her mentor John Dewey. "I would I told him, be at the university that summer," Elsie explained, "and would be happy if he could use my help. He said he would be glad to have me assist him again in his courses in Education at Teachers College. Then he pulled out of his pocket a crumpled piece of paper, saying, I found this note of yours, and I still do not understand what you meant by... and then and there we took up a discussion at the point where it had been left in 1912. It was heartening and reassuring to be back again in the world of intellectual interests and values."[20]

Elsie thoroughly enjoyed that summer working with Dewey although she did not record the nature of the work. "I think I have never enjoyed anything so much as my work with Dr. Dewey that summer," Elsie wrote. "To my astonishment, the practical work I had been doing for the past six years seemed to have deepened my understanding of philosophy of education, suddenly one day I found myself telling Dr. Dewey about my experiences at the Brooklyn Heights Seminary."[21] After recounting her experiences at Brooklyn Heights, Dewey suggested to Elsie that the criticism of her teaching may have been caused by jealously. Dewey blamed himself for not telling Elsie how much he admired her work before she left the university. Elsie was pleased with Dewey's reaction but angered with herself for being a "stupid, spineless fool."[22]

Elsie was able to meet her living expenses working for Lou Daniel and appreciated her kindness. "Cousin Lou, to whom I had outlined the situation was wonderful to me; in every way she tried to restore my confidence and self-esteem, having me eat with her and other faculty members and often inviting people to meet me. The job I did for her at Whittier Hall met living expenses so, for fun I took a Drama Writing course Minor Latham was giving over at Barnard."[23] Following the first summer session [1921], Elsie returned to Bar Harbor to sell the remaining merchandise from her store. On the way to Bar Harbor she stopped in Boston to check on an apartment for the fall term at Milton Academy. The prospective apartment was on Beacon Hill but was locked, and the owner, an antique dealer, was out of town. Elsie accepted the apartment sight unseen and upon closing the shop at the end of the summer moved to Boston, Massachusetts. "Waiting for my furniture to arrive," Elsie recalled, "I stayed with my cousin Amy Wentworth who lived in West Roxbury. I painted each of my rooms a different color, and though Amy was scandalized, the effect was quite pleasing. The house, probably once the stable of a Charles Street Mansion, was in an alley opening off Mount Vernon Street; when my trunks finally came the expressman just climbed on the top of his van and pushed them through the window into my second story rooms."[24]

Moving to Boston and teaching at Milton Academy were good experiences for Elsie. Milton consisted of a Boys and Girls School. Elsie taught in the Girls School that housed grades 6 thru 12. Milton also had a primary school attended by both boys and girls. Elsie taught eighth graders and described her new work. "Into my work at Milton I poured all my pent-up longing to teach, and to my surprise, found that I could as always. To the girls I taught I gave everything I had and my work with them went well from the start. As I taught there I became conscious of Milton's traditions; many of the people in the community were or had been at some time connected with this famous old New England academy. The school was at a crossroads on the outskirts of the town of Milton, a few miles from Boston. On one side of the road was the Boys' School, whose head was a Mr. Fields, a pleasant and able man; opposite was the Girls' School building which housed not only Grades 6 through 12, but also a small primary and elementary department attended by both boys and girls. Just down the road was Miss Goodwin's house, where two teachers and a dozen girls shared in entertaining the School's frequent guests."[25]

Elsie appreciated and admired Sara Goodwin's administrative abilities. "She seemed to value the personality and gift of all the different staff members," Elsie noted, "and we were made to feel that each of us because of what we were had something special to contribute. She was generous in appreciation, and I cannot recall a criticism."[26] Elsie's new situation was quite different from the harsh and critical environment Florence Greer had created at the Brooklyn Heights Seminary. Elsie thrived at Milton for the short time she was there and had the opportunity to practice her progressive pedagogy. Milton was friendly and supportive although Elsie believed she was the only "progressive" teacher on the staff. Occasionally teachers from the Boston area came to the school to visit Elsie's classes although Elsie believed the Milton administrators were concerned about her approach and methods of the "new education." Elsie described her students at Milton as a "good crowd to teach, wholesome and hearty and eager to learn." Elsie's eighth grade had a number of "lively and brilliant" members, and Elsie expressed her joy in working with them.[27] Putting her drama and art skills to work, Elsie directed the student performance of *Julius Caesar* for a unit on Roman history. "Miss Goodwin came to the performance," Elsie remembered, "prepared I think to be tolerant and was so enthusiastic that she insisted on a repetition of the play before an invited audience and that packed the little theater. To Miss Goodwin's surprise, I sat in the audience, and she was vastly entertained when one of the class came to me between acts and said, 'You don't have to stay through the play again if you don't want to, Miss Clapp. Everything is going all right.'"[28] Miss Goodwin was thrilled and surprised by the performance, but from Elsie's point of view "the best thing about the production was the fact that the entire class took part in it—some as actors, some as scene shifters, some in charge of properties and others running the lighting panel."[29] Elsie had turned her class into a true learning community. Everyone participated, using his or her specific talents and gifts to reach a specific goal. While the students learned Roman history, they also learned how to coordinate, communicate, and creatively solve problems, skills the students would need in life and the larger democratic society. Elsie's progressive ideals and ideas were now being put into practice. Even though she considered herself the only progressive teacher at the school, other teachers cooperated with her, and Miss Goodwin supported her approaches by not interfering. "Milton was a friendly place," Elsie wrote, "I was constantly being picked up as I walked to and from the trolley into Boston, or joining in a hike to the Round Hill Observatory, or going coasting with a group of parents and children. Toward spring as my acquaintances widened and included people in schools in and around Boston. Teachers would come to Milton and visit my classes. I was amused to find that, though the School valued the work I did with my students and appreciated their interest in museum collections and science materials, it was dubious enough about my 'progressive' teaching methods not to wish everyone to visit my classes. Though I did not represent the school's conservatism, I happened to have in my classes the daughter of Mr. Fields, head of the Boys School, and its distinguished teacher of Science and all the children were so enthusiastic about the work—as children are in free and active learning—that my rating was high. Even though I was the only 'progressive' at the school, other staff members cooperated readily with me; the Greek teacher went with us to the Boston Museum to view its replica of the Parthenon and its one piece of pentellic marble, and the hard-boiled and able Latin teacher often translated for the class transcriptions about which they were curious. Miss Goodwin was always pleasant to deal with, and I enjoyed seeing that she shared any incident that was educationally interesting."[30]

Elsie's success at Milton was emotionally supported by her new friend Ellen Steele, a teacher at the progressive Shady Hill School in Cambridge, Massachusetts. Ellen lived in the apartment above Elsie, and Elsie found her "warm and friendly" and "enjoyed her vitality and her absorbed interest in teaching." Ellen had grown up in Ohio and had graduated from Miami College in Miami, Ohio. Upon graduation Ellen took a job as a teacher in a rural Ohio school but soon left for a position at the University of Cincinnati. At the University of Cincinnati, Ellen met James and Edna Hopkins. James Hopkins was teaching art at the University and Edna made block prints. Ellen, Elsie and the Hopkinses would become part of the Provincetown summer art colony. "The works of the Provincetown artists are found throughout the world," wrote Mary Heaton Vorse in her description of Provincetown. "All schools have been represented here. It is impossible, without writing a long book, to appraise them or even list them. Even at present there is no art colony which has the importance of Provincetown."[31] Hopkins also helped fund Ellen's education at Teachers College, but Ellen was not content. In giving Ellen's history Elsie wrote, "Armed with her B.S. degree, she went to Boston, and persuaded the women starting the progressive school for children on Beacon Hill that they needed her on the staff."[32] This progressive school, known as Shady Hill, had begun under the direction of Katherine Taylor, herself "from Chicago and had grown up in the Francis Parker School there directed by Flora Cooke, once Colonel Parker's assistant." Katherine Taylor and the Shady Hill teachers joined a discussion group, and Elsie occasionally visited Shady Hill.[33]

These new relationships proved beneficial for Elsie. She was becoming part of a network of women progressive educators. These networks served as moral supports but also served as a mechanisms for the exchange of ideas and practices from all over the country for years to come. Ellen became Elsie's closest friend in Boston, but when Elsie spoke of her problems at Brooklyn

Heights, Ellen scolded her and pushed Elsie to forget and move on. Unfortunately, Brooklyn Heights was hard for Elsie to escape. On one of her frequent trips to New York, she was met by Florence Greer and Elsie described their meeting. "The outward forms of familiar relationship still held, but now had no substance or meaning. Brooklyn Heights Seminary seemed to have survived my departure, and I learned with amusement that three people were now covering the work I had done. Nothing was said about my present teaching at Milton."[34] For Elsie this meeting was a clear indication that she had made the right move to leave Brooklyn Heights and that Florence Greer thought only of herself and thus did not have Elsie's best interests at heart. If nothing else Elsie was being paid $1,800.00, twice the sum she had been paid at Brooklyn Heights. With Ellen's companionship, Elsie was enjoying her life in Boston. "My life in Boston was great fun," Elsie fondly recalled, " I cooked myself odd meals and talked education with Ellen and Miss Gannett, her principal, and various teachers in the schools around there."[35]

During the spring of 1922, Ellen Steele was offered and accepted a position at the City and Country School in New York under the direction of Caroline Pratt. Elsie returned to Milton Academy the following school year but continued to keep in close touch with Ellen. Elsie spent the summer of 1922 assisting Dewey in his course Special Problems in the Philosophy of Education, but exerted most of her time nurturing her interest in painting. Elsie kept a syllabus Dewey sent her while she was in Boston titled Types of Philosophic Thought. In the syllabus, Dewey sought to address the foundations of thought in experience and defined it as "an affair of doing-undergoing. As doing it reflected change in the environment."[36] This was not anything new to Elsie, but in the syllabus Dewey hinted at a broader, aesthetic approach to experience. He addressed in the syllabus the concept of community life, linking fine art and reflective behavior, thinking, inference, and rhythm. These, he believed could be transformed into shared activities such as dance, pantomime, decoration, story telling, poetry, and drama. Elsie was thinking along these lines and had integrated art and drama in her English literature classes at Milton, and from this point they became integral components in her future innovations in curriculum. Art was also personal for Elsie and she continued to nurture her interest.

Following the end of Dewey's course, Elsie and Ellen went to Provincetown, where Elsie was introduced to Fayette Barnum and Maude Ainslie, friends of Ellen's. Impressed by Maude's art work, Elsie and Ellen sought to improve their own technique. They convinced William Zorach, the art teacher at City and Country School to give them some art lessons. Although they had some experience, Ellen and Elsie requested Zorach teach them "as if they were children." Zorach accepted the challenge. "All right," Zorach acquiesced, "paint something and bring it to me."[37] Elsie painted an ocean scene of Race Point and Zorach shared his critique with her. "Zorach did a good teaching job," Elsie recalled, "never letting me think that what was bad was good, yet managing to commend something so that I had the heart to try again."[38] From this point in her life Elsie began a lifelong friendship with Zorach.

Born in Lithuania, Zorach and his family had immigrated to the United States in 1891. Extreme poverty forced him to leave school by the age of thirteen. Robert Sarlos writes, "He became a lithographer's apprentice and educated himself at the Cleveland Institute of Art and the National Academy of Design in New York."[39] Zorach first began his association with progressive education when he met Caroline Pratt in Yosemite, California, in 1920. Zorach was well known by this time and was one of the founders of the Provincetown Players. He sent his own children to progressive schools and "was fascinated by the natural ability of a child to express himself and in the problem of developing this ability, without superimposing methods."[40] From the meeting with Caroline Pratt in 1920, Zorach had made an arrangement to teach art at the City and Country School if the tuition for his children was waived. He soon found himself lecturing on progressive methods and teaching art to children. Zorach also taught at the Walden School, the Birch Walthen School, and for Elsie at Rosemary Hall in Greenwich, Connecticut.[41] Zorach's philosophy of art was pragmatic in the sense of his understanding of experience. He wrote, "That is all I really want from life, to be able to conceive and create my work out of myself and my life; to develop it to the extent of my ability at my own pace."[42] Elsie relished this artistic association and continued sketching upon her return to Boston. She enjoyed painting in the Commons near its lake, adorned by tiny islands and swanboats. "Each evening I would pin up these sketches and worship them; never since have I been so pleased with what I painted," a proud Elsie recalled. Painting became a necessary means for Elsie to express herself. Art, music, and drama gradually became important components of her Elsie's pedagogy. She made full use of the arts in her curriculum designs.

Elsie began her second year at Milton lonely without her friend Ellen Steele and with increasing responsibility. She now had charge of preparing the older high school girls for college, and though it was difficult, she enjoyed them. "They did not have the flair and the untamed vigor of the younger groups, I had taught the year before," Elsie noted, "but they were frank and likable, industrious and well trained by Milton standards."[43] One day, integrating art and literature in her class, Elsie asked the students to represent their emotions, such as fear or desire, pictorially. Elsie was impressed by her students' ability to express themselves and at home for Thanksgiving showed several of the pictures to Dewey, who was amazed at the maturity of the students. Shortly following the Thanksgiving break, Elsie scalded her hand, and her physician had difficulty treating it. Fortunately, Elsie's friend Agnes Carpenter from Bar Harbor visited Boston at the time and began to take care of Elsie. "She was so impressed by the agony I was obviously suffering that, without consulting me, she called Milton and arranged for a week's absence, then whisked me off in her car down to Providence, where Aunt Edith Clapp was in charge of a homeopathic hospital and left me in her care."[44] Agnes paid for all of Elsie's hospital expenses. Eventually, Elsie returned to work and began preparation for the Christmas play. Working with an artist at Milton, Elsie helped design the costumes. Rehearsal was difficult in the small theater behind Sara Goodwin's house due to the cold weather, but the play went off without a hitch, with many of Elsie's former eighth-grade students among the cast.

Due to being tired and still not fully recovered from the scalded hand, Elsie believed she contracted a cold during the Christmas holidays that eventually developed into pneumonia. Now back in New York, Dorothy Brewster and Ellen Steele helped nurse Elsie. "Ellen would drop in and talk about her new work at the City and Country School," Elsie noted, "and Dorothy Brewster kept me supplied with new books."[45] Elsie did not return to Milton Academy that spring. "The day I was to leave for Milton I stopped by Dr. Alsop's office for a final check up," Elsie explained, "and was forbidden to go back into Boston's damp winter climate, so I wired the school my resignation. Miss Goodwin herself came down to New York and offered to hold my place open until I recovered, but I was so weak and listless that Dr. Alsop could not tell when that would be and I had to refuse Miss Goodwin's offer."[46] One wonders if Elsie really wholeheartedly desired to return to Boston. Her teaching was highly successful and by Sara Goodwin's reaction to her illness, much liked and appreciated. Yet, in spite of these successes, Elsie felt lonely following Ellen Steele's departure and all her close friends were in the New York area. Since she was unable to pack her furniture in Boston, her mother traveled to Boston to facilitate the move back to New York.

Following the recommendations of her doctor, Elsie spent the spring of 1923 convalescing in a large house in Lake George, New York. Other guests included several war veterans and a nurse injured during the war. Breakfast and lunch were served in each patient's room, but dinner was a more formal affair held at seven each evening. "Although fires blazed in the hearths," Elsie noted, " the house was cold, even the long velvet curtains at the front of the stairway like a scene in Macbeth, could not shut out the icy winds that swept down the lake. Mornings I would waddle around in the deep snow sketching the evergreens. Afternoons, which I spent in bed, I painted literally on my chest."[47] Gradually, feeling better, Elsie went tobogganing with some of the men guests, but tore a ligament in her knee. As soon as Elsie could walk again she returned to New York where Ellen Steele had found a boarding house on West 16th Street. "Dreary weeks followed of limping around looking for a job to recoup my finances which had been depleted by my long illness," Elsie wrote. "I was not a cheery companion but, Ellen stood by faithfully."[48] One evening Florence Greer's sister Juliet visited Elsie. Elsie believed Juliet was on a mission from Florence, who knew full well that Elsie did not have a job. Florence offered Elsie a position managing museum trips for Brooklyn Heights students on a percentage basis. Elsie was insulted and enraged. "Enraged that they should try to get me back by taking advantage of my present need," Elsie explained, "I thanked her and said I had other plans."[49] Ellen was pleased Elsie did not surrender her hard-won freedom from Florence Greer and the Brooklyn Heights Seminary. Shortly after this incident, Elsie found work teaching five-year-olds in a Long Island School. "It was held in a remodeled farm house on an estate to which the pupils were brought by bus," Elsie recalled, "and whose staff came and went each day from New York. It was, I think, the only job on which I slacked; I could just about last out the half-day and that was all."[50] Fortunately, before the spring semester had ended, Ellen had persuaded Caroline Pratt and Lucy Sprague Mitchell of the City and Country School to offer Elsie a position for the fall of 1923.

Elsie accepted the offer, but before the fall term began she was able to further explore her interest in art. Ellen and Elsie spent the summer in Provincetown close to their friends Maude and Fay Ainslie and Edna and James Hopkins. "We held many swimming parties there, men and girls using the studio in town and consuming hot tea and store cakes on the porch afterwards. We spent many evenings up at Maude's house, which topped a sandy hill covered with rustling oak trees, and talked until the small hours."[51] All had a love for painting and Elsie learned much about art from Edna and James Hopkins that summer. "In the late afternoon Edna would appear with her walking stick and pick us up for a stroll about the town. To these walks I owe Edna an awareness of the beauty to be found in common things; she would notice the slant of a stairway, the thrust and interplay of roofs, or speak of the color of a shadow in a door or the value of a figure against the sun."[52] James Hopkins helped Elsie and taught her "to ignore the obviously picturesque and look for the more subtle beauty." She wrote, "I learned from him also something about selections of salient features in a landscape and about composition."[53] Elsie also began to work in oils under the tutelage of William Zorach, and he generally allowed her to experiment. Yet, one day Zorach dropped in on Elsie and Ellen painting a model in a Degas pose and criticized Elsie's work, suggesting that the art quality of her work was gone. Elsie challenged Zorach's critique of her work. "I insisted that I had a right to learn how to mix oils, that my sketch of the model showed my ignorance merely, and that nothing had ruined anything. Finally, people's emotions subsided and I went on painting as before—in oils now instead of watercolors."[54] At the end of the summer, James Hopkins accepted an offer to head the art department at Ohio State University, a financially stable position, and Edna Hopkins left for Paris. Elsie now believed more in herself.

Elsie's experience running her business gave her a sense of control, that she could make good business decisions relying on her own judgment. The support of her exclusive clientele added to her sense of importance, that her taste and judgment were appreciated and accepted. Elsie's limited role at the Red Cross Canteen showed she could be trusted with great responsibility and that her efforts were appreciated. She also felt the need to make a contribution to the war effort. Elsie's relationship with Ellen Steele provided emotional and professional support and began a lifelong friendship. Elsie cherished the emotional support she gained from her female friends, from whom she felt "empathy and lack of inhibition."[55] Elsie learned much from her work at Milton and appreciated the freedom that was given by Sara Goodwin to practice progressive methods. Through Milton Elsie regained her confidence to teach, but longed for a return to New York which tempered her success there, spending only one semester. During these six years Elsie's understanding of art matured. Clearly her work with William Zorach is significant, but also her interactions in the Provincetown art community where she observed artists expressing their own view of experience. Finally recovering from her bout with pneumonia, Elsie prepared herself to begin teaching at the well-known progressive City and County School under the direction of Caroline Pratt.

Chapter Eight

The City and Country School

Elsie began the 1923 school year with hope and excitement, living, working, and teaching with her close friend Ellen Steele. They roomed together on Grove Street in Greenwich Village. "Back of the houses on Grove Street and placed at a different angle was Grove Court," Elsie recalled, "a row of six small red brick houses topped with Dutch roofs—a reminder in this district of the days when the Village was one of the early Dutch settlements on Manhattan Island."[1] Located in a section of New York City west of Washington Square, Greenwich Village was a "haunt of Bohemian artists, writers and radicals who originally chose it as a place to live because of its cheapness. In former days, it had been a quaint, small village reached from the city in lower Manhattan by stage coach."[2] Ellen and Elsie began the year teaching at the well-known and respected City and Country School, founded in 1914 by Caroline Pratt and located in Greenwich Village on West 12th and 13th Streets. Ellen taught a "gifted group of nine year olds" and Elsie taught the twelve-year-olds. City and Country proved to be Elsie's first immersion into a progressive school. It shaped her thought and practice throughout her career although she does not attribute much influence to Caroline Pratt. Much like Elsie, Caroline Pratt sought to fit the school to the child rather than "fitting the child to the school."[3] Born into a middle-class family in Fayetteville, New York, in 1867, Pratt had begun her teaching career in a one-room school not far from her home. She enrolled in 1894 for a brief time in Teachers College and then taught manual training at the Normal School for Girls in Philadelphia. In Philadelphia, Pratt met her lifelong companion, Helen Marot, "a reform minded Quaker," who introduced Pratt to social justice, welfare, and labor issues.[4] Influenced by Marot, Pratt envisioned early childhood education as the first step to social reform.

Within this vision, Pratt viewed the school as a community, where the child learned to participate through play and manipulation. This was not the more mystical Froebelian approach or the structured Montessori, but one Pratt felt was practical. Pratt sought to connect practice with the experiences of the student. Through play, which Pratt saw as hard work for children, they learned how to "negotiate the world in which they live and to understand how life situations work and how people live together."[5] Pratt's play school sought to connect the school and the community through this form of a child's work. John Dewey and his daughter Evelyn described Pratt's play school *in Schools of To-morrow*, first published in 1915. They wrote, "This work, coupled with the fact that the constructions are almost always miniature copies of the things that the pupils see in their community, saves the work from any hint of artificiality. The children's constructions grow out of the observations already spoken of and give a motive for talking over what they have seen and making new, more extensive and more accurate observations."[6]

Influenced by Helen Marot and her own interpretation of progressivism, Pratt had originally begun her school in 1914 to work with poor children, tuition free. Unfortunately Pratt's desire to work with working-class children was not successful, largely due to parents who preferred a more traditional approach. In the distant future Elsie would also have difficulty convincing working-class parents of the value of a progressive education. Like most progressive schools, City and Country drew children from the intelligentsia, artists, and writers in the Greenwich Village community. Those who settled were made up of "professional people, social workers and teachers, drawn from cultivated families of old American stock who had occupied comfortable middle class or professional positions in widely scattered communities."[7] Village historian Caroline Ware offered her own interpretation of progressive schools. She wrote, "The progressive or experimental schools focused upon the personality of the individual child as the end and aim of their endeavor, little concerned with citizenship and still less with salvation. These schools regarded school life as a vital experience in itself. Living is a series of presents and not a continuous preparation for the future... eager to develop the capacity for independent thinking, they looked upon experience, never authority, as the only effective teacher, and liked to delay the teaching of reading so that the children would not become dependent on the authority of the printed page."[8] Although Ware is confused about some aspects of progressive education, her view offers some insight to the general public's perception of the "new education."

According to historian Susan Semel, the intelligentsia was "far more willing to embrace unconventional methods," such as progressive education.[9] Elsie Clapp's work in Kentucky and West Virginia was driven by the concern and acknowledgment that progressive education was elitist, urban, and largely associated with private schools.[10] By the time Elsie began work at the City and Country School, Pratt had expanded her interest from early childhood to include older children with some emphasis on more academic subject matter. However, Pratt believed the academic approach did not have to be dominated by teacher and text. She based her pedagogy on the experiences of the children, their interests, and coupled this with inquiry and experimentation.[11] Typical preschool children used block play, coupled with painting and woodwork, a carryover from Pratt's manual training days. Artistic expression was a vital component of Pratt's philosophy of education. Pratt biographer Mary

CHAPTER EIGHT 127

Hauser writes, "The arts were a counter to both the superficial aestheticism of the Victorian period and to the bleakness and spiritual aridity of the Industrial Revolution." [12] Caroline Pratt's interest in using play as the basis for learning came during an observation of a six-year-old boy playing in a nursery school. Pratt described the experience. "On this occasion I found the floor covered with a miniature railroad system. He was building with blocks, toys, old paper boxes and any material he could find. Some of it was obviously salvaged from the waste paper basket. As I watched him push his freight train onto a siding while a fast express soared by to stop at a station where lines of passengers and automobiles were waiting, as I listened to the uneasy accompaniment of happy noises in realistic imitation of train whistles and bells and automobile horns—it seemed to me that this child had discovered an activity more satisfying to him than anything I had ever seen offered to children."[13] As Caroline Pratt watched the child at play or at work, she believed he was seeking to understand the world by imitating it based upon experience. As children strove to understand the work around them, they used simple tools and imagination to construct this world. This discovery could not be found in text but through play, which Pratt interpreted as a child's work.

Older students built upon their earlier experiences with field trips to the city where the children linked the world of school to the real world. Children began to see work in its many capacities and the contributions individuals were making through individual gifts and talents. The older students, under the guidance of the teachers, tried to meet the needs of the school itself, approaching it as an "embryonic community" within a larger community. Progressives liked the term embryonic because it served as a metaphor for growth. Children were perceived as seedlings to be nurtured and cared for in a particular way for proper development. As far as the progressives were concerned, an embryo was always in development. This biological metaphor clearly meshed with Pratt's understanding of play.[14] Within the City and Country School these designs included a post office, a school store, and print shop, which also contributed to the needs of the school itself. The ultimate goal was for the children to link this embryonic community with the larger community. Caroline Pratt and her teachers believed this gave the students a sense of ownership. Through these types of activities the students developed a stake in what they were doing and by working independently and together learned to solve problems in an active experimental way. For these progressives this was learning, but it was also intelligence.[15]

Elsie wrote about her work at City and Country and her work with the children, whom she described as some of the more difficult ones at the school. "My group included several children who were difficult—John McCoy, tense and sensitive; Merle, a free untamed boy of Scandinavian parentage whom a professional woman had adopted; Fred, a Russian boy; John Farquar and Edward Hubbell, both children of divorced parents and emotionally insecure. Among the girls in the class I remember Sara Jane, an Eskimo girl whom Helen Garrett, a teacher there, had brought back from a summer trip to Labrador, and the two Donaldsons, gifted daughters of a commercial artist. This class, the first to attend the school, had both benefited and suffered from the enthusiasm. When I got them they were out of hand and bored, fed up, they said, with all this study of New York business; they could think of nothing they wished to study."[16] Prior to meeting her students Elsie had prepared some materials for a study of governments, approved by Caroline Pratt, but Elsie soon realized that approach would fail dismally with these children. Elsie probed them, and the children soon expressed an interest in what they would like to study. Dewey had defined interest as a "value, a dominant direction of thought and action."[17] The key to interest was to connect it with subject matter, itself accumulated experiences. Elsie sought to do exactly this. She discovered John Farquar was interested in African tribes and Sara in Eskimos, and another wanted to learn about polar expeditions. For a month Elsie "fed each on material on his or her interest" and the children shared information. The class asked Elsie to bring in a history book for a resource and she brought in several. The children chose to use a book titled *Our Ancestors in Europe* by Jennie Hall, a former teacher at the Lincoln School-Teachers College. Elsie described the text as a "short summary of events from the days of the Greeks and Romans through the Renaissance. Though somewhat sketchy, it is simply worded and contains the kind of material boys and girls of this age like; the classes at Milton had used it with enjoyment, I remembered."[18] As a teacher, Elsie had her students where she wanted, and "soon the class was demanding the geographical information they needed."[19] "And before long," Elsie recalled, "each child was making an individual notebook illustrated with drawings, maps, paintings, and costumes. Because their notes were unintelligible to them we started, at the children's request, work on sentence structure and on spelling as well as a writing period." Elsie praised the work of the Donaldson children, whose work stimulated the entire class to better their own efforts. This type of student-based research activity was common at City and Country and emphasized by Caroline Pratt. Pratt wrote, "We want them to develop strong habits of first-hand research, and to use what they find; we want them to discover relationships in concrete matter, so they will know they exist when they deal with abstract forms, and will have habits of putting them to use; we want them to have a full motor experience, because they themselves are motor; and to get and retain what they get, through their bodily perceptions."[20]

Although the students were actively engaged in their work, one visitor to Elsie's class seemed confused. "A woman from Teachers College visited us one day," Elsie amusingly recalled, "and after waiting all morning for a class recitation left saying, she 'would come back sometime when you're teaching, Miss Clapp'."[21] Overhearing the comment the children laughed, for they understood that "Miss Clapp" *was* teaching them. In light of this experience Elsie wrote, "When the group came to me, they were uncontrolled and rambunctious. The task of steering them through the day, especially through lunch and recess periods sent me to bed immediately after supper during the first three months I had the class. Finally I complained to them, saying that I knew much pleasanter things to do than to live each day in an uproar; I did not, I told them, have to spend my time with such disagreeable noisy people, and I was not going to. Realizing that I meant just what I said, the children stopped their fussing and quarreling."[22] To maintain the motivation and channel the energy of the class Elsie also integrated art, music, and drama. With Elsie's expertise in these areas, the class acted out Demeter and Persephone, a Greek myth that she had been reading to the class.[23] "I have never forgotten the way Harriet Hubbell helped the class compose the music for the play," Elsie wrote. "By mid-year life began to be much pleasanter for everyone."[24]

During the winter and spring sessions, Elsie spent two mornings each week assisting Dewey in his classes, an arrangement approved by Carolina Pratt. A substitute teacher taught in her place. She assisted Dewey in two courses, Logic and Educational Problems and Historic Relations of Philosophy and Education. Taking note of Elsie's absence, the children wanted to know where she was and asked if they could come with her. Realizing this as a teachable moment, Elsie took the children to Columbia University to work in the Main Reading Room and the Avery Art Library. Elsie proudly recalled that "The Avery librarian was hardly able to believe that twelve-year-old children could do such concentrated work."[25] John Farquar responded to the trip saying, "You know, I think this is a good idea—our coming with you to the university. Now I will know where to go when we grow up, and feel at home."[26] The children insisted on meeting their teacher's teacher so Elsie introduced them to Dr. Dewey.

Elsie's class expressed a keen interest in art so Elsie shared her own interest in art with the children and sometimes painted at school, although she felt she could not pay attention to the class while doing so. Yet, the children insisted she continue and were genuinely interested in her work. "Paint just as long as you want to," they responded, "we can manage ourselves." By mid-semester the class had matured considerably and Elsie wrote, "From February on, no one could have had a better group to work with."[27] Unfortunately in the spring of 1924, Elsie missed two weeks of class due to bronchial pneumonia. Each day a child from her class visited Elsie to discuss the daily assignments and "to the school's amazement, took entire charge of themselves and the work, and did a good job too."[28] Although successful with her students, Elsie never felt a part of the City and Country School. She explained her feelings. "Outside my work with the class, I was not much of a success at the School; I was never one of them, as Ellen was. I found staff meetings dull, and the attitude of discipleship toward Caroline Pratt distasteful. And Miss Pratt, I think, actually disliked me—chiefly because I handled my own discipline problems and presumed to believe I understood these children, who for years had been their special cases. My other crime was my college education. Miss Pratt, who had been a Manual Arts teacher was not a college graduate and, though she professed scorn of academic training, was self-conscious about this fact. She also resented my association with Dr. Dewey, who she told me 'had never paid any attention to the school.' When quite unexpectedly that spring I was offered and accepted the headship of Rosemary Junior School in Greenwich, she found in my willingness to leave the school further proof that I was not 'one of them'."[29] Elsie noted further her differences with Caroline Pratt and wrote, "No one, she believed, could really grasp their philosophy in just one year's time; she also held that an understanding of their methods was incomplete without the experiences of teaching younger groups."[30] On the contrary, Elsie believed she was successful in the classroom at City and Country and did have some sense of the methodology.

Pratt believed that the best teachers were those with social work backgrounds. Although lacking a social work background, Elsie certainly had experience with social welfare through her work with the children of the Paterson strikers and her own private investigations in white slavery in New York. Lucy Sprague Mitchell, a colleague of Elsie's and Pratt's, had her own view of Pratt, quite similar to Elsie's. Mitchell described Pratt as what "one might call aggressively individualistic, too much so to be a genuine sharer. She had an intense childlike, even belligerent belief in her own thinking that made disciples rather than thinkers of those who worked with her. At the same time, she lacked confidence and was upset unless she received the unqualified cooperation in which no one was free to express an opinion differing from hers. We could not question, we could only support."[31] But like Elsie, Mitchell greatly admired Pratt and expressed her admiration. Mitchell wrote, "I could not have learned as thoroughly or rapidly with anyone except Caroline Pratt. But she clipped my wings. I think she could not help it."[32] Like Mitchell, Elsie learned and owed much to Caroline Pratt and the experience at City and Country. "Miss Pratt, though irascible, was an arresting personality," Elsie explained. "She understood the use of tools and handwork and, backed by Mrs. Mitchell's intellectual and financial support, was making a contribution to education in her emphasis on a child's need to learn how to handle materials and through them express his understanding of the world about him. Due to Mitchell's influence, these materials included paint, dance and music; indeed no school at the time made fuller use of them. William Zorach, whose son and daughter were in the school, directed the children's art expression, and Ruth Doing, their rhythmic exercises. Harriet Hubbell and her friend and accompanist, Miss Osborne, gave me my first insight into the use of music in the education of children."[33]

One of the most significant aspects of Elsie's career at City and Country was her association with other women interested in the progressive education. The year at City and Country helped her become part of a network of professional women dedicated to the "new education." Elsie wrote, "Perhaps the best thing I gained from the year was coming to know well Jessie Stanton, then teaching the six-year-old group, who has ever since been my close friend. I watched with interests Edith Day's work with the three-year-olds and Lee Stott's teaching of the eights, and came to know Lucy Mitchell, whose contributions to staff meetings were always stimulating."[34]

Mitchell had financially and intellectually supported City and Country and had also established the Bureau of Educational Experiments that eventually became the Bank Street College of Education.[35] At the time Mitchell was most interested in children from fifteen months to three years. Mitchell viewed Pratt's play school as a laboratory "to observe and record children in the classroom and to carry out physical and mental tests."[36] The work of Mitchell at the Bureau of Educational Experiments gave legitimacy to Caroline Pratt's work *The Play School*. By the time Elsie arrived for her work at City and Country, Mitchell was well known for her book the *Here and Now Story Book*, first published in 1921. Mitchell based the storybook on her own observations of play. She tailored the stories to age and wished the children to use both cognitive and physical skills in acting out the stories as they interpreted them.[37]

The director of the nursery school at the Bureau of Educational Experiments was Harriet Johnson, then becoming an expert in early childhood education and whom Mitchell described as "enthusiastic, intelligent and imaginative."[38] Johnson pioneered the study of children through sustained observation. This data could then be used to "construct the school's learning environment and "add to the understanding of how children grow and mature intellectually." Both Mitchell and Johnson viewed their work as scientific, but they never lost their love and compassion for children, and even in an era of psychometrics and testing, they leaned to a more qualitative understanding of growth and development. Although Elsie's contact with Harriet Johnson was limited, she had some knowledge of the nursery school. Elsie wrote, "The Nursery school was located on the upper floor of the school building. To go up there was to enter a different world, a happy, peaceful world separated by a soundproof door from the main lower floors. I came into only occasional contact with Harriet Johnson, but her ideas, her meticulous attention to detail and her quiet competence in handing children, made a profound impression on me."[39]

One of Elsie's closest colleagues was Jessie Stanton. Like Elsie, Jessie Stanton was born in Brooklyn and spent time at Barnard followed by settlement work. Stanton spent ten years at the City and Country School, from 1919 to 1929, when she left to become director of the nursery school at the Bureau following the death of Harriet Johnson. Both Lucy Mitchell and Jessie Stanton had important influences on Elsie's understanding of early childhood education and both contributed significantly to Elsie's work in the Arthurdale School in West Virginia from 1934 to 1936.[40]

Elsie learned a great deal from her colleagues at the City and Country School regardless of the discipleship shown to Caroline Pratt. The teachers were innovative; the children made progress and Elsie admits she was genuinely interested in the children of the school. "Although the others [students at City and Country] were as boisterous and unruly as the ones I had," Elsie noted, "all the children had through their work at the School gained independence of thought and action and, once their restless activity was harnessed and their interest captured, were able to attack a problem with directness and intelligence. I remember how well and enthusiastically Ellen Steele taught her nine-year-old group, and I still recall the group's beautiful map of early trade routes and their medieval play in which shy, inhibited Jack Mitchell was so absorbed in his role of Knight that he emanated a happy confidence."[41] Elsie and the staff at City and Country had grasped Dewey's conception of thought as reflection, action, and intelligence. As Elsie had demonstrated with her own class, understanding a child's experience and linking interest to experience were key in motivating the pupil to pursue knowledge. Elsie had expressed her understanding of experience in notes sent to Dewey from a summer school class in which she assisted him titled Special Problems in Philosophy of Education. Elsie wrote to Dewey that "if experience is an affair of the convictions between what an individual does and what he undergoes, it follows that the experiencing individual is at once not only the doer, the sufferer, but also the converter?... always in the process of change of movement—development—in flux." The self Elsie surmised was formed in action, acting, and being acted on, and she was disturbed by the passive, stimulus-response as definition of the self, what Elsie termed, "the meager and misleading limitations of the conception of the behaviorists."[42]

Knowing was not a static entity, but an action, a process where one sought to relieve some question in what Dewey had earlier termed in *How We Think*, a felt difficulty. Elsie's tenure at City and Country proved invaluable and exposed her to some of the most innovative and provocative thinkers in progressive education. The influence of City and Country can be clearly seen in Elsie's best-documented work in Kentucky and West Virginia. She made use of art, music, block play, and manual training and understood the vital importance of the nursery school. However, Elsie differed with Pratt on the relationship between the school and the community with Elsie's emphasis on involving parents and others as part of the school as the center of community life. Elsie conceptualized the community school in broader terms, but the influence of City and Country is clearly evident and proved a valuable experience for her.[43] Although she spent only a year at City and Country, Elsie was now part of the "new education."

In the spring of 1924, Elsie gave a speech at a Mother's Weekly Luncheon at the Edgewood School, Marietta Johnson's school in Greenwich, Connecticut. Mrs. Charles D. Lanier, who served as president of the Foundation and financially supported the application of Marietta Johnson's ideas, founded the Edgewood School. Edgewood School is described by historian Joseph Newman as a type of "Organic School North." Marietta Johnson was the official director of the Edgewood School, but was not present most of the time, fund raising and remaining with the Organic School in Fairhope, Alabama.[44] Marietta Johnson was a popular figure in the New York area and publicity as early as 1913 in the *New York Times* stimulated "a group of prominent women in Greenwich, Connecticut, to form the Fairhope League which became the Fairhope Educational Foundation." Johnson held sessions in Greenwich exposing her ideas to parents, teachers, and anyone interested in her organic school concept. Immediately following the speech, Elsie surprisingly received an offer to teach at Edgewood and visited a few of the classes. Elsie felt that "although Edgewood was a friendly place, it was run as a hit-or-miss style. Those who were naturally good teachers did a fine job and those who were not, an exceptionally poor one."[45] Due to this observation Elsie decided not to accept the position.

Later that spring, suffering from a bronchial cold, Elsie received an inquiry from Caroline Ruutz-Rees, the headmistress of Rosemary Hall, a college preparatory school in Greenwich, Connecticut, inviting her to lunch at the Commodore Hotel. Elsie presented herself at the Commodore "in a new coat and hat bought for the occasion." Rosemary Hall was founded in 1890 when Mary Atwater Choate hired Caroline Ruutz-Rees to head a new school for girls. Rosemary Hall was named after the Atwater family farm. The school under the direction of Ruutz-Rees moved to Greenwich in 1900, and she directed the school until her retirement in 1938.[46] Elsie described her first exposure to Rosemary Hall. "I still remember the Tudor Houses in which the two Heads of Rosemary Hall lived and attending the English luncheon in Miss Ruutz-Rees' house in which an expert horseman and his wife were present and where the talk was about past and future horse shows at Rosemary Hall."[47]

Following the lunch, Miss Ruutz-Rees gave Elsie a tour of the grounds which housed the Rosemary Junior School, the elementary school for Rosemary Hall. Typically the children of the Junior School were the younger sisters of the girls attending Rosemary School. At the time of Elsie's visit the girls were being taught by two teachers whom Miss Ruutz-Rees described as "one who tended the blossoms and one who nipped off their heads."[48] The mothers of the girls were demanding progressive education for their children. Interestingly, this seems to be the reason Miss Ruutz-Rees was interviewing Elsie. According to Elsie, Ruutz-Rees had little interest in progressive education. During the short tour of the Rosemary grounds Elsie noticed the traditional facilities and was asked by Ruutz-Rees if the facilities were sufficient. Elsie immediately recommended the current buildings "be cleared of old furniture and equipped with light movable work tables and posture chairs and the kinds of teachings materials now used with young children."[49] A few minutes later, undeterred by Elsie's request, Miss Ruutz-Rees offered Elsie the position. Caught off guard, Elsie asked for two weeks to think over the offer and left for the train station. Elsie wrote, "I remember thinking as I waited for the train, that a wealthy suburban town like Greenwich was not the kind of place I ever wanted to live, least of all have a school. When I reached Grove Court, I found that Marjorie had unexpectedly dropped in for supper. She and Ellen were greatly amused because I had in my excitement put my hat on backwards."[50]

Elsie was familiar with elite preparatory schools for girls, for she had attended this type of school and also taught in them. However, at this point in her career she did not want to give up her progressive practices and enter a more traditional program. Still assisting Dewey in his classes at Teachers College, Elsie sought his advice. "I consulted Dr. Dewey," Elsie explained, "and to my surprise, he favored my taking the school. He said he thought it was time that progressive education broke into the Head Mistress type of school and that it would be interesting to see how children brought up in a progressive elementary school fared when they entered a conventional college-preparatory school. Certainly, he added there were few schools more conventional than Rosemary Hall, run by two Englishwomen, themselves scholars."[51] Elsie considered Caroline Ruutz-Rees and Mary E. Lowndes, the directors, to be bright and intellectually capable women. While a graduate student at Columbia, Elsie had heard Ruutz-Rees speak on Romance languages and comparative literature, an interest she shared. Elsie was also familiar with several monographs written by Mary Lowndes.

Supported by Dewey and not feeling a part of the tight-knit group of teachers at City and Country, Elsie accepted the position of head of the Junior School at Rosemary Hall. Ellen Steele agreed to leave City and Country and teach at the Junior School. Elsie also consulted the Young-Felton Employment Agency

CHAPTER EIGHT 135

to help her fill the other staff positions. Relying on her connections at Teachers College, Elsie consulted with Sara Patrick, Director of the Department of Industrial Relations at Teachers College. Elsie submitted her salary budget to Mary Lowndes, who soon summoned Elsie to Greenwich to explain her high salary figures. Taken aback and somewhat angry over being summoned, Elsie sought Dewey's advice. Dewey suggested Elsie speak with Mary Lowndes but let her do the talking. Elsie took Dewey's advice. "I presented myself to Miss Lowndes and waited silently for I think half an hour." Elsie recalled. "What shocked them, it seemed, was the teachers' salaries; to the amount I had put down for myself as principal, they made no objection at all. So I followed a suggestion Dewey had made."[52] Dewey had advised Elsie to submit her resignation if Rosemary Hall did not meet her salary demands. Apparently Rosemary Hall had advertised the change in philosophy for the new school, and Dewey did not believe they had the option to back down. Elsie won the gamble. "This trump card took the trick," Elsie wrote. "Before I left Miss Lowndes had accepted my salary budget, and, what was perhaps equally important, I had discovered that I would be dealing with two school administrators who might be scholars but also were hard-boiled business women."[53] Elsie had negotiated with Rosemary Hall during the spring of 1924 while still teaching at the City and Country School. She would begin the fall of 1924 as head of the Junior School at Rosemary, her first position as a school administrator.

Prior to beginning work at Rosemary, Elsie and Ellen took a vacation in Europe, spending time in England and France. Elsie described the trip over as a tempestuous one. Elsie and Ellen were relieved to disembark the boat and leave the "great grim dock and bare streets of Liverpool."[54] Traveling from Liverpool to London by train, Elsie and Ellen spent the next two days in bed trying to recover from the difficult crossing. On their summer trip the visited with friend and artist Edna Hopkins. Unfortunately Ellen became ill with a painful ear infection and was also diagnosed with an ovarian cyst. Elsie booked the return passage, but soon realized it was on the same ship they had made the original crossing. Elsie was not about to board this ship again and requested transfer to another boat. This was arranged, but further delayed departure for two weeks. Ellen and Elsie kept in contact with the Paris doctor who had diagnosed Ellen's condition. Finally the day arrived for the crossing and they departed on a cabin boat half-full. Elsie noted, "When I explained to the Purser how ill my friend was, he very kindly moved us without extra charge to a large first-class cabin and put us in charge of the best steward. The Ship's doctor visited Ellen each day, and both the Purser and the Captain were most attentive, enabling me to get the right food for Ellen and sending steward with books from the Ship's Library. This time we had a calmer passage."[55]

Prior to their arrival in New York, Elsie had cabled her family. Lawrence, who had been visiting Marjorie in Poughkeepsie, met the boat and drove Elsie and Ellen to Poughkeepsie. Ellen believed she needed to go to Boston to visit her doctor, but upon consultation the doctor advised Ellen not to make the trip. Ellen saw a surgeon at St. Lukes Hospital and had the operation. While Ellen recuperated in the hospital, Elsie stayed with her cousin Lou Daniel at Whittier Hall and also prepared the apartment at Grove Court for Ellen's return. The summer nearing its end, Ellen recovered enough to visit her sister in Cleveland, while Elsie spent some time with Maude and Fay Ainslie in Provincetown. "Renting a bicycle, I rode forth eagerly to sketch," Elsie recalled, " but going down a steep hill fell off and sprained my arm—weariness I suppose."[56] Tired, but relaxed, Elsie was able to further explore her interest in art and met two other artists, Jack and Janet Tworkov. The Tworkovs along with a friend, Peter Hunt, whom Elsie described as "exotic and extraordinary," convinced Maude and Fay to throw a Russian party. One afternoon upon returning from sketching, Elsie found the "stage all set in the living room." Not having a costume, Elsie improvised by wearing the gingham curtains in her room. Jack and Janet Tworkov served as Lord and Lady of the House and welcomed the "Russian gypsies" at the door. "Never was there such a party." Elsie recalled. "The music inspired various scenes and incidents, and finally broke into an irresistible rhythm that carried the revelers through several dance figures and then swept them out the door and down the steps into the moonlit garden."[57]

With the summer nearly over, Elsie prepared for her work at Rosemary Hall. The year had proved to be a significant one in Elsie's career. She had taught and participated in one of the most innovative progressive schools in City and Country. Unlike the Milton Academy, at City and Country Elsie was one among many teachers who practiced progressive education. She learned by watching and interacting with Caroline Pratt, Lucy Sprague Mitchell, Jessie Stanton, and Harriet Johnson. As a teacher she had explored the interests and experiences of the children to base her approach to curriculum and was becoming known in her own right. Elsie accepted the practice and importance of early childhood education so vital to the philosophy of Pratt, Mitchell, and City and Country. The role of block play and the nurturing of the imagination of children are clearly evident in Elsie's most documented work at the Ballard and Arthurdale School. Her classroom practices challenged the view that progressive education ignored the classics and was anti-intellectual. By the time of Elsie's departure from the City and Country School in 1924, her progressive philosophy of education was firmly grounded. According to historian Arthur Zilversmit, progressive schools in the 1920s were generally characterized by three traits: 1) "a progressive school was one that followed a children-centered rather than a subject-centered curriculum, a school which mobilized children's natural desire to learn," 2) "it was a school concerned with meeting the needs of the whole child, promoting children's emotional and physical needs as well as their intellectual development," and 3) "a progressive school was one in which children would play an active role in determining the content of their education."[58] Elsie did not see the dualism between a child-centered as opposed to a subject-centered approach. Her career at this point emphasized both. She paid attention to the social and psychological needs of her students and allowed them through interest to have a voice in subject matter content. Broadening Zilversmit's definition, Elsie had begun to develop and put into practice the conception of the community school, which for her was the essence of progressive education. Elsie theoretically accepted the basic principles of progressive education as she departed City and Country to become part of a more traditional school. But more importantly she had integrated theory and practice in attempting to meet the needs of the child and their understanding of their role in the larger society. Elsie had to build the progressive program at Rosemary Junior School from scratch and knew she needed support from parents, administrators, and teachers with the talent and ethic to work in this environment. This pioneering work allowed her to experiment, but it soon gave notoriety to her work, vital in shaping her career in the years to come and her conception of the community school.[59]

Chapter Nine

The Rosemary Junior School, 1924–1929: Greenwich, Connecticut

Following a tumultuous summer, beginning the 1924 school year at Rosemary did not seem so "stupendous or difficult" a task to Elsie. Her experience as an "unofficial school administrator" at the Brooklyn Heights Seminary was beneficial, but being the head of the Rosemary Junior School was a new experience. To prepare, Elsie went shopping with a friend to "find the kind of dress a principal would wear" and hoped this outward appearance might relieve some of the parents' skepticism. Elsie was under some pressure before the opening of the school year. Mary Lowndes had phoned Elsie and protested the expense of the movable worktables and posture chairs. "Their price, she said, was high," Elsie noted with dismay, "had I looked into the matter? I said I had and that this was the kind of furniture now used with class groups in elementary school. She made some rude remark and I finally hung up on her."[1] Now a more mature, fairly experienced, and confident educator, Elsie refused to back down and received her request. This was a different Elsie from the days of the Brooklyn Heights Seminary.

Ellen Steele reported for work but was still not well. Elsie recommended Ellen see a physician, who advised Ellen she could do the work and should stop thinking so much about how she felt. Nevertheless, Elsie allowed Ellen some time away from school until she felt better. Prior to beginning the school year, Elsie had consulted with Sara Patrick and Florence House, who headed the Department of Industrial Arts at Teachers College. Both helped Elsie select her teaching staff, and Florence House graciously agreed to teach for a week or two until Ellen recovered. Elsie and Ellen were staying at The Maples, a Greenwich hotel, to avoid the daily commute to New York.

Elsie described her handpicked teachers that first year. "Among the members of the staff that first year I recall Eunice Foster, a Canadian girl whom Miss House and Miss Patrick knew, who had our youngest group of four- and five-year-olds; Abbie Phillips, who came to us through the Young-Felton Agency, who had the sixes and sevens; and Elaine Dickenson, a student of Miss Patrick and Miss House from Teachers College, who had I think the eights and nines." Ellen Steele taught the tens and elevens, and Lettie Craig instructed the twelves, the oldest group in the school. Elsie persuaded Florence House to teach industrial arts on a part-time basis and praised her work. "It was due largely to her that the work made real progress that year, for she invigorated the teaching of the whole staff and was a bulwark of strength."[2] Ellen and Elsie also convinced friend and art teacher William Zorach to "come and guide us in the art work."[3] Maude Stewart, a friend of Harriet Hubbell at the City and Country School, taught music.

The students at the Rosemary Junior School ranged in age from four years old to twelve, but due to an enrollment of fewer than sixty pupils the first year, some of the age groups were combined. Elsie's experience, with the help of Ellen Steele and Florence House, guided the Junior School that first semester. Elsie described her new responsibility similar to "the sensation of trying to roll a heavy ball back uphill."[4] "The children, accustomed to maids and chauffeurs and to a weak and inefficient school," Elsie explained, "were both bad-mannered and indolent, and lacking in any work-habits or interests." One student responded to Elsie, "I'm sure I'd be glad to be interested in something if I knew anything to be interested in."[5] Elsie was incensed by this attitude and their general disdain for learning, something she had always loved and pursued.

Beyond student concerns, Elsie sensed a tension between the Upper School, essentially a high school, and the Lower School or Junior School she directed. Elsie did not believe the Upper School heads or teachers knew anything about early childhood education and were not as supportive as they could have been in the early stages of building the new progressive Junior School. Needing some relief from the stress of the first semester, Elsie and Ellen spent the week of Christmas vacation in Provincetown. "It was fun in the dusk of the winter evening to take the old-fashioned, brilliantly-lighted Fall River Boat and then board the leisurely train that ran down the Cape. In the long 'up-along' and 'down-along' street, the houses of the artists and writers where one may find good cheer and good talk around a blazing hearth-fire, blot out the boarded-up cottages of the summer residents."[6] Ellen and Elsie spent time sketching and interacting with their friend Janet Tworkov, with whom they ate Christmas dinner.

During the early spring of the first year, there was a meeting of the parents of the Junior School. Elsie described her perceptions of the school. "We had all the difficulties of our position as the Lower Department—and a progressive one, at that—of a highly regarded Upper School which, knowing nothing about the education of young children, left us to sink or swim. Some parents were hopeful, more doubtful, and a few hostile."[7] Elsie recalled her experience that day. "On my way out to Greenwich, I stopped at Altman's and bought a dress for the occasion—a beige silk-velvet trimmed in dark brown fur. It was a bitterly cold night, and few parents came out for the meeting, which was held in one of the large parlors of the Upper School."[8] Hostility soon surfaced. Sitting by the fireplace, Elsie began discussing the Junior School and had barely finished when a parent "recently come to Greenwich" stood up and lodged complaints about the school. His attack caught Elsie off guard. Several other parents supported his claims. Being present at the meeting, Caroline Ruutz-Rees listened to the parents "and then placed herself at the door where each parent would have to speak with her before leaving."[9] One of the supportive parents drove Elsie home that evening and tried to comfort her. "Greenwich, Miss Clapp," he said, "is filled with men who have, by fair means or foul, risen to the top; they are used to being the boss and are arbitrary and often unreasonable."[10]

Elsie called her staff together the next day, a Sunday, and discussed the criticisms with them. Although she thought the criticisms were "silly," she asked her staff to do what they could to eliminate them. Another parents' meeting was held a short time later, which, because the weather had improved, included a larger group of parents. This meeting was called by Miss Ruutz-Rees and by the parents who supported the progressive program of the Junior School. Although the "critics" were present, they said nothing at this meeting and it went smoothly. Still indignant over what she perceived as insignificant criticism of her program, Elsie wrote letters to the three families who had criticized the program and its methods. In the letters Elsie boldly stated her desire for their children to return only if the parents were satisfied with the school and its methods. Only one family decided to withdraw their children. Elsie explained to Miss Ruutz-Rees the intent of the letters, who was amused, surprised and approved the action. Elsie fondly recalled the months that followed "were inexplicably better at the Junior School...The children, now courteous and cooperative, were becoming interested in the work. It was I think, a combination of our unremitting efforts and the upswing of the spring."[11]

Later in the spring of 1925, Elsie again spoke to the parents of the children in the Junior School. She explained to them the general course of study that included arithmetic, language, history, geography, science, industrial arts, arts, music, and physical education. Elsie implied the approach of the Junior School was based on the old adage that "experience is the best teacher." "For we believe in education," she told the parents, "that one does not thoroughly grasp and know a fact unless one is able to use it. And therefore we plan as many opportunities as possible for a child to use and express what he learns while he is learning it."[12] This new approach did not ignore traditional subject matter, and Elsie gave examples of how she might teach Greek history, culture, and literature. Elsie informed the parents that this new approach would enrich learning and understanding, helping the students become independent learners. The parents were welcome to visit and conference with her and the teachers, but Elsie cautioned them not to interrupt the learning process.

During the spring Elsie prepared a catalogue containing information about the Junior School. It included descriptions of activities of the children, photographs of the activities, and a statement of educational beliefs. Elsie submitted the draft publication for the approval of Miss Ruutz-Rees and Miss Lowndes for moral and financial support. The teachers at the Junior School expressed a willingness to publish the information, even at their own expense. Lowndes and Ruutz-Rees were surprised at this level of cooperation and initiative among the staff of the Junior School. Ruutz-Rees responded, "I understand the cooperative attitude of your staff as little as I understand how you get from young children what I call scholarship."[13] The publication was approved and the teachers of the Junior School underwrote the publication. "By 1927, the first issue of the catalogue-bulletin was sold out," Elsie noted with pride, "and we published another, also illustrated with photographs, which was used as a school catalogue and sold as an educational bulletin."[14] The bulletin articulates Elsie's early vision of a community school. Following a brief description of the school and its curriculum, Elsie explained the philosophy of education for the Junior School. "The child's own activities and interests are taken as the starting point for individual and group and directed so that they lead him to an extending field of inquiry and investigation."[15] Learning was to be an active engaging process, leading to an enriched learning experience. Bulletin photographs show six-year-olds learning carpentry, and four- and five-year-olds constructing boats from block play. In breaking down some gender barriers, Elsie stressed new opportunities for girls. She wrote, "Girls receive the education that answers their own interests and that enables them to enter grades of Rosemary or other schools. Also they are enabled to gain those interests and hand-skills which have until recently, been the recourse of boys only."[16]

The curriculum was traditional but approached in a progressive way. All the children in the Junior School through seventh grade were exposed to French. A lunch was served everyday at one o'clock followed by a rest period. Physical development of the children was also stressed and the Rosemary School grounds afforded "ample play space; gardens, a meadow with a little canal and pond, a hockey field and track field."[17] Guest luncheons, afternoon courses for parents and teachers, and assemblies were also prominent features of the Rosemary Junior School. While the Junior School nurtured the development of the individual child, it did not ignore group activities. Elsie stressed that individuality was "to be gained through and in the process of participating with others in some shared and common activity. It is in associated activities, in a process of give and take, that a person realized himself and that those relationships receive direction."[18] Subject matter itself was couched in these terms. "Subject matter is the meaning of our associated life," Elsie explained, "as that has been worked out in the past in our cultures, our art and our skills, the stuff or material of civilization. Today in education we plan activities that involve and develop this meaning, these subject matters. And our Course of Study is in truth, the course which these interests run, the plan which is made for their on-going. We chart this process with regard for all factors that enter into it, but the point is not the charting but rather the process itself, the developing of these interests, the emerging of this meaning.[19] Each course of study was detailed in the bulletin, and at all times we attempted to link the subject matter to the experiences of the children. The Junior School course of study included mathematics, history, geography, literature, French, speech, English grammar, reading, writing, spelling, industrial arts, music and art.[20]

Elsie believed the bulletin served as a tool to share information and philosophy with other progressive educators. This desire to share ideas and practice is supported by a letter Elsie sent Gertrude Hartman, the editor of the journal *Progressive Education*. Elsie was also interested in what others were doing and believed educators needed a mechanism to share ideas beyond (and more accessible than) conferences and professional gatherings. Elsie wrote to Hartman, "Aside from these special moments in school work, we, as a school, would also be very glad to be kept in touch with the problems and studies, enterprises and researches that other schools have undertaken for the current year or terms... we therefore should like to propose that all schools who are interested send to *Progressive Education* news of what is going on for the coming quarter in the way of interesting enterprises among student or teachers, or news of events of interests educationally that have just occurred."[21] Hartman concurred with Elsie's request and asked readers to submit ideas and suggestions. Caroline Ruutz-Rees was so impressed with the work at the Junior School that she asked Elsie to tell her more "about the educational philosophy behind the methods and practices." Elsie noted Ruutz-Rees' interest, but she also observed that Ruutz-Rees was not willing to change her own way of teaching.

The Rosemary Junior School under Elsie's leadership was becoming known in progressive education circles. What did this mean? It meant that Elsie and her staff generally accepted and attempted to apply the seven principles of progressive education—the freedom of the pupil to develop naturally, that interest was the motive of all work, that the teacher was a guide and not a taskmaster, fostering the scientific study of pupil development, paying attention to the child's physical development, fostering cooperation between home and the school, and helping progressive education become the center of educational movements.[22] This acknowledgment of the Rosemary Junior School as progressive was apparent when Nell Goldsmith, one of the heads of the progressive Walden School in New York (founded by Margaret Naumberg in 1915) came to visit Ellen Steele's classroom. Like Elsie, Naumberg was a graduate of Barnard and an enthusiastic supporter of Dewey. Naumberg's Walden School was considered progressive although she paid more allegiance than most progressives to Sigmund Freud, Maria Montessori, and Carl Jung. According to historian Lawrence Cremin, Naumberg sought to create a school "in which the emotional side of education would have parity with the intellectual."[23] Unfortunately, when Nell Goldsmith came to visit Ellen's class, she was absent with a cold. Goldsmith was so impressed with "the way the children were running the class" that she hired Ellen to teach at the Walden Demonstration School that summer in California.[24]

Elsie spent the summer of 1925 again in, Provincetown art community, living on the "Portuguese" west end. Elsie convinced her summer landlord to make the apartment more of an art studio. Her friends Maude and Fay Ainslie were in Mexico and Ellen was teaching in California so Elsie concentrated on painting and writing. "The highlights of the summer for me," Elsie recalled, "were writing at request an article on Dewey for *The New Era*, the journal of the Progressive Education Movement in England and Europe and whose editor, an Englishwoman, I had met in New York; and an unexpected and extraordinary letter from Florence Greer, expressing sorrow at the wrong she had done me, to which I sent as pleasant and harmless a reply as I could compose."[25] Elsie was still hurt and troubled by Florence Greer's treatment of her at the Brooklyn Heights Seminary. Her contact with Florence and Edith Greer had been minimal since that time. Leaving Brooklyn Heights was an intellectual and emotional low for Elsie, but in reality provided her opportunities in progressive education she would not have had otherwise. Elsie's growing confidence in her ability to teach and even administer a program were far from the days of Florence Greer's criticisms and emotional trauma.

Although she was able to escape Florence Greer and the Brooklyn Heights Seminary, Elsie never seemed to escape her plaguing health problems. During the first year at Rosemary Elsie suffered from painful arthritis in both knees. A friend insisted Elsie try a new diet. "It was severe," Elsie recalled, "but I felt desperate: orange juice only for one week; then, for one of the three meals the second week, the juice of celery, carrots and lettuce boiled together; and for the third week, orange juice for breakfast, the juice for lunch, and the lettuce, carrots and celery for supper."[26] Apparently the diet with exercise worked, and in a few weeks Elsie had no more arthritis pain. X-rays confirmed the disappearance of the arthritis deposits. This wonderful news was coupled with Ellen Steele's return from California "completely disillusioned about the effectiveness of demonstration summer school."[27] As Elsie began her second year at Rosemary, 1925–1926, she and Ellen made a daily trip from New York to Greenwich, Connecticut. Tiring of the conditions and the travel from New York to Greenwich, Ellen often stayed with friends in Greenwich during the school week. Eventually, Elsie also tired of the long trip, and by mid-winter she and

Ellen had moved to Cos Cob, much closer to Greenwich. "It was," Elsie recalled, "despite the cost of cabs to and from school, a much easier living arrangement for us."[28] Elsie's sister Marjorie and her husband James Myers were living nearby, making the move to Cos Cob more personally satisfying. Elsie had described the first year at the Rosemary Junior School as like rolling a ball uphill. Now with one year of experience, with relief and satisfaction, the ball "began to roll of its own momentum." Due to the work of Elsie and her staff, "the children had come alive and were now deeply interested in what they were doing."[29] The teaching staff was much the same and like Elsie had matured during the first year. "Eunice Foster still had the four and fives," Elsie recalled, "and their block buildings filled their big room in the Upper Bungalow and the Court on which it opened. The sixes with Abbie Phillips were actively learning, and the village houses were set up on the Lower Court against the background of the Upper School Chapel whose side flanked this end of the Junior School buildings. Elaine Dickenson this year taught the sevens. Ida Perry, a teacher from White Plains who was an enthusiastic progressive, had joined us as an apprentice-teacher; she was particularly successful in working with eight- and nine-year-olds, and soon became a regular staff member in charge of this group."[30] A gifted student from Teachers College taught the tens; Ellen Steele taught the elevens, and Lettie Craig the twelves. The twelves under Craig's guidance connected Latin language studies with Roman history. This led to a field trip to the Metropolitan Museum, where the class studied Roman dress and culture. Elsie enlisted William Zorach to paint scenery for the twelves' performance of *Julius Caesar*. Music and drama were important elements in the progressive curriculum at the Junior School. Anita Darling and Maude Street worked with the children in music and rhythm studies for the younger children. Laure des Cherres, a teacher Elsie and Ellen met in France, also joined the staff and "proved to be very resourceful in connecting the work in French with the children's class studies and interests."[31]

During the year, Ellen Steele directed her elevens in a "study of Greek life in the pastoral period."[32] She published her experiences in an article "Freeing the Child Through Art," in *Progressive Education*. Ellen began the article by discussing freedom of the individual and freedom within a social context; the notion that freedom had two sides. "Educationally speaking," Ellen wrote, "the two aspects of freedom are working out the relationship for any given individual between the development of his powers so that he expresses himself through them."[33] In her teaching, Ellen had integrated art, drama, dance, and song. As part of the study students had read parts of the *Odyssey*, deciding to act out a harvest festival to Dionysius. They studied the forms of daily work in ancient Greece and paid special attention to weaving and spinning. Ellen showed the children slides from Greece, and they began to construct a stage to set the background for their school presentation. The children designed and painted a background of hills, rocks and vineyards and made their own costumes. Ellen wrote, "The most interesting feature of this experience was the way in which one act reinforced the other. The spirit of the Greek landscape found expression in the action, and the action called for some explanation through words... it is this kind of experience which privies the situation that places a value on art expression."[34] Although the stress was on art as expression, an interest Ellen shared with her students, there was much more complexity to this activity. A former teacher in the City and Country School, Ellen understood the importance the progressive school placed on proper comprehension of work and its connection with art. Most progressive schools at some point taught spinning and weaving, not as a vocation, but as initial activities in linking work with creativity, imagination, expression, and art. They believed it helped the students better understand how things came to be and the human force and energy that created them. In essence, art was a type of communal experience. Ellen Steele's students were learning about ancient Greece, but they also learned about themselves, how to cooperate and communicate in solving problems, the essence of the progressive view of learning and intelligence.[35] The arts were a significant component of the curriculum at the Rosemary Junior School.

Elsie described the Rosemary Junior School philosophy, including the use of the arts, in an article, "The Subject Matters in Experimental Education," published in *Progressive Education* during her third year at Rosemary Hall.[36] Elsie suggested that subject matter be chosen on the basis of inquiry and experience. She wrote, "Subject matter is the meaning of an associated life, as that has been worked out in the past in our culture, our art and our skills, the stuff or material of civilization, an integral part of our living today."[37] Elsie voiced a concern when subject matter became nothing more than facts or information for tests, because this usually opposed the interest and desires of the students. Children, she believed, needed to learn that they really educate themselves, "not individually, but as a social undertaking."[38] Elsie explained, "The specific problem of a child's education, is how, when, where, why he/she and we can come into possession of and further those subject activity interests. How, when where and why develop them in a developing universe?"[39] Traditional subject matter tended to ignore the interest and desires of the students, and Elsie believed student voices needed to be heard. She and her staff used the arts as a means to accomplish this. "We try to give children a conception of their contribution to the group, that they can create, and to gain for each member the strengthening and the stimulation that comes from a sense of his value to the group and of their appreciation of him. The arts offer us our readiest opportunity for bringing this to pass."[40] Elsie understood art as a means of

CHAPTER NINE 147

reshaping and re-creating the world, the artist fully integrated in the process, a type of harmonious interrelation.[41] The key for Elsie, and Dewey for that matter, was to "carry this idea from the realm of art and intellectual work over into living."[42] Elsie and Ellen Steele, both amateur artists, believed that art provided a means of self-evaluation and self-expression beyond words. It allowed a child a means to express feeling and emotion beyond the limited use of words. The stress on harmonious interrelation, interaction, and expression is clearly related to the democratic ethic and the concept of community.[43] Following the second year at Rosemary, Elsie and Ellen once again spent the summer in Provincetown, painting with Maude and Fay Ainslie. That summer Elsie enjoyed the "Art Salon," a weekly gathering of local artists who exchanged comments and ideas, often well into the night. Elsie enjoyed the relaxed atmosphere of Provincetown, conversing with friends about her art, although she never considered herself an accomplished artist.

As Elsie began her third year (1926–1927) as head of the Junior School, art was well entrenched. It was "an integral and natural part of the children's learning and experience." Ellen Steele shared her experiences with the art department at Teachers College. This was followed by a gathering of art teachers from the area at the Junior School. Students spoke to the visiting teachers about their artwork. One twelve-year-old student explained to the teachers, "You see, you paint a picture which is what you think and feel about something. And then, there it is, a picture which is something in itself, beautiful and it makes other people think and feel things."[44] This child fully grasped the notion of harmonious interrelation and the very nature of art as human experience and expression. The significance placed on art continued throughout the year as Elsie, staff and students prepared for the annual Christmas play. Elsie fondly recalled, "During the first year, the Christmas performance only attracted a few parents for the Junior School, as its fame spread, the performance was attended not only by all the mothers and fathers of the Junior School children, but also by the staff and students of the Upper School... although the play presented by the younger children of the Junior School lacked the force and gusto which had characterized its performance at Milton, it was sincere and moving."[45] Under the direction of Florence House and William Zorach, the children annually sent Christmas cards of linoleum block prints to their families and hung them on the school's Christmas tree. Students also explored during the Christmas season ancient rituals and celebrations for the changing season. This included studies and integration of Greek, Egyptian, and Nordic myths.[46]

By Elsie's third year at the school (1926–1927), Caroline Ruutz-Rees and Mary Lowndes had some remote understanding of the progressive education methods of the Junior School, but their personal teaching methods remained traditional. "They never did understand how it was possible for these young children to do such work," Elsie recalled.[47] The Heads of the Upper School continued to be disturbed by the higher salaries paid to the teachers of the Junior School and according to Elsie "were astonished to find that in progressive schools, such as ours, teachers occupied a far more responsible and independent position than held by any of their staff members."[48] Elsie believed the Upper School teaching staff was "built upon low-salaried inexperienced college graduates" whose chief mission was to prepare students for the college or the university environment. She described the situation. "If they tolerated our different practices," Elsie wrote, "it was because the Junior School's success was so to speak, another feather in their cap."[49]

Elsie sensed the Upper School's philosophy was not changing, and it was "none too easy to live with." She described her feelings. "The fact was, I suppose, that it had not envisaged the needs of a vigorous growing Junior School. Space in a little-used Rosemary Hall building was, for instance, yielded for the Junior School's lunch only on the agreement that the room and kitchenette be occupied for two and one-half hours exactly—a limitation that necessitated unusually quick preparation, service and clean up. The first two years I was given no space for an office, so I had no place in which to see parents or to dictate letters until after school hours. This third year an office of sorts was provided for me—a small, dark basement room in an adjoining Upper School Dormitory.... We our part, watched with amazement the working of the Upper School, the breathless racing of its students through a tightly packed schedule of recitations, study periods, test and games. The distinction Rosemary Hall enjoyed was conferred by Miss Ruutz-Rees and Miss Lowndes, whose own scholarship and social standing gave school events a kind of prestige and glamour, and who required from their staff and students vigorous college-preparatory work."[50] Although she was in the traditional mode, Elsie considered Miss Ruutz-Rees an excellent Latin teacher and once attended one of her summer classes. The class was translating Virgil while Miss Ruutz-Rees trimmed the hedges while making witty comments about the translation. Frustrated to a degree, Elsie reluctantly grasped that the Upper School was the central focus of Rosemary Hall and that the Junior School was generally perceived as a feeder school.

Enrollments in the Junior School declined during the third year and because of a lower enrollment the Junior School faced a deficit. Before discussing the problem with Miss Ruutz-Rees and Miss Lowndes, Elsie brought up the financial concerns with her staff. The next day and prior to the meeting with Miss Ruutz-Rees and Miss Lowndes, Elsie found on her desk resignations from her teachers, concerned about the budget deficit and not wishing to burden Rosemary Hall financially. Miss Ruutz-Rees and Miss Lowndes refused to

CHAPTER NINE 149

accept the resignations and believed the deficit could be addressed with a slight rise in Junior School tuition the following year. Elsie was relieved and appreciated the support. The staff of the Junior School remained intact.

Elsie's staff was hand picked and supported her. Staff meetings were held regularly and took the character of a graduate seminar study group. During the third year seminar topics included the Individual in His Social Relations, and the Subject Matters—Language, Literature, Mathematics and History. Other meetings were held to address science, industrial arts, arts, and music. On alternate weeks the staff worked with William Zorach in oils, watercolors, wood, and clay. Student teachers were also part of the life of the Junior School, many coming from Vassar College. Elsie described this environment as similar to contemporary professional development schools. "Individual programs were planned for each student teacher, but every program included observation of children, work on preparation of material with the group's teachers, supervised practice-teaching, and weekly conferences with me, participation in the staff seminar studies, visiting other progressive schools, work at Teachers College in Industrial Arts and in one of Dewey's educational courses, and in some subject of special interest to the student—Mathematics, History, Science, Geography, Language or Literature."[51] Elsie opened student teaching to college graduates, and graduates of accredited high schools with study in a normal school. She personally interviewed all applicants.

Ellen and Elsie once again spent their summer vacation in Provincetown. Their friends Maude and Fay Ainslie were there along with Jane and Arthur Allen from Louisville, Kentucky. All were drawn together by their interest in art. Once a week the "Art Salon" gathered to exhibit their work and exchange comments and ideas. "The Allens were kind about the paintings that Ellen and I made though they lacked all the techniques they were acquiring, and Maude and Fay were also encouraging. We all admired the work that Maude did and were interested in Fay's pictorial murals. However, whatever our differences, all of us enjoyed the art meetings and, since we had so much to say to each other, they lasted far into the night."[52] Suppers were sometimes a communal affair; Ellen and Elsie shared their studio room, and the Allens cooked on Elsie's two-burner oil stove.

The new school year was fast approaching, and Elsie had hired Luella Cruger, a friend of Ellen Steele's from the Shady Hill School, to teach the nine-year-olds; Marie Spotswood taught the tens, and Helen Lacy directed the work in athletics. Rosemary Lillard taught music and Ida Perry the eights. The work at the Junior School was becoming more visible in progressive education circles with staff publications appearing in *Progressive Education*. Ellen Steele and Rosemary Lillard published an article, "Creative Music in the Group Life," discussing the role of music in the eleven-year-old class.[53] Studying the Middle

Ages, the students decided to write a play about a legend surrounding Charlemagne. The students wrote the play, built and decorated the theater, and made costumes. Describing the activity Ellen wrote, "When it came time to putting the play together they found a number of places where music was needed, they were not able to find music that suited them, so there was nothing to do but make the music they wanted."[54] Ellen guided the children with writing the lyrics, and then they took their notes and ideas to Rosemary Lillard, the music teacher. In participating in this study the children integrated history, English, French, art, drama, and music. They were also learning to work together to meet a common goal. Ellen Steele believed this activity was clearly educational and wrote about how to enhance a child's imagination in this kind of creative environment She believed the teacher needed to be "sensitive to the child's creative impulses, and able to take an experimental attitude toward the child in his musical development."[55] Musical technique was not as important as creative expression.

During the spring of 1927 the elevens and twelves began studying the use of record keeping under the direction of Florence House. The students explored the Chinese use of silk and cloth scrolls and the Indian use of palm leaves. Other students studied and reported on the Egyptian use of papyrus and the cuneiform writing of the Sumerians, Babylonians, and Assyrians. As part of the study, students traveled to various libraries in the New York area where they observed Babylonian clay tablets, a manuscript on parchment, the Golden Gospels from Byzantium, wood blocks, and some early printed books. Field trips to local libraries were important components of learning at the Rosemary Junior School. The twelves under the direction of Ellen Steele made a study of the modern era. Elsie was clearly impressed and proud of this work and wrote, "They wished to find out how the modern world came about, they wanted to know how nations organized governments, how the countries got along together, and how they exchanged ideas, changed the ways of working, who the inventors were, and the development of power; about New York as the most modern city in the world and about Paris as an old-world city; about the literature that goes with modern times and about the artists, music, the theater and how it developed."[56]

This innovative use of subject matter was crucial to Elsie and her staff's philosophy of education. But Elsie, like many progressives, was concerned with how elementary students might fare when they entered a more traditional, teacher-text centered environment. Since the Junior School fed students to the Upper School this was an important issue to address. The first group of twelve-year-olds were now in their second year at the Upper School. Elsie noted her findings about the transition from the Lower School to the Upper School. "It was in the rating of students of average or below-average ability that the difference of the two schools appraisal was marked," Elsie explained. "Students who we considered superficial or lacking in intellectual or practical ability the Upper School rated higher than we did if they possessed acquisitive ability and memorized well, while our rating of students who were observant and thoughtful though inarticulate was higher than at Rosemary Hall, where ability was assessed chiefly through written tests and recitations."[57] Caroline Ruutz-Rees and Mary Lowndes, the Heads of the Upper School, admitted that the students from the Junior School were well read and had excellent study habits. Elsie concluded from her inquiry that "children who have average or better-than-average ability who had worked in a progressive elementary school could without difficulty handle the work of a rigorous college-preparatory school."[58]

Looking back over the last two years, Elsie knew she had made progress with the children. "It was surprising how alive, resourceful and independent the children now were, the interests and the handskill they had developed, and the degree to which their sterile culture had been broadened and enriched. With us in school where they were free to be their natural selves, they were engrossed in what they were doing and worked joyously and well. It was in fact the work they did that earned for the Junior School its growing fame in educational circles."[59] Elsie was largely responsible for the recognition of the Junior School in progressive education circles. She accepted speaking engagements to spread the gospel of the new education and the work occurring at the Junior School. Elsie had prodded Dewey to speak at some of these invitations, but he refused, suggesting Elsie assume the role of the educator in the community and she accepted the challenge. During her years at Rosemary she wrote several articles and made it her business to accept all invitations to speak and write. Elsie delivered what she considered her best speech for the Women's Club of Poughkeepsie, at Vassar at the invitation of her former English instructor, Laura Wylie, whom Elsie greatly respected. "You did pretty well, Elsie," Wylie responded following the speech, " but you told them only about your successes, not your failures."[60] This comment stimulated Elsie to think about what she could do better.

Despite the successes of the Junior School, Elsie did not feel she had adequately addressed the role of the school in the community and thought she understood why. "The cultural programs we had developed might enrich their learning," Elsie explained, "but they had little, if any, connection with their outside-school lives. And Greenwich, with its suburban residences, luxurious estates, country clubs, and shops that cater to such communities seemed to us to provide only scanty environmental study material." Elsie was truly bothered by this issue and grew restless and wanted to leave Rosemary. Once again she sought Dewey's advice. Dewey suggested Elsie remain because all schools had advantages and disadvantages and because at Rosemary, Elsie and the staff had a good chance to work on the selection and organization of subject matter material for use with children at each stage of their development at the Elementary Grades.[61]

This desire to leave may also have been stimulated by some staff problems at the Junior School. Luella Cruger, Ellen's friend and associate from Shady Hill, did not feel a part of the teaching cohort. "She was, I think," Elsie wrote, "jealous of Ellen's ability and reputation or she may, like many older teachers, have longed for a position of greater authority. Whatever the reason, she fomented discontent and succeeded in upsetting several other members of the staff." Attempting to head off a serious problem with morale, Elsie decided to replace Cruger and the discontented teachers. Ida Perry, Rose Lilliard, and Laure des Cherres were "not affected." Ellen Steele, Florence House, and William Zorach supported Elsie in her decision. Elsie blamed herself for not immediately recognizing the problem. "I was chagrined because, after my own experience at the Brooklyn Heights Seminary with Florence Greer, and after by work at Milton under Sara Goodwin, I should have known better. Teachers, especially older teachers, I now realized need reassurance and approval frequently expressed." Being a school administrator was difficult. On her way to spend the summer in Robinhood, Maine, Elsie stopped by the Milton Academy to express her thanks to Sara Goodwin for her support and what she had taught Elsie about administering a school. Goodwin responded, "I am not worried, you're a good learner."[62]

Elsie and Ellen spent the summer of 1927 with William and Marguerite Zorach in Robinhood, Maine. "After Provincetown, with its crowds of art students and tourists," Elsie recalled, "Robinhood, Maine seemed vast and silent, beautiful, but unpaintable. It was fun however living near the Zorachs, and we had a good time with them." Robinhood did not inspire Elsie to paint, but the free time allowed her to work on another Junior School bulletin. However, not all was quiet. Elsie and Ellen had been noticed by some of the conservative townspeople, who were shocked by their smoking and their bathing suits. Elsie recalled their gradual acceptance. "Finally an old eel-catcher, who had sometimes helped us fish our pail of milk and butter out of the deep hole under the trees which served as our icebox, came to call dressed in his Sunday best, and he and Ellen had a fine time talking about boats and rigging. He must have passed the word along that we were really all right, for the next day a neighbor left a pot of baked beans on the back step."[63]

Following a quiet and uneventful summer, Elsie began the 1927–1928 year at the Junior School with several new faculty and assistance from the student teachers from Vassar. As part of their training the students worked with experienced teachers on Elsie's staff. Elsie described her teaching assignments. "Bert

Whitehead worked with the sixes under Abbie Phillips. Elisabeth Sheffield helped Ida Perry with the eights and nines, Poggie Reese took charge of the children's athletics, and under the direction of Ellen Steele and Florence House, she and Kathie Day worked with the tens. This fall the theme of textiles was investigated by the entire Junior School. The eight-year-olds learned about flax and planted a garden on school grounds. Miss House showed the students how to spin and weave the flax fibers into linen cloth."[64] The elevens studied the Middle Ages, including the journals of Marco Polo, and made embroideries under the direction of art teacher William Zorach.

Ellen Steele wrote about her work with the twelves in an article "Twelve Year Olds Investigate the Textile Industry." The unit was stimulated by the interest the children had in learning more about the Industrial Revolution. As elevens, they had studied the Middle Ages and the Renaissance, but had difficulty connecting those historical periods with the modern era. Due to the textile and fashion industry in New York, the city provided an excellent area to learn about the textile industry which in England had stimulated the Industrial Revolution. The twelves visited the Metropolitan Museum to view prints from India, England, France and colonial America. They went to the Industrial Arts room where they "saw all kinds of spinning wheels and looms, including the big Jacquard looms."[65] Following this research the students exhibited their knowledge through paintings and reports. The goal of the study was not vocational, for Ellen Steele viewed it as a means to see how the contribution of one grows and eventually meets the needs of many. She taught the students that textiles played a significant historical role in the Industrial Revolution and also played an important role in their own lives. They now understood where the raw cotton at the docks came from and where it went to be processed. "I have been investigating this subject with the children," Ellen wrote, "helping them tap the resources of New York City to understand a great industry in a great city, and to glimpse some of the meanings that lie back of modern times...."[66] Ellen saw this study of textiles as a means to see how humanity was tied together through individual contributions. Although Ellen Steele was an excellent teacher, perhaps the best at the Junior School, there is no discussion in her article about the negative side of the textile industry in America. Working for the National Child Labor Committee, progressive photographer Lewis Hine had already documented prior to World War I the horrors of child labor in the textile industry and labor at large. Hine had studied sweatshops, mostly worked by recent immigrants to the United States. Ellen and Elsie's elite students needed to understand the Industrial Revolution, but they also needed to understand the sacrifices made by those less fortunate throughout the world who may have made the clothes they wore every day to school. It is unfortunate progressive schools rarely explored these forms of exploitation and oppression, but many of them were elite private schools, not radical forums for social discourse or reform.[67]

Following a quiet and uneventful summer in Robinhood, Maine, with the Zorachs, Elsie began her final year (1928–1929) at the Junior School. However in October, Caroline Ruutz-Rees decided that Elsie needed a rest, so she took a week off and returned to Maine to spend more time with her friend Marguerite Zorach. Historian Cheryl Black writes, "Marguerite Thompson Zorach was a native Californian," born into the middle class. "In 1910 she abandoned her plans to study at Stanford in order to study art in Paris. There she saw, and was immediately fascinated by, the unconventional use of color and line in Matisse, Picasso and others working in the Fauvist or cubist style." Marguerite met William Zorach in 1911 and they were married in 1912. Elsie believed William Zorach to be less sympathetic to her love for painting and her struggles than Marguerite. Elsie always enjoyed Marguerite's company. Also a member of the Provincetown Players, Marguerite will be best known for her work on embroidering tapestries.[68]

Upon returning from vacation to Rosemary, Ellen Steele met Elsie at the train station where they immediately went to a planning meeting for the Regional Progressive Education Conference to be held in the spring. Elsie believed belonging to professional associations was vital to her work. It served as a mechanism for supporting and sustaining the growth of progressive education. Elsie described her own desire to share her beliefs as similar to "a kind of missionary fervor."[69] But regardless of success in student excitement and achievement, Elsie believed that progressive education at large needed to be more firmly grounded "on the findings of scientists regarding physical and psychological growth, or one that demonstrated the part played in a child's development by his social relationship and the environment in which he lives."[70] In this last year Abbie Phillips had the sevens, and Ida Perry the eights. Roberta Whitehead taught the sixes, Elisabeth Sheffield the nines, Poggie Reese the tens, and Kathy Day the elevens. Mary Brock, a Vassar graduate, "successfully handled" the fours and fives and a replacement for Ellen Steele, a Mrs. Rogers, taught the twelves. "Florence House and William Zorach were," Elsie noted, "as always a mainstay and support, but we missed Ellen Steele's enthusiasm and the invigoration her work gave the rest of the staff."[71] Katherine Camp Mayhew, best known for her work at the Dewey Lab School in Chicago with her sister Anna Camp Edwards, was now on the staff of the Junior School as a science teacher. Excited at first by Katherine Mayhew's presence, Elsie soon had a problem on her hands and described the experience. "In an expansive moment, I invited her to share the ground floor apartment in the Cos Cob house which Ellen and I had been using, paying only for meals which, as before, we ate with the Vassar girls on the second floor. Because I was overbusy

CHAPTER NINE 155

and Mrs. Mayhew was a born chiseler, the arrangement proved a costly one for me; her adopted children visited her frequently, and laundry, telephone and taxi bills mounted. Although I managed to see the year through without unpleasantness, I ended it in debt."[72] On top of this, Katherine Mayhew's teaching was a disappointment. "Mrs. Mayhew," Elsie recalled, "like many older people, was critical of the younger teachers and the work in science, instead of illuminating class studies as we anticipated, turned out to be a separate and not-too-fruitful enterprise conducted by Mrs. Mayhew along lines she advocated."[73] As far as Elsie was concerned, Katherine Mayhew was not a team player and for the curriculum to be successful, teachers needed to work together as a community.

The work that year ended on the celebration of a May Day festival in which all the groups of students at the Junior School participated. The May Day festival was not simply entertainment but was perceived as a learning experience. The teachers and students linked history, literature, art, music, dance, drama, and even biology. All these were integrated as studies of the ancient civilizations and how these cultures celebrated the onset of spring and new life through the annual harvest. The festivities were watched by the Junior School parents and the staff of the Upper School and also out-of-town guests.

As Elsie concluded her work at the Junior School she viewed it as successful in its attempt to practice progressive pedagogy in curriculum innovation. Other progressive educators agreed. In 1928 Harold Rugg and Ann Shumaker in their noted work, *The Child Centered School*, acknowledged Elsie's work at the Rosemary Junior School as part of a new revolution in education. Rugg wrote, "The Junior School of Rosemary Hall, an old-line private academy was reorganized (1924) along modern principles with the help of Elsie Ripley Clapp, an assistant of Dewey."[74] Elsie and her staff had seriously attempted to address the principles of progressive education in their practice, but for Elsie there was something missing. Like many progressive educators, she sought to extend progressive pedagogy beyond lab schools and elite private schools like Rosemary. Progressive education needed to enter the public school, the schools in which the majority of American children attended. She noted that one problem for implementation in the public schools was class size and another the lack of trained teachers.[75] One incident focused Elsie's attention on the weaknesses of the Rosemary Junior School. A principal visiting from a New York City private school came to Rosemary, not to observe but to find the magic formula or magic program she needed to practice progressive education. Elsie and her staff knew this was not possible. "We ourselves were far from satisfied with them," Elsie told her, "and certainly would not advocate their use by a school in another locality working with children from a different background."[76]

This is a significant response for it shows Elsie's understanding of progressive education as a local community affair, deeply embedded in personal experience. It could not be packaged or copied by other teachers. It had a certain uniqueness, and that uniqueness varied with each individual community. There were no blueprints. Elsie must have thought and Dewey often articulated, with an education based on experience, how could it be otherwise.

Regardless of her success at the Junior School, Elsie still realized that she and her staff had failed in one major aspect, to make a connection between the school community and the community in which the children lived. "In Greenwich," Elsie wrote, "we had not seen how to change the separation of home and school. For the teaching staff had neither the means or motivation to lead the kind of social life that engaged the children and their parents, and the latter—however much they appreciated what their children were learning at the Junior School—had no desire to include the teachers in their own social activities. So the best we had been able to do for the children was to provide them with experiences children should have and to extend their cultural appreciation and understandings beyond the limit of dancing, music and riding lessons... Like all progressives, we talked about social relationships and their role in the children's development, but these relationships were actually those within the school community."[77] It is this perceived failure, the desire to merge the school community with the community at large, to truly build a community school that pushed Elsie to leave the Rosemary Junior School.

One opportunity that immediately came to Elsie's attention that last year was the plan for a progressive college-preparatory school at Vassar. During the final year at Rosemary the staff, under Elsie's direction, had begun studying subject matter centered on mathematics. Elsie addressed her ideas in an article "Children's Mathematics," published in *Progressive Education*.[78] Elsie suggested that the traditional approach to teaching young children about math was unsatisfactory and needed to be more inquiry based. This inquiry should "be based on other activities, and interests such as industrial arts, science, history, arts and music."[79] Using history, children could look into "how men long ago counted and measured, when they figured and measured, how they recorded it, how this helped them in their living and how it helped them to get food, to build, to exchange goods, to travel, to produce, to export and import... to improve conditions, to plan new things, to discover lands, to analyze, and to draw conclusions."[80] The ultimate goal for Elsie and her staff was to bring math and all subjects to life, to help children understand its value and its relevance in their daily lives. Math and its understanding was crucial in comprehending the human experience, how people used their imagination and solved problems. In preparing for the math studies with her staff, Elsie had made several trips to Vassar to consult with members of the math department and science department. Elsie found the Vassar faculty supportive and enthusiastic about her plans. On one of the visits President MacCracken of Vassar notified Elsie that some benefactors had left a gift to the College to establish a preparatory school under the auspices of the College. MacCracken proposed Elsie become the new director. "It was to be a progressive college preparatory school," Elsie explained, "and was to have connection with the Nursery School conducted by the Department of Euthenics and with its Home Economics course."[81] Vassar defined euthenics as "the direct application of the sciences to the betterment of living conditions with a view to the improvement of the individual, and, one hopes, indirectly of the race."[82] There is an element of progressive social meliorism here, to use science and the social sciences to improve the lives of all human beings. Vassar had begun a summer Institute of Euthenics in July 1926 that lasted until 1959 when it was discontinued for financial reasons.[83]

During the winter of 1929, while awaiting word from Vassar, Elsie and Ellen Steele were invited to visit Arthur and Jane Allen in Louisville, Kentucky. They were surprised at the "social eminence" and luxurious living of their Kentucky friends. Elsie described their home, a Georgian colonial in Glenview, about eight miles from Louisville. "One side of the house was a lawn shaded by tall trees, a tennis court and a swimming pool; and on the other a small red brick building which had been the children's playhouse and, further down the sloping hillside of walnut and beech trees, the garage and stable which housed the children's dogs and ponies." The Allens introduced Elsie to President McVeigh of the University of Kentucky and the luscious and beautiful bluegrass country, but Elsie seemed most impressed by the rural people. "Never before had I met people who expressed such love for their state, or who seemed to feel themselves an integral part of it."[84] Elsie and Ellen also spent some time with Maude Ainslie and Fay Barnum, who lived in the Louisville area and were part of the summer artist colony in Provincetown. Prior to Elsie's departure, Arthur Allen asked for advice regarding the school his children were attending in the Louisville area, the Roger Clark Ballard Memorial School. "The School," Arthur informed Elsie, "had run down over the years and they were troubled by it." Elsie replied that she could offer no advice until she had seen the school.[85] Accompanied by Jane Allen, Elsie visited the school. "It was a depressing place without life or interest," Elsie recalled, "a teacher in front of the class asking routine questions out of a textbook, while the children surreptitiously exchange notes, knives, etc... wherever we went, the children gathered around me as if they felt that here was someone alive, anyway the lunchroom was appalling—children pushing up to the counter with battered trays and exchanging greasy tickets for cups of their soup and desserts; while other children ate sandwiches and wedges of pie brought from home on one corner by themselves. No teacher was present, and while I was there several noisy food fights developed."[86] When the Allens asked Elsie about her observations, she responded that she had seen only one school worse than Ballard—on New York's Lower East Side.

The next day Elsie left for New York and Greenwich to begin the spring term. Approximately two weeks later, to Elsie's surprise, Jane and Arthur Allen arrived in New York. Seeking to improve the educational environment at Ballard, a committee had been formed in Louisville to find a new principal. Jane and Arthur Allen had come to New York to interview possible candidates. Elsie introduced the Allens to Dewey and William H. Kilpatrick. The interviews were held at Teachers College, and Elsie sat in on the interviews. She believed several of the candidates were very qualified and could serve to reform Ballard. Shortly before leaving for Louisville, Arthur, Jane, and Elsie had lunch when Arthur slipped Elsie a note asking, "Under what conditions, if any, would you take the school?" Surprised by the request Elsie responded, "None!" Elsie noticed the disappointment of her friends and suggested that she would think about it and tell them what she thought could be done to improve the school. "Thinking over what I had learned about the School from the interviews I had shared," Elsie mused, "and what I knew about the place and the people from my visit, I realized that here was a chance to develop in a rural countryside a real and functioning education in a public school, and I let myself dream of what a school could be in its community."[87]

Once again Elsie sought Dewey's advice. "I never dreamed you would be interested," Dewey responded to Elsie with surprise, "or I would have suggested you at once." Pondering the dilemma and looking out the window for a few moments, Dewey quietly said to Elsie. "I won't tell you to do this because I know it will be hard, but I will say that I always hoped that in my lifetime someone would do just that. We are going to need to know more about community schools in the country, and someone has to find out by doing it, just what a community school is and does."[88] Elsie knew this even before Dewey had responded to her, that here was a chance for progressive education to reach out into a rural public school, an opportunity to clearly link the school and community. Upon leaving Dewey, Elsie soon notified Arthur Allen what she thought Ballard needed to reform, adding ten thousand dollars to Ballard's budget for a start, plus financial and moral support from the school board.

With all this going on, Elsie was still deeply immersed in her work at Rosemary, trying to raise money for the Junior School. At the completion of a successful fund drive a dinner was held. Caroline Ruutz-Rees spoke at the dinner and said nothing about the work done by Elsie and her staff at the Junior School the last five years. Elsie was stunned and hurt. In retrospect she wrote, "Suddenly all the qualms I had felt about leaving vanished, for I saw clearly that the Junior School, whatever its achievements, was in point of fact regarded as an accessory, a feeder to the Upper School." Upon returning to Cos Cob that evening Elsie faced reality. "Realizing that my work at the Junior School was now over, and that I faced the task of trying to bring to pass my dream of a community school in a new and unfamiliar rural area, I sat there dismayed and disheartened. Following the fundraiser Elsie spent some brief time with Mrs. Ernest Hocking, the respected principal of the progressive Shady Hill School in Cambridge. During Mrs. Hocking's visit to Rosemary, Elsie bought up her concerns about leaving Rosemary and going to Kentucky. "Her advice was clear and definite," Elsie recalled, "your work here is done, go on to this new venture."[89]

Elsie knew there was some opposition in Louisville to reforming the Ballard School, "generally among certain well-to-do parents." Arthur and Jane Allen were not discouraged and believed the opposition could be kept under control. Elsie responded that she would gladly consult with any advisory group, including these people; however, all teacher appointments, the curriculum and educational procedures, and the running of the school were to be under her sole authority. Although some dissension was apparent, Elsie finally received the formal invitation offering her the position as principal of the Roger Clark Ballard Memorial School. Elsie postponed her final acceptance for two weeks to speak formally with President MacCracken of Vassar. MacCracken had received a wire from the Jefferson County Board of Education asking him to free Elsie and thus allow her to accept the position in Kentucky. MacCracken informed Elsie, that due to legal difficulties with the gift to Vassar plans for the progressive preparatory school had to be put on hold. Free to accept the position, Elsie sent in her letter of resignation to Rosemary. "I still remember," Elsie recalled, "the feeling and foreboding and despair that inexplicably seized me as I mailed my final acceptance in the post office on 125th Street on my way out of Greenwich. I was depressed by a premonition of the difficulties we would encounter, and it seemed to me that I had elected, for reasons that were not especially urgent, to bury myself in a far-away and unknown place."[90]

Upon receiving Elsie's resignation, Caroline Ruutz-Rees and Mary Lowndes asked Elsie who she might name as a successor. Without hesitation Elsie suggested Ellen Steele. Ellen was not as confident, but Elsie was certain Ellen would rise to the occasion. "Ellen knew her ground there, "Elsie noted, "and the desire of the Upper Heads, the parents and the children to have her as principal, was an incalculable advantage. She was the logical one to head the school she had helped to make, and the principalship was more of a professional advance for her."[91] Ellen Steele was an excellent choice for the position. She had articulated her ideas about teaching in a special issue of *Progressive Education* on "The Environment of Creative Education."[92] In the new position William Zorach, Ida Perry, and Florence House, Abbie Phillips, Roberta

Whitehead, and Elisabeth Sheffield supported Ellen in her role. The younger teachers of the Vassar group would form the nucleus of Elsie's Ballard staff.

Just as Elsie was readying herself for the move to Kentucky, the Allens informed her they were being attacked by the group opposed to reforming the Ballard School. The opposition contended Elsie had received the position due to her relationship to the Allens. "It was Jane, however, who foresaw the probable effect of this dissension on the parent group," Elsie noted, "and the problem it could create. However, we all agreed that there was nothing to do but go forward as planned." Returning to Kentucky during the spring of 1929 for another visit, Elsie went over the school thoroughly. "It was as before," she recalled, "a lifeless and slovenly place. I remember seeing an unwashed frying pan and a roll of toilet paper on the piano in the music room, and still recall my shock on entering the front door to see children waiting in line to go into the toilets and to be assailed by the acrid odor of urine."[93]

The teachers were anxious to meet Elsie, and she spoke to them about her plans for the school. The next day Elsie received a note they had all signed on to remain on staff under Elsie's leadership. Sensible of their plight, yet knowing full well that this would not be feasible, Elsie wrote, "I replied that I was bringing most of my staff with me. However, I realized that it would be desirable to have some Kentucky people on the staff, so I went in to see the Louisville Superintendent of Schools who was cordial and cooperative and introduced me to the Supervisor of Elementary Education." After visiting several classrooms, Elsie selected the Kentucky teachers to become part of her staff.[94]

The five years Elsie spent directing the Rosemary Junior School were valuable for her, progressive education, and the children of the school. Although in a difficult position of leadership and always under the auspices of the Upper School, Elsie believed she had professionally accomplished what she could. She and her handpicked staff had built a progressive school from the ground up, a school well known and respected in progressive education circles by 1929. She had based her methodology on the latest social/psychological research in early childhood education. Her curriculum was designed to be flexible and to free teachers to explore the interests and experiences of the children. The teachers under Elsie's watchful eye integrated subject matter and were clearly advanced in the use of the arts, which in many ways were the nucleus of the curriculum. The arts served as a tool for inquiry, reflection, creativity, imagination and expression although like most progressives of the era the teachers did not push to critical inquiry, challenging the dominant ideologies that led to class, racial, gender, and ethnic exploitation.

Now a confident and experienced educator, Elsie knew she needed and even desired a new challenge. That challenge, to build a community school in

CHAPTER NINE

a rural public school environment, moved her out of the elite private school or lab school dominance of progressive education. This challenge placed Elsie on the cutting edge: she knew it and her mentor, John Dewey, knew it. If progressive education was to become truly progressive, it had to move into the public schools which the majority of American children attended. She and her progressive colleagues had much to learn about education in a public school in rural Kentucky. But Elsie and her staff were not without support. Over the years she had become part of a network of professional women dedicated to promote progressive education. This network included Caroline Pratt, Harriet Johnson, Jessie Stanton, Marietta Johnson, Lucy Sprague Mitchell, Ellen Steele, and Agnes Hocking, to mention a few. Elsie had learned from all of these women and would need every ounce of experience to meet the challenges of reforming the Roger Clark Ballard Memorial School.

Chapter Ten

Ballard, Kentucky 1929–1934

Elsie's selection as principal at the Ballard School was not without controversy. At one point during the selection process, Arthur Allen, the chair of the committee, had been strongly instructed to send a note to Elsie stating that she was being considered among other candidates. Elsie responded, "I wired back at once that I was not, and never had been a candidate for the position. That, Arthur wrote me, had brought them to their senses. And I received a formal invitation to accept the principalship of the Ballard school."[1]

Elsie described her second trip to Kentucky where she relished the hospitality. "I had provided myself with some new clothes for the visit, among them a dress of lavender and red-violet which met with unexpected favor. As I sat by the tea table partaking of cakes and bonbons, passed by colored waiters in white cotton gloves, people were brought up to me—the men bowing and paying extravagant compliments."[2] Elsie enjoyed her special treatment but never voiced concern that people oppressed by Jim Crow were serving her. The children of the "colored waiters" could not legally attend the Ballard School. One introduction followed another, and Elsie soon attended a luncheon with the members of the County Board of Education. One Board member, a judge, said, "she sure knows her onions."[3]

With sadness and a sense of accomplishment, Elsie left the Rosemary Junior School and began new work in Kentucky. She knew she lacked experience in rural and public education, but she also desired to broaden and explore her conception of the community school. This desire was stimulated by her conversations with Dewey, and she received his support. "To me," Elsie noted, "the work at Ballard was still a challenging educational experiment which Dr. Dewey wished to have made, but I now realized that I would meet more difficulties than I had expected." Elsie believed and was correct that her appointment as principal had upset some of the wealthier parents who had influenced school policy. The group had attacked Jane and Arthur Allen. Elsie described the confrontation. "Arthur was deeply hurt that the efforts he and Jane had made to improve the school were interpreted by anyone as a desire to put in a friend of theirs as principal, and he bitterly resented the annoyance offered Jane and the resistance prepared against me. It was Jane, however, who foresaw the probable effect of this dissension in the parent group and the problems it could create. However, all agreed that now there was nothing to do but go forward as planned."[4]

In 1929, the American rural school was a challenging place to be. Historian Ellwood Cubberley had articulated his concerns about the rural school several years earlier. Cubberley wrote, "The county school lacks interest and ideas; it suffers from isolation and from lack of that enthusiasm which come only from numbers; and it realizes but a small percentage of its possible efficiency. Its site is usually unattractive; its building is too often a miserable, unsanitary box; it too often lacks the necessary equipment for proper instruction... its teacher is often poorly trained or entirely untrained, and is poorly paid." Cubberley considered the teacher in a rural school to be isolated culturally and professionally—how could they properly instruct children in the absence of libraries, museums, theaters, concerts, lectures, and reading circles?[5]

Elsie may have sympathized with Cubberley's literal description of the Ballard School and its facilities, but she refused to accept his assumption that good education was not possible in a rural environment. "To us, the School's location seemed ideal educationally," she noted. "Situated in the midst of farms and estates and surrounded by field and woods, it could use the teaching materials of its rural countryside and at the same time draw upon Louisville's industries, wholesale markets, shipping and freight depots, and its University, libraries, hospitals, and clinics." Surrounded by farms and estates, the teachers and students could see the Ohio River from the school grounds, teeming with barges and packet boats carrying supplies north and south to Louisville, about eight miles from Ballard. Initially built to house fifty to one hundred students, the school plant was less than adequate. "It has no science laboratory, no library, and no provision for teaching home economics," Elsie noted. "Cooking classes must be taught in a fenced-off corner of the Gymnasium without a sink, and shop work with large classes carried on in a small room. For physical examinations and dental work there is available only the principal's office which has no running water."[6]

Not deterred by the physical limitations of the facilities, Elsie and her staff began to study the area and history of Kentucky before beginning the school year.[7] The Ballard School, named officially the Roger Clark Ballard Memorial School, was twenty years old when Elsie and staff arrived. The school was built on donated land from Mr. and Mrs. Thurston Ballard and given to the Jefferson County Board of Education and named after the Ballard's late son. "The Ballards bore the major cost of erecting the buildings," Elsie wrote, "although the young parents and people in the community contributed, and the County Board of Education gave the proceeds from the sale of two one-room schools in the neighborhood." From its onset the Ballard community, rich and poor, had pooled together their resources and worked to sustain the school, "the mothers preparing lunches together, helping with physical examinations and with school suppers and entertainments, and the fathers contributed money for certain

CHAPTER TEN

school repairs and equipment and, occasionally also for additional teachers."[8] Elsie was fortunate to have this history of cooperation within the Ballard community although prior to her arrival it had deteriorated.

Just before the opening of the school year, Elsie and her handpicked staff visited many of the students' homes. From Elsie's observations, the families could be divided into two groups: "a large group including seventy-two families who had little or no economic security and ranged from poor to destitute, and a small group of perhaps twelve families who might be described as prosperous." The poor families tended to live in small cabins or shanties and made a living through farming small plots. Those somewhat better off worked as caretakers for large landholders in the area. Some were small merchants, truck drivers, clerks, gardeners, who often needed other jobs to supplement their incomes. Many homes did not have running water or inside toilets. Elsie described these people as "proud, gentle and self-respecting," just trying to get along. This group comprised approximately seventy-five percent of the school population. The other twenty-five percent was composed of professional and semi-professional families, some quite wealthy like Elsie's friends Arthur and Jane Allen.[9]

Elsie described the poorer children as "shy, bright, and tractable. Many of them learn well and easily; some of them, kept at home to help their fathers and mothers, do not get a chance to have much schooling." She described the children of the wealthier parents as "bright and gifted, most of them are indolent, and all of them are unaccustomed to work of any kind." She understood that the children of the elite had certain advantages in the traditional school. But in her understanding of the progressive community school, this type of "cultural capital" was no more valid than what the less fortunate children brought to school. She had great, even naive faith in what the community school could accomplish. She had been asked by the selection committee and the Jefferson County Board to make a good school, and that's what she was determined to do. "It was understood," Elsie wrote, "that we were to introduce modern methods of teaching, to foster the functions of the school in the community and, if possible extend them."[10]

There was much to be done in making Ballard a good school, a community school. Many of the children were one to three years below grade level. Literacy was a problem along with poor study habits. One of the poorer farm boys offered his opinion about book learning. "I don't learn that-a-way, I learns when I does things."[11] Elsie must have chuckled as she heard this for the young boy had articulated the progressive notion of learning by doing and had linked learning to his experience. As Elsie and her staff learned more about the children, they soon realized "these children had never made any connection between those things they knew and the facts school books contain. And our efforts that first year centered on helping them understand what they were learning in school through what they had experienced and on extending those experiences through class studies and activities."[12] Elsie and her staff constructed a curriculum based on the experiences and interests of the children. Neither the poor nor the elite children felt a kinship with school. For the school to be a successful community school, the community, the parents, the teachers, and the students needed to experience a sense of ownership, that the school was theirs.

School began early in September 1929, and even before the doors were open women and children were anxiously waiting outside. One hundred sixty-five children were enrolled, thirty more than expected. Elsie added a ninth grade to accommodate some of the older students. Already Ballard was a different school. Elsie and the staff had arrived two weeks early to prepare and clean the facility. She wrote, "With the consent of the county board we replaced the screwed-down-desks in the primary classroom with light, movable work tables and posture chairs; otherwise we accepted, and used the equipment we found. The job of cleaning the toilets, of obtaining school supplies and materials, and of making the schedule filled days with more activities than they could hold."[13] As principal, Elsie was also responsible for preparing a budget for the year. The ten thousand dollar request she had made prior to coming to Ballard was used to purchase the work tables and teaching materials. The five thousand dollars left went to supplement teacher salaries, cover running expenses, and pay for a school secretary. Jefferson County paid the rest of the teacher salaries, fuel, electricity, janitorial service, and school transportation via the trolley.[14]

Problems were evident from the start. The school library was poorly furnished and contained no reference books, a necessary resource for Elsie and her staff. Due to the small size of the cafeteria, Elsie created staggered lunch periods to avoid the chaos she had witnessed on her earlier visits. One of the mothers obtained a large used set of china along with utensils to help make the cafeteria more attractive, appetizing, and sociable. Elsie established a hot lunch program to meet the needs of many malnourished children even though it met resistance. "Resistance to this plan came," Elsie recalled, "surprisingly from the well-to-do parents who were, or we later discovered, accustomed to a light lunch and a hearty dinner at night for the whole family, including the youngest children."[15] Elsie overcame the resistance by explaining the importance of health to the entire school community, malnutrition being a serious issue for many of the children.

Elsie and staff spent the first few weeks trying to gain a sense of the students' ability levels and proficiency in learning skills. The children needed to have basic competencies in reading, writing, and math for Elsie and her staff to exploit the benefits of progressive pedagogy. But due to poor fundamentals,

CHAPTER TEN

Elsie and the teachers began work studying local Kentucky resources, her past and present. The need to strengthen the basics permeated the curriculum for several years. Poor morale and bad experiences at the school characterized the climate. The children felt no connection between their personal lives and the life of the school. Elsie believed and the children supported her belief that a study of the history, culture, geography and resources of Kentucky could overcome the poor morale. Although it took most of the first year, morale did improve as the children became engaged in exploring their interests. But it was not only the students who were learning. "Never before, I think," Elsie wrote, "had the teachers or I had to learn as much in as short a time. The most important, perhaps, of all the things we learned was to take as well as give, to listen as well as tell, to be willing and able to have things done as we never planned they should be, and finally, to get the point from each experience was to use it in the one that followed. If the story of the work is the story of our learnings, it is because they cannot be separated from our teachings."[16]

Elsie demanded a lot from her staff. The Ballard teachers were expected to be energetic, creative, inquisitive and excellent problem solvers. They were to live in and be part of the community, actively participating in community affairs. "From the outset the teachers all lived near the school and shared in the life of the neighborhood," Elsie noted. "The fact that our living as well as our teaching was done in the community needs perhaps to be stressed, for it was this fact that opened to us educational opportunities we would not otherwise have had."[17] The teachers were also learners, constantly setting examples for their students as they pursued knowledge. They were a handpicked, dedicated group of professionals, but due to limited funding and the county formula for teacher allotment, Elsie was not able to provide teachers for special subjects, so the elementary and high school teachers used their talents to cover these areas. Roberta Whitehead, Abbie Phillips, and Elisabeth Sheffield had followed Elsie from the Rosemary Junior School and were Vassar alumni. George Beecher and Carleton Saunders rounded out the high school staff. Louise Lawton, "one of the county's outstanding teachers of industrial arts," and Homer Howard, Ethel Carlisle, Mary Evans, Eleanor McArdle, and Mrs. A.B. Sawyer completed the Ballard staff that first year.[18]

Due to their inexperience in rural education, Elsie and her staff tentatively developed programs for the school. "We sought at every point," Elsie explained, "to engage in study of the environment and to make educational use of our surroundings. Our purpose in this was to gain with the children a basis for the understanding of their lives."[19] The educational engagement involved the entire community. Thirty-five extra children reported for enrollment for the first grade, and three-fourths of them were considered by Elsie to be underprivileged. Many of the children did not know how to stopper a sink or turn the water on and off. This group of first graders was shy and passive and remained so for the first semester. Even the children from the wealthier families seemed lost and confused. Abbie Phillips, the first grade teacher and a former teacher at Rosemary, was also surprised at the passivity of the children. Phillips, a trained musician and vocalist, began to sing and play for the children. At first they listened quietly, but eventually they began to participate, making up their own songs. This activity was followed with success through block play as the children constructed the farms, villages, and community around them. To meet the academic requirements of the county, the first graders began a study of farm life, connecting it to nutrition. The children grew corn, oats, barley, and wheat on a sand table in the class and made butter, cheese, custard, barley soup, and corn mush, a staple in the diet of many. The children also worked on phonetics and simple counting exercises, utilizing the resources they found on hand, such as seeds.

Ethel Carlisle taught the second graders, who studied village work and life. The second graders constructed and modeled their village on the nearby town of Prospect, Kentucky, where some lived.[20] The village, constructed largely of packing boxes, consisted of houses, a post office, a farmhouse, chicken house, and a bank, and to Elsie's delight the children also included a school. With observation and the help of the industrial arts teacher, Louise Lawton, the children constructed a bridge over a gully to the village. This may seem insignificant, but the children were required to use math concepts such as measurement to make the bridge. Feeling the need to put lighting in the houses, the students, under the advice of an electrician father, wired their village. Subject matter was not neglected in the building of the village. "The work in building the village," Ethel Carlisle reported, "required measuring—use of linear measure in cutting the doors and windows of the houses." The children also used math in selling groceries and transacting business at their bank. Elsie proudly noted, "This second grade, was an active, competent group and under the charge of a teacher, Ethel Carlisle, who was herself gifted along many lines and who knew how to enable children to carry on an organized activity."[21]

The third graders, under the tutelage of Mary Evans, studied native peoples who had lived in Kentucky. The children were interested in the everyday life of native people. Locating a nearby cave, the children created their own ancient campsite. The children studied survival techniques and with the help of shop teacher Louise Lawton, they learned how to make fire using different forms of tinder. "The third graders were more concerned in living out the experiences than in telling about them or recording them," Elsie noted, "but in one way or another they did a good deal of writing, describing the things they made in shop, and spinning many a yarn about their experiences as cave dwellers in trapping and hunting."[22] The children found traditional written

CHAPTER TEN 169

forms of expression unsuitable. Telling the story through narrative allowed them to express themselves and link their personal experiences. As a class the third grade was not as intuitive as the second grade in learning math concepts although they did gain some understanding of measurement in shop.

The fourth grade, under the guidance of Elisabeth Sheffield, studied pioneer life, a popular study in progressive schools, rural and urban. Elsie, Elisabeth Sheffield, and George Beecher wrote about their experiences with the fourth grade in an article, "Plays in a Kentucky County School," published in *Progressive Education*. They described the fourth grade's use of drama in their study of Kentucky life between 1775 and 1790. A local quarry near the school provided a place for the children to pretend to live, traverse, and survive in the wilderness. The children poured over pioneer journals from the time period, hoping to gain information about the trials and tribulations of pioneer life. To share their findings, the children wrote a play about the adventures of the Daniel Boone family. The theme of the play was the rescue of Daniel Boone's brother, Squire, who had left the safety of the fort to locate food during the winter. Squire is captured by the "Indians" and is rescued only through Daniel Boone's stealth and cunning. As typical of the time, the native people are depicted as violent savages bent on doing harm to the white man. There is no suggestion in the article that the native people were defending themselves from white encroachment and shooting the game they, too, needed to survive. The children did learn about aspects of pioneer life—how to prepare wool, card it, spin it and to make soap, dip candles, dye clothes, and tan hides. Unfortunately, their perspective was Eurocentric and gender biased. The girls tended to remain in the fort and were passive, usually weaving and cooking what the men brought home from the hunt. The men were the center of action. Fortunately, in the play the children did make some note of native suffering due to blinding snow and drifts. Apparently the children were also aware of the conflict over hunting and territory rights, but the report of the play does not reveal that this element was part of the overall drama.[23]

Elisabeth Sheffield spent a good deal of time practicing with the class members on addition, subtraction, multiplication, and division. Her room had a school store where pads and pencils were sold, and the children were required to keep track of their accounts. For English studies, the children kept notebooks/journals of their studies in wool and flax and the various field trips made. Elsie believed the fourth grade study helped both students and teachers grasp an understanding of Kentucky history and culture, allowing the children to connect their present with the past, giving them a sense of place.

The first year at Ballard was a learning experience for students and teachers and not totally free from behavioral problems. Behavioral problems included what Elsie termed "fussin," "tattle-tellin," "wraslin," and "roughhousing." Elsie believed as the children immersed themselves in the school routines, coupled with the teachers' "respect for justice" and patience, the behavior improved. By paying attention to the interests of the children, replacing busywork and rote learning with activity and inquiry, Elsie and staff further squelched behavior problems.[24] "The behavior of the fifth grade group," Elsie recounted, " would undoubtedly have presented a problem had the class been in the hands of a less skillful and experienced teacher."[25] Homer Howard taught the fifth grade class, mostly boys. Howard saw in this group "an inordinate desire for self-expression through the spoken word. It was pretty clearly indicated that the past history of the class was represented by unsuccessful attempts to repress both of these assets. My problem was to make use of them."[26] Howard discovered his students were interested in the diverse range of Kentucky's first European settlers. This led to a study of Western migration from Europe, one aspect being Nordic exploration of North America. The children improved their literacy and spelling and learned how to locate information. Maps, geography, and discussion of navigation were part of this curriculum. Under Carleton Saunders the children used fractions and decimals, drew graphs, and made scale drawings. This was the first year for these children in a progressive school, but they were adapting. Elsie believed they learned to trust their ability and that each of them had learned to try out new ideas and were not so afraid of failure.[27]

One of the more difficult classes the first year was the sixth grade, a class composed of primarily middle- and upper-middle class students. Elsie and her staff had planned a study of the settlements along the Mississippi Valley, including learning about the Spanish, French, and English. After observing the class, Elsie and the teachers realized this approach was "ludicrously inappropriate." The students, although many were privileged economically, were woefully lacking in study and research skills. Elsie described the majority of the class as "immature, indolent and ill-supplied with school learning." The teacher, Eleanor McArdle, wished to explore ancient Greece and Rome with the group, but this attempt proved disastrous. Morale disintegrated. Finally in the early spring the staff discovered the children had an interest in aviation, but they only carried their studies so far. Perhaps the strongest work of the class was in math because the students ran the school store. This included decimals, percentage, multiplication, and division. The students also explored ancient currency during their brief Greek and Roman studies. However, Elsie did not feel the experience was a successful one. "This experience with the sixth grade is worth recording because it illustrates the uselessness of program material which is irrelevant to children's interest and which demands for its appreciation a background of information they do not possess."[28]

CHAPTER TEN

The first year the Ballard School consisted of grades one through six, with seventh, eighth, and ninth grades being considered the high school. The high school teachers included Roberta Whitehead, Carleton Saunders, and George Beecher. Elsie believed that George Beecher carried the bulk of the load the first year. "When he joined the staff after graduate work at the University, he was, however, a competent linguist, a student of history, and a scientist. He had, besides an interest in art, musical ability, and skill with tools. What was still more important, he had a genuine farseeing interest in education, familiarity with farming and a liking for the kind of people and living found in Kentucky." It is clear why Elsie was so impressed by Beecher's skills because they shared many mutual interests.[29]

At first Elsie was not impressed by the children attending the high school, but they did have some admirable traits. "Although these boys and girls had no established habits of work and were accustomed to silly and noisy behavior at school," Elsie wrote, "they were, however, honest, responsive, and fundamentally gentle... we were not dealing with dull or intractable people. One and all were unusually quick witted, quite transparent and just naturally obliging."[30] The seventh grade class the first year consisted of thirteen students, with three students from disadvantaged homes. Beecher noticed early the class had a preference for handwork, or what might be now called hands-on work, over bookwork. "Reading aloud and note-taking was a painful process," Beecher, also the English teacher, explained. "The class did display an interest in the arts, largely painting and pottery." This interest fit with their study of Native American life in the Southeast and Southwest. In the far end of the quarry, the children constructed "a wattle hut, making the framework of bent saplings covered with brush and weaving mats of rushes to cover the top."[31] This class also constructed a Pueblo village and wrote a short play about Pueblo life. Beecher, the English teacher, used the play to enhance the writing and composition skills of the students, which were woefully lacking. While the children's interests had been captured, Beecher realized they still lacked fundamental work in spelling, handwriting, reading, grammar, and expression of their thoughts through writing. Elsie attributed the success of the class to Beecher's skills, particularly his temerity and ability "to treat the study of Indian civilization with this class from an intellectual as well as a creative and practical standpoint."[32]

Elsie described the eighth grade class, composed of twenty-four students, as teeming with interest, restless energy, wit, and humor. The class continued the study of Kentucky history, a central theme of the school curriculum the first year. This included pioneer life, mineral resources, and the industrial growth of Kentucky. Predating the Foxfire project of the early 1970s, the children published their own newspaper, the *Kentucky News*, telling about their studies.

The paper later served as a school paper that reported the activities of each class. The eighth grade class studied the decade between 1830 and 1840, paying close attention to the Ohio Valley. "The emphasis of the study was on the Jacksonian era," Beecher wrote, "which saw the rise of western democracy, the growth of rail and river boat communication, and the opening of the Mississippi Valley."[33] Through the help of shop teacher, Louise Lawton, the children also built models out of wood. These models consisted of a flatboat, a Conestoga wagon, and early trains. In his year-end report, Beecher wrote about his experience with the eighth grade class. "The history program was progressive in its attempt to suit subject matter to the temperaments and interests of the children and to use the local environment for making connections with historical material."[34] Beecher achieved this goal, but he did not explore the full extent of the Jacksonian era. From 1830 to 1850, native American power and property was broken and lost. In light of the school's interest in Native American studies, the children could have explored the forced migration of native peoples to "Indian territory" under the command of General Jackson, but these types of questions were rarely probed by Elsie or her staff nor by progressive educators as a whole. There were limits to progressivism.[35]

The ninth grade class was the smallest in the school, consisting of only nine students who were mostly middle and upper-middle class. The small number of students may have been due to the loss of the working-class farm children, who left school to help on family farms or go to work. While this attrition changed over the years, it did have an effect the first year. Due to state requirements in subject matter, Elsie and the staff wished to remain more traditional, giving the high school students adequate background in math, English, and Latin, preparing them for the tenth grade at more traditional schools. However, the children wished to explore the history of Greece and Rome. As part of their studies the children made a model of the Parthenon, learning about materials for construction but also proportion, and symmetry. To Elsie's delight, they also began to notice Greek and Roman architectural influences in Louisville. George Beecher sought to improve the students' understanding of Latin, and during the spring with his assistance, the students wrote a play titled *Horace and His Sabine Villa*. The play served as a drilling ground for the use of Latin but also was linked to Kentucky life and culture. Beecher wrote a short description of the play for the journal *Progressive Education*. "The rural side of Kentucky life offered in some ways a relation to the studies of Roman life," he wrote, "the final scene, the rural spring festival on the Sabine farm, was not a great leap for minds familiar with the rural setting of Kentucky."[36] Elsie and Beecher believed the use of the play by the children satisfied a desire and fulfilled a need. It served as a means for the children to make sense of their own environment, linking the past to the present.

CHAPTER TEN 173

At the end of the first year, Elsie and her staff thought they had succeeded in remotely connecting the school to the community. The first year stressed an understanding of local history, culture, geography, and other resources, and while these were valuable, Elsie believed they could have done better in integrating subject matter. The teachers needed to be more creative and imaginative in using subject matter and linking it to the interests of the children. "We did not that first year do more, really," Elsie wrote, "than glimpse the possibilities in the instrumental use of mathematics in the children's lives and education."[37] To remedy this, Elsie and the staff made a review of the history of math in their staff studies. She also shared some of the work done at the Rosemary Junior School with the newer faculty.

English studies also needed to be improved. Upon arrival in Kentucky, the teachers, the majority not from Kentucky, "seemed obsessed by the need and desirability of correcting speech and writing." With Elsie's expertise and George Beecher's understanding of linguistics, the staff was instructed "of the nature and structure of language, and of its growth and changes."[38] Teachers began to view the language the children used as more of a form of expression than a mechanism of proper grammar and social prestige. The Kentucky children enjoyed expressing themselves through play, story, art, painting, and music and tended to dislike writing and traditional composition. This observation led the teachers to integrate interest with subject matter in the following years. Elsie and her teaching staff had learned from their own experiences that first year, but the second year provided more daunting challenges.

During the summer of 1930, Elsie participated in the second Progressive Education Summer Institute at Vassar College. The conference leaders were Burton Fowler, president of the Progressive Education Association and headmaster of the Tower School in Wilmington, Delaware; Perry Dunlap Smith, headmaster of the North Shore County Day School of Winnetka, Illinois; and Katherine Taylor, director of the Shady Hill School in Cambridge, Massachusetts. By her inclusion in this group, it was evident that Elsie was now considered a clear leader in rural and community education among her progressive education colleagues. She was the only public educator among the four, again emphasizing the problem progressive education had in moving into the public arena. Each session of the institute lasted approximately three weeks and was devoted to discussing methods, material, and administration of the elementary school.[39]

During her second week session at the institute, Elsie discussed her work and experience at Ballard and Rosemary. Although her discussion is only available in outline form, we can still gain a sense of what she thought important to address. Elsie began by giving background on Ballard, its history, organization, and curriculum. She followed this by focusing on the curriculum for grades one through four. Elsie addressed subject matter as experimental in nature and the way it played out in a community school, a connection she was still forming. She exhibited some artwork from Rosemary and Ballard and emphasized the significant role art and drama could play in a progressive community school.[40]

In many ways progressive education as a movement, as loosely as it may have been constructed, was entering its heyday. By May 1930, *Progressive Education* was published eight times a year rather than quarterly. In his retiring address, President Stanwood Cobb of the Chevy Chase Country Day School briefly articulated his conception of the progress of progressive education. "In our own country educational progress has been rapid and continuous. Many new private schools have been founded along progressive lines, and many existing private schools have been growing more progressive in tendency. Splendid as are these gains, even more significant is the tremendous progress which the public school system of the country is making, especially in its elementary levels."[41] Cobb's optimistic and perhaps unrealistic view of the progress progressive education had made in the public school is notable. The "movement" was still dominated by elite private schools, and Elsie knew she was exploring uncharted territory. She was charting new ground in a different kind of environment with a different type of student. She was right on the cutting edge of this interest expressed by Cobb, expanding progressive education into rural public schools.

Elsie considered the second year at Ballard a continuation of growth and learning for herself, the staff, and the students. They had learned much about Kentucky, its history and culture, its rural nature, and what they could do to truly make Ballard a community school. A community school met academic needs, but perhaps more important it reached out into the community to bond learning with living. "We redoubled our efforts to make what they studied at school comprehensible and serviceable to them," Elsie explained, "introducing into their studies and activities information that would fructify their understanding." When the 1930–1931 year began, Elsie and staff sought to "expand and deepen the children's understanding of the environment in which they lived." For the high school children, a major goal was to "use and develop their ability and capacities by extending their acquaintances with other lands and peoples and bridging them in contact with their ideas and experiences, also to expand their own social and cultural resources."[42]

Connecting learning with living, Elsie thought that one of the most significant achievements of the second year was the focus on health and nutrition. Many of the children were malnourished and lacked adequate access to health care. Elsie and her staff sought to remedy this as best they could. They began by working closely with the mothers in charge of the school lunch program. Through home visits, Elsie and her staff had some understanding of the poverty in the community, now growing because of the effects of the Depression. This group of mothers took over the lunch program, bought the food, prepared it, and served it to the children. Teachers and a few wealthier parents helped subsidize the lunches for the more undernourished and poor children. By allowing these women to run the lunch program, Elsie believed she had learned to "take as well as give, learn as well as teach...Working with and through people meant, as we should have known, starting where they were, using what they knew and sharing work and responsibilities with them."[43] Elsie and the staff had been in charge of the lunch program during the first year but had made some mistakes in selecting foods for Kentucky palates and overpricing the meals. The mothers felt left out. By making them part of the program and eliminating some of her own administrative duties, Elsie believed the lunch program improved the second year. The children were receiving nutritious meals at least once a day, and the mothers more easily identified with the school community.

Upon medical examination in the second year, over half the children were suffering from some form of malnutrition. Examinations took place in October 1930 and were more than revealing. The school had requested each family meet with their family doctor for an examination. "Out of 208 children in school," Elsie reported, "140 were unable to have this done by a family doctor." Most of the families had no family doctor and could not afford to make this visit. With the help of the Parent Teachers Association and a local physician, the school office was turned into an examining room. Through these exams, Elsie and the staff realized the social welfare issues of their community were serious. They believed there was no separation between the child's health and learning and growth. The school did what it could to meet the needs of the children, but at the time this was a foreboding task. Elsie wrote, "All through the year the School did whatever it could to alleviate the poverty and distress of many of the School's families, which had been accentuated by the summer drought and by a bond failure that, curtailing the income sources of the well-to-do group, cut off the odd jobs by which many of the disadvantaged families supplemented what they could earn."[44] The Depression brought dire suffering to many of the families in the Ballard School, and there was no safety net other than local charity to catch them. "The more prosperous farm families, as well as the wealthier parents," Elsie wrote, "shared what they had with those in need, and between us we managed to take them over the worst stretches." Elsie herself secured grocery credits for the most needy families and got some help from a farm relief fund administered by a Jefferson County judge. By the end of the year, she believed Ballard had "become a closely knit school and community."[45]

Meeting the social welfare needs of the children was fundamental to living and learning. During the first year, Elsie had realized that subject matter had become secondary to getting the children interested in school. Staff studies during the second year addressed this need to nurture interest and to more fully utilize math and language studies throughout the curriculum. This meant that Elsie and staff needed to relate math and language to real life. In terms of language, the teachers had discovered the Ballard children enjoyed expressing themselves, largely through art, drama, and music. They enjoyed sharing their experiences with other classes and parents. They excelled in story telling but did not enjoy writing stories down—perhaps due to literacy problems. The desire to express themselves was natural, and Elsie and staff sought to build upon this starting point to improve literacy and basic composition. For example, high school teacher George Beecher, in his year-end report of 1930–1931, wrote of his work with the eighth graders. "At the beginning of the year, the class' written expression was quite scant and colorless. Oral composition however flourished on several occasions during the fall." Beecher used this knowledge to his advantage. "Late in the Year," he observed, "we experimented with creating stories orally before writing them down. An outline of the ideas as they were told was taken down and the written composition based on this outline."[46] The work of the eighth grade that year included a reading of most of Homer's *Odyssey*, Melville's *Typee*, and Morley's *Where the Blue Begins*. Elsie knew that Beecher "was able to foster and develop the language confidence of the eight graders, who lacked and needed words to use to express their learning and their ideas, impression and imaginings."[47] This class also used artwork to express their understanding in the history and migration of various peoples to America. This study was directed by Helen Post, the new high school member of the staff. Fay Barnum, Elsie's friend who lived in the Louisville area, taught art. Some work was also done in pottery, and the students visited the Louisville Pottery Company. This use of art allowed the children to express an understanding of subject matter they could not express through the written word—perhaps Elsie and her staff understood a picture is worth a thousand words.

Another class that improved their language skills was the second grade under the guidance of Ethel Carlisle. The previous year this group of students had come to Ballard lacking confidence and was very passive and shy. As soon as they arrived for the second year they actively began to construct their own village just as they had observed the second grade class the year before doing. Along with creating the village by using packing boxes, the children began to study irrigation. Due to a summer drought, many of the farm families were unable to grow sufficient crops for the winter, extremely important during these Depression times. The children studied the transportation of foodstuffs by rail, and they traveled to the railroad yard where they observed loading and unloading of material. A field trip to one of the river docks provided further information. The children kept journals, detailing what they had seen, writing down what they experienced. Elisabeth Sheffield wrote, "The language the second graders used in these reports has, it is evident, been expanded by their experiences. They have tried, one can see, to say in words exactly what they saw, and their description is both clear and vivid." At the end of the year Carlisle reported that "the children get a great amount of satisfaction from being able to write well; they love to write down their ideas and feel perfectly free in expressing them."[48] Carlisle was surprised to see the group quickly grasp and use numbers. She believed this was due to their participation in the village construction, where they had to use addition and subtraction in measuring. Like their predecessors, they were interested in lighting their village and discovered a resource book by Katherine Keelor, a teacher at the Lincoln School at Teachers College. Keelor discussed how she had used electricity in her class. By reading the book the second graders at Ballard were able to devise a battery to light their home. They did this with the assistance of Carleton Saunders, who taught math and shop. Ethel Carlisle had succeeded in capturing the interest of her students, which motivated them to utilize subject matter as a part of their effort to construct the village.[49]

Carleton Saunders used the eighth graders' interest in athletics to teach them math concepts. With the help of Louise Lawton, the students constructed a plane table as they prepared to survey the property site to build an athletic field. "The work," Saunders reported, "included practically the mathematical principles we were studying—number relationships, balance, whole and part relations and of course, geometry." In the spring the students used their skills to lay out the school gardens. Students throughout the Ballard School benefited from the school's math museum, where the students could see examples of earlier currency, such as fur, coal, grain, beads, tobacco, and Confederate currency. The museum also included scales and other types of measurement. Elsie and Saunders believed the museum allowed the students to show how math was used in the everyday aspects of human life, making it relevant to the students.[50]

By the end of the second year, Elsie described what she thought was a progressive school. "We have in progressive schools been finding out how to engage children in enterprises that will further their growth. We have arranged to have them learn activity in doing and making and in reliving the experiences of the people they are studying. We have chosen for them activities that would further their understanding of the world around them. This learning about actual events or processes, about life and living, has I think been all to the good. The children have grown in it and through it, and their experiences have been enriched by it."[51]

Shortly following the beginning of the third year at Ballard (1931–1932), Elsie proposed to the teachers that together they attempt to formulate a conception of a community school. Basically she asked her faculty to describe "the kind of school Ballard was, and the education that went on there." The teachers expressed that Ballard provided an excellent opportunity for education due to its location and cultural resources. Ballard, they asserted was a socially functioning school, a descriptive term Elsie would frequently use. "The social functioning of the school," the teachers pointed out, "occurred in the children's relations with each other at school and in the relation between the teachers and children. It occurred also, they said, in the teachers' relations with the families, and in the parents' relations with the school and its work."[52] To continue to meet the school's social and educational activities and in need of financial support, Elsie along with some members of the staff wrote a grant at the invitation of a foundation.[53]

Writing the grant request proved to be a good exercise for Elsie, the teachers, and the parents because it allowed them to articulate the social and educational aspects of a community school. It allowed them to state a sense of their mission and their vision. Following a brief history of the school and the accomplishments thus far, Elsie suggested several necessary changes that receipt of the grant could provide: 1) a science laboratory for more sophisticated work in physics, chemistry, geology, botany, and biology; 2) a shop equipped with the machinery to teach carpentry, plumbing, electricity, printing, and metalwork; 3) a library for use by the community to house Ballard's growing collection; 4) an art and music room for chorus and orchestra but also for painting, pottery, block printing, and exhibitions; and 5) a business room to house the math museum, bank, and school store. Going beyond the physical plant of the school but still linking the school and community Elsie also requested 1) a health care center for medical exams and dental work; 2) a model kitchen for home economics and canning; 3) an open-air pavilion for class rest periods and for play on rainy days; 4) a cooperative market for school families to sell produce and 5) a child care center. Elsie's most unusual requests were the child care center and the cooperative market. The child care center could serve as a place where mothers could leave their babies and small children when they came to school, and where the older girls could receive instruction in their care and feeding. This center would be used as a psychological laboratory for examination of, and remedial work with children of special needs.[54] Elsie requested $20,000 from the foundation to begin expanding her notion of the community school. Unfortunately, the grant was not funded because the grant officials believed Elsie was already doing what she was requesting. This was only partially correct.

CHAPTER TEN

Ballard clearly lacked adequate facilities to house a growing school population during the Depression era, and the failure to receive the grant hurt the working-class children who needed exposure to certain subject matter areas and remediation if they were to continue their education. By the late high school years, the children of the wealthier parents were typically in private schools or in the high schools in Louisville. There was still much to be done in meeting the health and child care needs of the school and community. Elsie showed a great deal of insight in making these requests, many which are now characteristics of the contemporary public school. A few years later, Elsie would be asked to tell to the federal planners of the Arthurdale homestead community what was needed to make a community school. She reiterated the requests she made at Ballard and in essence received all of them. While she was attempting in the grant to clarify Ballard's needs, she, in reality, was exploring what she believed was the very nature of the community school. Part of the duties of a community school was to address health and dental care. The Ballard children received exams at least once a year. Elsie sought to teach the children that rest, exercise, good posture, and eating your vegetables made you a healthier and better student. Harry Carlson taught shop and the eighth grade, Lucille Clark, a Kentucky teacher, taught the fifth grade. They were assisted by three student teachers from the University of Louisville.

In most cases, students chose to participate in the same work as their predecessors. For example the new second graders still built a village, and the fourth graders continued to study pioneer life. It is apparent that Elsie and her staff noted what activities worked with the children, and there seemed to be at least some guidance from the teachers to continue the activities of the previous class. It is within that context that the interests of the children were being addressed. The first grade continued with block play and made several field trips. The second grade constructed their own village in the quarry and developed a rudimentary form of a town council. The third grade participated in weaving and studying native life and living conditions. The fourth grade continued with the study of pioneer life; the fifth grade studied New England colonial life, and the sixth grade studied early American history and government. The seventh grade studied the opening of the Mississippi River and making a pathway west to the Pacific Ocean. An interesting facet of this study, under the direction of Homer Howard, was that the class actually "studied the government's attempt to remove the Indians from the path of the whites, the disregard of the Permanent Indian Frontier by the incoming settlers, and the constant trouble with the Indians because of these encroachments on their land."[55] Homer Howard's class was on the verge of some real critical/reflective thinking. Howard wrote about his experiences in "Mapping Out a Small School Activities Program," in *The Nation's Schools* in 1931. "In the active life of the progressive school we use the spirit of adventure, the desire to explore, that is part of the make-up of every child. But an adventure into the far-away in either time or place is understood fully only in the light of the here-and-now and takes on meaning only in terms of the child's experience." He continued to explain how the curriculum worked at Ballard. "We try to have them form good habits of first-hand research into the known in their environment, to make use of what they find in discovering concrete relationships." The classroom was to be an active environment and not driven by subject matter outside of the experiences of the children. Subject matter should be alive and not remote information from texts. Unfortunately Howard did not discuss how far the students went in their discussions on the conflict between whites and the Native Americans, and such exploration could only have enhanced a study of pioneer life. Elsie also does not describe the nature of the discussion, but at least students were investigating and probing the issue. The students seemed to grasp that the native people were simply trying to protect their way of life. This stimulated the students to explore the geography of the white migration and further explore Native American life at the time.[56]

The eighth grade constructed a log cabin, an activity they had started the previous year. Harry Carlson, the new shop teacher, assisted the students, and the cabin soon became a home for study in pioneer life. This study involved the entire school. Under the guidance of Helen Post, the ninth grade made a study of textiles and manufacturing. They wrote a play and studied the invention of the cotton gin by Eli Whitney, which helped stimulate textile manufacturing in the North and slavery in the South. There is no indication that any connection was made between slavery and the growth of American industry. The new tenth grade had studied the Renaissance to the Industrial Revolution. The previous year they had investigated the Middle Ages with George Beecher. The ninth and tenth grades sometimes met together due to the shortage of teachers. They worked on more advanced science and geometry and also made a study of industrial geography, material resources for industrial production and agricultural issues. The older girls were given classes in physiology and hygiene, and boys were taught glass cutting and the general use of tools in shop. There was a clear gender differentiation here, as the girls were sent to learn about sexuality and becoming good mothers while the boys were in shop class. The gender bias at Ballard seemed to be tightly drawn as the children reached high school age. This is interesting in light of the fact that Elsie and other women in progressive education, some on her staff, saw themselves as professionals, and they understood that marriage usually meant giving up their careers.[57]

Although she had marched in suffragist parades, Elsie was not a revolutionary radical and had developed her own version of feminism. Some insight into this issue can be seen through Elsie's reaction to George Count's speech at the Annual Meeting of the Progressive Education Association held April 17–20, 1932, in Baltimore, Maryland. Ann Shumaker, co-editor of *The Child Centered School* and editor of the journal *Progressive Education*, had suggested Counts as a potential speaker at the convention. Counts chastised the PEA in his speech and challenged them to move from their idealistic child-centered approach and truly become a force for social change. For Counts this meant more of a social democratic stance that clearly challenged capitalism and led to some form of socialized economy.[58] The April 1932 issue of *Progressive Education* contained an article voicing Counts' concerns titled, "Dare Progressive Education Be Progressive?" In the article Counts declared the great weakness of progressive education was that it "elaborated no theory of social welfare, unless it be anarchy or extreme individualism."[59] This article was followed shortly by Counts' publication of the pamphlet, *Dare the School Build a New Social Order?* In this pamphlet, Counts "introduced his highly controversial doctrine of imposition and indoctrination."[60] Counts wrote, "If Progressive Education is to be genuinely progressive, it must emancipate itself from the influence of this class, face squarely and courageously every social issue, come to grips with life in all of its stark reality, establish an organic relation with the community, develop a realistic and comprehensive theory of welfare, fashion a compelling and challenging vision of human destiny, and become less frightened than it is today at the bogies of imposition and indoctrination. In a word, progressive education cannot place its trust in a child-centered school."[61] The article clearly was an attack on the child-centered progressives, and they responded in kind.

Although Elsie did not consider herself among the child-centered progressives or the social reconstructionists, she responded to Counts in an essay, "Learning and Indoctrinating." What disturbed Elsie was Counts' call for indoctrination. She appreciated his challenge to the Progressive Education Association, pushing them to recognize "their responsibility as educators for social change and betterment."[62] Elsie believed through her work at the community school at Ballard, by attacking health and poverty concerns, that she had addressed a serious social issue and helped build an "organic" relation with the community. She saw Ballard as a community where the rich and poor had come together for the betterment of the children. Professionally she believed she had taken a rural public school and helped it become progressive, moving it out of the dominant strain of middle-class private schools and the child centeredness Counts so vehemently criticized. However, she could not accept the indoctrination of children. In her response to Counts, Elsie suggested that education itself was revolutionary "in the process of living and learning and doing."[63] While conscious and unconscious indoctrination was taking place in the education process, indoctrination was opposed to the very nature of the "child's own learning and experiencing." Both Counts and Elsie viewed the school as a tool for social reform, but Elsie preferred to approach reform gradually, with each child, each class, and each school that reaches into the community. "Perhaps Professor Counts' challenge may persuade us to accept our responsibility as educators to participate in changing the social conditions we live in," Elsie wrote. "I know of no more potent way to condition the child and make him a social person, now, in his childhood."[64] To Elsie, social change began one step at a time, essentially with the individual child. She did not view herself in the camp of the child-centered progressives, whom, she believed, like Counts, did ignore the social aspects of education. Elsie's notion of the community school places her in neither group. She was attuned to the social welfare issues of the time—poverty, malnutrition, disease, and social inequity. However, she was not a radical calling for the demise of capitalism and a socialized economy. During the Depression, even with her experience in social welfare and labor concerns, Elsie does not engage or ever articulate a political ideology.[65] With all her heart and soul she believed the community school was the key to making the progressive education truly progressive, not Counts' call for social reconstructionism and a new social order. This should be no surprise. Elsie had always centered her social welfare concerns in the interests of the child such as her personal investigation into "white slavery" in New York and her participation in the Paterson Strike. It was not the system that fostered white slavery that Elsie was concerned with but the needs of each individual. It is the individual and social needs of the child that drove Elsie's pedagogy.

In April 1932, Elsie participated in a special weekend meeting at Vassar College to discuss education and the possibilities for social reconstruction. Elsie's friend William Heard Kilpatrick chaired the discussion. Leaders of the PEA attended the meeting.[66] John Dewey, Harold Rugg, and John Childs were not present. Other PEA notables included Wilfred Aiken, Rachel Ervin, Frederick Redefer, Gertrude Hartman, Lois Meek, Jesse Newlon, Morris Mitchell, and Ann Shumaker. Agreeing with Counts, the various groups came to the conclusion that the progressive school must broaden its focus beyond being child-centered and "develop an adequate social perspective."[67] The group described progressive education students as critical and poised but self-centered and indecisive. There is almost a sense of fatalism among this notable group of educators because most progressive students were from homogeneous environments and were not exposed to diversity or conflicting points of view. Although the specifics of the individual perspectives are not available, the failure to engage differing points of view threatened the very nature of democracy and the need for critical-reflective inquiry so strongly argued by Dewey on numerous occasions.

We have no record of Elsie's thoughts about the meeting as she returned to Ballard to close out her third year. It does seem clear that her practices at Ballard were not altered by the events taking place in progressive education at the national level. She reports that at the end of the third year progress was made in science instruction in the second, sixth, ninth, and tenth grades; work in home economics had been expanded for the girls and the boys were being schooled in home and school repairs. Elsie described the students as "eager and enterprising," rapidly learning, self-reliant, and competent.[68] She shared her experiences by teaching extension courses at the University of Louisville. Through this opportunity she was able to share with public school teachers in the Louisville area what was happening at the Ballard School.[69]

Elsie summarized her three years of work at Ballard in an article "Social Education in a Public Rural School," in the journal *Childhood Education*.[70] Besides giving a brief description of Ballard and its history, she also discussed her concept of a socially functioning community school. Elsie addressed the importance of history and social studies and how they served as a case to integrate English, math, science, art, music, and industrial arts. She also expressed her view of the school as a social center—paying attention to the health needs and recreational aspects of the school and in the community that included preparing healthy lunches, cooking and sewing, gardening, home visits, and medical and dental examinations. Perhaps most important, Elsie described the reason behind her work. "We are attempting to establish a model rural school which will demonstrate to rural schools and to rural school educators the social-education possible to and demanded of country schools."[71] As Elsie and her staff closed out the third year, she believed Ballard had provided a good example for others to follow, not a blueprint, but an illustration of how a rural school can fully utilize its surrounding resources. This success was based on cooperation of the teachers, parents, students, and community at large. Elsie described education as growth, and growth for her took place in gradual steps, not through radical political movements or social reconstruction.

At the beginning of her fourth year at Ballard, the effects of the Depression were clearly evident in Kentucky. "This year a series of bank failures and the business depression," Elsie noted, "which depleted the resources of the wealthy and well-to-do parents and curtailed business and family operations, affected all the school families in the low-income group, especially those who lived always close to the safety margin."[72] The school facilities were crowded, with no adequate lab for science instruction, and many of the poorer children could no longer pay for the hot lunches. These children were helped by a special fund from Mrs. Thurston Ballard, by school funds, and from county relief funds.⁷³ Due to school's failure to receive a grant and salary reductions due to the Depression, teacher morale was suffering. Only the progress and enthusiasm of the students and the strong support of the parents sustained the teachers.

Due to the lack of funds for activities and curriculum, the teachers had no choice but to fully utilize the resources around them. Ethel Carlisle guided the third graders in their study of Native American life. Elisabeth Sheffield taught the seventh graders as they investigated the expansion and settlement of Western territory. Due to the significance of the local bank failures on the community, Carleton Saunders helped the students establish a school savings bank, as students learned how a bank actually worked. The eighth grade under Harry Carlson studied the history of Great Britain. Integrated in this study was language and math. George Beecher worked with the students in understanding Old English and linguistics, and Carleton Saunders introduced the concept of taxes, wages and prices, war debt, and inflation to the students. Ballard now supported an eleventh grade that had only two students but stretched the teaching staff. Elsie believed the expansion was evidence that the working class and farm families were now valuing education. ⁷⁴

In March 1933 she published in *Progressive Education* her most extensive discussion of her work at Ballard. Elsie saw the rural school as unique, "a neighborhood linked by intimate relationships and informal friendly intercourse. A rural school shares those interests and enters into them."⁷⁵ She described how Ballard had achieved "their community school" by meeting both academic needs and social needs. Elsie was clearly proud of the school's assistance in meeting the medical, dental, and recreational needs of the community. Although her conclusion is debatable, Elsie believed her school had brought rich and poor together, an impossible task for most progressive schools, which catered only to the upper-middle classes. Elsie conceptualized the community school in the following statement: "A community school foregoes its separateness. It is influential because it belongs to its people. They share its ideas and ideals in its work. It takes from them as it gives to them. There are no bounds so far as I can see to what it could accomplish in social reconstruction if it had enough wisdom and insight and devotion and energy."⁷⁶ Elsie saw the community school as a social change agent. It could bring people together in a true sense of shared interests where people contribute to the common good. The teachers played a crucial role in the community school, and Elsie addressed this issue in "The Teacher in Social Education," also published in *Progressive Education* later that spring. A community school had to be firmly grounded in a cooperative effort by parents, teachers, health officials, school administrators, and other resources. Elsie described the teachers as sharers in "the wider world of the school" and as participants in the community itself. "The teachers

CHAPTER TEN

are residents, neighbors," she wrote, "their comings and goings are part of the happenings."[77] Elsie's teachers were dedicated individuals and students themselves as they learned about the history and the culture of the area. A community school must have socially conscious "tough-minded" teachers willing to accept the enormous responsibility of teaching in a progressive community school. "There is no ease, little leisure, much work, great happiness," Elsie explained, "no aloofness, take and give; learning and living, expanding work," and answering growing needs.[78] It took a talented, dedicated, resourceful, and versatile teacher to be part of Elsie Ripley Clapp's staff. It must have been difficult for these teachers to find a private space when they were "on call" virtually twenty-four hours a day. Elsie respected her teachers and applauded their work and dedication. They were a unique group of professionals.

In recalling her final year at Ballard, Elsie recognized her staff. The teachers over the last four years had helped make "indolent and unaroused children… competent and self-reliant."[79] The students, under the guidance of their teachers, now took the initiative and assumed the responsibility for much of their own education. A prime example of this for Elsie in her last year was the location of a second-hand printing press by Harry Carlson. After cleaning and resetting the type, the high school students put the press into action, publishing a newsletter, *The Ballard News*, and also a community magazine. The newsletter reported on school news and individual classes. Both the newsletter and the magazine were to reach into the community with information about the school. They were made available to the public and placed in local stores for a minimal price. Ironically *The Ballard News* reported on Elsie's invitation from the Subsistence Homestead Division, Department of the Interior to meet with Eleanor Roosevelt about the plan for a community school in a new type of community. "They asked her to go into West Virginia, to Morgantown," the paper reported, "to study conditions there and advise them about the right kind of school… the miners and the Government want a community school like our school, and called in Miss Clapp for advice."[80] While in West Virginia Elsie had wired Carleton Saunders to go and measure several of the rooms at Ballard so she could plan the new homestead school. Saunders enlisted the help of the students who soon realized their own facility could see some sprucing up and repair. The students painted, mended plaster, did small carpentry work, and cleaned up the school grounds. The newspaper served as a communication device for linking the school and the community. The students also learned grammar, and literacy skills in its production.

As Elsie recounted the last year, she emphasized how the children had gained ownership over their education. They were now active in school and community affairs, and they had learned how to learn. Now that they had become acquainted with the "resources that were theirs and understood them, they were ready and eager to use them and go forward. They can, they know, do it."[81] Elsie's trip to West Virginia to advise the federal authorities, including Eleanor Roosevelt, would change the Ballard School. Impressed by Elsie's expertise in rural education and with strong recommendations, Eleanor Roosevelt offered Elsie the position of principal of the school and director of community affairs for the new homestead community in West Virginia. To a degree, Elsie believed her work at the Ballard school was complete, finished, "but in another way it had just begun."[82] A new challenge was before her, to create from the ground up, the actual community school she had recommended. Elsie accepted the position in West Virginia with the stipulation that she could bring most of her experienced staff with her. The new principal of Ballard wanted to bring in his own staff, so Elsie could, in effect, take most of her staff. "So Elisabeth Sheffield, Ethel Carlisle, Kathryn Ash, and Eunice Jones who had been with us during the past year," Elsie noted, "George Beecher, Carleton Saunders, Harry Carlton, Alice Bowie and I slowly accustomed ourselves to the idea that we would no longer be working in Kentucky but must now use what we had learned there for a group that needed our services even more than the children and families we had long known and cared for."[83]

Elsie wrote, "We did not go to Kentucky with any full conception of a community school. We had a vision of what such a school might be and do, but the understanding of this kind of school we have gained as we have lived it out. Working in a school that really functions in its community, however, I have come to believe that such functioning is the primary business of education not only here in Kentucky, but in all places, city or country."[84] What were the characteristics of Elsie's functioning school? One crucial characteristic was the teachers, dedicated and experienced in applying progressive methods. They were philosophically supportive of the philosophy of progressive education. The teachers made full use of the local environment in introducing subject matter and paying attention to the traditions and customs, the culture of the community. The functioning school paid attention to the health concerns of the children, a serious concern due to malnutrition and the inability of many families at Ballard to take their children to the doctor. Last, a functioning school centered itself in the life of the community; it served as a connection for sharing experiences. But there were still lessons to learn; Ballard was in Jim Crow Kentucky where African American children went to separate but not equal schools. There is no mention by Elsie or any teacher of any attempt to connect these two communities, a necessary step in the building of true democratic community. New challenges in a new environment were ahead. With her conceptualization of the community school, Elsie and her staff readied themselves for north central West Virginia, to participate in the first federal homestead subsistence project of the New Deal.[85]

Chapter Eleven

The Arthurdale Community School (1934–1936)

In the midst of the Depression, Elsie and her teachers traveled to north central West Virginia to begin another community school. They now had five years of experience in rural Appalachia leading progressive education into uncharted territory. The challenges at Ballard were multiplied enormously at Arthurdale, largely due to the economic devastation of the coal industry, increasing poverty, apathy, and health problems such as malnutrition, dysentery, typhoid, diphtheria, and tuberculosis. Elsie became part of a highly politically charged environment at Arthurdale due to her position as principal and director of community affairs. Arthurdale was the first federal homestead subsistence project of Franklin Roosevelt's New Deal. The subsistence projects were funded through Section 208 of Title II of the National Industrial Recovery Act of 1933.[1] This act gave President Roosevelt and Secretary of the Interior Harold Ickes the authority to distribute twenty-five million to "aid in the redistribution of population from industrial centers. It did so by providing loans or other aid to enable families to purchase subsistence homesteads."[2]

New Deal historian Paul Conkin argues that during the Depression the homestead subsistence idea made sense. In theory it allowed an individual to farm a small plot of land, providing enough food for his family and not threatening an already glutted agricultural market. The subsistence homestead was to provide at least part-time employment for the farmers in the form of wage labor in small local service industries or factories. While the subsistence homesteads were designed to keep demographic and economic pressure off urban areas, there was also a strong social/philosophical component to the idea. This more ambiguous but fundamental ideal behind the subsistence planning was to build community, not simply getting people to relocate outside of urban areas but to create a bond, where they felt empowered, where they felt they contributed, and where they felt a sense of ownership.[3]

There was a strong Jeffersonian tone to this back-to-the-land movement. The democratic concept of community, including fraternity, equality, and solidarity, was a part of the ideology of community planning at Arthurdale.[4] This emphasis on democratic community is deeply embedded in the planning of the school and also a thread throughout the curriculum. Known first as the Reedsville Experimental Project, the community eventually became known as

Arthurdale after the family from whom the government purchased the land. The homestead plan called for building one hundred sixty-five houses for displaced coal-mining families in north central West Virginia, most notably from the vicinity of Scotts Run, a mining area devastated by the Depression.[5]

The dire suffering and poverty of the Scotts Run area came to the attention of Eleanor Roosevelt through her friend, Associated Press reporter Lorena Hickok. On August 18, 1933, Eleanor Roosevelt drove her own car to Scotts Run to see the conditions for herself. The people did not recognize her and thought she was an acquaintance of the social workers. After viewing the suffering and plight of the people, she returned to Washington deeply determined to help the residents of Scotts Run.[6] In October she received a letter from a group of women in the Scotts Run area who had heard about the plan for a local homestead in the area. The mothers emphasized how important it was for a school to be built in the new community. They also requested "a community house which could be used as a kindergarten on week day mornings, for a recreation and reading room in the evenings, and a place for worship on Sundays."[7] Eleanor Roosevelt, herself a former teacher, believed the new community needed a new type of school, because for her education was the foundation of democratic society.[8] She envisioned the new school as the center of community life, an experimental school for an experimental community.[9] She wrote, "This conception, I think grew out of the fact that there has been accepted for some time the fact that rural life has actually not held sufficient attraction for youth because of the lack of opportunity for both recreational and educational activities, and community life which would be of real social value was practically impossible under our present rural social conditions. Under this head I put the nursery school, recreational facilities, the connection between school and community centers, handicraft work and certain adult education plans which might lead to more satisfactory living."[10]

Following one of Elsie's visits to Scotts Run, Mrs. Roosevelt asked her about her thoughts on the community and the proposed school. Elsie responded, "Last week when I talked with you I recommended a community school because of our experience in Kentucky. Now I know that nothing else will do. It must be the community's school and the homesteaders must have a voice in making it."[11] Apparently Mrs. Roosevelt agreed. The plan for the Arthurdale School, drafted by the Arthurdale Advisory School Committee and voted on by the homesteaders, clearly stated: "It is proposed that, just as the organization of this community represents an experiment seeking to discover means of needed adjustment in our social and economic life, likewise let this be a new school, providing for its citizens of all ages richer and more adequate educational opportunities."[12] Elsie was not alone in this daunting challenge to build a community school in a socially planned community. She was supported by

CHAPTER ELEVEN 189

the Arthurdale Schools National Advisory Committee that included Eleanor Roosevelt, E.E. Aggers of the Resettlement Administration, Fred Kelly of the United States Office of Education, Clarence Pickett of the American Friends Service Committee, W. Carson Ryan, Lucy Sprague Mitchell, and John Dewey.[13]

Elsie was also supported at the local level by the West Virginia Advisory Committee. This committee included the following: Floyd B. Cox, superintendent of Monongalia County schools; Justus Deahl, superintendent of Preston County schools; Jasper Newton Deahl, retired dean, College of Education, West Virginia University; W.W. Trent, state superintendent of schools; George Colebank, principal of University High School; Dean F.D. Fromme of WVU's College of Agriculture; Robert Clark, assistant superintendent of schools; Howard B. Allen and L.B. Hill of WVU's College of Education; Alice Davis, county welfare administrator; C.H. Ambler, historian and president of the Monongalia County School Board; Eric Gugler, the architect for the project; Earl Hudelson, Dean of WVU's College of Education, and Mary Jo Barrett, a teacher.[14] According to the plan, the government was to take care of initial costs of constructing the school plant. When the homesteaders were economically stable and could pay property taxes, the school would revert to the control of Preston County. It was clear from the beginning of the project that the school at some point would become part of the Preston County system.

Regardless of her prior experience and this illustrious support, Elsie wrote, "No one, including myself, really knew the function of a school in a homestead community. I believed that a school would be serviceable here, as in other communities. Our work in Kentucky has shown us that health and recreational services-made a good community relation."[15] Due to the poverty of the north central region the school plant was constructed at government expense. The schools in the local area were not able to handle the influx of homesteader children moving into the county. The Arthurdale school was really a corporate school in the sense that it received federal, state, local and private funds for operation but public in the sense it allowed access from the surrounding areas.[16]

Elsie began her work in Arthurdale by seeking to meet the needs of the children. She had visited on several occasions during the spring of 1934 and knew the conditions the people in Scotts Run were living under. She was aware of the work of Clarence Pickett of the American Friends Service Committee and Alice Davis as they tried to feed, clothe, and meet people's basic needs. Elsie had seen the "scrawny children" who played in "sulphur stained puddles." She saw the look of apathy and disillusionment in the faces of the people. She remembered the hundreds of black shanties without running water and electricity following the departures of the coal companies. She knew Scotts Run offered no hope for the people; as one miner said to her, "You ain't never goin' to make notin of us. We're like them old apple trees out there, all gnarled and twisted."[17] Elsie was determined to prove the frustrated miner wrong. She believed her socially functioning community school could help reconstruct the lives of these people and certainly improve the lives of their children. "And help them we must, for the children's sake as well as their own. For on their ability to make good hung the children's chance for growth and development, even survival."[18] Even more so than the Ballard children, Elsie believed these children needed special care, nurturing, and attention, both physically and emotionally, and that is how she began to build the Arthurdale community school. This meant paying particular attention to early childhood education along with health and recreation.

Much of the planning began in earnest during the summer of 1934 as Elsie met with Milburn L. Wilson, head of the Division of Subsistence Homesteads, and project architect Eric Gugler.[19] Elsie was assisted in the early childhood education planning by her close friend, Jessie Stanton of the famed Harriet Johnson Nursery School. Stanton had consented to serve as the director of the nursery school at Arthurdale.[20] Since the nursery school was to play an integral role at Arthurdale, Elsie took Jessie Stanton to Scotts Run. Stanton's eyes were opened as she viewed the horrible conditions of the devastated mining camps. She was shocked at the sight of a malformed baby, lying down and covered with flies with little chance to survive. Noting her friend's consternation, Elsie immediately drove Stanton the twenty-five miles to Arthurdale, "where there was still hope."[21] When they arrived, Arthurdale was bustling with activity, a great contrast from Scotts Run. Elsie and Stanton observed road construction and the building of the town center, the forge, the administrative offices and the workmanship of the Mountaineer Craftsmen's Cooperative Association. The Mountaineer Craftsmen's Cooperative Association had begun as part of the relief efforts in Morgantown as the unemployed miners had learned to make furniture for their homes. This cooperative labor produced functional handmade furniture, reproducing simple American patterns. They also made the furniture for houses in the homestead, which provided a source of income for a small group of homesteaders. Using sample cots, chairs, tables, and building blocks brought in by Stanton as models, the craftsmen began to construct furniture for the nursery school.

The architectural plans for the school were complete, but by midsummer 1934 a disappointed Elsie knew the school plant would not be ready for use the first year. In addition to this disappointment, Sarah Ripley Clapp passed away at the age of eighty-three. The funeral was held at the First Presbyterian Church in Brooklyn on Friday, August 10. Elsie left no personal recollection of her mother's death, but they had grown closer over the years, and her mother's passing must have affected her. Yet, Elsie knew she had a job to do, and she immersed herself in readying the Arthurdale School.[22] With Jessie Stanton's help, Elsie located temporary buildings for the school within the Arthurdale community. The primary and elementary grades would meet in the old Arthur mansion, the shop and high school in construction sheds, and the nursery school in a one-story building near the town center. Elsie had arranged with the project manager, O.B. Smart, to clean the sheds and the Arthur mansion and create the temporary nursery school.[23] Still seeking to fill staff positions, Elsie left for New York to meet with Mary Elizabeth Sedman, whom Stanton had recommended to Elsie to run the daily operation of the nursery school. Arriving back in Arthurdale three weeks before school began, Elsie was disheartened to see nothing had been done to prepare for the beginning of the school year. Realizing the homesteaders were discouraged by the lack of progress on the school, Elsie enlisted them and the teachers as part of work teams to aid in the preparation for the school. "No one grumbled about the work," Elsie recalled, "indeed they all felt relieved and reassured that there was someone around who believed in having things right for the children."[24] As the teachers began arriving they, too, pitched in. Harry Carlson and George Beecher built a workbench, a cabinet for shop tools, and a staircase. The homesteaders installed water fountains in the Arthur mansion and drywalled the sheds, and Alice Bowie set up the school office in the town center. Still a few days before school began there was no furniture and no instructional materials although Elsie had ordered the necessary equipment several months in advance. Finally, a Washington official "authorized the making of some deck-benches," Elsie noted. "Sunday evening, these were finished and, while the entire population of Reedsville looked on, were unloaded at the Mansion and divided among the classrooms." With little help from the federal planners in cutting red tape, Elsie, with the help of the homesteaders opened school on time the next morning. For Elsie and the homesteaders "it seemed a miracle—a school on the homestead at last, and children in it happily learning. Nothing else really mattered even the fact that we had virtually no equipment, few if any books, a scant number of pads and pencils, and for blackboards, sheets of brown wrapping paper tacked up on the walls."[25] From the first days, the homesteaders began to see the school as theirs and a central part of the community.

An integral part of the community school was the nursery school, which opened in the fall of 1934 with thirty-two children, two teachers, and a dietician. Elsie believed that the nursery school was one of the most significant contributions of the homestead. It helped create a sense of pride, joy, and hope for the community. However, it took some time for the children to overcome the devastation of Scotts Run. "The children in Nursery School in September looked like no little children we had ever known," Elsie recalled. "Aged, wizened, wan and lifeless, they all showed the sufferings they had undergone.

Most of them had either impetigo or scabies." The initial project nurse was overwhelmed by the poor health conditions of the children and in taking care of pregnant women and sick babies. Fortunately, following the departure of the first nurse, Elsie was able to hire Kay Plummer, a nurse with experience in the Henry Street Settlement in New York and familiar with social welfare issues. Rest, fresh air, nutritious food, cod liver oil, and tomato juice were considered adequate remedies at the time and by spring the children had shown significant improvement.[26] However, the health problems were serious, and Elsie sought to locate a doctor to be part of the school staff. Kay Plummer, like her predecessor was becoming overwhelmed and Elsie also spent time securing and distributing milk to pregnant mothers and sick babies.[27] Finally, one of the homestead women had a dangerous miscarriage, and as Kay Plummer was not trained to handle this type of problem, a doctor became a necessity. Elsie contacted Clarence Pickett of the American Friends Service Committee and an advisor to the school. Through Pickett's help, Elsie was able to secure the services of Dr. Harry Timbres, who brought experience, tolerance, skill, wisdom, and seriousness to the job—exactly what the homesteaders needed. Elsie believed Dr. Timbres saw the homesteaders as human beings and not as relief cases, a physician for the people and one they learned to trust. The mining camps had taught the homesteaders to distrust the company physicians. Company physicians often came to the mining camps only in emergencies and were typically indifferent and unsympathetic.[28]

As director of community affairs at Arthurdale, Elsie not only tried to meet health needs but was also in charge of recreation and social events. The Labor Day celebration in 1934 allowed the homesteaders to gather together, eat, hear speeches, and enjoy a ball game. Halloween also gave Elise and staff the chance to get teachers and mothers together. Saturday night square dances also provided a forum for community gathering and conversation. Elsie believed the square dancing was one the community's most important social gatherings.[29]

The school served as the center of the health care programs and recreational programs. They "needed not only warm clothes, food, health and vigor," Elsie commented, "but fun and companionship with other children, and interests—the very kind of interests a countryside offers." The new homestead community gave the children the opportunity to grow, and for Elsie the homestead was "the best place imaginable to gain knowledge."[30] The teachers had poor facilities, no books, and few instructional materials. One might argue they were forced to use the resources in the community around them to begin to educate the children. However, this was not the disaster it may have seemed, because Elsie and her experienced staff from the Ballard School knew how to use the local resources as the basis for curriculum development. The first grad-

CHAPTER ELEVEN

ers under the direction of Ethel Carlisle studied the farming at Arthurdale, an important study in a subsistence homestead community. Since families were to grow their own food for subsistence, this study allowed the children to share with their parents what they were learning at school. The children observed their parents and other homesteaders plowing fields, threshing buckwheat, digging potatoes, and husking corn. Parents interrupted their work to share with the children what they knew and were doing, and the children continued their discussion back at school. The younger children used block play and mimicked their parents in the building of their own village. The children's village contained barns and houses, just like the community they saw growing up around them. They watched the planting of oats, the milking of a cow, and the raising of chickens. However, subject matter was not neglected, as Ethel Carlisle noted: "We spend time each day on reading, writing and number work. We do large manuscript writing and the children now form their letters and space their words quite well." She reported the first graders were enthusiastic, alert, and eager to learn, played well together and needed little disciplining.[31]

Eunice Jones guided the second graders whom she described as "not always well and still undernourished and ill-clad but cooperative and responsive, eager and quick to learn."[32] Under Jones' guidance the group decided they wanted to build the village of Arthurdale. The children did not have strong basic skills so Jones sought to nurture interest first and then strengthen their basic skills. The children were thorough in their preparation for building the village. Together they decided their village needed a store, bank, barn, and post office. In constructing the village with scrap lumber collected throughout the project, the children learned to measure and use a square and level. In the process they enhanced their understanding of fractions, addition, and subtraction. They also learned to work together for a common end, and this meant cooperation and communication to solve problems as they literally built the village. They constructed maps of their village, price charts for their store, and eventually made deposits at the bank. They learned cents and decimals in the process. They elected a mayor, assistant mayor, and town council and according to Jones did so "with good sound judgment."[33] By the end of the first year, the children had increased their competence and self-reliance, so much that they took control over their learning, consulting Miss Jones only when necessary.

Due to the delayed arrival of the West Virginia teachers, Elsie had placed the third graders in the first and second grades. Sara Liston, a West Virginia teacher, took over the third graders when she arrived in December. She was not initially trained in progressive methods, but Elsie helped her develop an activity-oriented unit on Native American life. The students constructed a small village, built a teepee, built meat-drying stands and collected berries for dyeing. Liston learned pottery from Ethel Carlisle and weaving from Elizabeth Sheffield to enhance the study of native life. These studies were popular among the children as they learned and researched the tribes that had lived in western Virginia.

The fourth grade under the direction of Elizabeth Sheffield began the year with "one broken table, four temporary desk-benches, twelve pencils and a filler of lined paper."[34] Stimulated by the location of a log cabin, the fourth graders decided to study pioneer life. For Elsie their study was important not just in learning history; she hoped and believed it gave the children a connection to their past. Elsie contended, as did many of the federal planners, that the life in the coal camps was disruptive, resulting in the loss of a sense of sharing, belonging or community. For Elsie, learning about pioneer life enabled the children to transcend the dark days of the coals camps, giving them a sense of understanding and pride in their Appalachian heritage and culture. This goal is deeply embedded throughout the curriculum at Arthurdale, and Elsie refers to it frequently in her publications about Arthurdale. Elsie believed this type of study gave the children a sense of place, a connection to the past, so important to the Arthurdale community and her pedagogy.

The children began the year by cleaning out the old log cabin, believed to be the former residence of Colonel John Fairfax's boss slave, Watt. The children dyed wool, dipped candles, ground corn, and read everything they could find about life and the history of the early settlers of the area. Reading and writing improved in the first few months, and eventually the children wrote a play about pioneer life which they shared with the school and community.[35] "They had gained too," Sheffield noted, "in their ability to think with numbers. More quickly than many fourth graders, they grouped the relationships between parts and wholes, and had no special difficulty manipulating fractions and mixed numbers."[36] Perhaps stimulated by Sheffield's own weaving skills, the children kept wool notebooks, including detailed guidelines for fluffing, carding, and weaving. They also kept flax and history notebooks, read through the diaries of pioneers, and used this information for their drama. As they did at Ballard, Elsie and the teachers saw "art and drama as an expression of hands-on learning, creativity, cooperation and interdisciplinary study."[37] The study of the log cabin offered an opportunity for the school to reach out into the community. Families joined in with the fourth graders, and the cabin inspired them with what Elsie described as "an appreciation of that simple home life of which their mothers told them."[38] As far as Elsie was concerned, the school was becoming the center of community life at Arthurdale; like the study of pioneer life, it was to help children and adults gain a sense of place. This meant knowing who you were and feeling a sense of contribution. The homesteaders viewed themselves as pioneers in creating a new type of community—they, too, were forging through a wilderness of sorts. Elsie noted this was a powerful contrast to the physical and mental lethargy of the coal camps.

The fifth and sixth graders, generally eleven and twelve years old, had not attended school regularly in Scotts Run. "Ill fed and ill-clad," as Elsie described them, "they had spent their days playing around the slag piles and tipples and along the sluggish stream that crept through the Run. Naturally they found regular work in school and the demands of school community living somewhat difficult." Testing had shown the children to be two grades below level. During the first three months of school Harry Carlson and Carleton Saunders taught the children—Carlson in history and shop and Saunders in math, English, geography, and science. Under the guidance of Carlson and Saunders, the children began a study of West Virginia history, geography, geology, and culture. "It proved a good choice," Elsie noted. "The children liked the West Virginia study and were quick to see that all things they were learning in one way or another contributed to it."[39] West Virginia teachers Inez Funk and Katherine Kimble arrived in early December 1934 to separate the classes according to age. The teachers used the interest of the children in building handcrafts and musical instruments. The students constructed a loom, hornbook, flutes, a seed box, and dug-out canoes. Fletcher Collins, the teacher in charge of art and music, also helped them, teach the students. Elsie described these children at the end of the first year. "Caught up in new activities and endeavors," she wrote, "they began to find abilities they did not know they possessed and discovered interest and enjoyments they did not dream life held."[40]

The seventh and eighth graders were part of the high school at Arthurdale and were taught the first year by Fletcher Collins.[41] Collins sought to reach these children through studying their cultural heritage, which he believed was "still in their blood" but "layered over by coal dust." "Their experience in the mine camps," he wrote, "brief though it had been, had obscured to them their cultural heritage; and being in the shadow of urban Monongalia, they had also been disturbed by the radio, the movies, and by bourgeois cultural standards."[42] Here Collins clearly stated the progressive concern over the loss of identity due to industrialization and its effects, but he went further than Elsie or any member of the staff in criticizing the consumerist/materialist character of American middle-class culture. Politically, Collins leaned more to a democratic socialism, more along the lines of John Dewey. Collins believed Arthurdale to be a unique social democratic approach to community planning, and that is why he chose to be a part. Under the guidance of Collins, the students began work on a large-scale map of the Arthurdale community. This effort helped unite the students, and the map was admired and seen by the entire community. The map study led the children into science through work in geology as they studied rocks and geological formations in the area. The children further enhanced their writing skills by scripting a play detailing the years in Scotts Run and the new adventure in Arthurdale. Seeing that the children enjoyed expressing themselves, often through singing Scotch-Irish folk tunes and ballads, Collins led them into a more sophisticated study of poetry focusing on the English romantics Shelley, Wordsworth, Keats, Coleridge, and Americans Emerson and Whitman. Collins had a personal interest in collecting folk ballads, and his expertise enhanced the study.

Square dancing, often incorporating folk tunes and ballads, was a popular forum for entertainment on the homestead, and some of the students expressed an interest in learning how to make and play fiddle and guitar, the primary instruments used for playing for the dances. Collins invited a violin craftsman, Bert Nicholson, to come and teach the boys interested in making their own fiddles. Nicholson showed the boys how to select the proper wood, usually spruce or maple, and how to craft it using only a chisel, handsaw, and penknife. The seventh and eighth graders also cleaned out an area in the woods for a park, and built an outdoor fireplace and tables and benches for the community and school. Elsie was impressed by Collins' work with these children and wrote: "It is, I think, quite clear that one of the services which Mr. Collins rendered these seventh and eighth grade students was to make accessible to them musical, literary and dramatic expression. The first was their heritage from their Scotch-Irish ancestry; the second was this group's native gift; the third they enthusiastically made their own."[43] Collins had connected interest as a basis for enhancing cultural understanding. Both Elsie and Collins understood that to form a community, people had to have a sense of self, where they belong and where they fit. Understanding cultural heritage was a central component of self-realization.

The upper high school grades the first year consisted of nineteen students who ranged in age from fifteen to twenty-one. Although there were few students, the age range created some difficulty for the teachers. George Beecher served as principal of the Arthurdale High School although he was under Elsie's supervision.[44] The high school teachers during the 1934–35 school year were George Beecher, Adolph Ipcar, Carleton Saunders, and assistant teacher Henry Easterley. Fletcher Collins taught music and drama, Harry Carlson taught shop, and Alice Bowie, the school secretary, taught office skills and typing.[45] The high school teachers surveyed the nineteen students to try and discover their interests and prior school experiences and knowledge.[46] Elsie grouped the students by interest. "The grouping of students in the beginning not by high school grades, or by age, but by the lines on endeavor was an experiment undertaken because it seemed more likely that any other plan to organize—or reorganize—high school work along fruitful lines. It succeeded."[47]

Elsie and George Beecher sought to structure the high school curriculum to meet the needs of the students and the community, with some success and some failure. The group of students interested in science began a study of botany with George Beecher. With no lab available the students utilized the environment with some botany manuals obtained from West Virginia University. The group collected, classified, and mounted various specimens found in their surroundings. They also met and discussed agricultural problems with Bushrod Grimes, who served as the federal advisor for subsistence farming in the community. Harry Carlson directed a group of students in a study of electricity, amplifiers and radios. Another group constructed a coal mine and studied geologic facts associated with mining. Fletcher Collins led his group in a study of poetry, mostly Emerson, Shelley, Wordsworth, and Whitman. This traditional study led to a study of ballads, stories in poetry form. Some of the children wrote their own ballads based on stories they had heard or learned. Collins viewed this as an educational activity that helped the Appalachian children use their own life experiences for expression and storytelling. Poetry and song combined to help the children relate subject matter to their real world.

Similar to the studies at Ballard, subject matter work often expressed itself through art, music, or drama. During the first year the high school students, largely under the direction of Adolph Ipcar and Fletcher Collins, wrote a play, *The Gold Rush,* and staged it in the outdoor amphitheater. This amphitheater had been cut out of the local woods by the students and was an ideal site due to the sloping hillside, which made seating and good visibility possible. Elsie believed this activity was successful due to "the fact that the apathetic, meagerly equipped group of boys and girls who came into this high school in September had during the year come alive, acquired varied skills and much information, and gained new interest and new enjoyments."[48]

As director of community affairs of Arthurdale and as an educator, Elsie with her staff also sought to meet the needs of younger and older adults on the homestead. "This group of forty-three young people, whose ages ranged between fifteen and twenty-six years," Elsie explained, "were the ones who had left school before or shortly after, coal production in West Virginia petered out."[49] Although some of the students had enrolled in the high school, most dropped out and were not able to find work in the homestead or in the surrounding area. After meeting with her staff and then the students, Elsie began night school classes for those interested. The students studied carpentry, electrical work in the shop, practical math, typing, science, reading, and writing, pottery, home economics, and also participated in athletic events. Their for the studies improved as the students were able to connect their schooling to work, which gave them some hope. Elsie saw this group of young adults as "responsive, sensitive and insecure, and just naturally obliging," but they lacked endurance and persistence.⁵⁰ "Harmed as they unquestionably were by idleness and by life in the cesspool conditions of the abandoned mine camps," Elsie noted, "they had an innate sweetness of nature and an unquenchable and infectious gaiety."⁵¹

Elsie claimed that scholars in the Arthurdale community school ranged from two to seventy-two. In many ways this was true. During the first year, the adults were largely taught how to manage and farm their homesteads. For both men and women this included learning about animal husbandry, and budgeting for the purchase of food, cows, pigs, or chickens. "Their classrooms," Elsie wrote, "were home and school kitchens, gardens, club meetings, square dances—wherever and whenever we happened to be together. And our teaching, intentionally was done informally in day by day work and living."⁵²

Fletcher Collins directed the Arthurdale Men's singing group and an adult drama group. "The Men's Singing Group met once a week all winter," Collins reported. "They sang gospel songs and they sang from oral traditions, not from notation." Being a musician, Collins made an attempt to teach the men music theory, but when some gradually dropped out, he learned that held no interest. Some participated in making flutes, guitars, and violins. The adult drama group produced six plays during the first year, one being a satire on the life at Arthurdale and how the newspaper reporters saw them and how the homesteaders saw themselves. There was some interest in black-face comedy among the group, and the drama group did perform *The Battle of Rolling Bones*, based on an African American's experience in World War I. Collins tried to move the homesteaders away from this prejudiced form of mocking entertainment and preferred that the group write their own plays.⁵³

Teachers in a progressive community school were to be an active part of that community. Teachers served or assisted on the fire committee, Men's and Women's Club, the farm cooperatives, and the well-baby clinics held at the nursery school. Teachers at Arthurdale worked during the summer of 1935. One of the most significant events was the Music Festival held in July, largely under the direction of Collins. He sought to involve the Reedsville and Arthurdale communities. Mrs. Roosevelt also attended this festival. Eleanor Roosevelt was considered by the homesteaders as their savior and in reality she was. She financially supplemented many of the projects at Arthurdale through her radio broadcasts. The Associated Press reported her philanthropy: "One half year's salary to Miss Elsie Clapp, teacher of the Reedsville, W.V., subsistence homestead, $3500; for incorporation of the Reedsville cooperative, $111; for handicraft, $6000; for Logan, County health work, $6000; scholarships for girls at Kentucky and West Virginia educational camps, $500; general work of Friend's Committee, $8000. Total, $19,111."⁵⁴ Eleanor Roosevelt had a deep love and compassion for these people, and she used her time and her generosity to make their life better. She championed the progressive education experiment at Arthurdale and the cause of the homesteaders and she enjoyed her visits to Arthurdale, particularly the square dancing.

The festival she attended was characterized by a fiddler's contest, jig dancing, ballad singing, mouth harping, and a square dance contest.[55] But for Fletcher Collins, the music festival served an educational purpose. "The musical culture latent in the people of Arthurdale," he wrote, "and the region was encouraged and dignified by the emphasis of the Festival. The music and dancing were the peoples' own and they knew it."[56] At the close of the first year of school in Arthurdale, Elsie supported Collins' view that the program of the schools and community had given the homesteaders a sense of ownership. As part of a community, the people needed to feel this sense of ownership. The school served as a source of this feeling for the homesteaders had few possessions to call their own and rented their homes from the government. The school was the major social institution in which the homesteaders felt some control. The activities of the school brought the people together in a common interest.

The school was functioning as a community school, but Elsie believed the second year was just as difficult as the first and beset by problems the school alone could not overcome. "The second year was in fact, as challenging educationally as the first," Elsie reported, "for the homesteaders, struggling to find and maintain their stance as villagers in the growing community of Arthurdale, were uneasy and unsatisfied, beset by middle-class ambitions and harassed by economic problems. And the sudden and rapid development of organization and services created by the Government for their benefit seemed to increase rather than lessen their confusion and discomfort."[57] Elsie blamed much of the malaise and discontent on the homesteaders' previous years in the mining camps. She rationalized that during the boom years of the coal industry, the miners had spent freely and had received higher wages than they were now receiving working on the homestead project building the homes. The arrival of winter made things worse because it slowed and then ended home construction until the spring. The homesteaders sensed that any work stoppage threatened their survival, as it had in the mining camps. "They fell this year again into grumblings and complaints," Elsie wrote, "and believing any rumor, however wild and fantastic, that seemed to confirm their doubts and suspicions."[58] To remedy lack of employment, the federal planners established homestead cooperatives, like the furniture-making Mountaineer Craftsmen Cooperative. Elsie believed the people simply did not understand how the cooperatives could help them. It was in this climate that Elsie and her staff began the second year.

Fortunately, the new school plant was complete when the 1935–36 school year began. Elsie had worked closely with project architects Eric Gugler and

Steward Wagner. The school designs were to be simple, "homelike in character and allow the maximum amount of sun and air."[59] They were also designed to meet a shrinking federal budget. Although Elsie and the federal planners cut school construction costs to one-third of the original plans, she believed the school genuinely reflected the character of the community. The school buildings were similar to the houses and detached to prevent the spread of disease and leave room for future expansion. The plans called for playgrounds, gardens, and proximity to the woods but separate from the community center complex, yet close enough to the community for walking.[60]

The school plant consisted of a recreation building closest to the main access road, the school center/administration building, the elementary school, the high school, the primary school building, and the nursery school. "The school was," Elsie wrote, " a little village in itself."[61] The recreation building was designed for the school and community functions and included a full-size basketball court, showers and dressing rooms, a large stage for plays and set construction. It was near the main access road to make it accessible to the community. The high school was placed near the recreation building for full usage and also housed a greenhouse and the school community library. The school center building housed the school cafeteria, kitchen, home economics rooms, a canning kitchen, the doctor's office, school bank and bookstore, and Elsie's office. The younger children were housed in the primary, elementary, and nursery school buildings, more secluded and further from the main access road. Elsie described the primary and elementary buildings as identical, long, one-story buildings, "open to the sun and air on all sides, containing five large classrooms, so that there could—at need—be a division of two of the three grades."[62] All the rooms were provided with running water and had alcoves off the main classroom for special work and study.

Jessie Stanton, along with Elsie and Wagner, designed the nursery school. More than any structure in the school plant, the nursery school embodied progressive pedagogy in its basic design and curriculum. Constructed to provide light, airy areas where children could rest and play, each classroom had its own exit to a playground and sheltered area that allowed children to play outside during inclement weather. The nursery school served the community in numerous ways—teaching parents about hygiene, nutrition, and child development. It sponsored well-baby clinics in the form of preventive medicine. Early childhood education was an important component of the curriculum. Block play was considered a key to nurturing creativity and imagination as students often reproduced what they saw on their field trips through the village. For Elsie the nursery school was the core of community education at Arthurdale, and it improved the physical, social, and emotional lives of the students. She wrote, "The need at Arthurdale for the child care which a nursery school especially can give was obvious; proclaimed by every soul on the homestead. The results of what the Nursery School did for the children were things which the mothers and fathers understood very well indeed. In an emphatic and persuasive way, the Nursery School was the heart and spring of community education at Arthurdale."[63]

The entire community, including teachers, students, and parents, was excited at the opening of the 1935–36 school year. Although materials and equipment were still lacking, the school plant was ready for occupancy. First-grade teacher Ethel Carlisle once again guided her students in a study of farm life. During the previous years these children had attended the nursery school and Elsie reported that the eighteen six-year-olds were well adjusted to group play and work. Under Eunice Jones, the second graders continued building the village of Arthurdale. The children, twenty-four in all, decided to work in fours to build a store, post office, hospital, two houses, and a farm. The children observed the construction around the community, found saws and hammers and other scrap material, and began to build. Jones used this interest to build basic skills of reading, writing, and math. Elsie believed this class to be "unusually competent and knowledgeable. They worked hard and were willing to correct mistakes and learned from them. The village houses they built were well constructed and a remarkable achievement, really, for seven-year-old children. And in their reading and writing and work with numbers, the group showed the same perseverance and the same ability to learn."[64] West Virginia native Sara Liston taught the third grade, and Elsie was pleased with her progress teaching in a progressive school environment. "She perhaps more consciously made connections between activities and learning from books," Elsie reported, "and followed recommended methods in reading, writing and arithmetic, but her diary records an active and interested participation by the children in the processes of Indian life."[65]

Under the guidance of Elizabeth Sheffield, the fourth graders, like the previous class, studied pioneer life. Sheffield believed the previous year's studies of Native American life under Sara Liston had prepared these fourth graders for such a study. Sheffield described the group as cooperative, independent, and capable of self-management. She attributed much of this to the improved living conditions of Arthurdale, including better nutrition and health care. During the year the children kept notebooks, more like journals in history, math, reading, geography, and weaving. They made a sophisticated study of textiles and visited the local Engelhardt Woolen Mill to enhance their study. Elsie believed the children had made considerable progress not only in learning but "in understanding themselves and others, and in using their abilities."[66]

The fifth grade under Katherine Kimble, another West Virginia teacher, investigated the colonial era in western Virginia. "Mrs. Kimble had a personal interest in this period, and," Elsie noted, "helped by Miss Sheffield in bibliography, in the use of material and of local resources, she assembled primary facts and many articles and, with the children, made illustrative implements and utensils, furniture, samplers, etc.," of the colonial period. Leonard Bramble taught the group of sixth graders, typically several years below grade level. Elsie considered it important for these children to receive adequate instruction in reading, writing, and math. Bramble also exploited the interest of the children in early native culture, particularly native burial customs. Inez Funk taught a combined group of fifth and sixth graders whose families had just moved into the community and had not attended school in Arthurdale the previous year. These children came from the surrounding areas of Preston County. Elsie described them. "They came from families of Preston County who had been miserably poor, but whose needs were not as desperate and whose background not as wretched as those of the first homesteaders from Scotts Run."[67] These children thrived in the new environment and under the calm and sympathetic care of Inez Funk. Funk guided the students as they studied West Virginia history and culture. This included early settlement, growth, and the struggle during the Civil War for statehood. Notable efforts during the year were topographical maps made by the children and the artwork in pottery and clay.

The high school staff during the 1935–36 school year consisted of Carleton Saunders, Fletcher Collins, Adolph Ipcar, George Beecher, Harry Carlson, Susan Gross, Nell Rider, and Carson Ryan.[68] Ninth grade students attended the high school, and Elsie described this group as creative and curious. The students expressed an interest in studying the Middle Ages, an interest Elsie considered appropriate because of the similarities between Arthurdale and medieval life. Through such a study the students could better understand how to divide and use land, how to use labor, how to market goods, and how to entertain through the use of drama and music. Team taught by Beecher, Collins, Ipcar, and Carlson, the students studied Old English, history, math, botany, drama, and also made use of musical instruments. One aspect of curriculum integration included music and math. The students experimented with tension, sound, tones, and scales. They also worked with local violin craftsman Bert Nicholson. Elsie contended the success of the ninth graders was largely due to a disciplined, creative, and compassionate group of teachers. Elsie considered their success an example "of what boys and girls eager to investigate and discover, and teacher can accomplish."[69]

The tenth-grade class was composed of fifteen students, seven students from the previous year, three new students to the homestead, and five boys from night school, who had previously dropped out of school. The theme of study for this group was the late Middle Ages and the early Renaissance. English teacher George Beecher noted that the group was less activity oriented and more passive than some of the other high school groups. They preferred to learn from books and in more traditional formats. There were also some discipline problems from some of the older boys and Beecher described them: "Our irregular boys, are being misfits just now in drama and bookstore and, to some extent, in biology—the classes which most tax the ability to move about with consideration for others."[70] Beecher along with Adolph Ipcar sought to find some interest to stimulate the boys to learn. This largely came through a study of bookkeeping, which the teachers felt complemented the gradual growth of cooperatives at Arthurdale. The teachers tried to make schooling relevant to the students and give them something they could immediately use. The boys were frustrated by their school experiences and saw no connection of learning and reality. This reality was amplified by an extremely tight job market during the Depression.

The eleventh and twelfth grades studied the history of industry, centering their exploration on the growth of the textile industry. This study of industry was considered important due to the effect of industry on the economy of the area, many of the children coming from former mining families. The group also used a printing press to publish a school newspaper. These classes were also in charge of the school bank with the idea of helping the students to become thrifty and also to teach the basic math skills. In chemistry the students made a study of glass and glass making, a prominent industry in the north central West Virginia region. The students conducted extensive experiments to determine the proper temperatures for the furnace they constructed. They also experimented with different types of glass for etching. The study included looking into the history of glass through ancient to modern times—Egyptian, Assyrian, Babylonian, Greek, and Roman to the modern era. Both boys and girls in the class "emerged from their year's work knowing that research, experiment and a spirit that does not admit defeat are needed in solving science problems."[71] Elsie knew this group would soon need their problem-solving skills following graduation whether they remained in the community or continued their education. There was some optimism that glass making might serve to employ some of the homesteaders, but Arthurdale lacked the capital to test the project and thus its prospect of employing the people.[72]

Though lacking in traditional skills, Elsie reported that the older students excelled in printing, publishing the school/community newspaper, and producing a dramatic production. Fletcher Collins directed both activities. During the 1935–36 school year the community population of Arthurdale was around eight hundred. Collins believed that a newspaper could serve as the primary source for the dissemination of information. Beecher, Ipcar, Carlson, and Collins worked to pull the project together. Collins also contended the publishing of the news could help stop the rumor mill, which fed distrust, dissension, and depression. The school served as the chief means of information for the community in disseminating school and community events and reporting fact rather than rumor.[73]

The high school students produced several plays, including *The Three Strangers, The Cherry Tree Coral, The Masque of the Red Death,* and *John Brown's Body.* Elsie seemed impressed by the "native ability of these boys and girls, their zest for new knowledge and new experience, their quickness in laying hold of essential facts, their power to address themselves to a task and the patient and unflagging efforts they put forth day after day."[74] She was proud of the efforts of the high school teachers and the students. Although the high school did not receive state accreditation until 1938, two years following Elsie and her staff's departure, most students responded positively to their experience at Arthurdale. One student wrote, "Not only did it give us the experience, but it gave us enough freedom to use our own ability and initiative. And our teachers were friendly guides and not absolute rulers. They taught us to be proud of our community, to utilize the resources and strive to make it the best community that we could. Our education was not divorced from life studies but was an integral part of our lives."[75] However, some Arthurdale students did not feel their high school experience prepared them for the more traditional environment of college.[76]

The positive high school student captured the essence of Elsie's community school. Based upon the freedom to explore, to ask questions, to reflect, and to initiate, with teachers serving as guides seeking to capture the interest of the students and integrate traditional subject matter as part of the process, the ideal community school was a living, vital component of the community and met the educational, health, and recreational needs of the people it served. Elsie saw no dualism between learning and living, and the school was to serve as an agency of sharing, mutual effort, and transformation. The community school was a society itself, and, as John Dewey had articulated in *School and Society*, it "is a number of people held together because they are working along common lines in a common spirit and with reference to common aims."[77]

In January 1936, Eleanor Roosevelt brought a party of fifteen to see Arthurdale and its school. They visited the old mining camps in Scotts Run and Jere and then rode to Arthurdale, where Elsie greeted the contingent. Elsie showed mothers preparing lunch for the children, all volunteers. The vegetables for the lunch were all grown by the homesteaders through subsistence farming. They also visited the wood-working shop and the forge and observed looms being set up to teach weaving. Supper that evening was held at Elsie's home, followed by a dance.[78] Elsie and her staff viewed the school as a means where people could find common ground and common purpose, but this goal was made more difficult by the social, economic, and political forces

CHAPTER ELEVEN

surrounding the Arthurdale community as the first federal subsistence homestead. As director of community affairs, Elsie found herself in the midst of these forces. She was the intermediary between the homesteaders and the federal officials, dealing with electricity rates, construction schedules, clinic operations, and the basic subsistence needs of food clothing and shelter for the people.[79]

Being the first subsistence project, Arthurdale was in the spotlight and the frequent target of Republicans, who saw much of the New Deal as socialism. Ironically, one of the most vehement critics of the Arthurdale project was William Wirt, the well-known superintendent of the Gary Schools in Gary, Indiana. Wirt had referred to Resettlement Administration head Rexford Tugwell as a revolutionary trying to overthrow the government. He had also made comparisons between President Roosevelt and Alexander Kerensky. There is no response in Elsie's record, if she made one, but Wirt was brought before a House Committee looking into his charges.[80] Elsie attempted to remain politically aloof and refused to respond to questions about Arthurdale while in Washington for a Progressive Education Association meeting. Although she refused to be quoted, she did tell the journalists that the children were "working with their hands."[81] This seems like an interesting comment for her to make considering the curriculum at Arthurdale was far from controversial. Perhaps it speaks more to Elsie's moderate political stance and her refusal to embroil the school in the numerous controversies surrounding Arthurdale. It also speaks to the highly politically charged environment of Arthurdale and the media interest in anything that went wrong at the project.

Economic forces were always present at Arthurdale and affected the school and community in many ways. The idea of subsistence homesteading at Arthurdale was successful in terms of the homesteaders growing enough food for themselves. However, Arthurdale homesteaders still needed wages in order to buy goods such as clothing and pay their rents. Once the housing construction ended, jobs for wage labor began to dry up in the community, and this led to apathy and discontent. The cooperatives were seen as supplements to already received wages, not substitutes for them. Numerous attempts were made by the federal government and Eleanor Roosevelt to bring factory employment to Arthurdale such as a factory for making furniture for the U.S. Postal Office, a vacuum cleaner factory, a shirt company, and a tractor factory.[82] All of these efforts failed for one reason or another. According to Arthurdale historian Stephen Haid, "the lack of permanent employment proved to be the most corrosive and unsettling influence of the community. The success of the project assumed at least permanent part-time employment as a prerequisite."[83]

The failure to attract employment to Arthurdale gradually pushed philanthropist Bernard Baruch to withdraw his financial support, a crucial blow to the school. Baruch and Eleanor Roosevelt funded the operation of the nursery school through private contributions, and they helped supplement teacher salaries. Elsie described the dilemma: "At the end of the second year, the donor of the largest amount of money that sustained the education experiment decided together with the Director of the School and those interested in the experiment, that the time had come to transfer the School to the direction of the State and County school authorities."[84] Under these conditions, Elsie, her staff, Eleanor Roosevelt, and the West Virginia Advisory committee all knew the project could not continue.

Social forces also proved powerful at Arthurdale and were dominated by classicism and racism. The Roosevelt Administration was well aware of the potential for class conflict in the mining camps of Scotts Run in the late 1920s. Fighting between the United Mine Workers and the communist National Miners Union resulted in Scotts Run being nicknamed Bloody Run.[85] Knowledgeable of this conflict in the area, federal planners with the support of Eleanor Roosevelt and FDR decided to create a community free of conflict. The dire conditions of Scotts Run and its potential for conflict led to north central West Virginia becoming chosen for the first federal homestead project. The selection process for becoming a homesteader was rigorous, and homesteaders were carefully chosen according to Eleanor Roosevelt.[86] Eleanor Roosevelt preferred a more open selection process and may have opposed the background checks, but she was not able to overcome the discrimination and power of Jim Crow politics in 1930s West Virginia. Surveyed on their knowledge of farming, carpentry, animal husbandry, dairy farming, physical fitness, mechanical knowledge as well as attitude and ambition, only twenty percent of applicants were selected for Arthurdale. Only native-born whites were selected, mostly from Scotch-Irish or Pennsylvania German "upbringing and social background."[87] African Americans lived and worked in Scotts Run and made application for the new homestead, but all of them were denied. The NAACP protested the exclusion, with W.E.B. Du Bois leading the charge, but the complaints were dismissed by the federal authorities.[88] Approximately twenty-five percent of the applicants to Arthurdale were African American. One reason for the apparent denial of access was due to West Virginia law that followed *Plessy v. Ferguson* and the separate and equal doctrine. The Jim Crow laws of 1930s West Virginia demanded that African Americans be segregated and thus in the homestead a separate school would have to have been built. There was also some hostility between white and black miners, with white miners seeing the African American miners as strike breakers. Homesteaders also expressed an unwillingness to live in an integrated community. There is no available written record of Elsie's opinion on the selection process, but she, like Eleanor Roosevelt and federal planners, wished the project to be a success. During her two years at Arthurdale the community remained all white; apparently social segregation was perceived a normal part of existence and was not questioned in the community.

Of course, there is a problem here in making sense of the notion of community, particularly democratic community. Elsie and her staff stimulated the students to imagine, create, reflect but not critique in the sense of challenging class, power, and racism. The exploitation and oppression of the coal-mining families in Scotts Run, which the homesteaders understood, could have stimulated a discourse on racism and how it too was exploitative and oppressive socially and economically. The high school children came close to this in their play *Spade*, the drama of a slave who escaped the bondage of the plantation to experience the bondage of the factory. This is where Elsie and her teachers could have pushed the envelope to truly begin to achieve democratic community—to help the children understand. Regardless of their skin color, these working-class children were closer to Spade than they were to the coal barons who exploited their labor and their culture and environment. While some fraternity, equality, and solidarity existed at Arthurdale, it did so within a homogeneous, segregated community.

The combination of political and economic forces eventually ended the educational experiment at Arthurdale. Politically, the homesteads were becoming a headache for the democrats and FDR. The inability to find consistent work for the homesteaders resulted in the withdrawal of Baruch's substantial contribution. "Let us not put these people on their feet," he wrote, "unless it is humanly possible for them to stand by themselves when the helping hand is removed."[89] Elsie also recognized the situation and wrote to Eleanor Roosevelt that without "industry and security our education enterprise cannot go on here."[90]

Elsie had taken on the Ballard and Arthurdale projects to bring progressive education to the rural public arena. She and her teachers showed that poor working-class children could benefit from progressive education and that it should not be limited to elite private schools and lab schools. As director of community affairs, Elsie sought to nurture an environment where people had a voice. This is evident through the various clubs and associations at Arthurdale. Arthurdale historian Stephen Haid suggests that no one recognized the importance of community more than Elsie Clapp.[91] Elsie defined community education as a "growing idea, born in the interaction of thinking and learning, shaped in part by events. A community school is made with the people whose school it is. In the making, teachers lead as fellow workers."[92] A community school seeks to meet the needs of living and learning. Through meeting the health, recreational, and educational needs, Elsie was successful in linking the needs of living and learning. However, the politically charged atmosphere of

Arthurdale, the failure to provide economic sustenance for the homesteaders, and the racism and classicism present undermined the attempt to create a true democratic community. True progressivism had its limitations, much like the New Deal. It was designed to work within the capitalist system rather than change it. As Elsie and her staff prepared to leave Arthurdale, they continued to work with the community during the summer of 1936. Students continued to work on many of their projects begun during the school year such as planting a vegetable garden, playing in the miniature Arthurdale village and the log cabin, practicing musical instruments, and testing the local water. Adults participated in the Men's and Women's Clubs, music and drama activities, and crafts. The Arthurdale school was still functioning for the entire community from dawn until the late evening hours.

Two important events took place in June 1936, one, the high school graduation attended by Eleanor Roosevelt who delivered the commencement address, and the other the music festival.[93] Eleanor Roosevelt arrived at Arthurdale on June 24 around 6 PM and participated in the opening of a factory at the homestead designed to build vacuum cleaners and provide employment for some homesteaders. Following the ceremony, she went to Elsie's for supper, then to the gymnasium for the music festival highlighted by a fiddle contest. "I was to give out the ribbons to the winners in the music festival contest," Mrs. Roosevelt reported. "There was an audience of some eight hundred men, women and children, and their approval of the programs was attested by the quiet in the hall as each contestant played his contribution." Eleanor Roosevelt noted the musicians took pride in their playing and their craftsmanship. She finished the day visiting the baby clinic, garden club, and a Four H project.[94] The people of Arthurdale had a caring and compassionate champion in Eleanor Roosevelt and they knew it. The other important event was the 1936 music festival begun the summer before. This second festival proved to be a huge success. On both nights the festival held in the recreational building was filled to capacity, with over 1,000 people attending each night.

On July 8, 1936, Elsie, several teachers, and the West Virginia Advisory Committee met with Eleanor Roosevelt to discuss the future of the school. Mrs. Roosevelt recalled the discussion. "It has become necessary, from Miss Clapp's point of view and mine," she wrote, "to make certain changes, and we wanted to discuss them with the committee and set the machinery in motion for a transition period."[95] Following the meeting, Elsie and her staff knew for certain they would have to leave Arthurdale. For two years she and her staff struggled, sometimes against the odds with inadequate materials and facilities, apathy, and government red tape and inefficiency. Although we do not have the recollections of Elsie about leaving, she seemed to feel positive about the work accomplished during the two-year span. She had not expected the experiment to end so quickly and wrote, "To all of us it seemed almost impossible to cease upon the instant, as it was, the many and interrelated school and community activities which had both immediate and long-range benefits in view. The children, we felt confident however, could and would now go forward in the learning. And the adults, whose hardihood had won them the chance to make a new start in life, would in all probability gradually gain stability and composure as time brought healing and perspective."[96]

Unfortunately short in duration, Arthurdale was Elsie's most significant attempt to fully develop a community school. Although she and her staff knew from the start that the school would eventually become a county school, she did expect to stay more than two years. According to Adolph Ipcar, one of the high school teachers, Elsie was not frustrated at the early departure but did express some disappointment.[97] Elsie needed time to heal from departing one of the most significant rural experiments in progressive education, but she had to be heartened by John Dewey's belief that the Arthurdale school program was one of the best public schools in the nation. From April 6 to the 8th, in three dreary days of inclement weather, John Dewey had visited Arthurdale with the National Advisory Committee, including Dean William Russell of Teachers College, Lucy Sprague Mitchell, Clarence Pickett, and Eleanor Roosevelt. Elsie described the visit. "It was Dewey's first visit to the homestead and the School, and he spent several days with us."[98] Dewey not only visited the Arthurdale school but requested to see one- and two-room schools surrounding Arthurdale in rural Preston County. Dewey was impressed with what he saw at Arthurdale and what his pupil had accomplished. In a note to J.A. Rice of Black Mountain College, Dewey claimed that the Arthurdale School was one of the best public schools in the country.[99] Elsie was proud of her work in West Virginia and contended the experience "showed us ways in which the education a school can provide may inform and enrich living. I hope that other teachers may find, as we have, that these facts and ways are as useful and potent in other and usual situations as they were at the homestead at Arthurdale."[100] She did not see her work as a blueprint but as a way for other educators to build socially functioning community schools, meeting the educational, health, and recreational needs of the community, making the school the center of community life.

Chapter Twelve

The Later Years

The last twenty-nine years of Elsie's life are difficult to chronicle. Following Arthurdale there is no evidence she ever directed or developed another community school. By all indications she desired to do so. Although the progressive education at the Arthurdale experiment ended for her far too early, she felt a sense of accomplishment from 1929 to 1936 due to the work in Kentucky and West Virginia. Elsie had brought progressive education to the public arena in Appalachia. Elsie spent the year following departure from Arthurdale writing a book about her experiences in Kentucky and West Virginia.[1]

Elsie left Arthurdale in the late summer of 1936 and returned to New York City. Her staff of experimental progressive educators also departed and went their separate ways. Elsie wrote to Eleanor Roosevelt that her proposed book was "an attempt to describe concretely what a community school is and does."[2] "Dewey has approved the manuscript," Elsie continued, "and will write the Introduction—in another fortnight. I shall be trying my luck with a publisher. Mr. Pickett will read it to be sure that it is discreet." Eleanor Roosevelt had recently returned from Arthurdale and Elsie had asked her in previous correspondence about the community. "I found everything at Arthurdale quite encouraging," Eleanor informed Elsie, "Mr. Nine is doing a good job in the school and, while of course it isn't as good a school, the people do seem able to go along on their own initiative. I was given some money for books which the school needed and do hope they will continue to be as interested. The nursery school is to continue and the chief thing now for which money is needed is the medical end. The Women's Club handled the Christmas party and I think, on the whole, the people are happy and satisfied." Elsie felt some comfort in what she had accomplished, but disappointed that she school had moved away from progressive education to a more teacher/text centered approach.[3]

Elsie had two professional opportunities following Arthurdale. W. Carson Ryan Jr., President of the Progressive Education Association from 1937 to 1939, had offered her the editorship of the journal *Progressive Education*.[4] Dean Arps and James Hopkins at Ohio State University also offered her a position in the art department. The job at Ohio State fell through when the Ohio legislature adjourned without appropriating the funds for the position so Elsie accepted Ryan's offer to serve as editor for the journal. "The appointment is for a year only," Elsie wrote, "at my request, as I still wish if and when opportunity offers to be used on some phase of community education in rural or developed areas.

During the year I hope to gain more information as to where and what the needs are educationally in our country."⁵

Elsie located an apartment on 71 Washington Square South in New York City and shared it with her friend Jessie Stanton. Unfortunately in July 1937 Elsie lost her beloved brother Lawrence who passed away after what Elsie termed a "tragic illness." The loss was difficult for Elsie and she went to spend a few days with Eleanor Roosevelt at her cottage at Hyde Park. Elsie also spent August 3, 1937, with Mrs. Roosevelt and Eleanor described Elsie's visit. "Today Miss Elsie Clapp, who has taken the editorship of *Progressive Education* for this year, is lunching with me. She did a wonderful job at the Arthurdale, West Virginia, school–not only in planning and starting it as a progressive school, but in helping to draw the community together and in making the school the center of almost every community activity–that I believe she can do a very great service to education through the magazine. I wish her every success."⁶ Following her stay, Elsie felt a "renewed courage and serenity" and expressed so to Mrs. Roosevelt.⁷ Elsie now immersed herself in editing the most important mouthpiece for progressive education.

Progressive Education Association historian Patricia Alberg Graham describes the change in the journal when Elsie became editor. "Miss Clapp's selection gave support to those Association members who urged the organization to limit its principal activities to those directly connected with education and the school. Along with Carlton Washburne, Miss Clapp had been opposed to unqualified endorsement of the report of Counts' Committee on Social and Economic Problems."⁸ The October 1937 issue of *Progressive Education* was the first under Elsie's leadership. Lois Meek, the Director of the Children Development Institute of Teachers College, introduced Elsie to the readers. "We are fortunate to have Elsie Clapp as a member of the staff of the PEA, she has been connected so long with the work of the Association and was the first woman to be elected as Vice-President. We are anticipating a new emphasis in the Journal from her rich experience in making education an integral part of the lives of children and adults."⁹

This anticipated new emphasis began with the October 1937 issue, subtitled, "Where Is Education Going?" "It seems to me a momentous and pressing question," Elsie noted in a letter to Eleanor Roosevelt, "as I wrote you earlier, my especial interest is to further the Association's realization of the wider aspects of education, and the imperative problems it faces in view of what is happening in our society."¹⁰ Elsie asked Eleanor Roosevelt to write down her thoughts on the most pressing issues facing American education. Mrs. Roosevelt agreed and posed questions on the rural and urban school, the purpose of education, the role of the nursery school, the problems of citizenship, the training of teachers, child development, and free texts.¹¹

CHAPTER TWELVE 213

Elsie solicited various educators to respond to Mrs. Roosevelt's concerns. Respondents included Dr. Herbert Stolz, Assistant Superintendent of the Oakland Public Schools; Josephine Roche, Assistant Secretary of the Treasury; Caroline Zachry, the Director of Research of the Commission on Secondary School Curriculum of the Progressive Education Association; Milburn Wilson, Undersecretary of Agriculture in the United States Department of the Interior and Eduard Lindeman, Professor of Social Philosophy of the New School for Social Research and National Director of the Iowa Child Welfare Research Station at the University of Iowa.[12]

Elsie's first edited issue of *Progressive Education* clearly showed her influence. The cover photo was a picture of a young girl climbing, symbolic of the issue theme, 'Where Is Education Going?" Topics included health, the use of leisure, the role of the classroom teacher, agricultural education, human relationships and community, and the concept of the nursery school. Through her experiences at Ballard and Arthurdale, Elsie had used these ideas to build her own conception of the community school. One is immediately struck by the photographs of children, some taken by noted photographers Arthur Rothstein and Dorothea Lange. Children are shown playing, swimming, resting, and sitting alongside their parents. Many of these children lived in inadequate housing, and did not have access to recreational facilities or access to health care. As she had always done, Elsie centered her focus on the needs of children and the best means to meet their needs.

The fall of 1937 was a busy time for Elsie as she edited her first issue and attended professional meetings associated with progressive education organizations. In October 1937 Elsie attended the Francis Parker Centennial Celebration in Chicago held at the Palmer House. The December 1937 issue of *Progressive Education* included many of the presentation and committee reports from the Celebration. In November Elsie traveled to Ann Arbor, Michigan, for the Michigan-Ontario-Ohio regional meeting of the PEA along with William Heard Kilpatrick of Teachers College and Alice Keliher, chair of the Commission on Human Relations and Growth. The theme for this conference was "Community Schools–An Objective for a Democracy." This theme was selected by the conference planning committee "because they believe that organized education in a democracy must serve the changing needs of the community."[13] In December Elsie traveled to Tulsa, Oklahoma, for the Southwestern Regional conference of the PEA, which included members from the states of Missouri, Kansas, Oklahoma, Arkansas, New Mexico, Arizona, and Texas. Public school teachers and parents participated in the conference. Conference participants included Caroline Zachry and Wilfred Aiken of Ohio State among others. Elsie followed this meeting, attending the Central Mission Regional conference in early December, which held meetings in neighboring communities prior to the meeting.

Under a tight time line Elsie edited the December issue dominated by a photo of Colonel Francis Parker. Focal pieces in the issue included Flora Cooke's article, "Colonel Francis Parker and His Influence on Education," and Jesse Newlon's article "Democracy and Education in Our Times."[14] During the Centennial conference Elsie had participated on a panel, discussing the Outlook for Youth in America, to examine problems confronting youth in America. The panel included Emory Filbrey, vice-president of the University of Chicago; Paul Hanna of Stanford University; and William Hinckley, president of the American Youth Conference.[15] Panel members voiced concern that the traditional focus in education was not meeting the needs of most students. In her discussion, Elsie stressed the problems of unemployment, the difficulties faced by youth out of work and with no place to live.[16] Speaking from her experience with the Works Progress Administration and the National Youth Administration, Elsie warned educators not to falsely assume other agencies would meet these needs. Educators should be attuned to the opportunities and resources offered and available in the local community.

Elsie had always centered her view of the community school on meeting the needs of children. The January 1938 issue cover was a North Carolina sharecropper's child wearing a burlap sack. Noted photographer Arthur Rothstein took the photograph. Honorary Vice-President of the PEA and Ohio State Professor Boyd Bode wrote the central article, "The Concept of Needs in Education." This issue is notable for its attention to drama, art, and poetry, all clear interests of Elsie's. The issue included a poem from Marni Mitchell, the daughter of Lucy Sprague Mitchell, and also work from Dahlov Zorach, the daughter of William Zorach.[17] The issue included articles on pioneer life, native life, mathematics instruction, banking, and summer theater, all topics Elsie had explored and continued to emphasize.[18]

Elsie contributed an article to the February 1938 issue titled "Schools Socially Functioning." She began the article by quoting a familiar passage from Dewey's *My Pedagogic Creed*. "Education being a social process," Dewey wrote, "the school is simply that form of community life in which all these agencies are concentrated that will be most effective in bringing the child to share in the inherited resources of the race, and to use his own powers for social ends."[19] She emphasized the moral duty to educate and believed that it is through education that society can shape, give it purpose, organize its resources, and move in the direction it wished. In a more radical twist Elsie quoted John Childs from *The Educational Frontier*. In a clear challenge to American capitalism, Childs had suggested that society employ science and technology in the direction of social rather than mere private ends, which required "the cooperative use of intelligence on a social scale in behalf of social values."[20] In the midst of economic depression, Elsie challenged schools and teachers they could not evade or deny their social responsibilities and these responsibilities could be addressed through the community school. Elsie saw the journal as a mechanism to share ideas and examples on "socially functioning community schools." For Elsie the goal of this issue was to "make clear the nature of the social function of a community school, in both city districts and rural areas. Education is seen to be a creative enterprise, a democratic process."[21] The role of the school was to reach out into the community, enhancing civic organization, participation, and an understanding various problems.

Clarence Pickett of the AFSC and former member of the Arthurdale School Advisory Committee also contributed an article.[22] Pickett wrote, "Community itself means communing, sharing, the passing of something from one to another, the experience the pouring forth of the inner life." Describing the community school was central to this issue, and Elsie solicited articles from George Beecher, Fletcher Collins, and Carson Ryan, former teachers at Arthurdale. Beecher and Collins were teaching at Elon College in North Carolina. Beecher wrote, "Resources for Learning in Alamance County, North Carolina." Collins contributed a piece on "Cultural Resources in America." Carson V. Ryan, now working on the Cherokee Reservation in North Carolina, authored "Science with the Eastern Cherokee Indians."[23]

Elsie continued to explore her interests in the March 1938 issue, "Resources in Education." She included photos of handicrafts, food, pottery, and woodcarvings from various parts of the United States, emphasizing cultural diversity. Photographs included work from Native Americans, Appalachians, African Americans, and Hispanics. Contributors to this issue were far less diverse, but included notables in progressive education such as Lucy Sprague Mitchell, M. L. Wilson, and Howard Odum, but also Max Lerner, George Counts, Ernest Hocking, John Dewey, Franz Boas, and James Harvey Robinson. Several authors were responding to themes on the interpretation of the work of political scientist Charles A. Beard. Beard along with John Dewey, Wesley Claire Mitchell, Thorstein Veblen, and James Harvey Robinson had worked together to form the New School for Social Research in 1919. According to Dewey biographer George Dykhuizen, the "New School" was to be "a center for learning where pressing political, economic and social problems could be discussed by adult men and come in an atmosphere of genuine freedom, without fear of recrimination."[24] Unfortunately Dykhuizen left out the women who were facing day-to-day social, economic, and political forces shaping their lives and the lives of their school children. This list included Lucy Sprague Mitchell, Caroline Pratt, Ella Flagg Young, Marietta Johnson, and Elsie Clapp. These women challenged the status quo in their own ways in their own type of feminism.

The April 1938 issue focused on rural education with the journal cover picturing young boys sitting on tree stumps reading at their rural school in the Cumberland Mountains. Wearing overalls, barefoot, obviously poor, they were all engrossed in reading. In 1938 there were still many one-room schools in the United States. The major theme of this issue was rural school housing, although there were three articles on reflective thinking of high school students. Elsie contributed a piece titled, "School Housing; Facts and Figures." Elsie's information and concern had grown from a report issued in January 1935 by the Research Division of the National Education Association in Washington, D.C. The report provided information on the age and shortage of adequate facilities in rural American schools.[25] From her childhood Elsie had exhibited an interest in architecture, but her interest here was not Gothic church architecture, but school architecture and its importance in meeting the needs of the child and community integrating the school plant with pedagogy, health, and recreation. "In recent years there has been a well-defined movement towards the school as a vital center in the life of our people," Elsie wrote. "In many cities, the schools are in use all of every day and evening for normal education work and for adult education and recreation."[26] Good citizens needed to be educated in proper surroundings. Elsie summarized the report's concerns; unsafe facilities, part-time attendance, portable and temporary structures and the age of school buildings. Approximately eighteen thousand school facilities in use at the time had been built before 1900. Upon viewing these facts, Elsie wrote, "One wonders why every conference of this past year that has discussed social education has not concentrated on this problem which so drastically discloses the imperative need to put the theory of social education into practice, a need that will not await the advent of a new social order."[27] There is no doubt here that Elsie was suggesting the discourse of the social reconstructionists was more theoretical than practical. It was simply out of touch. For her school people needed to talk about issues influencing the lives of the children daily. Elsie envisioned that if school was a socially functioning community school the needs of the child and community could be met. In her view there was no need for a new social order, "just one awakened to full use of its resources."[28]

Steward Wagner, the architect of the Arthurdale School, contributed an example of rural school architecture. In his article, "School Buildings: Arthurdale, West Virginia," Wagner emphasized his desire to design the school buildings to be an integral part of the community and "believed they increased the vitality and the life and work of the community." Most likely Elsie contributed a good portion of this article. As far as she was concerned here was clear evidence of a school system built on a tight budget, but containing facilities for science instruction, the arts, recreation, canning, and meeting the medical/dental needs of the community. The Arthurdale School buildings could become models for school districts throughout out the country, setting the stage for community schools.²⁹

The May 1938 issue continued to show Elsie's influence and interests. On the cover of the journal was a sculpture titled, *Flight*, which "interpreted through form the upward motion of a flying bird." The sculpture was by artist Jose Ruiz de Rivera, and a part of the Federal Art Project sponsored by the Works Progress Administration.³⁰ Although John Dewey contributed an article on "What Is Social Study?," the theme of the issue was art as it functions. The title rings of Dewey's pragmatism and his own view of art as communicative by nature, representing human experience. Dewey had suggested in *Experience and Nature* that art represented consumatory human experience and should not be confined to elite culture or in traditional art forms such as plays, paintings, sculpture, etc. Art was not something outside of human experience, but truly a form of transaction or interaction between artist and viewer. By its very nature art was communicative. Art, like life, for Dewey was "an ongoing transaction between an organism and its environment."³¹ In linking this to her own interest in the community school, Elsie included a quote from Dewey's *Art as Experience* published in 1934. "Works of art that are not remote from common life, that are widely enjoyed in a community, they are signs of a unified collective life. The remaking of the material of experience in the act of expression is not an isolated event confined to the artist and to a person here and there who happens to enjoy the work. In the degree in which art exercises its office, it is also a remaking of the experience of the community in the direction of great order and unity."³²

Writing the lead article in this issue was sculptor William Zorach, who supported many of Dewey's concerns. Zorach viewed the artist as expressing the ideas and aspirations of humankind and cautioned that one should be leery of compromising or commercializing the expression. "The greatest value of art work in education," Zorach wrote, "is in the part it plays in the development of a human being and the power it gives him of expressing his contacts with life."³³ According to Elsie and Zorach art was something of use and should be explored by all educators from early childhood to adult. Experience by its very nature, art could give us insight into our own humanity, a necessary step in understanding community.³⁴

During the period of Elsie's editorship, the journal was not published during the summer months, but the summer of 1938 was a busy one for members of the Progressive Education Association, with the annual meeting slated for Hawaii from June 19 through June 25. Association membership was at its highest with thirty-eight thousand.³⁵ From June 27 through August 5, Teachers College at Temple University and the PEA sponsored a summer program titled, "Elementary Education for the New School." The program was held at the

Oak Lane Country School and was to serve as an opportunity for participants to observe a demonstration school. Elsie participated at the conference in the afternoon sessions along with other progressive notables such as Laura Zirbes from Ohio State, W. Carson Ryan Jr., Gerald Craig of the Lincoln School, and Bess Goodykoontz, United States Assistant Commissioner of Education.[36]

Publication began again with the October 1938 issue and Elsie continued to explore her deep interests in the education of young children. The cover photo included a father sitting with his daughter and children from a nursery school. Elsie's experience at the nursery school at Arthurdale was clear.[37] Mrs. Roosevelt contributed a piece titled, "Education: A Child's Life." Mrs. Roosevelt was a strong advocate of the nursery school at Arthurdale and a champion for early childhood education. "The nursery school from my point of view," she wrote, "teaches the lesson which we need to learn; namely, what is real education for little children. It is not a question of some academic achievement, it embraces the whole of a child's environment. Every minute of the day and night is part of their education. The environment in which a child lives, the type of house, the type of living conditions, the people with whom he comes in contact–they all have a part in his education."[38] Mrs. Roosevelt went on to address her concerns about adequate health care, sanitation, disability, and accessibility as well as the need for recreation. She envisioned this form of social activity as a means to develop character, and all these components were necessary for true equality of opportunity. Eleanor Roosevelt expressed concerns relevant to contemporary education–the over stressing of academic achievement, embracing the environment of the child, and understanding what might be termed the formal, informal, and non–formal aspects of education. As one author expressed, the nursery school was a child welfare center in the sense that it met psychological needs, but also attempted to deal with the emotional, a combination of the psychological and sociological.[39]

The November 1938 issue continued to explore the theme of childhood education, but examined the period of middle childhood to early adolescence. Many of the articles expressed a concern for the lack of research in this area, and that middle to early adolescence was a distinct period in the life of a child. The authors emphasized the need to understand the years of transition from childhood to young adulthood and educators needed to pay attention to the transition.[40] The final issue of the year was the December 1938 issue, which explored early and late adolescence. With the Depression still entrenched, the cover exhibited a photo of an adolescent migrant worker by Dorothea Lange and a young child by Arthur Rothstein. For Elsie, understanding this period in a child's life was important in terms of directing and designing appropriate curriculum. The next publication of the journal was themed Adolescents in College and attempted to characterize the nature of American higher education. In the introductory editorial, W. Carson Ryan challenged the traditional approach of Robert Hutchins, president of the University of Chicago, who advocated a "segregated type of schooling."[41] The Eight Year Study was still in progress at the time and there was concern among progressives about how well students in progressive schools might do in a more traditional academic setting. Progressive themes were evident in articles written by college and university administrators such as Stringfellow Barr of St. Johns, Robert Leigh of Bennington, James Wood of Stephens College, David Bailey of Black Mountain College, and Constance Warren of Sarah Lawrence College. Progressive themes included viewing the institution as a community of learners, improving guidance, developing a more student, centered curriculum, seeking political and social equality, gender equity, and freedom coupled with responsibility.

The February 1939 issue was themed Education's Present Responsibility for Interpreting Democracy, with a photo of John Dewey on the cover. Authors included leaders and theorists in progressive education such as William H. Kilpatrick, George Counts, Merle Curti, John Childs, Alice Keliher, and Jesse Newlon. The authors were clearly aware of events in Europe with the rising tide of National Socialism and fascism and the threats they posed to democracy. Counts expressed his concerns writing "It (fascism) reduces the individual to the status of a slave of the state–a pawn to be used in the military aggrandizement of the nation and the apotheosis of the dictator. It mocks all the values which in the minds of men have come to be associated with the concept and practice of democracy."[42] All the authors emphasized the challenge and the important role education needed to play in protecting American democratic values. Alice Keliher suggested in her article, "Frontiers of Democracy," that "we must see that the essence of all living engages the democratic way in a truly democratic society."[43]

With the world moving closer to war, the March 1939 issue changed direction and focused on the Educational Use of Resources, a theme that will characterize Elsie's final contributions to progressive education. The devastation of the Depression had pushed educators and local communities to make better use of resources. These resources included health, recreation, housing, food, but also talent, culture, history, and folklore. George Beecher and Fletcher Collins contributed articles about the use of local resources. Collins wrote about "Local Resources from the Tobacco Country." George Beecher contributed "Local Resources from the Sciences and Social Studies." Beecher was involved in Alamance County, North Carolina, in a cooperative study of teacher training as they attempted to integrate science and social studies through an understanding of local resources. While the thrust was obviously on natural resources and how best to use them, the most vital resource was human in an era of growing inhumanity to man. Frederick Redefer, the executive secretary of the

Progressive Education Association, closed the issue by emphasizing renewed dialogue on discussing the philosophy of progressive education. This was a necessary task in light of the world circumstances where democracy seemed under attack from all sides. Progressive education was also coming under attack, perhaps the most significant critique being Dewey's own *Experience and Education* that challenged the excesses of traditional and progressive education. Dewey attacked the anti-democratic stance of the traditionalists who preferred a teacher/text-centered environment. But he also criticized the romantic side of progressivism, which failed to truly understand the responsibilities associated with freedom and democracy.[44]

The April and May 1939 issues were the last under Elsie's editorship. Elsie's friend and mentor William H. Kilpatrick graced the cover of the issue themed Teaching and Understanding Children. Elsie must have smiled as she viewed another photo of a young girl sitting at her desk holding a paper flower she had made. Her eyes were wide and bright, exuding excitement and pride with her creation. The photograph was simply subtitled *Ready*.[45] Three of Elsie's closest friends and colleagues made contributions to the issue. Jessie Stanton wrote, "What Is Education for the Child Before He Is Six?," Ellen Steele Reece, still the director of the Rosemary Junior School, contributed, "An Interesting Age to Teach," and George Beecher contributed a book review. Stanton emphasized the need to understand early childhood education, the nursery school being the primary place to educate "the whole child."[46] Elsie's close friend Ellen Steele Reece wrote about her experiences with eight- and nine-year-olds and how she worked to capture their interests, nurturing their curiosity and imagination. Photographs for both articles show hands-on activities, an active approach to learning. Redefer once again closed the issued describing the current educational scene. American schools were changing and European teachers now had to teach children civil defense and safety, learning first aid and how to wear gas masks.[47]

The March 1939 issue was Elsie's last as editor, and it focused on an issue dear to her heart, Art in Education and Art in Human Relations. The cover page showed a young four-year-old boy painting with intense concentration. Carson Ryan in his editorial pointed out Elsie's special contribution to this issue and wrote, "It would be difficult to find any one in the United State, as richly equipped by training, experience and point of view to organize a group of papers on this subject as Elsie Ripley Clapp, Editor of *Progressive Education*. If the papers in this issue make some contribution to the art of human relations, and if they succeed in making us a little more conscious of the deepening influence of the arts in our culture, they will have justified the time and energy that Miss Clapp has put into the task of reviewing appropriate articles and arranging them for our use."[48] A concern at the time was the manipulation of art by the National Socialists and Fascists and the threat to creative talent and democracy it made. The arts were a means of human expression and a necessary and vital component of any progressive education program.[49] While numerous pictures in the issue show the creative, imaginative, and communicative capacity of human beings, two of the most striking photos are of children living in dire poverty. With all the talk of war, Elsie refused to forget the human element in the necessity of meeting the needs of these children. The creative products and the pictures of the children were communicative in that they conveyed something about human relations and the human spirit.

Progressive Education during Elsie's short tenure emphasized what she felt were the primary issues affecting education. She had addressed many of the concrete issues surrounding rural education, such as school housing, the vital use of local resources, and the needs of children in rural poverty. She had emphasized the need to integrate art in the curriculum and to allow children the freedom to express their creativity and imagination. But most characteristic of Elsie's tenure as editor is the attempt to further articulate her conception of what she termed the "truly functioning community school." As she had stated in *Community Schools in Action* a community school "foregoes its separateness." It should be a vital part of the community and community was central to democracy as an ethical type of association.

Elsie published her most extensive work in community education in 1939, *Community Schools in Action*. In writing, Elsie utilized the diaries of Mary Elizabeth Sedman and Ethel Wadsworth, who headed the nursery school at Arthurdale. Teachers contributed several of the chapters, such as Jessie Stanton's discussion of the Arthurdale nursery school. Elsie also fully utilized reports written by Fletcher Collins, the Arthurdale director of drama and music, and George Beecher, the head of the Arthurdale high school.[50] It should be no surprise that Elsie dedicated the book to John Dewey, "whose philosophy and whose vision of the school as a social institution promoted our efforts to create a community school and to participate in community education."[51] Elsie noted the special contributions of Eleanor Roosevelt, whom she described as "sympathetic, insightful, fair, and courageous in the face of obstacles." She thanked W.W. Trent, State Superintendent of Schools in West Virginia during her work at Arthurdale, and also the Jefferson County Board of Education, which had oversight of the Ballard School. "The book is dedicated to children," Elsie wrote, "the boys and girls and to the families with whom and for whom the schools were established."[52]

Elsie asked Dewey to write the foreword to the book and he obliged. "It is a pleasure," Dewey wrote, "because reading the book has vividly recalled to me many stimulating conversations with its author in which the two schools were mentioned, and because of a most enjoyable visit to one of them, that at

Arthurdale."[53] Dewey seemed impressed by Elsie's ability to integrate theory and practice in fashioning a community school. A school was more than a formal institution; it provided a source to nurture and understand the human experience; "a school not only for, but of and by the community; the teachers being leaders in the movement, since they are themselves so identified with the community."[54] He championed how the Ballard and Arthurdale schools had based the curriculum and the community activities on the "basic instruments of life." He saw a link between the subject matter interest and experience and how the students began to see themselves as contributing members of the community. Dewey ended his comments with a powerful statement: "The report is a demonstration in practice of the place of education in building a democratic life."[55] Dewey could not have given Elsie or anyone else a higher compliment.

Although Dewey responded favorably to Elsie's chronicle of the Ballard and Arthurdale community schools, one reviewer challenged Elsie's book in the *Curriculum Journal*. The reviewer, Samuel Everett, a professor at Northwestern University, considered the book "a contribution to the growing literature on community education" and wrote, "It should be most useful to administrators and teachers because of the sympathetic understanding of the immediate vital problems faced in this type of education, and the story of the practical ways and means developed to solve these problems."[56] Everett challenged the book because he believed it had no concrete social philosophy. "The book is rich in suggestions of practical methods," he noted, "and rich in the quality of human contacts which is at the heart of everyday life in a democracy."[57] Everett believed that while Elsie had explored the practical in terms of curriculum in community programs, she had failed to relate the communities of Ballard and Arthurdale to the larger "social problems of modern America or of the South of which local problems are an inextricable part." "The programs described," Everett continued, "are not sufficiently intellectualized. Issues such as those of race, farm tenancy, unionization, conservation of human and natural resources, unemployment, paternalism, dictatorship, nationalism, the maldistribution of wealth and income in work, the sickness of an acquisitive society–are noticeable for their almost entire absence." Everett contended that Elsie's work should and could have been much richer if she had applied more critical analysis. Everett's view of the community school was one that led children to think through the major issues of the day, which he perceived as threats to democratic living.[58]

There is no record of Elsie's reaction or response to Everett, but Dewey responded to him in a letter dated April 29, 1940. Dewey wrote Everett in order to "clear up what seems to be a misunderstanding on your part of with the point of my introduction or of the text of Miss Clapp's report."[59] Dewey suggested to Everett that there was an underlying social philosophy in Elsie's work, the same philosophy he had expressed in *The Public and Its Problems* and the last chapter of *Freedom and Culture*. "I don't say this," Dewey wrote to Everett, "to indicate Miss Clapp's got the philosophy of her book from these writings, but on the contrary, to point out that the education policy of the school as she conducted it is a beautiful concrete exemplification of what I state in very general terms–the necessity of beginning with the local face to face community and developing the potentialities and resources, human and otherwise, if any serious attack is to be made upon the problem of larger society." Dewey continued to attack Everett's view suggesting that he held an opposing social philosophy to his, one that was too abstract, verbal, and controversial "instead of helping it get down to its vital tasks." Dewey ended the letter stating, "Please understand I shouldn't have written criticizing your review if it hadn't been that in your quotation from me you seemed to give it a turn the opposite of what was intended by me."[60]

Dewey's response to Samuel Everett seems much more than a teacher protecting one of his students. However, even a cursory reading of *The Public and Its Problems* and *Freedom and Culture* shows Dewey held an interest, like Everett, in dealing with the political, economic, and social forces that potentially undermined community and thus democracy. It does seem clear as Dewey insinuates, that Elsie's educational policy was not based on these works, certainly never a challenge to the capitalist order. Although Elsie certainly had the social welfare and political experience to offer cultural analysis she does not. A radical critique of the powers to be or the capitalist order never appears in any of her published writings, public correspondence or her personal memoirs. As Charlene Siegfried points out in her work *Pragmatism and Feminism*, Elsie was not a radical feminist and like her friend Lucy Sprague Mitchell both developed their feminist versions of pragmatism. Siegfried implies that Elsie did "not retreat to a women's sphere, but deliberately chose childhood education as a way of radically reinventing the social and political goals of the nation by developing the habits of thought and action before prejudices were hardened."[61] This is an accurate assessment.

Elsie's notion of the community school rested its foundation on meeting the needs of the individual child and this included education, health, and recreation. The school could serve as a social institution that could literally build community from the ground up. In this sense Elsie did view the school as a tool for social reform, but it was patient and one step at a time. While she seems to understand the community and democracy are deeply intertwined, she never articulates how the larger social concerns of racism, inequality, and paternalism undermine community. Dewey's support of Elsie's conception of the community school can be understood by examining such works as

The Public and Its Problems also published in 1939. Dewey strongly suggested that the great community went hand in hand with the realization of the local community, a goal that Elsie seems to have accomplished. Dewey wrote, "Democracy begins at home, and its home is the neighborly community."[62] Although not without their problems, Ballard and Arthurdale center the school in building, integrating and nurturing the neighborly community. But there is a problem here for Dewey and Elsie, and Samuel Everett articulated it. Historian and Dewey biographer Robert Westbrook suggests that Dewey in the late 1930s gave us little guidance in how to overcome the problems that undermined community, including those mentioned by Everett. Dewey's work is vitally silent on racism, although he did allow his name to be used to challenge social injustice.[63]

Elsie did receive a more positive review from Eduard C. Lindeman, professor of social philosophy at the New York School of Social Work. Lindeman praised the book in the sense that it helped him clarify the relationship between pupil, teacher and community. He wrote, "So far as I can learn from the material presented, in this volume in terms of curriculum the primary teacher-pupil relations, these teachers never lost sight of the fact that their fundamental responsibility was towards the organic growth of the pupils in their charge."[64] Lindeman suggests these took place in the attempt to link school projects with sanitation, agriculture, household crafts, recreation, parental education, cooperatives, cultural heritage, and civic responsibility. "Elsie Clapp and her colleagues have done something more," Lindeman wrote, "than to present a romantic tale of two progressive schools. They have furnished a vast amount of detail which is the hand book material for progressive teachers."[65] Both Everett and Lindeman saw the book for what it really was, a handbook for how to develop a community school. Elsie never saw the book as a blueprint, but she did see it as a chronicle of how two schools paid attention to the basic needs of children and to their experiences in developing curriculum. The needs of the child are related to the needs of the community.[66] She never envisioned the school as a tool for radical social reform.

Elsie was now living at 158 Waverley Place in New York City where in January 1940 she acknowledged a Christmas gift sent to her by Eleanor Roosevelt. Elsie wrote Mrs. Roosevelt and thanked her for the "goodies" and then detailed her future plans. "I have been in West Redding doing some writing on the educational use of resources," Elsie wrote Mrs. Roosevelt, "which Dr. Dewey believes should follow the record of the two community schools just published. I am of course eager to know if you approved of the record of the community school at Arthurdale. I tried to present a concrete, actual record and hope I included nothing that could in any way hurt the homesteaders or Arthurdale. As soon as the weather permits I am going down to Elon College in North Carolina to try to lay the foundation for a genuine kind of adult education in Alamance County, and to gather data with Fletcher Collins and George Beecher for presenting education use of resources."[67]

Elsie soon moved to Chapel Hill, North Carolina, near the University of North Carolina. *Community Schools in Action* had just gone into a second printing and Elsie felt justified in expanding her conception of the community school. "So it seems there is a public for this kind of education," a pleased Elsie wrote Mrs. Roosevelt.[68] Elsie spent much of her time working and researching in the University of North Carolina library, but she was far from content. She desperately wanted to be part of another community school and expressed that concern to Eleanor Roosevelt numerous times throughout the war years. However, times were changing and the United States was at full mobilization following the attack on Pearl Harbor, December 7, 1941. One month later Elsie wrote to Eleanor inviting her to visit her new residence in Burlington, North Carolina, near Fletcher and Margaret Collins' home. Feeling a need to contribute to the war effort, as she had in World War I Elsie wrote, "I wonder if I could not perhaps be used in community organization, a community education in the non-exclusive sense." Elsie graciously offered her services but had suffered a health problem that had drained her financial resources so any job offered had to meet her living expenses. "I laid up to acquire a fresh reserve of energy," Elsie wrote, "now my wise doctor says I am quite ready for active work again."[69]

Elsie developed a heart condition during the early 1940s, but was still attempting to complete her work on the use of resources. Back in New York in 1943 Elsie once again appealed to Eleanor to help her locate work. "I am well again," Elsie wrote to Mrs. Roosevelt, "and long to be used on some piece of work; I care very little about what the work is called. For the last three months I've been writing a book, prompted by John Dewey, trying to describe the resources people have and daily use—in themselves and in their relations with others, and in the particular place in which they live, and to tell about education's responsibility in helping people to use these resources intelligently and well. But I think—and this is why I am writing you—that if I know enough to write such a book, I shouldn't be writing at all but doing it, now, when it needs to urgently to be done."[70] In an attempt to help her friend, Eleanor Roosevelt put Elsie in contact with Edgar Kaiser, Charles Taft, and Dr. James Brunet for employment consideration, but their funding depended on the Thomas Bill in Congressional Committee, which was terminated June 30, 1943.[71]

By mid-July, Elsie still had no steady employment and she remained in New York. Elsie spent time in libraries at Columbia University and Teachers College. Still seeking full-time employment, she applied for a position at Connecticut State Teachers College at the beginning of the fall semester, but she did not take a position.⁷² A year later Elsie was assisting Dr. Frank Cyr during the winter term in his class on rural education at Teachers College. Elsie needed financial assistance and sought funding for her writing and research project from the John Simon Guggenheim Foundation and the Whitney Foundation. Both turned her down. Elsie's friend Eduard Lindeman suggested Elsie contact the John Dewey Society to see if they might be willing to financially support her writing project on the use of resources in education even though he was not a member of the Society at the time.⁷³ On April 8, 1947, Elsie followed Lindeman's suggestion and wrote a letter to Ernest Melby, dean of the School of Education at New York University. Elsie asked Melby if he thought the John Dewey Society would be interested to make possible the completion of her manuscript, *The Use of Resources in Education*, an "expression of Dr. Dewey's educational philosophy."⁷⁴ Dewey believed the book was needed, Elsie argued, "as a specific account of the ways in which these community schools enabled the children, boys and girls, and adults to comprehend and develop their resources in and through school studies and community activities." Elsie continued in her inquiry to Melby to explain what she meant by use of resources. "Essentially, the book is a description of Dewey's educational philosophy in action. For the work of these schools in the educational use of resources was an attempt to execute an understanding of the educative process gained through my years of association with Dr. Dewey, as a student, and later as assistant in the courses he gave at Teachers College and Columbia University in Education and Philosophy." Elsie informed Melby that Drs. Edmund deS Brunner, William H. Kilpatrick, and John Dewey would also be writing to him to discuss her work.⁷⁵ Upon receipt of Elsie's letter, Melby agreed to bring it to the attention of the John Dewey Society at the next meeting of the board of directors.⁷⁶

By mid-summer Elsie had not heard from Melby, who apparently did not acknowledge the letters sent by Brunner, Kilpatrick, and Dewey. Dewey tried to phone Melby in July, but could not reach him. Dewey was on his way to Hubbards, Nova Scotia, and had just married Roberta Lowitz Grant and shared with Elsie a personal note. "I am glad to report that I seem to be in a very good state of health. Married life agrees with me; as I suppose a dozen persons or more have remarked to me that they had not seen me looking so well for years."⁷⁷ A month later, Dewey wrote Elsie that Melby had responded, although the news was not encouraging because the Society had limited funds. Dewey suggested to Elsie that she write a synopsis of the work expressing her knowledge of progressive education. Dewey was angered that the Guggenheim and Whitney Foundations would not support her work. "The Foundations seem as bat-blind to where their support might best go—or maybe it is cockeyed, as Boards are inclined to be. As the Boston philanthropist said, Boards are hard, long and narrow."⁷⁸ No doubt Elsie chuckled at Dewey's sense of humor.

Thanking Dewey for his kind and supportive advice, Elsie developed a synopsis of the book and sent a copy to Dewey and the John Dewey Society. Elsie expressed to Dewey her concerns and wrote, "I feel so far away from Progressive Education, now that I feel that I have nothing to say about it. Its principles I have long assimilated, and the movement of which I was an active part seems now to have flowed into other channels." Elsie had sensed that progressive education had passed her by and she was correct in that assumption. She was a member of the old guard, many, whom were now aging and not as active in the association. Regardless, Elsie refused to capitulate and continued to pursue her project. [79]

Finally, Elsie received word from I.N. Thut, executive secretary/treasurer of the John Dewey Society, that the proposal was under consideration. Thut also informed Dewey that the proposal was receiving serious consideration.[80] Thut suggested to Elsie that if she published with the Society that the book serve as the John Dewey Society Yearbook.[81] Elsie immediately sent the letter to Dewey to get his response. "I know practically nothing about the John Dewey Society," Dewey ironically responded to Elsie, "and the only point on which I can form an opinion of the matters you bring up is the evident desirability of your finding out just what is meant by joint authorship."[82] Prior to the board meeting of the John Dewey Society, Elsie sent Thut a description of the nature and content of her proposed book. She explored the possibility of the Yearbook and also requested six hundred dollars for the grant and a fifty percent share of royalties.[83] In the proposal Elsie emphasized that she had targeted the book to teachers and explained to Thut, "The book I have in preparation is an account of how a group of teachers, working in public schools in two different rural areas, became acquainted with the resources the children and their families used daily as they lived, and helped them understand and developed these in studies in school and in community activities."[84]

In late October Thut responded to Elsie and informed her the Board would meet on November 10 and 11 and Thut asked her if she could complete the entire manuscript by early June 1948. Taken aback by Thut's request, Elsie indignantly wrote back, "As you probably know, it is not easy to gauge the time necessary to complete a book. My first book, comparable in size, took me a year and a half to write, and I think this one will take approximately the same time."[85] After responding to Thut, Elsie fired off a letter to Kilpatrick, stating she refused to submit a "hasty and unfinished piece of work." "Although I am willing of course to fit as far as possible into the Society's publication requirement," Elsie wrote, "there is no sense in promising something which cannot be done."[86] Elsie had stopped writing at the time and needed the grant to support herself financially and to dedicate the time to finish the task. Kilpatrick responded to Elsie attempting to keep her on task. Kilpatrick was scheduled to be present at the Board meeting of the John Dewey Society and agreed to oppose the June deadline. He also suggested that if Elsie could convince Dewey to write the introduction it might greatly enhance her proposal request.[87] With the strong support Elsie received from Dewey and Kilpatrick, the John Dewey Society decided to publish *The Use of Resources in Education*. Dewey wrote the Board thanking them for supporting the work and he agreed to write the introduction to the work. Thut suggested that Harper and Brothers might be the best publisher.[88] Elsie finally received, some financial support for her work in the sum of seven hundred and fifty dollars to be paid in quarterly installments at her request. Dewey seemed pleased that Elsie was awarded the grant and requested from her the first half the book so he could write the introduction.[89]

Elsie directed her work to teachers, to staff of teacher training institutions, to departments of education, rural educators, sociologists, and social workers. She saw *The Use of Resources in Education* [hereafter URE] as a sequel to *Community Schools in Action*. While Elsie had been in touch with several possible publishers for the work, including Viking and Macmillan, Thut insisted on Harper and Brothers.[90] Elsie seemed content that Harper and Brothers was interested. She was spending the winter with Mrs. Daniel Hartwell in Exeter, New Hampshire. Thut expressed his willingness to visit Elsie in New Hampshire and also indicated his interest in her work. "I am very much interested in the materials you have in preparation," he wrote Elsie, "but above all I anticipate with much pleasure the possibility of meeting you personally. We have a great many friends and acquaintances in common."[91] This must have surprised Elsie since she thought many of Thut's requests were unreasonable and demanding.[92]

Elsie expressed to Kilpatrick in the early fall of 1948 that she was experiencing difficultly in completing the final portions of the book and cutting portions of the text. "This may sound promising, " Elsie wrote to Kilpatrick, "but at the moment, I feel further off from the end that I did in the beginning."[93] Dewey had been ill and had not reviewed the manuscript so Elsie was writing to Kilpatrick to reaffirm her purpose in writing URE. She was still having difficulty financially and even sold one of her paintings to buy writing materials. Elsie did not feel she could ask Thut to give her additional funds for the project. Dewey finally wrote to Elsie and discussed his ideas with her for writing the introduction. "I have thought quite likely that I would say something about the main practices generally and the need for a new and constructive examination of education theory and practice, in the direction of the kind of community connections you report."[94] In closing the letter Dewey wrote, "In any case I can't improve on your linking of living and learning–and the resulting benefits to each of the links." Kilpatrick responded, "I don't think

CHAPTER TWELVE

that I can make any helpful suggestions. The plan as you describe it sounds very good. The book, I believe will prove very useful. When you get it ready I shall be glad myself to see the manuscript."[95] Illness slowed Elsie's progress, not only her own, but Dewey's. While kindly probing him to see if he had time to work on the manuscript Elsie constantly asked about his health. "I am glad to be writing you because I always feel a little anxious when I have not heard from you in some time. I hope you are well and that people like me do not bother you too much."[96]

By early October 1949, Elsie had finished her first draft of the manuscript and sent copies to Kilpatrick and Dewey. Dewey apologized to Elsie for not finishing the introduction he had promised to write but had just returned from Jamaica and was finishing an introduction for a new edition of *Experience and Nature* to be printed by Beacon Press. Dewey was ninety at the time and beginning to experience serious health problems, although he sought to remain active and sincerely wished to help Elsie.[97] Elsie was not only concerned about Dewey's health, but the future of progressive education. She had expressed earlier that she felt left out and that the movement was moving without her. There is much truth to her assumption. She had a deep love for Dewey as a mentor, but also a faith in his pragmatism. Dewey sent Elsie an article, "Philosophy's Future in Our Scientific Age," from an issue of *Commentary*. Elsie replied to Dewey suggesting, "I don't know that you wish to do it, but there is no one but yourself who can develop the methods of inquiry into human conditions for one thing the ground has been cleared and prepared in your *Logic*. And who else so conceives philosophy? You have pointed out the road and indicated its course and direction–but who but yourself can now take it? What I am suggesting is perhaps not too arduous–this article in *Commentary* to be followed by others describing the control and reaches of human knowledge."[98] Elsie closed the letter on a more personal note. "I hope that the birthday party was not too strenuous and that you enjoyed the people there and their expression of honor and admiration."[99] Elsie needed Dewey to help pull her through once again, to bolster her confidence, but in reality she cared deeply about him even when he informed Elsie he had lost all his notes to her manuscript and needed her to send previous correspondence to jog his memory.[100]

Soon Thut notified Elsie of the upcoming board meeting of the Executive Board of the John Dewey Society and asked her about her delay. Thut knew Elsie was behind in finishing the manuscript and offered help and assistance. Once again Elsie's health had plagued her and now she was experiencing back problems coupled with the heart ailment. Elsie informed Thut that the manuscript was now in the hands of Dewey and Kilpatrick.[101] Although Dewey, Kilpatrick, deS Brunner, and Lindeman had the manuscript by February 1950, none had offered analysis of any kind. Events were moving too slowly for Elsie. Lindeman had been ill, deS Brunner had been out of the country, Kilpatrick overworked, and Dewey was exhausted from the birthday celebration and other writing projects.[102] Now finished with the manuscript, Elsie spent much of her time painting New Hampshire landscapes. Kilpatrick and deS Brunner soon finished their reviews, but Lindeman and Dewey had not responded. It was Dewey's judgment that mattered most to Elsie. Lindeman responded in May 1950; although he had not finished the work he expressed enthusiasm for it.[103] That same month the manuscript was in the hands of Harper and Brothers without Dewey's introduction. Age and illness had prevented him from writing, but he was still determined to help Elsie. One evening Dewey awoke in the middle of the night expressing his concern to Roberta that he needed to finish the work he promised. Elsie soon began to converse with Roberta, who considered Elsie a dear friend of the Dewey family.[104] Elsie's work was now in the hands of the publishers and soon she heard critique from the Harper and Brothers editor Ordway Tead. Tead praised Elsie's conceptualization of the work, but believed the reader would get lost in the detail. He suggested a summary of each chapter to clarify points. "Presumably, the major audience of this volume is teachers," Tead wrote Elsie, "and I confess I feel they will get lost in the trees without seeing the woods." Tead believed the work was too long, larger than a normal yearbook and thus more expensive to produce.[105]

Irked at Tead's request, Elsie replied to him, but not until she had heard from Kilpatrick with whom she shared Tead's letter. Kilpatrick advised Elsie to pay attention to Tead's advice and experience, but not allow him to dictate the content of the manuscript. Elsie agreed that the text was lengthy, but urged that it was a source book and contained actual teacher reports and daily entries, making the work longer than normal. She grudgingly agreed to cut the work by fifty pages and believed that would allow for greatly clarity, negating the need for chapter summaries. Still fuming about Tead's comment Elsie wrote Kilpatrick, "His [Tead's] comments however indicate that he is not conversant with the educational philosophy the book expounds. Accustomed to the mere usual style of educational writing, and unaware evidently of the interests among educational circles in resource use education, the book seemed to him I think wearisome and filled with uninteresting and unimportant detail."[106] Regardless of her feelings, Elsie made the necessary cuts and Tead seemed generally pleased and offered her a contract on the book. Tead was anxious to have Dewey's introduction to finalize plan for publication. Elsie knew Dewey's contribution was a central component of the book and wrote a note of concern to Roberta Dewey. "Perhaps I can say to you," Elsie wrote Roberta, "as I can't to Dr. Dewey, that I do not think it is incumbent upon him to write a long or full introduction. If he feels able to write a few paragraphs, and is content to do that, he will have done all and more than anyone has a right to expect. He should do as he wishes and I have no wish to dictate, only a desire to spare him."[107] Elsie was not sure Dewey could compete the task and the deadline was fast approaching.

Due to the delays Elsie did not sign an official contract with Harper and Brothers until November 20, 1951. She agreed to have the complete manuscript, with Dewey's introduction, at the publishers by February 1, 1951.[108] The deadline came and went with no materials from Dewey. Elsie wrote him in Honolulu, Hawaii. "I judge, since I have received no material, that it did not prove possible to write as you had hoped to do. And I am writing to say that I shall be far more content if you will now dismiss this piece of work from your mind and not let it trouble you anymore." Elsie reiterated in the note that *The Use of Resources* was really a dedication to his philosophy. "There is no way to express my lifelong indebtedness to you for your guidance in my thinking, and in whatever I have been able to do with and for the children and parents and teachers with whom I have worked. I have been, and still am, your eager student."[109]

It was November 1951 before the publishers had Dewey's introduction. Dewey never completed the introduction he had originally planned. Joseph Ratner had assisted Roberta Dewey in pulling together notes Dewey had taken on Elsie's book. Elsie continued to read proofs while still residing in Exeter, New Hampshire. She communicated with Kilpatrick and thanked him for his gracious support and patience. By April 1952 the book had been published and Elsie sent a copy to Dewey, Kilpatrick, deS Brunner, Lindeman, and Eleanor Roosevelt.[110] Elsie suggested that Ordway Tead send review copies to *Childhood Education, Elementary School Journal, Parent's Magazine, the Nation, Schools Educational Forum, Curriculum Journal, Journal of Adult Education,* and the *Louisville Courier Journal,* a newspaper that might have interest in the Ballard School. Elsie did not request a copy be sent to *Progressive Education* nor was the work ever reviewed by that journal.[111] Elsie made arrangements with Tead to have the book sent to various State Departments of Education, Colleges of Education, and State Superintendents and Supervisors of Rural Education. Elsie also wrote Dewey expressing her appreciation for his help and that *The Use of Resources in Education* was an attempt to integrate his philosophy of education into practice. "I am mindful how you taught me during the years I worked with you," Elsie wrote, "and how that without your guidance and encouragement I would not have undertaken and could not have carried through efforts such as those the book describes. It is then, with gratitude and deep abiding love that I am sending this transcript to you."[112]

Elsie's last contribution to progressive education was now in the public domain. Harper and Brothers' announcement described the book as a report "of the ways in which two public rural schools helped children and adults use and develop their resources." The targeted audience for the book included teachers and principals, early childhood educators, teacher training institutions, rural educators, adult educators, sociologists, social workers and health workers. The announcement also built upon Dewey's reputation and Elsie's association with him and quoted from the introduction. "Miss Clapp has not only given a full, vivid and convincing description of the practical phases of the work, what was done anyhow; she has also given a clear and illuminating interpretation of its theoretical content and meaning; the purposes that inspired it, the leading principles that guided it, the educational philosophy of which it is an expression and embodiment."[113]

Regardless of the announcement and Elsie's expectations, the book sold slowly. Between June 1952 and December 31, 1954, only 1,114 regular copies had been sold with seventy-five copies sold at a special discount. The total sale for the period was 1,489. Another 1,011 copies needed to be sold before royalties increased according to the initial contract. Due to slow sales Elsie wanted to contribute her share of the royalties to the John Dewey Society to repay the writing grant. She also arranged that year upon her death royalties were to go to the John Dewey Society. As president of the Society, Kilpatrick responded to Elsie's desire and refused to accept her royalty check for $127.34 until she assured him she was financially stable. She responded to Kilpatrick in confidence. "Thank you for your letter of May 10th. To answer your question: Confidentially at the moment my needs are, with the help of family, adequately met so I am able this year to use the royalties on the book as I see fit. What will be true in ensuing years I do not know."[114] Elsie expressed hope that the sales of the book would increase, suggesting that *Community Schools in Action* also had a slow start. She closed her letter with a sense of reality. "Aside from the merits or defects of *The Use of Resources in Education*, its publication took place just after Dr. Dewey's death, appreciably at the close of an era in education. Whether or not there will be a revival of interest in its subject I do not myself know."[115] Elsie sensed the loss of the prophet meant the demise of the movement.

Kilpatrick accepted Elsie's check and sent it to Thut. Thut showed a great deal of compassion and concern for Elsie. "The society had not intended that you guarantee the return of the advance," Thut wrote Elsie, "but had hoped that you would look at this arrangement as a mutual undertaking in the interests of better education. I know you have been deeply disappointed in the sales of this book, but as any publishers can tell you, all sale has been exceedingly slow in recent years. Our yearbook sales have been especially disappointing of late, and, indeed, it has become difficult for us to recover the cost of preparing

CHAPTER TWELVE 233

them. I offer this information in the hope that you will not look upon your effort to bring forth this significant and worthwhile publication as a failure, or that your book in any way unusual, since sales have not lived up fully to your original expectations."[116]

No doubt Elsie appreciated Thut's kindness, yet she was deeply disappointed at the sale of *The Use of Resources in Education*. As she correctly sensed, perhaps the slow sales of the book was clear evidence that American education was entering a new era and she had been left behind. Elsie had planned to continue writing, exploring a history of how Americans as a people had come to make "use of their resources" and actually began to write, but never finished the project. Her health was declining and she knew the times had changed. Elsie was suffering from back pain, bursitis, and heart problems. Her physical suffering was compounded by the loss of a dear friend, the journal *Progressive Education*. From 1937 to 1939, Elsie had labored and given her all to conceptualize the community school and how schools and teachers come to fully utilize their community resources. American Education had entered a new era, not one conducive to building community schools and democracy, but one driven by Cold War conservative political and market economic forces. Perhaps in an effort to understand herself and to explain her work, Elsie began to write her memoirs. In the last decade she had lost two dear friends, her mentor John Dewey and the journal *Progressive Education*. Times were tough for Elsie Ripley Clapp and progressive education.[117]

Chapter Thirteen

Epilogue

Despite constant concern about health, Elsie published *The Use of Resources in Education* at age seventy-three. She knew the world had changed and so had progressive education. In the Cold War climate of the 1950s the prospects of a book on community schools were not promising. Progressive educators were clearly on the defensive. Articles in the January 1952 issue of *Progressive Education* included, "Meeting Attacks on Public Schools," "Essentialism in Education," "Anticipating Progressive Education Attacks," and "The Charges Against American Education: What Is the Evidence?"[1] Progressives were more interested in defending themselves against the attacks of essentialists and realists such as Mortimer Adler, Robert Hutchins, James B. Conant, Arthur Bestor, and Hyman Rickover. Cremin described the changing times in *The Transformation of the School*. "The search for Gemeinshaft of the nineties had become the quest for pluralism of the fifties, while the rampant individualism that Dewey so earnestly feared was now widely applauded as nonconformity. The economy had entered upon an era marked by the harnessing of vast new sources of energy and the rapid extension of automatic controls in production, a prodigious advance that quickly outmoded earlier notions of vocational education."[2]

For Cremin as well as Dewey and Elsie, Gesellshaft seemed to be the order of the day. Growing individualism had the potential to fragment community, not unite it. Elsie envisioned the school as the center of community life, the nucleus of the community, even though postwar cultural norms and mores were favoring the atomistic individual. Dewey had viewed the school as a means to help the child understand its place in the community and saw the school as a tool to saturate the student "with the spirit of service and providing him with the instruments of effective self direction."[3] Social pragmatist George Herbert Mead championed this notion, stressing that we are who we are based upon our membership in the community.[4] Progressive educator Joseph Hart wrote, "The democratic problem is not primarily one of training children; it is the problem of making a community in which children cannot help growing up to be democratic, intelligent, disciplined to freedom, revered of the goods in life; and eager to share in the tasks of the age."[5]

Community was the foundation from which democracy was built, but it was under girded by an ethic. This ethic, what Dewey termed sympathetic character, was what guided ethical association, the interactions between and within a collective of people. The collective by itself did not make community and that was the fear of Gesellshaft. So how does one learn to be part of the community? For John Dewey and Elsie Clapp education helped serve that purpose. As they saw it, individuals needed to be socialized to the ethic of sympathetic character; they were not born with it. Education by its very nature, like life, was experimental. As James Campbell states, "This experiment can be enhanced by the recognition that the well-being of each individual is bound up with the well-being of others within the community and throughout the world."[6] The self is not a given; it emerges through experience, transaction and interaction in the environment.[7] Self-realization is communal.

Dewey was a philosopher; it was his students like Elsie Clapp who sought to nurture community, to put the ideas they read and learned in class into practice. Interestingly, Samuel Everett, who criticized Elsie's book *Community Schools in Action*, supports this view. Everett argued in 1938 that there was a separation of theory and practice in the public schools, in essence a dualism. He sought through his own work to unify theory and practice, just like Elsie thought she was doing with the community school. She was successful in many facets.[8]

Two months after the publication of *The Use of Resources*, Carmelita Hinton, the director of the Putney School in Vermont, "a coeducational college preparatory boarding school," published an article in *Progressive Education* titled, "A School that Attempts to Be a Community." Hinton described her community school as a place where "rural and city children learn first hand about country life. They treasure it and are made wholesome by it," and eventually are "better able to understand the impact of adult tensions."[9] Hinton made no mention of Elsie's work on community schools. Later that year, the October issue of *Progressive Education* was dedicated to John Dewey in honor of his passing. Contributors included Max Otto, Boyd Bode, William H. Kilpatrick, Eduard Lindeman, Herbert Schneider, Jerome Nathanson, and H. Gordon Hullfish. No women were apparently asked to contribute to the issue, a gross oversight by the editorial leadership. No serious educational journal reviewed Elsie's book except *School and Society*. Here the reviewer applauded Elsie's "painstaking accuracy" and suggested the book had much to offer environments similar to Ballard and Arthurdale. He also praised the "subject matter index." Another review appeared in the *Springfield Republican*. It implied the book was for "all who are concerned with modern elementary education, this important pioneer work with community schools will be of great interest."[10] Elsie's work was never reviewed by *Progressive Education* and *The Use of Resources in Education* was not listed by the journal as a book of special interest to teachers. This issue listing the works of special interest was dedicated to responding to Arthur Bestor's *Educational Wastelands*.[11] Progressive education was clearly entrenched. In the July 1957 issue of *Progressive Education*, H. Gordon Hullfish, a professor at Ohio State and executive treasurer of the John Dewey Society, announced the issue to be the last. "Readers of progressive education will not be surprised," Hullfish wrote, "to discover that the magazine end as it started, as a constructive critic of educational thought and practice."[12]

That same year the Soviets launched Sputnik and according to Cremin "a shocked and humbled nation embarked on a bitter orgy of pedagogical soul-searching."[13] Cremin suggests progressive education was a victim of its own success, but one wonders if Elsie saw herself as a victim of success at this point in her life. Probably not. She was frustrated at the lack of response her work had received, but she also believed she had made a significant contribution to education, and she had. America was now a superpower along with the dreaded Soviet Union. While Dewey and many of his followers, including Elsie, sought community, the war generated economy fostered individualism, a new kind of pioneer spirit more attuned to rugged individualism. This pioneer spirit was not the spirit of barn raising or the New England town meeting Dewey remembered, but one lost in a growing crass materialism and consumerism. The new movement fostered the growth of suburbia and the building of interstates with more cars that used more energy and created more pollution. People lived inside their homes in a type of insular isolation and entertained themselves with a new technology called television. The neighborhood, the community, became more of a geographical designation than a communal one.

In the late 1950s Elsie's old energy was renewed when she began corresponding with Una Sait, also a former student of Dewey's. They began to correspond on two issues, one being the centennial celebration of Dewey's birthday (1959) and the other working on collecting memories and materials from former students on Dewey. Following several discussions, Elsie and Una decided that the centennial celebration was beyond their physical capabilities. "And though the idea of a 100th anniversary memorial celebration has many possibilities," Elsie wrote Una, "I can see that the difficulties of organizing and carrying through such a celebration are enormously increased by the many deaths that have occurred and the fact that those of us who knew and worked with Dewey are in no shape physically to undertake the labors involved."[14] Elsie and Una began to collect materials they had on Dewey. Elsie collected materials to be sent at some point to an archive for possible future study about progressive education and how Dewey's thought was applied through her work. Elsie was most attracted to the suggestion of collecting Dewey's work, notes, letters, and memorandum, which were largely in the hands of his former students, colleagues, and his wife Roberta Dewey. Elsie suggested to Una Sait at the time that Columbia University be the major depository/recipient of the materials. Elsie's own library contained approximately 30 books by Dewey, numerous reports of journal articles, journal articles, lecture notes, and a scrapbook of clippings.[15] Elsie spent the last years of her life writing her own memoirs and painting. Unfortunately, the memoirs exist only through 1929, the year she left for Louisville to direct the Ballard School in Kentucky. Most likely Elsie wrote her memoirs for family members, and she always held an interest in genealogy. Yet in reading what she termed autobiographical notes, it seems clear she was trying to reach a wider audience. Elsie wanted to be understood. She wanted the student of progressive education to have access to her work and attempt to understand how she interpreted Dewey's philosophy and had applied it in practice. She believed *Community Schools in Action* and *The Use of Resources in Education* described her and clarified what she believed should be the relationship between the school and the community.

Politically Elsie was a liberal, although she was not a radical feminist even though she often associated with many. Elsie's feminism was grounded through her pragmatism out of which grew her own "ethic of caring." As discussed by modern theorists such as Carole Gilligan and Nel Noddings, this ethic was related to responding to a perceived need. Judy Long in *Telling Women's Lives* writes, "This ethic of care is an expansive orientation, representing women's sense of responsibility and concern for a widening circle. It is a morality not limited to the family or the household; women's leadership in many areas of public and community life is motivated by this ethos... Indeed, the ethic of care makes women responsible for the well-being of the world," fostering the link of relationships.[16] But Elsie's ethic extends beyond her gender. She was what Charlene Siegfried calls a "pragmatist feminist." "A pragmatist feminist," writes Siegfried, "assumes the social construction of gender, one which avoids the negative aspects of equating care with biological functions by emphasizing the conceptual basis for the perceived differentiation rather than the gender basis."[17] Elsie built this ethic into her conception of the community school. For her social welfare and meeting the needs of the child went beyond political or ideological affiliation, it meant becoming part of the community, personally and professionally. A true community school for Elsie was one that engaged people working with people for people, and the school served as the key institution by which to build this solidarity.

For Elsie Clapp community was best formed through education, not through violent social class conflict or revolution that might, as Charlene Siegfried suggests, keep "old habits, such as sexism and racism, unchanged."[18] Elsie always saw education as the key to social reform even as early as 1913 when she participated in the Paterson Silk Workers Strike, not through indoctrination or intimidation as advocated by George Counts. This holds true for her work in the suffragist's movement, supporting birth control, investigating white slavery, and helping the children of the workers and the poor displaced by the Depression. Elsie developed her own version of feminism, a type of welfare liberalism.[19] However, regardless of Elsie's focus on community and the school she never lost sight of the children and their basic human needs and those needs took many forms. The child needed access to health care, proper nutrition, and forms of recreation, but there was more; the child needed to feel a part of something This was the role of the community school. Children were children, not miniature adults, and needed to be treated as such. Elsie believed children by nature desired to express themselves and should be allowed the freedom to do so through art, construction, play drama, and music. As a progressive Elsie tried to make education humane, to capture the human spirit. This does not confirm that Elsie was "child centered," for she never separated the child from its social needs. The child was an individual, but also a member of a community. Where many progressives failed, including Elsie and Dewey, was the failure to extend the boundary of community to challenge vestiges of sexism, racism, and social class. Regardless of these shortcomings, and they are serious, Elsie made significant contributions to progressive education.

Cremin describes Elsie's view of the progressive school in *Transformation of the School*. "First it meant helping the program and function of the school to include direct concern for health, vocation and the quality of family and community life." It further meant "applying in the classroom the pedagogical principles derived from new scientific research in psychology and the social sciences." Lastly it meant the curriculum needed to be attuned to the "different kinds and classes of children who were both within the purview of the school."[20] Elsie's major thrust was in rural education, although she believed her ideas could work in urban settings. For her urban teachers could certainly build community schools and fully utilize the resources surrounding their communities.[21] Like Dewey wrote in *Democracy and Education*, upon which Elsie had commented, community was characterized by "unity of purpose, loyalty to public ends and mutuality of sympathy." It was in community where "sympathetic character" could be nurtured, where one gained an understanding of self and developed empathy for the other.[22] This is what contemporary educators need to understand. This is Elsie's greatest contribution to American education. While there is always conflict and misunderstanding in human interaction, educators need to work to foster an environment where children learn to be themselves, but also that they have responsibility to others. Education needs to become more compassionate and cooperative, and less competitive. The school should be a place where one learns to become a better human being. As Dewey suggested and Elsie fostered through her work, it is "mutual respect, mutual tolerance, give and take, the pooling of experiences."[23]

Elsie struggled with health problems the last years of her life. She spent her last years in Exeter, New Hampshire, under the care of Mrs. Daniel Hartwell, who provided room and board. Elsie continued writing and painting.[24]

On July 28, 1965, at the age of 86 Elsie's heart failed and she passed away. *The New York Times* carried her obituary on July 31. It described her as a special assistant to John Dewey and Teachers College "who put into practice his theories on progressive education at the Ballard Memorial School, Jefferson County, Kentucky from 1929–1934, and as a Director of Arthurdale School and Community Activities, Arthurdale, West Virginia from 1934 to 1936." The obituary carried a special heading, "Miss Elsie Clapp, 86, Aide of John Dewey." For Elsie no better epitaph could have been written.[25]

Illustrations

Figure 1. William Gamwell Clapp in 1879, the year of Elsie's birth
(Courtesy of Barbara and Sheldon Rahn ©2004)

Figure 2. Elsie posing with her chinchilla muff
(*Courtesy of Barbara and Sheldon Rahn ©2004*)

Figure 3. Elsie and her younger sister Marjorie
(*Courtesy of Barbara and Sheldon Rahn ©2004*)

Figure 4. Elsie, her mother Sarah Louise Ripley Clapp, Marjorie and Lawrence Circa 1897
(*Courtesy of Barbara and Sheldon Rahn* ©2004)

Figure 5. A nine-year-old Elsie posing with flowers
(*Courtesy of Barbara and Sheldon Rahn* ©2004)

Figure 6. Elsie as a young girl
(*Courtesy of Barbara and Sheldon Rahn* ©2004)

Figure 7. Elsie in her later teens
(*Courtesy of Barbara and Sheldon Rahn* ©2004)

Figure 8. Elsie in her basketball letter sweater from Vassar
(Courtesy of Barbara and Sheldon Rahn ©2004)

Figure 9. Elsie as a young woman ready to begin her career as a teacher
(Courtesy of Barbara and Sheldon Rahn ©2004)

Notes

Introduction

*Portions of this chapter were presented as "Telling the Life Story: Intentions and Caveats" at the International Society for Educational Biography, April 2000, Chicago, Illinois.

1. Samuel Johnson, "The Rambler," No. 60. In *Dictionary of Quotations*. Edited by Bergen Evans (New York: Crown, 1968), p. 59.
2. For the source of Emerson's quote, see Craig Kridel, *Writing Educational Biography: Explorations in Qualitative Research* (New York: Garland, 1998), p. 7. I have stretched Stephen Oates' categories for biographical research, which include the scholarly chronicle, critical study, and narrative. I have attempted to combine the best of each approach. I have used the traditional historical method and rigor, have attempted to use her voice, critiqued her when she did not live up to the vision of democratic community, and have tried to capture the "warmth of a life being lived." See Stephen Oates, *Biography as History* (Waco, Tx: Mankam Press Fund, 1991), p. 11. I owe this insight to Craig Kridel's introduction in *Writing Educational Biography*, pp. 9–10.
3. See George Herbert Mead, *Mind, Self, and Society* (Chicago: University of Chicago Press, 1934). Mead writes: "one cannot take the attitude of identifying himself with the other without in some sense tending to set up such communities. It is a particular function of history to enable us to look back and see how far such social reconstruction has taken place...," p. 297. See also Jack Campbell, "Inside Lives: The Quality of Biography," In Robert Sherman and Rodman Webb, *Qualitative Research in Education: Focus and Method* (Philadelphia: Falmer Press, 1990), p. 70.
4. Diana Moyer uses the term "dutiful daughter" in her Ph.D. dissertation, *Sentimentalists and Radicals* (Columbus: Ohio State University Press, 2001).
5. Thomas Hutcheson, *The Process and Content of Community Education for Participatory Community Planning in Two Towns in Massachusetts* (Ph.D. diss., University of Massachusetts, 1993), p. 19.
6. Catherine Surdovel, *Community Education: 1890 to the Present* (Ph.D. Diss., Rutgers University, 1985), pp. 63–64.
7. Diana Moyer, *Sentimentalists and Radicals*, p. 137. This point should also make us leery of the categories of administrative and social progressive used by David Tyack in *The One Best System* (Cambridge: Harvard University Press, 1974). In my own studies of Lawrence Peter Hollis, the superintendent of the Parker School District in Greenville, South Carolina, I found he often used the rhetoric of the social progressives but usually acted out as an administrative progressive. Through his experience as a welfare capitalist, he appeared to move between both categories, meeting the needs of the workers but also the needs of the textile mill owners. For understanding of Elsie Clapp's work up to the Arthurdale years, 1934–1936, see Sam Stack, "Elsie Clapp and the Arthurdale School," in Sadovnik and Semel, *Founding Mothers and Others: Women Educational Leaders During the Progressive Era* (New York: Palgrave, 2002), pp. 93–110.

8. Charlene Siegfried, *Pragmatism and Feminism* (Chicago: University of Chicago Press, 1996), p. 58. I thank Barbara Thayer-Bacon for drawing my attention to this work. Siegfried presents an accurate picture of Elsie Clapp relying only on materials in the Elsie Ripley Clapp Papers, Collection 21 [hereafter ERCP]. Special Collections-Morris Library, Southern Illinois University. Some of her professional materials are available in the Elsie Ripley Clapp Papers. It is unfortunate that the papers at SIU do not contain the more personal anecdotes found in her autobiographical notes. Collection 38 at SIU contains photos from Elsie's work at Ballard and Arthurdale. At present Elsie's later correspondence is privately held. I will refer to her correspondence as Elsie Ripley Clapp Correspondence [hereafter ERCC].
9. See Charles Taylor, *Resources of the Self* (Cambridge: Cambridge University Press, 1992). Also see Erzsebet Barat, "The Discourse of Selfhood: Oral Autobiographies as Narrative Sites for Construction of Identity," in Allison Donnell and Pauline Polkey, *Representing Lives/Women and Autobiography* (New York: St. Martin's Press, 2000), p. 165–173. This book derives from conference papers given at Nottingham Trent University, July 23–25, 1997. Barat discusses the way human beings "make sense of the world and another by the stories we tell," p. 165.
10. See Judy Long, *Telling Women's Lives* (New York: New York University Press, 1999), p. 29. Long addresses why women write biography.
11. Elsie Ripley Clapp Memoirs [hereafter ERCM], unpublished. On loan to the author from the Clapp family. Elsie describes her life from childhood to just prior to her move to Louisville, Kentucky, to direct the Ballard School. She wrote the notes in the late 1950s. It appears in writing the memoirs that she had access to correspondence and other primary materials which are no longer available. I suspect she may have kept a diary and used it with other correspondence to write her memoirs, but these materials have not been discovered.
12. See Barbara Finkelstein, "Revealing Human Agency: The Uses of Biography in the Study of Educational History," in Craig Kridel, *Writing Educational Biography*, pp. 55–56.
13. Ibid.
14. Janet Miller, "Biography, Education and Questions of the Private Voice," in *Writing Educational Biography*, p. 227.
15. Kathleen Weiler, "Reflections on Writing a History of Women Teachers," *Harvard Educational Review* 67 (Winter 1997), p. 635.
16. For a discussion of the descriptor "practical visionary," see Mary Hilton and Pam Hirsch, *Practical Visionaries: Women, Education and Social Progress: 1790–1930* (New York: Pearson, 2000), p. 3. This work examines nineteenth and twentieth century women from England and continental Europe.
17. Ibid.

Chapter One

1. *This Is Brooklyn: A Guide to the Borough's Historic Districts and Landmarks* (Brooklyn: The Fund, 1990), pp. 13, 17. The growth of the Heights was enhanced with steamboat transportation which became reliable in 1820. Hicks Street was named for one of the original

NOTES

landowners. The architectural style of the Heights varied with federal urban row houses being prominent during the late nineteenth century. See also *Elsie Ripley Clapp Memoirs* [ERCM].
2. Many prominent women and later acquaintances of Elsie's struggled with identity around this time, e.g., Eleanor Roosevelt and Lucy Sprague Mitchell. Elsie came to know both women well. ERCM, p. 3. They would work together largely through a mutual interest in progressive education. See Blanche Wiesen Cook, *Eleanor Roosevelt* (1884–1933) Volume I (New York: Viking, 1982), pp. 56–78. Also see Joyce Antler, *Lucy Sprague Mitchell: The Making of a Modern Woman* (New Haven, CT: Yale University Press, 1987), pp. 3–21.
3. ERCM, pp. 3–4.
4. ERCM, p. 4.
5. ERCM, p. 1.
6. ERCM, pp. 6, 10.
7. See Maxine Schwartz Seller, *Immigrant Women* (New York: SUNY Press, 1994), pp. 85–94. Women immigrants to America outnumbered male immigrants in the nineteenth century. For a detailed description of the experience of many Irish immigrants, see Reverend John Francis Maguire, *The Irish in America* (New York: Arno Press, 1969). Originally published in 1868. Elsie borrowed this description from a book, a source she does not note.
8. ERCM, pp. 5–6.
9. ERCM, p. 7.
10. Ibid.
11. ERCM, p. 8.
12. Hannah Bass Penniman passed away on September 4, 1898, according to genealogical records prepared by Elsie Ripley Clapp on the Ripley and Clapp families. Private possession of family. ERCM, p. 8.
13. In her autobiography, Elsie gives much more detail about her life with her grandparents than with her own parents. She was very close to her maternal grandparents, the Ripleys, although not close with her mother for some time. ERCM, p. 9.
14. ERCM, pp. 10, 11.
15. ERCM, p. 12.
16. Ibid.
17. With irony Elsie wrote in her autobiography that the Home Life Insurance Company, Grandfather Ripley's company that he built and served as president, refused to insure him. ERCM, p. 13.
18. ERCM, p. 13.
19. Marjorie was born on April 4, 1884, and died on August 20, 1979. Lawrence was born in 1886 and died in 1937. Elsie also had a younger brother, Russell, who lived for only one year, 1881–1882. The family plot is located in the Greenwood Cemetery in Brooklyn, New York. Elsie is also buried in this cemetery. ERCM, p. 14.
20. Later Elsie would recall studying with Professor James Harvey Robinson at Columbia University. According to Elsie he used a similar technique to link the history of ideas with events. Elsie gave Professor Robinson the credit for "pulling up the forces erected during high school and college... separating man's geographic and scientific discoveries, their agriculture, religion, and philosophy and their literature, art and music." ERCM, p. 14.

21. I have not been able to document this monitor as a participant at the Battle of Mobile. Most likely she is mistaken about the presence of a monitor named *Sunapee* at the Battle of Mobile.
22. According to Elsie, George Moseley Clapp spent his later years fighting the government seeking payment for the second monitor that was built but not put into service due to the war's end. According to Elsie's memoirs, he never received just compensation, which resulted in debt and declining fortunes for the foundry. The memoirs suggest that Elsie was more in touch with and closer to her maternal grandparents, the Ripleys. George Moseley Clapp was born August 24, 1825, and died July 24, 1897. Grandmother Clapp was born in 1828 and died in 1906. ERCM, p. 30.
23. ERCM, p. 19.
24. Elsie refers to her mother in her memoirs as Sally Ripley Clapp. According to Elsie's niece, Barbara Myers Rahn, Elsie never referred to her mother as "Sally" while her mother was living. According to the convention of the time, this would have been viewed as disrespectful. ERCM, p. 11.
25. ERCM, pp. 17, 19.
26. See Barbara Welter, *Dimity Convictions* (Athens: Ohio University Press, 1976), pp. 21–41. See also Jean Strouse, *Alice James: The Life of the Brilliant but Neglected Younger Sister of William James* (Boston: Houghton Mifflin, 1980). Alice James' intellect was submerged in this era of male domination. Elsie also saw this in her mother, a woman of great musical talent that was totally obscured in this Victorian family. Elsie resented her mother's refusal to resist. Elsie's response to this situation was written after her association with numerous women reformers who resisted the cult of womanhood in one way or another such as Eleanor Roosevelt, Margaret Sanger, Elizabeth Gurley Flynn, Crystal Eastman, and Lucy Sprague Mitchell.
27. ERCM, p. 16.
28. Ibid.
29. Ibid.
30. Ibid.
31. ERCM, pp. 21, 22.
32. Ibid.
33. ERCM, pp. 21, 36.
34. Ibid.
35. ERCM, p. 15.
36. Elsie occasionally uses the term "Aunt" to describe friends of the family who were not blood relatives, e.g., Auntie May Nelson. ERCM, pp. 16, 17.
37. Maresi's was a well-known local caterer. ERCM, p. 18.
38. ERCM, p. 22.
39. Ibid.
40. ERCM, p. 24.
41. ERCM, p. 25.
42. ERCM, pp. 31, 26.
43. Hall directed the funeral of Elsie's father, William Gamwell Clapp, at the First Presbyterian Church in Brooklyn. William Clapp died on December 14, 1914. Sarah Ripley Clapp's funeral service was also held in the church. She died while Elsie was working at Arthurdale.

Elsie's sister Marjorie married Jim Myers in this church as well. ERCM, p. 34. Elsie never discusses her personal religious beliefs. Her participation may be linked more to tradition and ceremony than spirituality.
44. ERCM, p. 38.
45. Elsie probably does not record the actual dates of the summer excursions because she could not recall them. She most likely wrote the memoirs in the late 1950s. ERCM, pp. 36, 41–42.
46. ERCM, p. 26.
47. ERCM, p. 42.
48. Her description of the trip is ironic in the sense that almost a decade later the most famous ship of the White Star Line, *The Titanic*, would meet an unfortunate fate with an iceberg in the North Atlantic. ERCM, p. 43.
49. ERCM, p. 44.
50. Ibid. See also Barbara Finkelstein, "Revealing Human Agency: The Uses of Biography in the Study of Educational History," in Kridel, *Writing Educational Biography*, p. 55.
51. See Blanche Wiesen Cooke, *Eleanor Roosevelt 1884–1933* (New York: Viking, 1992), p. 12. Clapp's struggles as a young woman are very similar to Eleanor Roosevelt's. Both grew up in the world of privilege, were concerned about their appearance, and fought against the Victorian image of women. Later in life they would become close friends, largely through the Reedsville Experimental Project, known as Arthurdale, and their mutual interest in progressive education.
52. Charlotte Siegfried, *Pragmatism and Feminism* (Chicago: University of Chicago Press, 1996), p. 266.
53. John Dewey, *LW* 14: 96–97. (Carbondale, Southern Illinois University Press,). These volumes cover 1925 through 1953.

Chapter Two

1. ERCM, p. 45.
2. ERCM, p. 46.
3. Elsie Clapp was plagued by various health problems throughout her life. At times they seem to be brought on by stress or psychological trauma, but at this stage in her life may be associated with her struggle for self-identity. Elsie expresses some concern in her memoirs that her father's family had a history of mental illness. She does not explore this further. ERCM, pp. 49, 50.
4. Brooklyn was an excellent location to nurture this interest in Gothic architecture. ERCM, p. 46.
5. Elsie attended dance class with friend and future colleague Jessie Stanton. Also born in Brooklyn, Stanton spent some time in settlement work and eventually taught at the City and Country School in New York. Her interest was early childhood education and she worked closely with Elsie at the Arthurdale School from 1934 to 1936. ERCM, p. 46. Stanton also organized a nursery school in Harlem in 1943 and served as a consultant to Bank Street College under the direction of Lucy Sprague Mitchell. See ERCP 21/3/11 Misc. fragment and biographical information on Jessie Stanton. Writing in retrospect as

an experienced educator, Elsie emphasized the importance of non-formal education. As a mature woman she also understood the incredible opportunities her social class and status afforded her. She noted reading Voltaire and Marcus Aurelius gave her a feeling of sophistication.

6. ERCM, pp. 47, 48.
7. ERCM, p. 48.
8. ERCM, p. 49.
9. ERCM, p. 50.
10. Ibid.
11. This is not to suggest personal appearance does not continue to be an issue as she approaches adulthood. ERCM, p. 52
12. ERCM, p. 53.
13. It is important to note that Elsie Clapp digresses at this point in her memoirs to make sure the reader understands the nature of her upbringing. She wanted to help the reader comprehend the incredibly comfortable and protected little world in which she lived. ERCM, p. 53.
14. ERCM, p. 54.
15. ERCM, p. 55.
16. This digression is vital in understanding Elsie Clapp as she looked back at her own life as a mature woman. The Great Depression also changed her life and gave her a broader perspective about life, poverty, democracy, and the role of education in dealing with these. ERCM, p. 55.
17. Michel Beaud, *The History of Capitalism* (New York: Monthly Review Press, 1983), pp. 117–144. Chapter Four of the text is titled, "The Great Depression to the Great War, 1873–1914."
18. Elsie Clapp's future mentor, John Dewey, would be an acute observer of the Pullman strike in Chicago. For his reactions see Robert Westbrook, *John Dewey and American Democracy* (New York: Cornell University Press, 1992), 86–91.
19. Elsie consistently misspells Backus as "Bachus" in her memoirs. ERCM, p. 58.
20. ERCM, p. 55.
21. Ibid.
22. ERCM, p. 59.
23. Marjorie Nickerson, *A Long Way Forward: The First Hundred Years of the Packer Collegiate Institute* (Brooklyn, New York: Packer Institute, 1945), p. 19.
24. The Packer School still exists as a coed prep school. ERCM, pp. 52, 33.
25. Nickerson, *A Long Way Forward*, p. 42. According to Nickerson this was the largest sum given for the higher education of women until 1850. Nickerson's work is the most comprehensive history of the Packer Institute.
26. Ibid., p. 111.
27. Ibid.
28. Ibid.
29. Ibid., p. 98.
30. Ibid., p. 107. During Elsie's era, Packer had an active social life that included the Glee Club, Banjo and Mandolin club, Dance Association, drama and various lectures.
31. Ibid., p. 101.

NOTES 257

32. There were strong connections between Vassar and Packer with Backus being a former instructor at Vassar. Elsie's mother was an alumna of Vassar.
33. ERCM, p. 56.
34. At the time, Packer was also experiencing some financial stress due to decreasing enrollment. According to Dr. Backus this was due to competition from several schools in the Brooklyn area: the Girls High School, the Manual Training High School, Erasmus Hall, and the State Normal School at Jamaica. See Nickerson, p. 127.
35. "Newport's Opening Days," 23 June 1895, *New York Times*, p. 12.
36. "Mrs. Brice Gives a Dinner at Newport," 3 July 1895, *New York Times*, p. 4.
37. "Entertainments in Newport Cottages," 13 July 1895, *New York Times*, p. 4, "Dr. Brice Not to Buy a Newport Villa," 25 July 1895, *New York Times*, p. 4.
38. ERCM, p. 56.
39. Nickerson, *A Long Way Forward*, p. 248.
40. ERCM, pp. 58–59.
41. Description of Kate Morgan Ward by Adelaide Gill, in Nickerson, p. 247.
42. Nickerson, *A Long Way Forward*, p. 248.
43. ERCM, p. 59.
44. ERCM, pp. 58, 59.
45. ERCM, p. 62.
46. Ibid. As an educator, Elsie will clearly link the influence of social forces and interaction. This is evident in her interest in the school as the center of community life.
47. ERCM, p. 60.
48. Nickerson, *A Long Way Forward*, pp. 239, 154. Regardless of Elsie's portrayal of Amy Dunlap, she proved to be a significant instructor at Packer. She is described as "kind, idealistic, courageous, vivid, vital, a very handsome woman with lovely color, twinkling eyes and lilting voice, thoroughly alive." p. 239. Dr. Edward J. Goodwin, Packer, encouraged Amy to continue her education when he discovered her talent and realized she was not content with her current role as registrar and head of the bookstore. Upon completion of her degrees, Goodwin awarded Amy a teaching position at Packer. Amy taught sociology, economics, and European history.
49. Ibid.
50. "Newport at the Theatre," 5 September 1896, *New York Times*, p. 5.
51. ERCM, p. 57.
52. Ibid.
53. Ibid.
54. ERCM, p. 58.
55. Ibid.
56. ERCM, pp. 62, 63. The Spanish-American War was the first United States war against a European power since 1814. There was strong American sentiment for war following the "mysterious" sinking of the U.S.S. Maine. This "splendid little war," as it was often called, resulted in the acquisition of Puerto Rico, Guam, Philippines, and eventual Cuban independence in 1901. See Joseph Strayer, *The Mainstream of Civilization* 2nd ed. (New York: Harcourt Brace, 1974), p. 685.

57. "Mrs. F.O. French Entertains: Dinner at Her Newport Cottage Followed by a Dance," 10 August 1898, *New York Times*, p. 7. Noted guests at this event were Miss Elsie Clews and Julia Dent Grant.
58. ERCM, p. 56.
59. Ibid.
60. ERCM., p. 62.
61. One wonders if the family specifically arranged for the scholarship for Elsie although this cannot be documented. It does suggest her family's financial problems were serious. ERCM, p. 64.
62. Zorach will be described later in more detail. ERCM, p. 52.
63. ERCM, p. 65.
64. Ibid.
65. ERCM, p. 66.
66. Ibid.
67. ERCM, p. 67.
68. Ibid.

Chapter Three

1. Cornelia Raymond, *Memories of a Child of Vassar College* (Poughkeepsie, New York: Vassar College, 1940), pp. 44–45. Dean M. Rogers, Special Collections Assistant at Vassar College, recommended this book.
2. During Elsie's years at Vassar, the student government was granted a new charter giving the students more legislative power. ERCM, pp. 67-68. Jane Addams spoke to the students on March 20, 1902, on the topic of college women. In 1903 a more liberal course curriculum was put in place, and the number of free electives was increased. These were exciting years to be at Vassar. See Dorothy Plum, *The Great Experiment: A Chronicle of Vassar* (Poughkeepsie: Vassar College, New York, 1961), p. 81. According to Dean Rogers, Special Collections Assistant, Elsie is considered "ex. Vassar 1903." According to the Vassar Alumnae Biographical Register of 1939, Elsie attended Vassar from the fall of 1899 to April 1902. She did take classes with the Class of 1903 and considered herself a member of that class. She does not appear in the yearbook nor are there images of her for the Class of 1903 photos. Email correspondence from Dean Rogers to S. Stack, 28 August 2002.
3. Nickerson, *A Long Way Forward*, p. 250.
4. Ibid. Laura Wylie taught Latin and English, and she had an interest in entering settlement work, but chose to begin teaching at Vassar instead in 1897, retiring in 1924. She remained in Poughkeepsie until her death in 1932.
5. ERCM, p. 68.
6. Ibid. Upon reading Elsie's freshman English examination, Laura Wylie referred to Elsie's writing as a mixture of "Shakespeare and the Old Testament."
7. ERCM, p. 69.
8. Ibid. Writing in the late 1950s, Elsie failed to note her unfortunate reference to the colored cook and the struggle of African Americans for equality of opportunity. Elsie was

NOTES

always served by her Irish maids in her younger years and failed to see the hegemonic nature of this service based on gender, race, and ethnicity. This begs the question about her own understanding of democratic community and what characteristics it entailed.
9. Ibid.
10. ERCM, p. 70.
11. Ibid.
12. Ibid.
13. Ibid., p. 71.
14. Nickerson, *A Long Way Forward*, p. 238.
15. ERCM, p. 72. This is the only reference I have ever found regarding Elsie's romantic interests.
16. Ibid.
17. ERCM, pp. 72, 73. Lucy Burns continued her debating and political skills as a active contributor to the suffragist movement in years to come.
18. ERCM, p. 73.
19. ERCM, p. 74.
20. Ibid.
21. ERCM, p.75.
22. Ibid.
23. ERCM, p. 75.
24. This was Elsie's second year at Vassar, 1900–1901. ERCM, p. 76.
25. Ibid.
26. Ibid.
27. Ibid.
28. As part of the complications Elsie claimed to have developed phlebitis. ERCM, p. 77.
29. Ibid.
30. ERCM, p. 78.
31. Ibid.
32. ERCM, p. 80.
33. Although Elsie's description is brief, Bawden's approach seems related to the new approach of James and then Dewey.
34. George Dykhuizen, *The Life and Mind of John Dewey*, p. 68.
35. Lawrence Cremin, *The Metropolitan Experience, 1876–1980* (New York: Harper and Row, 1988), p. 400.
36. William James, "Remarks on Spencer's Definition of Mind as Correspondence," from James' *Essays in Philosophy* (Cambridge, MA: Harvard University Press, 1978), p. 116. Originally published in 1904. See also Charlotte H. Siegfried, *Class and Context: A Study in William James* (Athens, OH: Ohio University Press, 1978).
37. Dewey's critique of traditional education is most clearly stated in *Experience and Education*, which he published in 1938, but when Elsie met him, he had already expressed his concerns about traditional education in other books and articles.
38. ERCM, p. 80.
39. ERCM, p. 81.
40. ERCM, p. 82.

41. ERCM, p. 88.
42. ERCM, p. 83.
43. This porcelain is still sold as an Irish product and is considered to represent excellent craftsmanship. Elsie uses a different spelling than the current "Belekware."
44. Ibid. Elsie had been given ten dollars for the trip to New Jersey by Mrs. White.
45. ERCM, p. 84.
46. At the 1913 reunion of the class Elsie reunited with Marion Judson and Crystal Eastman. This is the only reunion of the Class of 1903 Elsie attended.
47. Dykhuizen, *Life and Mind of John Dewey*, p. 94.
48. Ibid., p. 95. See also John Dewey, "Psychology of Elementary Curriculum," *Early Works* (1900).
49. John Dewey, *The School and Society* (Chicago: University of Chicago Press, 1899), p. 28. *The Child and the Curriculum* (Chicago: University of Chicago Press, 1902). For information on the Lab School from two participants, see Katherine Camp Mayhew and Anna Camp Edwards, *The Dewey School* (New York: Atherton, 1966).
50. ERCM, p. 86.
51. This description is from a memorial service held for Anis Ford Eastman. A Baptist minister, Z.R. Brockway of the Elmira Reformatory, gave the address. See Max Eastman, *Heroes I Have Known: Twelve Who Lived Great Lives* (New York: Simon and Schuster, 1942), p. 14. Eastman includes among his heroes Mark Twain, Carlo Tresca, Sigmund Freud and John Dewey. Isadora Duncan is the only woman included besides his mother. See also Eastman's chapter, "The Making of a Woman Minister," written by his mother and included in his *Enjoyment of Living* (New York: Harper and Brothers, 1948), pp. 68–71. Anis Ford Eastman was the first ordained woman in the Congregationalist Church.
52. Crystal's brother was Max Eastman who will be discussed later in this text. Crystal Eastman always fascinated Elsie. ERCM, p. 87.
53. ERCM, p. 86.
54. Ibid.
55. Ibid.
56. ERCM, p. 87.
57. Ibid. Elsie mentions Florence Keyes, Laura Wylie, Grace McCurdy, Abby Leach, a Miss Burch and Professors Baldwin and Bawden as being strong intellectual influences during her Vassar years.

Chapter Four Notes

1. This information comes from a website on Katherine Bement Davis, a New York suffragist and corrections commissioner who had ties to Brooklyn Heights Seminary. http://www.correctionhistory.org.
2. Henry Stiles, *History of Brooklyn*, p. 885. This is an online text located at http://www.panix.com.
3. ERCM, p. 88.
4. Ibid.
5. Ibid. Lawrence's behavior may also have been the source of the move to Mexico. Elsie notes he lived in a fraternity house and was not showing the necessary maturity for serious study.

NOTES 261

6. ERCM, p. 89.
7. *This Is Brooklyn*, p. 41.
8. All of Florence's older sisters were associated with the Department of Domestic Science at the Pratt Institute. ERCM, p. 90.
9. Elsie notes in her memoirs that following the Great Fire of San Francisco that Chickering came to the East to raise money for the rebuilding of the city. ERCM, pp. 92, 93.
10. ERCM, p. 93.
11. Detailed in a later chapter, Elsie would become principal and director of community affairs for the Reedsville Experimental Project, also called Arthurdale. Arthurdale was the first federal homestead subsistence project as part of the National Industry Recovery Act. She worked on the project from 1934 to 1936.
12. This simple incident points to the difficulty women teachers had in supporting themselves on their salaries. ERCM, p. 93. For a discussion of these issues see Margaret Haley, "Why Teachers Should Organize, *Addresses and Proceedings* (St. Louis: National Education Association, 1904), pp. 145–152, and Grace Strachan, *Equal Pay for Equal Work* (New York: B.F. Buck, 1910), pp. 117–122.
13. Frederick Paul Keppel, *Columbia* (New York: Oxford University Press, 1914), pp. 111–114. Keppel was dean of Columbia College [later known as Columbia University]. Elsie's advisor, George Krapp, served as the editor of this book series.
14. Elsie notes that at the time there was some concern in both the English and philosophy departments about a student taking courses across the disciplines. Elsie did not understand interdepartmental politics and the effects they might have until several years later. ERCM, p. 94.
15. ERCM, p. 95.
16. Ibid.
17. ERCM, p. 96.
18. Dykhuizen, p. 120.
19. ERCM, p. 95.
20. Ibid.
21. ERCM, p. 94.
22. Elsie recalled an incident when, traveling home for the Christmas season, her brother Lawrence gave up his berth to a small family. In doing so, he got little sleep on the trip. Elsie saw her brother as a kind, generous and compassionate man. ERCM, pp. 96–97.
23. Dykhuizen, *The Life and Mind*, p. 122.
24. Lawrence Cremin, *Transformation of the School* (New York: Vintage, 1964), pp. 170–171, and James Earl Russell, *Founding Teachers College: Reminiscences of the Dean Emeritus* (New York: Teachers College, 1937), p. 6.
25. Lawrence Cremin, David Shannon, and Mary Evelyn Townsend, *A History of Teachers College, Columbia University* (New York: Morningside Heights Press, 1954), p. 71. Cremin's primary sources for Butler's report is Frank Fackenthal, *Columbia University and Teachers College: Documents and Correspondence* (New York: Columbia University Press, 1915). During Elsie's early years at Teachers College (1907–1912), the reach of Teachers College was greatly enhanced by its popular summer school, which attracted students from all

over the country. From 1910 to 1914 summer school students increased from 2,632 to 5,590. By this time it was largely a graduate professional school for teachers and other professionals.
26. Elsie's intellectual relationship with Dewey will be explored in the next chapter. ERCM, p. 97.
27. Barnard allowed Elsie to take "12 points a semester" to make up the 24-point deficit. She finished with 26 points. Ibid., ERCM, p. 98.
28. Ibid.
29. Elsie and Max Eastman were both involved in the Paterson Silk Workers Strike of 1913. ERCM, p. 99. Eastman would serve as editor of the radical periodical *The Masses*. For an account of his life, see Max Eastman, *Enjoyment of Living* (New York: Harper and Brothers, 1948) and Milton Cantor, *Max Eastman*, (New York: Twayne Press, 1970). Max Eastman humorously recalls his appointment in philosophy in his *Enjoyment of Living*. He was recommended for the position to Dewey by Simkovitch to teach Principles of Science.
30. ERCM, pp. 97–98.
31. ERCM, p. 99.
32. Elsie Ripley Clapp, *Transcript from Barnard College (1907–1908)*. This transcript lists Elsie's date of birth as 13 November 1879 and in the upper-right corner has her deceased in 1965. Elsie was given credits from Vassar in English, elementary German, history, mathematics, philosophy, Latin, elementary French, algebra, including plane geometry and quadratics, and elementary physics. Her Latin courses included studies in grammar, composition, Cicero, Virgil, advanced composition and sight translation.
33. In her memoirs she suggests that her uncle had been right and that she did not fully understand the nature of the work required for the Doctor of Philosophy. While there may be some truth to this, she did understand her discipline but not departmental politics and personality conflicts in the English Department at Columbia which eventually undermined her pursuit of the degree. ERCM, p. 100.
34. ERCM, p. 100.
35. Cremin, *A History of Teachers College*, p. 100. Cremin challenges the notion that Horace Mann was truly an experimental school. It generally attracted children of high intelligence and social class and became more of a college prep institution over the years. It was a model school, as he and Butler imply, and was chiefly a showplace for Columbia and did draw visitors from all over the world.
36. Elsie's initial contract for Horace Mann was from 16 September 1908 to 2 June 1909. ERCM, p. 102. Employment and biographical data. Elsie followed her good friend Una Sait in the role of secretary for the journal. ERCP. Personal data. 21/1/2. Subscription for the journal was $3.00.
37. Elsie Clapp, Book review of Stanley M. Bligh, "The Direction of Desire: Suggestions for the Application of Psychology to Everyday Life," *Journal of Philosophy, Psychology and Scientific Method* 8 (1911), pp. 407–411.
38. Ibid., p. 411. See John Dewey and James Tufts, *Ethics*, Part II, Theory of Moral Life (New York: Henry Holt, 1929), p. 201. Originally published in 1908 and a very popular text on ethics. Elsie also noted Dewey's *How We Think* (New York: Houghton Mifflin, 1998). Originally published in 1910.

NOTES

39. Elsie Clapp, Book review of Willystine Goodsell, "The Conflict of Naturalism and Humanism," *Journal of Philosophy, Psychology and Scientific Method* 9 (July/December), pp. 413–415. This book was part of a series titled, Contributions to Education, no. 33, and was published by Teachers College.
40. Ibid., p. 414.
41. Ibid. See also Goodsell's *The Conflict of Naturalism and Humanism*, p. 17.
42. Ibid., p. 415.
43. See John Dewey, *Ethics*, 1929, p. 262. See also Dewey, MW 6: 381–388. Here Dewey gives a definition of character in his contributions to the *Cyclopedia of Education*, edited by Paul Monroe.
44. Dewey, MW 7:217. In this contribution to the *Cyclopedia of Education*, Dewey defines both humanism and naturalism.
45. ERCM, p. 102.
46. ERCM, p.103.
47. Ibid. Elsie attended one of James's lectures on pragmatism at the Horace Mann School during this time. "Even in a snow blizzard," Elsie noted, "The Horace Mann Auditorium was crowded with celebrities...." Max Eastman recorded his interactions with James in his work, *Enjoyment of Living*, pp. 286–287.
48. Due to the marriages of Florence and Anna Ripley, Elsie's sister Marjorie was now the owner of the Leather Studio on Irving Place. ERCM, pp. 104–105.
49. Sidney Hook, *Out of Step* (New York Harper and Row, 1987), pp. 82–83. For further commentary on Dewey's classroom behavior see Alan Ryan, *John Dewey and the High Tide of American Liberalism* (New York: Norton, 1995), p. 38.
50. Max Eastman, *Enjoyment of Living*, p. 310.
51. ERCM, p. 105.
52. Ibid.
53. During her research travels Elsie was able to visit relatives such as Walter Ballou in Providence, Rhode Island, whose family had a farm there. She also visited with John and Hattie Kneeland in Boston. ERCM, p. 107.
54. Solipsism is a theory holding the self can know nothing but its own modification and the self is the only existing thing. It is a doctrine that suggests "there is a first person perspective possessing privileged and irreducible characteristics, in virtue of which we stand in various kinds of isolation from any other person or external thing that may exist." ERCM, p. 109. See *Cambridge Dictionary of Philosophy* (Cambridge: Cambridge University Press, 1999), p. 751.
55. ERCM, p. 110.
56. Elsie believed her work on English grammar could be enhanced by study in England. Although she was invited to stay with a visiting professor from Oxford, she did not believe she could leave her father and mother. There were also financial concerns in taking such a trip. Recalling the professor's invitation she wrote: "I have never forgotten his generous concern with an unknown American student." Elsie was interested, yet disappointed with Trent's course on Eighteenth Century Literature and Krapp's course on English Literature and stated both "were concerned with the minutiae of their subjects." She took the courses because she thought they would help in writing her dissertation. ERCM, pp. 110, 111.

57. Elsie's professional papers include several materials from this course. ERCM, p. 111. See Notes outlining Dewey's course, Philosophy and Education in Their Historic Relations October 1910. ERCP 21/1/6. See also ERCP 21/1/8 Course notes for Philosophy and Education in Their Historic Relations, 18 May 1911.
58. ERCM, p. 112. Van Doren also served as the literary editor of *The Nation* (1919–1922) and helped edit the *Literary Guild* and *Living Library*. Van Doren's brother Mark was also among Elsie's acquaintances among the graduate students in English. See *Readers Encyclopedia*, p. 1047.
59. This interaction is explored later in an attempt to understand Dewey's influence on Elsie and her reaction to his ideas. He also benefited from this interaction. ERCM, p. 113.
60. Ibid. Elsie notes that at the time she was also exchanging notes with Dewey on *Democracy and Education*, which he would first publish in 1916. This exchange is noted by Dewey in the preface to the book. Typed excepts from John Dewey's book, *Democracy and Education*, 1916. Elsie notes in her memoirs that she hoped her work would be available for the student of intellectual history to analyze and study. ERCP 21/2/36.
61. ERCM, p. 115.
62. ERCM, p. 106.
63. ERCM, p. 116–117.
64. ERCM, p. 117.
65. ERCM, p. 118.
66. ERCM, p. 119.
67. Ibid.
68. ERCM, pp. 119-120.
69. ERCM, p. 120.
70. Aunt Edith meant a great deal to Elsie. Edith had once studied to be an opera singer, but due to the illnesses in her family, she had gravitated to a career in nursing, specializing in what might be called today psychiatric nursing. Edith later headed the State Hospital in Englewood, New Jersey, from 1915 to 1919 and served as field secretary to the American Nurses Association from 1926 to 1930. She retired from nursing in 1935. When in need of medical advice or treatment, Elsie often relied on Aunt Edith. While Edith did well in her career, it is another example of how young women were expected to drop all goal/ desires to nurse ailing relatives. For another example of the enormous responsibility many women felt and how they were expected to care for family members, see Antler, *Lucy Sprague Mitchell*, pp. 34–41. Lucy had to take care of an ailing father. Elsie suggests that mental illness was characteristic of her father's family.
71. ERCM, p. 121.
72. ERCM, p. 125.
73. Excerpts from letter to Elsie Clapp from Dorothy Brewster, no date, ERCM, p. 124. In writing her memoirs, Elsie seems to have direct access to this letter. It is not found in her professional papers or her later correspondence but only paraphrased by her in the memoirs.
74. ERCM, p. 127.
75. ERCM , p.128.

76. ERCM, pp. 129–130.
77. ERCM, p. 130.
78. Elsie's first topic for the dissertation was "Creative Imagination," an extension of her master's thesis. ERCM, p. 132. I have not been able to locate a copy of this thesis.
79. Ibid, p. 132. Dewey had asked for leave for the spring semester of 1912, and his leave was granted. See Dewey chronology, Center for Dewey Studies website.
80. John Dewey to Elsie Ripley Clapp, 1 October 1911. Enclosing report of first lecture. ERCP 21/1/17.
81. Joyce Antler, *The Educated Woman and Professionalization: The Struggle for a New Feminine Identity* (1890–1920) (New York: Garland, 1987), pp. 334, 418.
82. It is interesting to compare Elsie's life with that of Lucy Sprague Mitchell. Both come from upper-class families, had similar interests in education and architecture, both felt a deep need to meet the needs of family members, and both were influenced by working with Caroline Pratt. However Elsie never expresses the personal angst of dealing with marriage and the loss of identity that Mitchell does. Mitchell's struggle is chronicled by Joyce Antler in *Lucy Sprague Mitchell* (New Haven, CT: Yale University Press, 1987). Unfortunately, Elsie did not write nearly as much as Lucy Mitchell.

Chapter Five

1. Academic Records and Academic Correspondence. List of courses by John Dewey attended by Elsie Clapp. From 1907 to 1908 Elsie took the following courses: Social Life and the School Curriculum, Practicum and Philosophy of Education, Modern Ethical Ideas and Types of Logical theory. From 1908 to 1909—Psychological Ethics and Logic as Applied to the Problems of Teaching. From 1909 to 1910— Philosophy of Education and Kant. From 1910 to 1913—Philosophy and Education in Their Historic Relations. From 1911 to 1912—Analysis of Experience and Theories of Experience. She assisted Dewey during the 1911 and 1912 summer sessions: 1912 Social Aspects of School Curriculum and Foundations of Method and in 1912 Foundations of Method and Selected Philosophic Problems. She may have planned a biography of Dewey due to the variety of collected materials. She also developed a catalogue list of Dewey books she possessed. ERCP 21/1/1.
2. The years 1907 to 1913 were productive ones for Dewey and can be considered the years in which he was laying down his foundations for pragmatism. See MW volumes 4–7 for the scope and breadth of this work. See also Dykhuizen, *The Life and Mind of John Dewey*, pp. 116–152, and Westbrook's *John Dewey*, pp. 117–149, biographical and intellectual aspects of Dewey's life during this time.
3. Elsie's professional papers do not include materials prior to 1910; thus there is no discussion of her courses from 1907 to 1909.
4. Fragment concerning the Dewey Lab School. Elsie expressed her anger at the closing of the Lab School, perhaps after some discussion with Dewey. "Its end was precipitated by the President (William Rainey Harper), of the University who," she noted, "anxious of the impeccable acclaim the school received, contrived a merger with the Cook County Normal School, an outgrowth of the Chicago Institute headed by Col. Parker."

ERCP 21/2/32. Dewey never discussed the more personal aspects of the closure, and it is reasonable to assume Elsie got her information from him. See Westbrook, *John Dewey*, pp. 110–113 for more information on the closure of the Lab School and the politics involved.

5. See John Dewey, *School and Society*, Middle Works 1: 25, 30. *The Child and the Curriculum* (1902) Middle Works 2: 276. The comparison between traditional and progressive education is clearly pointed out in *Experience and Education* (New York: Macmillan, 1938).

6. John Dewey, *School and Society* (Chicago: University of Chicago Press, 1971), p. 14. Originally published in 1899.

7. John Dewey to Elsie Clapp, Exchanged notes on valuation, 13 October 1911. ERCP 21/1/22.

8. John Dewey, MW 9: 3. For a discussion on Dewey's failure to acknowledge women, see Charlotte Siegfried, *Pragmatism and Feminism* (Chicago: University of Chicago, 1996), pp. 45–52. Dewey referred to *Democracy and Education* in 1911 as a textbook in Philosophy of Education. See MW 6: 515. Letter John Dewey to Elsie Ripley Clapp, 2 September 1911. ERCP 21/1/11. Enclosing a paper amendatory of the original outline. Dewey does acknowledge Alice Chipman Dewey, Jane Addams, and Ella Flagg Young in Jane Dewey, "Biography of John Dewey," in *The Philosophy of John Dewey*, ed. Paul Schilpp (Evanston, IL: Northwestern University Press, 1939), pp. 28–30.

9. For a brief discussion of ethics, happiness and democracy, see Sam Stack, "John Dewey's Theory of Happiness," *Journal of Thought* 31 (Summer 1996), pp. 25–35.

10. Notes outlining Dewey's course Philosophy and Education in Their Historic Relations. Elsie also assisted Dewey with this course from 1923 to 1925, and on several other occasions. ERCP 21/1/6. Dewey had addressed the ethical nature of democracy in *Ethics*, originally published in 1908 and revised in 1932. LW 7. Enclosing report of November 2 lecture. See John Dewey to Elsie Clapp, 2 November 1911, on Dewey's concern on reaching his class in understanding desire. Dewey Paper on Self and Want. ERCP 21/1/12. He also suggested Elsie contribute to his preparation for this class. John Dewey to Elsie Clapp, 18 September 1911. Enclosing remarks on Tolstoy's attack on science and philosophy. ERCP 21/1/15.

11. Ibid.

12. Class notes Philosophy and Education, 4 October 1911. In this class Dewey spent some time on the ancient Greeks—Socrates, Plato, Aristotle, and the Sophists. He also spent some time discussing the concepts of desire and good—or that is what made an impression on Elsie. ERCP 21/1/6.

13. Elsie Ripley Clapp, *Community Schools in Action* (New York: Viking, 1939).

14. John Dewey, MW 6: 424. From Dewey's contributions to the *Cyclopedia of Education*, a five-volume work published from 1911 to 1913 and edited by Paul Monroe of Teachers College. Dewey made approximately 120 contributions to the *Cyclopedia*. The *Cyclopedia* is an excellent source for understanding Dewey's definitions of terms.

15. Lecture Notes. 15 August 1911. Summer courses were popular at Teachers College at this time and allowed full-time teachers to attend. Teachers came from all over the country. ERCP 21/1/9. See Keppel, *Columbia*, 135–136.

16. John Dewey, MW 6: 447. From *Cyclopedia of Education*.

17. John Dewey, MW 7: 328. From *Cyclopedia of Education*.

18. John Dewey, MW 6: 177–356. This volume includes *How We Think*.
19. John Dewey MW 6: 78. This essay was first published in *Science* 13 (1910), pp. 121–127 and was reprinted in the *Journal of Education* 71 (1910), pp. 95–96, 427–428, 454.
20. John Dewey, MW 7: 339. *Cyclopedia of Education*.
21. Ibid.
22. Notes referring to a Dewey lecture. 15 August 1911. ERCP 21/1/9.
23. John Dewey, *How We Think* (New York: Houghton Mifflin, 1988), pp. 100–101.
24. John Dewey MW 6: 185.
25. Ibid., p. 188.
26. Max Eastman, Book review of *How We Think*, *Journal of Philosophy, Psychology and Scientific Methods* 18 (1910), pp. 244–248. Boyd Bode also reviewed the book in *School Review* 18 (1901): 642–645. See also Textual Commentary from MW 6: 518.
27. Boyd Bode, "Review of Dewey's *How We Think*," *School Review* 18 (1910): pp. 642–645. See textual commentary from MW 6: 518.
28. John Dewey, MW 6: 212–215. See the introduction to this volume by V.T. Thayer and H. S. Thayer MW 6: xxiii. Also George Dykhuizen, *The Life and Mind of John Dewey* (Carbondale: Southern Illinois University Press, 1973), pp. 139–140, and Robert Westbrook, *John Dewey and American Democracy* (Ithaca, NY: Cornell University Press, 1991), p. 142.
29. John Dewey to Elsie Ripley Clapp, 2 September 1911. ERCP 21/1/11.
30. Notes regarding theories of experience. Fall 1911. ERCP 21/2/22. See also John Dewey to Elsie Clapp, summary of lecture on experience. 15 December 1911. Enclosing summary of last few lectures. ERCP 21/2/19.
31. John Dewey, MW 6: 447. *Cyclopedia of Education*.
32. John Dewey, MW 6: 448. *Cyclopedia of Education*.
33. Elsie's notes regarding theories of experience, p. 3. ERCP 21/2/22.
34. John Dewey, MW 6: 434. *Cyclopedia of Education*.
35. John Dewey, MW 6: 449.
36. John Dewey, MW 7: 224.
37. John Dewey to Elsie Clapp. Notes on the Peculiarity of Knowledge. ERCP 21/1/15.
38. John Dewey to Elsie Clapp. Notes regarding Knowledge. 10 October 1911. Enclosed report of third lecture. ERCP 21/1/20.
39. John Dewey to Elsie Clapp. Notes on Knowledge and Ignorance. 21 October 1911. Enclosing report of first lecture. ERCP 21/1/17.
40. John Dewey, MW 6: 450.
41. Thomas Alexander, "The Art of Life: Dewey's Aesthetics," in Larry Hickman, *Reading Dewey: Interpretations for a Postmodern Generation* (Bloomington: Indiana University Press, 1998), p. 18.
42. John Dewey, paper on Self and Want. ERCP 21/1/12.
43. Transcription of Dewey lecture, "One and Many." ERCP 21/1/14.
44. James Campbell, "Dewey's Conception of Community," in Larry Hickman, *Reading Dewey: Interpretations for a Postmodern Generation*, p. 35. See also James Campbell's *Understanding John Dewey* (Chicago: Open University Press, 1995). Another informative volume on Dewey's view of community is Feodor Cruz, *John Dewey's Theory of Community* (New

York: Peter Lang, 1987). Both authors argue the centrality of community in Dewey's democratic theory, but few educators have explored this concept in light of how it is practiced in progressive schools. Elsie's work helps clarify their interpretation. Both views have been informative to this project in better understanding the concept of the community school.

45. Ibid. Dewey's most ideal example might be Jane Addams of Hull House, but he was most likely aware of women in the New York community like Lillian Wald, Florence Kelly, Mary Richmond, etc. See Antler, *Lucy Sprague Mitchell*, pp. 135–158 for a discussion of these women in New York. Dewey was knowledgeable about settlement work in New York. He also supported women's right to vote. Alan Ryan, *John Dewey and the Rising Tide of American Liberalism*, p. 161.
46. Dewey will address the individual role in democratic society more thoroughly in works like *The Public and Its Problems* (New York: Henry Holt, 1927), *Individualism: Old and New* (New York: Minton, Balch, 1930) and *Freedom and Culture* (New York: G.P. Putnam, 1939).
47. See John Dewey, MW 9:89. *Democracy and Education*.
48. Notes regarding interests. 8 February1912. ERCP 21/2/23. According to a schedule of Dewey's activities at this time he was on leave during the spring semester of 1912.
49. Notes outlining Analysis of Experience. ERCP 21/2/24.
50. This notion of connection is vital to understanding pragmatism and its links to progressive education. This was clearly brought to my attention by one of my Philosophy of Education classes, which stressed that education by its very nature was connection; if proper it was our connection with our own experiences as well as how these engage those of others. This is important to keep in mind in light of our discussion of community and the role of the school.
51. John Dewey, MW 7: 262.
52. John Dewey, MW 11: 44, and James Campbell, "Dewey's Conception of Community," p. 40.
53. John Dewey to Elsie Ripley Clapp, 15 December 1911, enclosing summary of last few lectures. John Dewey to Elsie Clapp, Notes on Experience. See Notes regarding interests, 2 February 1912. ERCP 21/2/23.
54. Ibid.
55. Clapp, *Community School in Action*, p. 49.
56. John Dewey, MW 6: 425.
57. See John Dewey, LW 7: 243 and MW 11: 57. In these works Dewey discusses the necessity for education to prepare the individual for living with others, that the role of education is to nurture good citizens "in furthering the general good, so that they will find their won happiness realized in what they can do to improve the conditions of others."
58. John Dewey, MW 6: 418.
59. John Dewey, *The Ethics of Democracy* (Ann Arbor, MI: Andrews, 1881).
60. James Campbell, "Dewey's Conception of Community," p. 24.

NOTES

Chapter Six

1. ERCM, p. 150. Employment and biographical data. ERCP 21/1/2.
2. There is no mention in Elsie's autobiographical notes or professional papers of her early exposure to socialist thought prior to her interaction with socialists during the Paterson Silk Workers Strike of 1913. She did seem interested by this time in social justice issues as they pertained to children and women's suffrage. Early exposure may have occurred under Laura Wylie at Packer but most certainly occurred through various associations at Columbia, such as with Max Eastman. ERCM, pp. 150–151.
3. Ibid.
4. Ibid. The Civil War, better known in Charleston as the War Between the States, had been over for only 48 years when Elsie was in Charleston, and sectional feelings were still strong with the city's intense involvement during the war and its symbolic meaning. ERCM, p. 152.
5. Ibid.
6. ERCM, p. 153.
7. ERCM, p. 164.
8. Barbara Petrick, *Church and School in the Immigrant City: A Social History of Public Education in Jersey City (1830–1930)* (Dissertation: Rutgers University, 1995), p. 311.
9. Ibid., pp. 314–315. In 1920 the majority of graduates at the high school went into the workforce and not to college. That year 224 graduated and 71 went to college, p. 314.
10. Ibid. The high school was noted for its location in Jersey City, overlooking the city. The school boasted a 2,000-seat auditorium with a stained glass window ceiling. The auditorium served as a place for community gatherings, and often-notable speakers were invited such as Woodrow Wilson, then of Princeton University and Nicholas Murray Butler of Columbia University, p. 312.
11. ERCM, p. 153.
12. Elsie's attempt to break the large classes into small discussion groups is similar to a tactic used by William Heard Kilpatrick in his large classes Teachers College. ERCM, p. 154. See Sam Stack, "William Heard Kilpatrick and Teaching Methods," In James J. Van Patten's *Watersheds in Higher Education* (Lewiston: Edwin Mellen Press, 1997), pp. 111–122.
13. Philip Foner, *History of the Labor Movement in the United States, Volume 4, The Industrial Workers of the World (1905–1917)* (New York: International Publishers, 1968). Steve Golin, "Defeat Becomes Disaster: The Paterson Silk Workers Strike of 1913 and the Decline of the I.W.W.," Labor History 24, (Spring 1983), pp. 223–238. Christopher Lasch, *The New Radicalism in America, 1889–1963: The Intellectual as a Social Type* (New York: Alfred Knopf, 1965), Steve Golin, *The Fragile Bridge* (Philadelphia: Temple University Press, 1988). Golin's work challenges much of the historical work on Paterson, particularly the effect of the Pageant. Golin supports the view that the strike had a strong democratic temper and that the Paterson strikers really controlled the strike although they were greatly assisted by the IWW and Greenwich Village intellectuals. The strike, according to Golin, helped create a bridge between the intellectuals and the workers.

14. Golin, *The Fragile Bridge*, p. 67. On the Lawrence strike see Donald B. Cole, *Immigrant City: Lawrence, Massachusetts 1845–1921* (Chapel Hill: University of North Carolina Press, 1963). Henry Bedford, *Socialism and the Workers in Massachusetts, 1886–1912* (Amherst: Massachusetts, 1966). Also see the periodicals *Solidarity* and *Survey* from 1910 to 1912 which contain numerous references to the Lawrence strike.
15. ERCM, p. 138.
16. See "Giovanniti's Address to the Jury," 23 November 1912, Salem Court House, Salem, Massachusetts. Special Collections and Archives, W.E.B. Du Bois Library, University of Massachusetts-Amherst. This speech was published by the Boston School of Social Sciences, 27 January 1913.
17. Anne Tripp, *The I.W.W and the Paterson Silk Workers Strike of 1913* (Urbana: University of Illinois, 1987), p. 80. Max Eastman will pattern his character Jo in *Venture* after Bill Haywood. See also Peter Carlson, *Roughneck: The Life and Times of Big Bill Haywood* (New York: W.W. Norton, 1983), pp. 194–195.
18. Flynn's romantic interest at the time was Carlo Tresca. Elsie may have been confused by Flynn's association with Tresca in describing her as Irish-Italian. ERCM, p. 141.
19. Tripp, *The I.W.W.*, p. 83. Haywood, Flynn, and Sanger wrote their autobiographies. See William D. Haywood, *Bill Haywood's Book: The Autobiography of Big Bill Haywood* (New York: International Publishers, 1929); Elizabeth Gurley Flynn, *I Speak My Own Piece: Autobiography of a Rebel Girl* (New York: International Publishers, 1955) and Margaret Sanger, *An Autobiography* (New York: W.W. Norton, 1983).
20. *New York Globe*, 2 April 1913, p. 10.
21. ERCM, p. 139.
22. Steffens spent a restless youth and is best remembered as a journalist. He served as managing editor of *McClure's Magazine* from 1902 to 1906 and associate editor of the *American Magazine* and *Everybody's Magazine* from 1906 to 1911. His social reformist works include *The Shame of the Cities* (1904), *The Struggle for Self-Government* (1906), and the *Upbuilders* (1909). Readers' Encyclopedia, volume 2, p. 960.
23. See Lincoln Steffens, *Autobiography* (New York: Harcourt-Brace, 1931) and John Reed, *The Education of John Reed: Selected Writings*, John Stewart, ed. (New York: International Publishers, 1955). ERCM, p. 138.
24. Vorse was part of a group of actors and actresses called the Provincetown Players. This group included Eugene O'Neill, George Cram Cooke, Susan Glaspell, John Reed, Louise Bryant, and artists William and Marguerite Zorach, who would later teach Elsie about art and painting. The Players were known for encouraging native writers and playwrights around World War I. Originally organized in 1915 in Provincetown off Cape Cod, they would move to New York in 1916 and continue their work. O'Neill (1888–1953) was the most famous of the group. ERCM, pp. 139–140. Vorse's autobiography is titled *A Footnote to Folly: Reminiscences of Mary Heaton Vorse* (New York: 1935). Vorse was actually in Europe during the Paterson Strike although she kept in close touch with her colleagues in the labor movement.
25. Golin, *The Fragile Bridge*, p. 133.
26. See "Tie Silks Getting Scarce," 5 April 1913, *New York Times*, p. 17, and "Paterson Prepares for a Long Strike," 13 April 1913, *New York Times*, p. 9. "Paterson Strike Goes On,"

13 April 1913, *New York Times*, p. 15. In this article the manufacturers refused to deal with the IWW.
27. ERCM, p. 137. For information on how the evacuation of children was carried out in Lawrence, see C.C. Carstens, "The Children's Exodus from Lawrence," *Survey*, 28 (April 6, 1912): 70–71. "Children of a Strike," *Survey*, 27 (February 24, 1912): 1791–1794.
28. Mary Heaton Vorse, *A Footnote to Folly: Reminiscences of Mary Heaton Vorse*, p. 4. Vorse also notes that the children of Lawrence had one of the highest rates of tuberculosis in the nation in 1912.
29. Golin, *The Fragile Bridge*, p. 135. For a brief piece on the Lawrence children, see "Strikers' Children Coming," 10 February 1912, *New York Times*, p. 6. This article announced that 150 children from the Lawrence, Massachusetts, mills would arrive and be marched down 5th Avenue to Union Square where they would be assigned to families. Flynn commented: "All the people who are adopting the children are workers. There are no rich people among them," p. 6.
30. Ibid., p. 133.
31. ERCM, p. 142
32. Ibid.
33. ERCM, p. 143. Elsie's view of prejudiced journalism is supported by Tripp in *The IWW*. *The New York Times, the American Federationist*, and the Paterson city newspapers were generally in support of the employers. The strikers were supported by the IWW's, *Solidarity*, the *Internationalist Socialist Review*, *The Masses*, and *Survey*, p. xiv.
34. ERCM, p. 143. Francis Bret Harte (1836–1902) was an American short story writer, novelist, editor, and poet. Harte was best known for short stories such as, "The Luck of Roaring Camp," and "The Outcasts of Poker Flat," and his colorful western writing. *Readers' Encyclopedia*, p. 443.
35. The five-cent house was a boarding house for the children of the strikers, more along the lines of an orphanage than an actual home. Most of the children Elsie worked with were the children of Italian immigrants who worked for the lowest wages in the silk industry. Typically, the higher-paid silk workers were English-speaking ribbon workers. This created some tension. ERCM, p. 144–145. Florence Greer had persuaded St. Mark's rector, a Dr. Guthrie, to allow them to use the upper floor of the Parish House as a school. Elsie and Florence furnished the school with discounted items from Saulner's Oriental Store on Fulton Street. ERCM, p. 144.
36. ERCM, p. 146.
37. ERCM, p. 145.
38. ERCM, p. 148.
39. Elsie learned this story about Francesca's activity from Frederick Howe, a friend who visited Elsie at Arthurdale, WV, to discuss Cooperative Credit Unions at the federal subsistence homestead. ERCM, p. 147.
40. Best expressed by Paulo Freire, *Pedagogy of the Oppressed* (New York: Seabury, 1993).
41. Dodge's memoirs are *Intimate Memoirs. Volume 3. Movers and Shakers* (New York: Harcourt, Brace and Company, 1936). ERCM, p. 148.
42. ERCM, p. 147.

43. "Haywood's Pageant Cheers up Strikers," 9 June 1913, *New York Times*, p. 18.
44. "Violence Renewed in Paterson Strike," 13 June 1913, *New York Times*. One must keep in mind the *Times* was not considered friendly to the strikers. Haywood had trouble getting the paper to pay any attention to the strike. Elsie also believed the *Times* to be biased.
45. Tripp, *The I.W.W.*, p. 154. Vorse in *A Footnote to Folly* wrote, "the workers were puzzled and angry because they had made no money." p. 57.
46. "Deficit at $1996 from Strike Show," 25 June 1913, *New York Times*, p. 18. Frederick Summer Boyd supported Ashley in this article that there were not misappropriations and gave figures to the *New York Times* for publication. Receipts were disappointing for the Pageant, but at least 3,000 of the 15,000 in attendance paid no fee. With only one performance, it was impossible to pay all the bills.
47. Ibid., p. 279. Golin argues against Flynn's interpretation of the Pageant as being the downfall of the strike. He suggests that publicity was the major goal of the Pageant and this was achieved. Financial backers knew they might lose money. See Steve Golin, "The Paterson Pageant: Success or Failure?" *Socialist Review*, 69 (May–June, 1983), pp. 45–78. The Pageant may be one of the most researched aspects of the Paterson strike. For further information, see Linda Nochin, "The Paterson Strike Pageant of 1913," *Art in America*, 62 (May–June, 1974), pp. 64–68. For coverage at the time of the strike see "Pageant of the Paterson Strike," *Survey* 30 (June 28, 1913), pp. 428 and "The Pageant as a Form of Propaganda," *Current Opinion* 55 (July 1913), p. 32.
48. ERCM, p. 147.
49. I have no documentation to support Elsie's contention. Margaret Sanger placed the blame for the failure of the strike on Bill Haywood. She believed he was too soft, too political, and too inexperienced to lead the strike at Paterson. She also believed the strikers' economic position could be enhanced through proper attention to birth control. Having too many children placed an enormous demand on the working- class family. See Sanger, *An Autobiography*, p. 84. Sanger also believed the needs of women were being ignored during the strike. She wrote, "Furthermore, I was enough of a feminist to resent the fact that woman and her requirements were not being taken into account in reconstructing this new world about which all were talking. They were failing to consider the quality of life itself." Sanger, p. 85. Sanger correctly assumed that lack of access to birth control and sexual mores kept women oppressed.
50. Mary Heaton Vorse, *A Footnote to Folly*, p, 52.
51. Elsie lost all track of Marco and Emilio. Francesca was located after a long search, "marching round and round the dirty backyard of a Catholic School with thirty others under the stern eyes of two blackclad sisters," Elsie wrote. "And Francesca, wan and dirty, looked at us out of vacant and hostile eyes with no sign of recognition." ERCM, pp. 148–149. According to Golin, *The Fragile Bridge*, 427 children were in New York by the end of May 1913 and 116 were in Elizabeth, New Jersey. See *Paterson Evening News*, 31 May 1913, p. 1 and *Solidarity*, 7 June 1913, p. 4. Golin also notes when New York families went on their summer vacations, the children were often placed with families paid to keep them, which took money away from the strike fund, p. 270.
52. ERCM, p.149. The end of the strike was more complex than Elsie remembered and did not occur overnight. Bomb threats were not considered the downfall of the strike. Flynn

NOTES

dated the end of the strike on July 28, 1913, although the IWW never officially called off the strike. The failure of the strike also had to do with basic economic competition within the silk industry in Pennsylvania and growing ethnic tension among the English and Italian workers in Paterson. See Tripp, *The I.W.W.*, pp. 209–243.

53. Tripp, *The I.W.W.*, p. 178.
54. Golin, *The Fragile Bridge*, p. 135. During the Lawrence strike the attempt by authorities to stop the children from leaving created sympathy for the workers. This sympathy filled the coffers of the relief fund. This did not happen in Paterson.
55. See Arthur Zilversmit, *Changing Schools: Progressive Education Theory and Practice, 1930–1960* (Chicago: University of Chicago Press, 1993), p. 3. Elsie's ideas about the emphasis on meeting the needs of children was considered "progressive" although this is an impossible concept to define. Historian Zilversmit, attempting to define it, writes: "Their first priority was to create schools in which children would find a nurturing environment that would allow them to develop their individual capacities." Elsie's work certainly fits this conception, but her vision of the community school was much broader as she integrated a larger social vision that what was traditionally considered "child-centered progressive."
56. ERCM, p. 162.
57. Others of note who were part of this organization include Elizabeth Gurley Flynn, Mary Heaton Vorse and Alice Paul. Crystal Eastman was very active in the feminist movement, helping organize the Feminist Congress in New York in 1919. Issues for the Congress included the right to vote, equality in employment, access to birth control, and moving to end double moral standards. See Sue Heinemann, *Timelines of American Women's History* (New York: Perigee, 1996), p. 43.
58. ERCM, p. 154.
59. ERCM, pp. 155–156.
60. ERCM, p. 156.
61. ERCM, p. 157.
62. Margaret Sanger, *An Autobiography* (New York: W.W. Norton, 1938), p. 118. Sanger had received the following notice from the NYC postmaster. It read, "Dear Madam, you are hereby notified that the Solicitor of the post Office Department has decided that the *Women Rebel* for March 1914 is unmailable under Section 489 postal laws and regulations."
63. ERCM, pp. 157–158.
64. ERCM, p. 158.
65. This experience came about when Elsie and Florence were trying to find an apartment. They made a mistake and ended up in the red-light district. "We sensed something wrong," Elsie recalled, "partly because of the questions they asked whose purpose we did not understand, and partly because while we were there several odd-looking men and women came into the room." ERCM, p. 158.
66. ERCM, p. 160.
67. ERCM, pp. 162–163.
68. ERCM, p. 164.
69. *Obituaries, New York Times*, December 17, 1914. This issue reports the death of Elsie's father. He actually passed away on December 16, 1914. The short obituary suggests that

his passing was from a long illness although Elsie does not mention it in her memoirs. He is buried along with Elsie and other family members in Greenwood Cemetery in Brooklyn. ERCM, pp. 164–165.
70. ERCM, p. 166.
71. Elsie lived about two years with her mother at Gramercy Park. ERCM, p. 167.
72. Elsie reported that her friend Ellen Yale Stevens had been politically forced out as principal of the Brooklyn Heights Seminary and Florence Greer appointed in her place. ERCM, p. 168.
73. In her memoirs, Elsie gradually begins to refer to Florence Greer as "Miss Greer." Perhaps as she sat to write her memoirs she began to rethink her association with Florence and the tensions between them during these years.
74. ERCM, p. 169.
75. Elsie does not explain why her family "deserted" her, but she seemed irritated by it. ERCM, p. 170.
76. Elsie's mother and sister may have sensed this early, and this may explain why they left Elsie alone to recuperate. ERCM, p. 174.
77. ERCM, pp. 174–175.
78. Steve Golin, *The Fragile Bridge*, p. 199.
79. ERCM, p. 134. This is an interesting term for Elsie to use and may have come from the influence of William H. Kilpatrick. Kilpatrick had substituted "learning by living" for "learning by doing," which he felt better described Dewey's philosophy. See the Kilpatrick Diaries, 16 November 1917, 3 July 1914, 1 January 1916. Also view William Heard Kilpatrick, "We Learn as We Live," Conference Proceedings, Pasadena City Schools, 13–20 July 1949, p. 38. Original source for this information is John Bienke, *The Life of William Heard Kilpatrick* (New York: Peter Lang, 1998), p. 402.

Chapter Seven

1. See Loretta Turner, *When Bar Harbor Was Eden* (Dover, NH: Arcadia Press, 1995), pp. 7, 97. This book of photographs chronicles the history of Bar Harbor. It makes quite clear the elite nature of this summer colony. The book lacks photos of the business district, where Elsie had her store. Elsie seemed to be able to move easily within this type of community and also relate to her more radical friends in social settings such as the Provincetown Players in Cape Cod, many of whom held IWW connections.
2. Richmond Barrett, *Good Old Summer Days* (New York: Appleton-Century Company, 1941), p. 306. Barrett writes like a social reporter and chronicles the havens for the rich, including Newport, Saratoga, and Bar Harbor.
3. ERCM, p. 176.
4. ERCM, p. 178.
5. *Annual Report of the Red Cross*. June 30, 1918. (LaCrosse, WI: Brookhaven Press, 1918), p. 75. For a brief history of the Red Cross see Charles Hurd, *The Compact History of the American Red Cross* (New York: Hawthorn, 1959). For a more detailed portrayal of the Red Cross during the war see Foster Rhea Dulles, *The American Red Cross: A History* (Westport, CT: Greenwood, 1971).

NOTES

6. Ibid. Elsie notes the Canteen was under the direction of a Mr. and Mrs. Roswell, "two young able and socially prominent New Yorkers." ERCM, p. 183.
7. ERCM, p.178.
8. ERCM, p. 179.
9. Ibid.
10. ERCM, p 180.
11. ERCM, p 181.
12. Elsie does not discuss how difficult it must have been to run the store and still work at Brooklyn Heights. ERCM, p. 182.
13. ERCM, p. 182.
14. ERCM, p. 183.
15. Ibid.
16. ERCM, p. 188.
17. Ibid.
18. ERCM, p. 187.
19. ERCM, p. 188.
20. ERCM, p.189.
21. It is interesting that Dewey kept the note for almost ten years. No doubt he had word that she was coming to see him in New York. ERCM, p. 189.
22. Ibid.
23. Ibid.
24. ERCM, p. 190.
25. ERCM, p. 191.
26. Ibid. Elsie did not believe Sara Goodwin had contacted Florence about professional references. She wrote: "I took some comfort from the fact that in engaging me she had depended on my University record and had not, as far as I knew, consulted Florence Greer—or if she had, it made no difference."
27. ERCM, p. 192.
28. Ibid.
29. Ibid. Elsie was following in a tradition set for her by previous teacher Adelaide Nichols, the former head of the English department. Under Nichols the department had built up a reputation for good dramatic performance. Plays took place in a small theater built behind Miss Goodwin's home.
30. ERCM, pp. 192–193.
31. Mary Heaton Vorse, *Time and Town: A Provincetown Chronicle* (New York: The Dial Press, 1942), p. 212. Provincetown was Vorse's home town, and she describes the history of the community in this work. She mentions that Zorach was considered a part of the community along with Eugene O'Neill, Charles Demuth, and Arthur Fiske. The Provincetown Players were at the time performing in New York.
32. For information on the Shady Hill School, see Edward Yeomans, *The Shady Hill School: The First Fifty Years* (Cambridge, MA: Windflower Press, 1979) and Sue Ettelson, "The Parker School Legacy," in Marie K. Stone, *Survey I and Survey II of Twenty-five Current Francis W. Parker Faculty on Teaching at the School for Twenty or More Years*. April 1993, June 1994. ERCM, p. 195.

33. ERCM, p. 195.
34. Ellen most likely told Elsie about her family, and Elsie wrote about the family in her memoirs. Ellen's grandfather had immigrated from Ireland to attend Princeton University. Ellen's mother was a southern socialite by Elsie's description and met Ellen's father while he was practicing law in Washington, DC. He left Washington to move to Hillsboro, Ohio, where the family lived a small-town existence; an existence Ellen's mother never adjusted to. Ellen was the youngest of five girls. As a young girl she spent a great deal of time with her older sister Mary, who had married Lyman Beecher, the nephew of Henry Ward Beecher, pastor of the Plymouth Church in Brooklyn Heights. ERCM, p. 193–194.
35. ERCM, p. 196.
36. Syllabus for Types of Philosophic Thought. Course taught at Columbia University, 1922–1923. Elsie wrote on this folder, "given to me by John Dewey, year in Boston, 1922–1923." While working at Milton Elsie was receiving a salary of $2,500.00 as head of the English department under a five-year contract. ERCP 21/2/25.
37. As Elsie recalled, Ellen had a tougher time taking criticism and wrote, "Ellen discouraged easily, and grieved because the paintings she made were childlike and naive..." ERCM, p. 197.
38. ERCM, p. 197.
39. Robert Karoly Sarlos, *Jig Cook and the Provincetown Players: Theatre in Ferment* (Amherst: University of Massachusetts, 1982), p. 199. Sarlos does not mention that Zorach taught in progressive schools but does briefly sketch his later career. "Zorach painted until in the 1920s he was commissioned to do *The Spirit of Dance* for Radio City Music Hall, and in 1954 he sculpted four large figures for the Mayo Clinic," p. 199.
40. William Zorach, *William Zorach* (New York: American Artists, 1945). The book contains no page numbers but does exhibit Zorach's varied artwork.
41. John Baur, *William Zorach* (New York: Praeger, 1959), p. 24. Zorach's longest teaching assignment was at the Arts Students League, where he began teaching in 1929. He received the Logan Medal for sculpture in 1931 and for watercolor in 1932 from the Art Institute of Chicago. See Zorach, *William Zorach*. Elsie took some of her paintings over the Thanksgiving holidays to the home of William and Marguerite Zorach, then living on West 10th Street in New York. "I tried to tell them how I felt about painting," Elsie explained, "and Marguerite, of whom I stand in awe, surprisingly seemed to comprehend and sympathize." ERCM, p. 197.
42. Zorach, *William Zorach*. This explanation may be one of the reasons Zorach and his wife Marguerite left the Provincetown Players because the Players preferred to focus on realism while the Zorachs preferred creativity and imagination.
43. ERCM, p. 198.
44. Ibid.
45. ERCM, p. 199.
46. Ibid.
47. ERCM, p. 200.
48. Ibid.
49. ERCM, p. 201.

NOTES

50. Ibid. The school in Long Island was run by one of Dewey's admirers, a Mr. Bulkey. Elsie does not detail her experience there.
51. ERCM, p. 201.
52. ERCM, p. 202.
53. ERCM, pp. 201–202. According to Elsie, Edna Hopkins was not happy about the move to Ohio State. "... Edna was unhappy about the arrangement. She was a modern in art, and in spirit, and James' acceptance of this position seemed in some way to confirm her fear that, gifted and eminent an artist as James was, he was fundamentally a conservative. She was that summer suffering from inability, after a long illness, to start her own work again. The idea of life in Columbus, Ohio, froze her soul; she was by no means through with Paris, which she loved, and in the fall she returned there." ERCM, p. 204.
54. ERCM, p. 203.
55. See Nancy Fix Anderson, Review essay "Righting Women: Interpretations of the Lives of Anglo-American Victorian Women," *Nineteenth Century Prose* 22 (January 1995), p. 158.

Chapter Eight

1. ERCM, p. 204.
2. *Readers Encyclopedia*, p. 422.
3. Caroline Pratt, *I Learn from Children: An Adventure in Progressive Education* (New York: Simon and Shuster, 1948), pp. 26–27. For more specific biographical information on Pratt, see Pat Carlton, *Caroline Pratt: A Biography* (Unpublished dissertation, Teachers College, 1986). For a more contemporary brief biography of Pratt, see Mary Hauser, "Caroline Pratt and the City and Country School," in Semel and Sadovnik, *Founding Mothers and Others* (New York: Praeger, 2002), pp. 68–69. The later work chronicles the contributions of women educators, many who espoused progressive education as their philosophy of education.
4. See Lawrence Cremin, *The Transformation of the School*, pp. 203–204. Cremin's work is still the starting point for any serious study of progressive education. Marot became known for her work with the Women's Trade Union and her editorial work on *The Dial*. Marot's influence on Pratt is evident through the early attempt to use education as a tool for social reform in helping poor working-class children. See also Joyce Antler, *Lucy Sprague Mitchell*, p. 237. Antler details the relationship between Pratt and Mitchell, p. 237.
5. Susan Semel, "The City and Country School," in Semel and Sadovnik's *Schools of Tomorrow: Schools of Today* (New York: Peter Lang, 1999), p. 125. One of the earliest progressive attempts to understand work was evident at Hull House, where Jane Addams had a museum of simple tools. She believed work and labor through the Industrial Revolution had dehumanized the creative aesthetic nature of work. Work was linked with creativity and expression, and the individual needed to be in charge. The link between Addams, Dewey, and Pratt and their understanding of work needs further investigation. Recall Pratt's own interest in settlement work and surrounding herself by teachers like Lucy Sprague Mitchell and Jessie Stanton, both experienced in settlement work. See Jane Addams, *Democracy and Social Ethics* (New York: Macmillan, 1902), pp. 180–181, and

Twenty Years at Hull House (New York: Macmillan, 1910). Christopher Lasch, ed. *The Social Thought of Jane Addams* (Indianapolis: Bobbes-Merrill, 1965).

6. John Dewey, MW 8: 286. A photograph is included in "Constructing in Miniature the Things They See Around Them," (Play School, NYC), p. 285. Elsie's work in Kentucky and West Virginia will exhibit many of these characteristics. Dewey also notes in *Schools of To-morrow* the growing interest in drama being used by progressive schools which will become an integral component of Elsie's pedagogy.
7. See Caroline Ware, *Greenwich Village: 1920–1930*, (Boston: Houghton Mifflin, 1935), p. 245. Ware argues the intelligentsia were attracted to schools like City and Country and in doing so "the Villagers acted consistently with their own repudiation of long accepted values," p. 342. Ware claims the Villagers did little to interact with the Irish and Italian communities who had preciously settled the community. Ware's critique challenges the Villager's understanding of democratic community although the innovative progressive schools often articulated such.
8. Ibid., p. 327.
9. Semel, "The City and Country School," p. 126.
10. The elite nature of progressive schools is further documented by the Eight-Year Study under the direction of Ralph Tyler from 1932 to 1941.
11. Ibid., p. 127. See also Caroline Pratt, "Learning by Experience," *Child Study* 11, 1933, p. 70.
12. See Mary Hauser, *Caroline Pratt*, p. 70. See also Lawrence Cremin, *Transformation of the School*, p. 204.
13. Cremin, *Transformation of the School*, pp. 203–204. Cremin in a later work, *American Education: the Metropolitan Experience* (New York: Harper and Row, 1988), accurately described the progressive education movement as pluralistic and contradictory, p. 228. See also Pratt, *I Learn from Children*, p. 23. Chapter Five of Dewey's *Schools of To-morrow* is an essay on the City and Country School, called at the time The Play School, a name which Pratt felt best described her philosophy of early childhood education.
14. This conception of the child coupled with the necessity of nurturing can be found in the work of Comenius, Rousseau, Pestalozzi, and Froebel, all familiar to most progressive educators.
15. Semel, "The City and Country School," p. 130. One can find similar approaches to curriculum in The Gary Schools in Gary, Indiana, and later in Elsie's Arthurdale schools. It was important for the progressives to see the school as a community itself although they sometimes differed on the nature of that community in linking it with larger democratic society.
16. ERCM, pp. 204–205.
17. John Dewey, MW 7: 259. From Dewey's contribution to the *Cyclopedia of Education*, edited by Paul Monroe from Teachers College.
18. ERCM, p. 205.
19. Ibid.
20. Mary Hauser, *Caroline Pratt*, p. 69. Original source is Caroline Pratt, *Experimental Practice in the City and Country School* (New York: E.P. Dutton, 1924), p. 32.
21. ERCM, p. 206.

NOTES 279

22. Ibid.
23. Demeter was the Greek goddess of corn. As the story goes, Demeter's daughter Persephone was abducted by Hades, who snatched her away in his chariot.
24. ERCM, p. 207.
25. Ibid.
26. Ibid.
27. Ibid.
28. ERCM, p. 208.
29. Ibid. Elsie noted that Caroline Pratt believed no one could possibly comprehend the philosophy of City and Country within a year. Elsie believed she did understand it.
30. ERCM, p. 208.
31. Antler, *Lucy Sprague Mitchell*, p. 245. This quote is from Mitchell's unpublished autobiography.
32. Ibid., p. 301. See also Lucy Sprague Mitchell, *Two Lives* (New York: Simon and Schuster, 1953), pp. 412–413. *Two Lives* is the story of Lucy Mitchell and her husband Wesley Mitchell, a well-known and respected scholar and economist. "It was her most experimental and least didactic book, her deepest, most colorful and natural piece of writing." Antler, *Lucy Sprague Mitchell*, p. 342.
33. ERCM, pp. 208–209.
34. ERCM, p. 209.
35. Antler, *Lucy Sprague Mitchell*, p. 284. Lucy Sprague Mitchell, *Here and Now Story Book* (New York: E.P. Dutton, 1921).
36. Ibid., p. 243.
37. Ibid., p. 250. Mitchell had an intense dislike for sagas, myths, and fairy tales, "because they violated the processes of ordered thinking and confused young children who could not understand their symbolic meaning."
38. Ibid., p. 286.
39. ERCM, p. 209.
40. Jessie Stanton directed the nursery school staff at Arthurdale from 1934 to 1936. Mitchell served on the National Advisory Board to the Arthurdale School. See Elsie Ripley Clapp, *Community Schools in Action* (New York: Viking, 1939), pp. 397–398.
41. ERCM, p. 209. Jack Mitchell was Lucy Mitchell's son who was born in 1914.
42. John Dewey Papers. Collection 102. Special Collections, Morris Library, Southern Illinois University, Carbondale. "What I Recall from That Class," Elsie Ripley Clapp's recollection of the 1922 course Special Problems in Philosophy of Education. JDP 102/71/14. Elsie served as Dewey's assistant for the class during the summer session of 1922.
43. See Mary Hauser, *Caroline Pratt*, for Pratt's views of parental involvement at City and Country, p. 72.
44. See Joseph Newman, "Marietta Johnson and the Organic School," in Semel and Sadnovik, *Founding Mothers and Others* (New York: Praeger, 2002), p. 27. The connections in Greenwich eventually led to Marietta Johnson's school coming to the attention of John Dewey, who chronicled the school with his daughter Evelyn in *Schools of To-morrow* (New York: E.P. Dutton, 1915). For a more contemporary history of the school, see Joseph Newman,

"Experimental School Experimental Community: The Marietta Johnson School of Organic Educations, Fairhope Alabama," in Semel and Sadnovik, *Schools of Today, Schools of Tomorrow: What Happened to Progressive Education* (New York: Peter Lang, 1999), Chapter 3.
45. ERCM, p. 211.
46. This information comes from the website of Choate Rosemary Hall, now in Wallingford, Connecticut. http://choate.edu. Ruutz-Rees taught Latin, Greek, French literature, history and "feminism by indirection" during her tenure at Rosemary.
47. ERCM, p. 212.
48. Ibid.
49. Ibid.
50. ERCM, p. 213.
51. Ibid. Dewey's concern about how well progressive education students might do in a traditional program was a significant issue of the time and although explored in the Eight-Year Study is still debated. The focus on the Eight-Year Study was the transition of progressive students into the college environment, in which it was concluded they did just as well as traditionally schooled students. Progressives saw this as a victory. Its publication during World War II and the changing political climate made it "dead on arrival."
52. ERCM, p. 214.
53. Ibid.
54. ERCM, p. 218.
55. ERCM, p. 224.
56. ERCM, p. 226. Elsie and Ellen had leased the Grove Court apartment for the summer. Due to their early arrival from Europe they had to move back in. Elsie made note of the "courtesy of the tenants" in their willingness to move. ERCM, p. 225.
57. Ibid. Jack Tworkov (1900–1982) immigrated to the United States from Poland at the age of thirteen. He studied at the Art Student's league and Columbia University. He was well known in New York art circles as an abstract impressionist. See http:// usbr.gov/museumproperty/art.
58. Arthur Zilversmit, *Changing Schools: Progressive Theory and Practice 1930–1960* (Chicago: University of Chicago, 1993), p.18.
59. To suggest that all progressive schools followed the same pattern is a mistake, and there was never a pure progressive education movement. This is clearly documented in David Tyack, *The One Best System: A History of American Urban Education* (Cambridge: Harvard University Press, 1974), Ronald Cohen and Raymond Mohl, *The Paradox of Progressive Education* (Port Washington, NY: Kennikat Press, 1979), Ronald Cohen, *Children of the Mill* (Bloomington: Indiana University Press, 1990), Larry Cuban, *How Teachers Taught: Constancy and Change in American Classrooms, 1890–1980*. (New York: Longman, 1984), pp. 43–44. Raymond Callahan, *Education and the Cult of Efficiency* (Chicago: University of Chicago Press, 1962). Some of the most clear early evidence is in John and Evelyn Dewey's *Schools of To-morrow* (New York: E.P. Dutton, 1915). Even as early as 1915 progressive schools showed a great diversity due to differences in location, culture, philosophy, and leadership. This was Dewey's vision, but it also led to confusion.

NOTES

Chapter Nine

1. Elsie noted she kept one of the former Heads of the Rosemary Junior School on staff that first year, a decision she later regretted. Elsie believed she made a "rallying point for the resistance and the disgruntled among the parents." At the end of the year Elsie informed Miss Ruutz-Rees that she could no longer work with the former head, who soon left. ERCM, p. 227.
2. ERCM, p. 228.
3. Ibid.
4. Ibid.
5. ERCM, p. 229.
6. ERCM, p. 230.
7. ERCM, p. 229.
8. Ibid.
9. Ibid. Elsie does not detail the content of the criticism but did not feel it was serious.
10. ERCM, p. 230.
11. Ibid., p. 231.
12. Elsie Ripley Clapp, "Talk Given at the Parents' Meeting on 2 February 1925, Rosemary Hall." Vassar Alumnae Library Papers, Vassar College, Poughkeepsie, New York.
13. ERCM, p. 232.
14. Ibid., Reading the bulletin years later, following the years spent in Kentucky and West Virginia, Elsie believed the work clearly illustrated their thought and practice at the time.
15. Elsie Ripley Clapp, *The Rosemary Junior School Bulletin*. Vassar College Alumnae Collection. Vassar College Library. This bulletin was updated version from a previous version and is dated 1928, p. 3.
16. Ibid., p. 6.
17. Ibid., p. 11.
18. Ibid., p. 15.
19. Ibid., p. 18.
20. Elsie was particularly proud of the art program and wrote, "The Junior School is fortunate in having as its art director William Zorach, whose interests in education makes it possible for us to have working with us a great artist, which is in itself an invaluable experience for children." Ibid., p. 30.
21. Elsie Ripley Clapp to Gertrude Hartman, Correspondence. *Progressive Education* 3 (January/February/March) (1926), pp. 89–90. The subject of this issue was called "the new child study" and focused on early childhood education. Elsie and her staff were right in the midst of this new view of the child using the best psychological and sociological information available to base the education of the young child.
22. For a detailed description of "The Principles of Progressive Education," see *Progressive Education*, 2 (July/August/ September 1925), p. 129.
23. Cremin, *Transformation of the School*, p. 211. In comparing Naumberg with Caroline Pratt, Cremin wrote, " Margaret Naumberg attempted in the Children's School [later the Walden School] to build an education that would take proper account of psychological principles; likewise, Caroline Pratt undertook in the Play School to generalize the notion that chil-

dren comprehend the world most vividly through play activities." For information on the Walden School in the 1920s, see Margaret Pollitzer, "Foundations of the Walden School," *Progressive Education*.2 (1935), pp. 15–18. This short piece describes the philosophy of the Walden School: "a conscious educational philosophy that balances and correlates the life of each child with the life of the entire social group," p. 18.

24. Ellen Steele may have been the best-known progressive teacher at Rosemary and often expressed her views in the journal *Progressive Education*. Goldsmith had heard of her reputation and visited in order to fill out her staff for the summer demonstration school.
25. ERCM, p. 233.
26. Elsie learned about the diet from her friend Diana Storm, "and her actor husband, Arthur Holt." ERCM, p. 234.
27. Ibid. Elsie does not explain why she thought Ellen was disenchanted with demonstration schools.
28. ERCM, p. 235.
29. Ibid.
30. The activities of block building and village construction will be seen in Elsie's later work in Kentucky and West Virginia. ERCM, p. 236.
31. Ibid. Rosemary Lilliard would replace Maude Stewart. Elsie described Lilliard as "a brilliant young musician just returned from Europe" and was "interested to find ways to make music a vital part of the children's work experiences." p. 236.
32. ERCM, p. 237.
33. Ellen Steele, "Freeing the Child Through Art," *Progressive Education* 3 (April/May/June 1926), p. 168.
34. Examples of student art from the Rosemary Junior School can be seen in the journal *Progressive Education* 3 (April/May/June 1926), p. 129. See also in that issue Lucy Sprague Mitchell's article, "Maps as Art Expression," pp. 150–154. This article contains artwork from an eleven-year-old student at the Rosemary Junior School captioned, "The Period of Exploration and Expansion." ERCM, pp. 237–238.
35. The focus on weaving and spinning is documented in early photographs of the Dewey Lab School in Chicago. Elsie's later work at Ballard and Arthurdale shows this activity, grasping the basic concepts of work. Dewey addressed this notion as consumatory experience in *Experience and Nature*. Dewey wished to challenge the distinction between fine art and useful art. His definition of art included "all action that deals with materials and energies outside the body, assembling, refining, combining, manipulating them until their new state yields a satisfaction not afforded by their crude condition." *Experience and Nature* LW: 283–284. V.1. (Originally published in 1925). For a more detailed discussion of art by Dewey, see Robert Westbrook, *John Dewey and American Democracy*, pp. 337–341.
36. Elsie Ripley Clapp, "The Subject Matters in Experimental Education," *Progressive Education* 3 (October/November/December 1926), pp. 370–375.
37. Ibid., p. 371.
38. Ibid., p. 372. Note John Locke's similar discussion in *Some Thoughts Concerning Education* when he implies a key to education is to get the child to ask to be taught.
39. Ibid.
40. Ibid., p. 374.

41. This predates Dewey's philosophy of art by at least eight years when he will publish *Art as Experience* in 1934. John Dewey, *Art as Experience* (New York: G.P. Putnam's Sons, 1934). Elsie mentions in her article Dewey's contribution to her own thinking.
42. Clapp, "The Subject Matters in Experimental Education," p. 374.
43. Music and Poems of Children, "Creative Music made in connection with other class studies, Rosemary Junior School, Greenwich, CT." There is a postmodern concern here about the limits of language. See ERCP, 21/3/1.
44. ERCM, p. 238.
45. Ibid., p. 239. Elsie had performed this play while at the Milton Academy and asked permission to use the script and stage designs.
46. Elsie does not record if their pagan studies created any concern at the Rosemary Junior School. The studies were seen as part of the learning process and attached to the individual class studies. For Florence House's use of the artwork, see Florence House, "Creative Expression Through the Use of Block Print," *Progressive Education* 3 (April/May/June 1926), pp. 134–135. House discusses how block printing can help children express themselves and how materials such as linoleum or wood can be used in a study of cultures, East and West.
47. ERCM, pp. 241–242.
48. Ibid., p. 242.
49. Ibid.
50. Ibid.
51. ERCM, p. 244.
52. ERCM, p. 245.
53. Ellen Steele and Rosemary Lillard, "Creative Music in the Group Life," *Progressive Education* 4 (January/February/March 1927), pp. 45–49. Elsie used a notebook from Rosemary Lilliard to compose this section of her memoirs, but the work is not available. New teachers at the time were Marie Spottswood, who taught the tens, and Helen Lacey, who directed athletics.
54. Ibid., p. 46.
55. Ibid. Examples of the verse the children wrote can be found on pp. 47–48 of this article. Titles included "Song to Charlemagne," the "Jester's Song," the "Song of the Bard," and "The Potter's Song." Ellen Steele mentions in the piece that some of the twelves were studying Chinese culture and the use of music.
56. ERCM, p. 250.
57. ERCM, p. 252.
58. Ibid.
59. ERCM, pp. 252–253.
60. Ibid. Laura Wylie passed away in June 1932 and had been a professor of English at Vassar from 1895 to 1924. See Dorothy Plum, *The Great Experiment: A Chronicle of Vassar* (Poughkeepsie: Vassar College, 1961), p. 55. This work chronicles events in Vassar history with brief descriptions of each. Elsie's sister Marjorie and her mother were living in Poughkeepsie at this time.
61. ERCM, p. 254.
62. ERCM, p. 255. Elsie does not name the teachers involved in the discontent other than Cruger.

63. ERCM, p. 256.
64. ERCM, p. 288. Flax is from the genus *Linnum* and the family *Linaceae*; a slender plant with blue flowers cultivated for its fiber. It can be used for spinning, which is why it was put to use by Elsie and other progressives.
65. Ellen Steele, "Twelve Year Olds Investigate the Textile Industry," *Progressive Education*, 5, (July/August/September 1928): pp. 238–241. The children also put lyrics to music. One song addressed the spinning of an Indian woman, another a Mississippi dock worker, and another a pier where they were unloading cotton. What a wonderful opportunity to explore the difficult working class lives of these people as they contributed to textiles.
66. Ibid., p. 241.
67. For how Hine used his camera as a progressive artist, see Lewis Hine, "Baltimore to Biloxi and Back—The Children's Burden in Oyster and Shrimp Canneries," *The Survey* 30 (May 3, 1933), p. 170. Eugene Provenzo, "The Photographer as an Educator: The Photo-stories of Lewis Hine," *Teachers College Record* 83 (Summer 1982). See also Judith Mara Gutman's *Lewis Hine, Two Perspectives* (New York: Grossman Publishers, 1974).
68. Cheryl Black, *The Women of Provincetown (1915–1922)* (Tuscaloosa: University of Alabama, 2002), pp. 15, 29. Black argues that it was Marguerite who was the dominant member in the relationship. Her work with William on set design with the Players was innovative and extraordinary in an era in which there were few women set designers.
69. ERCM, p. 264. At the conference Jessie Stanton presented some of her work on block building at City and Country, Avah Hughes of the Lincoln School described a milk-study at the Lincoln School, Ellen Steele described her study of cotton, and Sara Patrick led the group in a panel discussion, ERCM, p. 263.
70. ERCM, p. 265. Clearly Lucy Sprague Mitchell was trying to do some of this through the Bureau of Educational Experiments. Mitchell and Harriet Johnson saw their work as scientific.
71. Elsie does not state where Ellen Steele was at the time.
72. ERCM, p. 266.
73. Ibid., For Mayhew's description of the Lab School, see Katherine Camp Mayhew and Anna Camp Edwards, *The Dewey School: The Laboratory School of the University of Chicago, 1896–1903* (New York: D. Appleton, Century, 1936). Dewey collaborated with Mayhew and Edwards in writing the book.
74. Harold Rugg and Ann Shumaker, *The Child Centered School* (New York: World Book Company, 1928), p. 51. Lawrence Cremin published the book again in 1969 as part of his American Education Series. Elsie's *Community Schools in Action* was also published as part of the series.
75. Elsie mentions that the Lincoln School had made some progress in teaching large classes through active learning. She believed some success could be had with large classes.
76. ERCM, p. 272.
77. Ibid.
78. Elsie Ripley Clapp, "Children's Mathematics," *Progressive Education* 5 (April/May/June 1928), pp. 131–135.
79. Ibid., p. 134.

NOTES

80. Ibid., p. 132.
81. ERCM, p. 274. The journal *Progressive Education* announced Vassar's interest in initiating a new department for the education of women in 1925. See News and Comments, *Progressive Education* 2 (July/August/ September) (1925), p. 181.
82. Ibid. On these trips to Vassar, Elsie stayed with her friend Winifred Smith, a teacher in the English department.
83. Dorothy Plum, *The Great Experiment*, p. 81. Jessie Stanton directed the summer institutes at Vassar from 1929 to 1931. See also ERCP 21/3/11. Misc. Material. Some of this material contains biographical notes on Jessie Stanton. Stanton was considered an experienced nursery school instructor and an expert of the progressive approach to early childhood education. See ERCP, 21/3/1. Stanton was a strong proponent of block play, evident at Rosemary, Ballard, and Arthurdale. See Jessie Stanton, "Six-Year-Olds Explorations in New York City," *Progressive Education* 5 (July/August/September 1928), pp. 224–228.
84. ERCM, p. 275. Elsie described the relationship of Maude Ainslie and Fay Barnum. "Fay Barnum, also was born and brought up in Louisville, had spent some years in New York where she and Edna Hopkins had shared an apartment before Edna married James Hopkins, Fay designing stage costumes and scenery and Edna working at the Art Students League. Returning to Louisville, Fay made her home with Maude Ainslie. It was a unique relationship; to Maude, Fay brought her vitality and her abounding interests; to Fay, Maude gave a background of security and devotion. Both artists, they each had an ever-fresh sense and appreciation of the other's gifts and qualities." ERCM, p. 275.
85. ERCM, p. 276.
86. ERCM, p. 271.
86. ERCM, p. 278.
87. Ibid.
88. Ibid.
89. ERCM, p. 279. Agnes Hocking and her husband Ernest were close friends of Lucy Sprague Mitchell and her husband Wesley. Agnes Hocking had started Shady Hill School on the front porch of her home "when they could find no suitable instruction for their young children." See Antler, *Lucy Sprague Mitchell*, p. 277. Hocking is described as eccentric, spontaneous, devoted, and unyielding. As Antler notes, she also believed in fairies.
90. ERCM, p. 282.
91. ERCM, p. 283.
92. Ellen Steele, "The Teacher as Part of the Environment," *Progressive Education* 4 (April/May/June 1927), pp. 110–112. ERCM, p. 285.
93. Ibid.
94. Ibid.

Chapter Ten

1. ERCM, p. 280.
2. ERCM, p. 281.
3. ERCM, p. 282.

4. ERCM, pp. 284–285.
5. Ellwood P. Cubberley, *The Improvement of Rural Schools* (New York: Houghton Mifflin, 1912), pp. vi, 13.
6. Elsie Ripley Clapp, *The Use of Resources in Education* (New York: Harper Brothers, 1952), p. 11, 129. [Noted hereafter as URE]. Elsie Clapp dedicated this book to John Dewey "for it is the philosophy he has expounded that has enabled education to serve people in their living and their learning by helping them comprehend their resources and expand them," p. v. Elsie wrote the book as a guide for other progressive educators but did not see it as a blueprint to be simply copied. It is the last known published description of her work in Kentucky and West Virginia. See also *Manuscript of the Ballard School*, 21/4/1 (hereafter MBS), ERCP, p. 2. This manuscript explores much of the material included in Clapp's *Community Schools in Action* and *The Use of Resources in Education*.
7. Elsie and staff read N. S. Shaler, *Kentucky: A Pioneer Commonwealth*, Cecil B. Hastings, *Life and Times of Daniel Boone*, W.D. Funkhouser and W.S. Webb, *Ancient Life in Kentucky*, A.B. Hulbert, *Path of Inland Commerce*, F.A. Ogg, *The Old Northwest*, Malcolm Keir, *March of Commerce* and *Epic of Industry*, URE. p. 9. It is evident how much these books served as resource guides for the teachers and influenced the curriculum at Ballard for several years.
8. Clapp, URE, p. 8. For a concise description and history of Ballard, see Elsie Ripley Clapp, "Social Education in a Public Rural School," *Childhood Education* 9 (October 1932), pp. 24–26
9. Clapp, URE, p. 16.
10. Ibid., p. 17.
11. Ibid., p. 18.
12. MBS, p. 3.
13. Clapp, URE, p. 12.
14. Teacher salaries the first year were $1,800 plus their supplement. Half of the $10,000 came from the community, largely from the wealthier parents. URE, p. 41.
15. Ibid., p. 13.
16. Ibid., p. 23.
17. Ibid., p. 42.
18. For a complete list of Ballard faculty from 1929 to 1934, see *Community Schools in Action*, pp. 395–396. This also included the student teachers, who were prominent members of the teaching staff. The majority of student teachers came from the University of Louisville.
19. Clapp, *Community Schools in Action*, p. 21. See also MBS, p. 8.
20. MBS, p. 11.
21. Clapp, URE, p. 47. The industrial arts program under the direction of Louise Lawton was integrated throughout Ballard, including the elementary school and high school. This typically involved some form of agricultural education or manual training. Activities included planting gardens, canning, and taking care of the physical plant by the students. See MBS, p. 8.
22. Ibid., p. 50.

23. Elsie explains the work of this class in some detail with the notes from Sheffield. See *Community Schools in Action*, pp. 29–32. For the original article that reports on several plays written at Ballard, see Elsie Ripley Clapp, Elisabeth Sheffield, and George Beecher, "Plays in a Kentucky County School," *Progressive Education* 8 (1931), pp. 35–39. For a more realistic description of the active and significant role women played in pioneer life, see Sandra L. Myers, *Westering Women and the Frontier Experience, 1800–1915* (Albuquerque: University of New Mexico Press, 1982). Myers attacks the stereotypes that pioneer women were "sunbonnet saints," "gentle tamers," and "silent partners."
24. See MBS, p. 7. Here Elsie emphasizes the importance she and the staff placed on nurturing subject matter interests.
25. Clapp, URE, p. 59.
26. Homer Howard, Year-End Report in *Community Schools in Action*, p. 35.
27. Howard wrote about his experiences with the students in "Mapping Out a Small School's Activities Program," *The Nation's Schools* 8 (December 1931), pp. 65–69.
28. Clapp, URE, p. 65. Elsie accepted some of the responsibility for the failure. Eleanor McArdle was not on the staff the following year.
29. Clapp, URE, p. 67. Elsie described no other teacher that way in the first year. She considered Beecher a gifted and talented teacher, perhaps the best on the staff at the time. Recall Elsie's own interest in art, history, music, and linguistics.
30. Ibid., p. 68.
31. Ibid., p. 70.
32. Ibid., p. 71. See also Clapp, Sheffield, and Beecher, "Plays in a Kentucky County School," pp. 35–39.
33. Ibid., p. 36.
34. Clapp, URE, p. 75.
35. For an interesting discussion of Jackson's rise to power and his treatment of native peoples, see Paul Johnson, *The Birth of the Modern: World Society 1815–1830* (New York: Harper and Row, 1991), pp. 225–231. Information on the federal policy of removal can be found in Bernard Sheehan, *Seeds of Extinction* (Chapel Hill: University of North Carolina, 1973). Alexis de Toqueville also made observations of the removal of native people in his landmark work *Democracy in America*.
36. Clapp, Sheffield, and Beecher, "Plays in a Kentucky County School," p. 38. The focus on Latin was due to its importance for college admission, and also it was taught in the local Louisville high schools, where many of the students would continue their education.
37. Clapp, URE, p. 87.
38. Ibid., p. 87–88.
39. For a brief description of this institute and its participants, see J. Allen Hickerson, "The Summer Institute of Progressive Education," *Progressive Education* 7 (October 1930), pp. 301–303. Perry D. Smith also served on the faculty of Winnetka Teachers College with Carleton Washburne and Flora Cooke of the Francis Parker School. See Arthur Zilversmit, *Changing Schools: Progressive Education Theory and Practice, 1930–1960* (Chicago: University of Chicago Press, 1993), p. 66.
40. For Elsie's session outline see Hickerson, "The Summer Institute of Progressive Education," p. 302. This summer institute was held in 1930 in conjunction with Vassar's Summer Institute of Euthenics directed by Elsie's friend Jessie Stanton.

41. Stanwood Cobb, "Retiring President's Message," *Progressive Education* 7 (May 1930), p. 180.
42. Clapp, URE, p. 103.
43. Ibid., p. 92.
44. Ibid., pp. 93, 95.
45. Ibid., p. 95.
46. Ibid., p. 122.
47. Ibid., p. 123.
48. Ibid., pp. 106–107.
49. See MBS, p. 11. This manuscript contains more specific information on how the students used electricity. One can also see photographs of models of their work in the Clapp collection in Special Collections 38, Morris Library.
50. Elsie started the Math Museum when she had observed on a trip to New York a similar museum in the Chase National Bank. She brought the idea back to Saunders, and the students named it the Math Museum. There are numerous examples in Chapter Two, *The Use of Resources in Education*, that describe how the teachers approached improving math and language studies at Ballard and integrating them throughout the curriculum.
51. MBS, p. 9.
52. Clapp, URE, p. 128.
53. Elsie did not note the name of the foundation from which the invitation came to write the grant, but she was disappointed when they did not receive it.
54. Ibid., p. 130. This work is very reminiscent of the work Lucy Sprague Mitchell was performing at the Cooperative School for Student Teachers and through the later work at Bank Street.
55. Clapp, URE, p. 137.
56. Homer Howard, "Mapping Out a Small School Activities Program," pp. 65, 69.
57. I can find no evidence that professional careers for girls were discussed at Ballard. There is evidence of some manual training for boys, but girls were placed in a more home economics or domestic economy track.
58. George Counts, "Dare Progressive Education Be Progressive?" *Progressive Education* 9 (April 1932), pp. 257–263. For a brief view of the effect of Count's speech at the convention, see Patricia A. Graham, *Progressive Education: From Arcady to Academe* (New York: Teachers College Press, 1967), pp. 63–75; and Cremin, *The Transformation of the School*, pp. 258–264.
59. This essay is also included in George Counts, *Dare the School Build a New Social Order* (Carbondale: Southern Illinois University Press, 1978), pp. 4–5. Wayne Urban, pp. v–xiv, writes an excellent historical introduction.
60. Graham, *Progressive Education*, p. 65.
61. George Counts, *Dare the School Build a New Social Order?* (New York: John Day, 1932), p. 9.
62. Elsie Ripley Clapp, "Learning and Indoctrinating," *Progressive Education* 9 (April 1932), p. 269.
63. Ibid., p. 270.

NOTES

64. Ibid., p. 271.
65. Elsie did not totally agree with Augusta Alpert's definition of progressivism. Alpert, a New York psychologist "insisted in an article in *The New Republic* that the word progressive in progressive education never carried political or sociological implications or obligation, that it is descriptive only of educational techniques which progress in keeping with psychological and other relevant findings." See *The New Republic*, v. 72, p. 75. See Cremin, *Transformation of the School*, p. 259. While it can be argued she neglects the political she does not neglect certain sociological aspects of linking education and social welfare.
66. In his diaries Kilpatrick has Counts and Bode present. Kilpatrick made a note in his diary about the meeting. Elsie did not recall Counts being at the Vassar meeting. Kilpatrick biographer John Beinke writes, "Teachers were ready to listen because there appeared to be no escape from the grinding economic conditions they were enduring." See John Beinke, *And There Were Giants in the Land: The Life of William Heard Kilpatrick* (New York: Peer Lang, 1998), p. 201. Regardless of their willingness to listen, most teachers were willing to work within the system rather than replace it. Elsie left no recollections of the meeting. Most likely she was one of few women present.
67. Graham, *Progressive Education*, p. 7.
68. Clapp, URE, p. 142.
69. Louise Lawton, the shop teacher at Ballard, also instructed part time at the University of Louisville.
70. Elsie Ripley Clapp, "Social Education in a Public Rural School," *Childhood Education* 9 (October 1932), pp. 24–26.
71. Ibid., p. 25.
72. Clapp, URE, p. 144.
73. Mrs. Thurston Ballard was the chief benefactor of the school, and when Elsie asked her to help she complied. She occasionally gave Elsie advice, but we do not know the nature of it.
74. The students in the later years in high school were typically the children of the working classes of small farmers. The wealthier students tended to go to private school or to Louisville high schools.
75. Elsie Ripley Clapp, "A Rural Community School in Kentucky," *Progressive Education* 10 (March 1933), pp. 123–128. Curti described Dewey's intellectual growth in *The Social Ideas of American Educators*. He wrote, "A democratic neighborliness and a sort of nonconformist individualism modified the social conservatism of the Vermont community in which he lived, factors that may well have contributed to his independent and democratic temper." Merle Curti, *The Social Ideas of American Educators* (New Jersey, Littlefield, Adams and Company, 1968), p. 500.
76. Ibid., p. 128.
77. Elsie Ripley Clapp, "The Teacher in Social Education," *Progressive Education* 10 (May 1933), pp. 283–287.
78. Ibid., p. 287.
79. Clapp, URE, p. 154.
80. Ibid., p. 156.
81. Ibid., p. 159.

82. Ibid.
83. Ibid., p. 155. During the 1933–1934 year at Ballard, Sheffield, Beecher, Carlson, and Saunders made up the high school staff, and all followed Elsie to Arthurdale. Three of seven of the elementary teachers followed, which included Ash, Jones, and Carlisle. Alice Bowie was the executive secretary who also went to Arthurdale. See *Community Schools in Action*, p. 396, for a complete listing of Ballard faculty from 1929 to 1934.
84. MBS, p. 13.
85. I owe much insight in this chapter to Dr. Sheldon Rahn as he evaluated Elsie's contributions from the perspective of social work. While a student at Union Theological Seminary, Dr. Rahn attended a class in educational foundations taught by Ernest Johnson, William Kilpatrick and George Counts. He was also a member of a small club on democratic socialism at Union Theological Seminary. Sheldon Rahn to Sam Stack, 27 April 2002. His wife is the niece of Elsie Clapp, Barbara Myers Rahn.

Chapter Eleven

1. United States Congress. Resettlement Administration Program. 74th Congress, 2d Session, 1936. Document 213. Washington: United States Government Printing Office. See also United States Department of the Interior. Division of Subsistence Homesteads. General Information Concerning the Purposes and Policies of the Division of Subsistence Homesteads, Circular 1. National Archives. Washington, D.C. 1933, p. 1. For the original press announcement from the federal government about the Reedsville project, see Record Group 96 Entry 9. Records of the Farmers Home Administration 1933–1935. Box 13. National Archives, Washington, D.C.
2. Paul Conkin, "Arthurdale Revisited," In *A New Deal for America* edited by Bryan Ward. (Arthurdale: Arthurdale Heritage Inc., 1995), 46. This work includes proceedings from a conference held at Arthurdale on subsistence homesteads. It is a concise source of information on the Arthurdale project and the homestead movement. For a more thorough analysis of the larger federal homestead movement, see Paul Conkin, *Tomorrow a New World: The New Deal Community Programs* (Ithaca, NY: Cornell University Press, 1959). The most comprehensive work on the Arthurdale project is still Stephen Haid's, *Arthurdale: An Experiment in Community Planning* (Dissertation: West Virginia University, 1975).
3. Federal Emergency Relief Administration Document on Organizing Communities. Archives and Manuscripts 1646. Folder 4. West Virginia Regional Collection [WVRC], West Virginia University Libraries.
4. For a well-known critique of the subsistence homesteads, see Russell Lord and Paul Johnstone, eds. *A Place on Earth: A Critical Appraisal of Subsistence Homesteads* (Washington, D.C.: United States Bureau of Agricultural Economics, 1942), pp. 17–19.
5. Scotts Run is spelled without an apostrophe. This use is supported by the *West Virginia Gazetteer of Physical and Cultural Place-names*. See Ronald Lewis, "Scotts Run: America's Symbol of the Great Depression in the Coal Fields," in *A New Deal for America*, pp. 1–23. Scotts Run was a creek that ran along the various coal-mining communities that could turn into a raging torrent during storms and flood the area, creating problems in sanitation due to pollution.

6. Lois Scarf, "First Lady/First Homestead," in *A New Deal for America*, p. 45. See also Lois Scarf, *Eleanor Roosevelt: First Lady of American Liberalism* (Boston: Twayne, 1987). The most comprehensive works on Eleanor are Blanche Wiesen Cooke's, *Eleanor Roosevelt (1884–1933)* v.1 (New York: Viking, 1992), pp. 449–476. Cooke discusses the relationship of Eleanor and Hickok. See also Nancy Hoffman, *Eleanor Roosevelt and the Arthurdale Experiment* (North Haven, CT: Livet Press, 2001). This book is directed to a younger audience. Some of Eleanor's own recollections are included in Eleanor Roosevelt, *This I Remember* (New York: Harper Brothers, 1949), pp. 126–127.
7. Letter from potential homesteaders to Eleanor Roosevelt, 18 October 1933. Archives and Manuscripts 2178, WVRC.
8. Blanche Cooke, *Eleanor Roosevelt*, p. 403.
9. Eleanor Roosevelt's ideas can be seen in a proposed article for *Liberty Magazine*, pp. 1–12. This piece was a response to an article in *Harper's* April 1935 issue attacking the homestead concepts and comparing it to "a state of serfdom." p. 1. Eleanor Roosevelt Papers [ERP] Franklin Delano Roosevelt Presidential Library, Hyde Park, New York. In this piece she gives a concise history of how Arthurdale came to be.
10. Eleanor Roosevelt, "Homesteaders—W.Virginia," An article for possible publication in *Liberty Magazine*, 1935. United States Department of the Interior. Record Group 48 1-277 Box 503. National Archives, Washington, D.C., p. 3.
11. Elsie Clapp, *The Use of Resources*, p. 8.
12. Elsie Clapp, *Community Schools in Action*, p. 72, *The Use of Resources*, p. 8. The Morgantown newspaper, the *Dominion News*, had an article on the plan, 12 February 1934.
13. *Community Schools in Action*, p. 397. Agger represented Rexford Tugwell, head of the Resettlement Administration, Division of Subsistence Homesteads. Pickett headed Quaker relief efforts in the north central region of West Virginia. Through the efforts of the AFSC, the displaced miners had learned about subsistence gardening and furniture making. Ryan and Mitchell were well-known figures in progressive education.
14. *Dominion News*, 12 February 1934. Another article, "First Lady Will Return Again to Farm," *Dominion News*, 26 February 1934, lists this rather large group. The list was a Who's Who of West Virginia educators at the time. See *Community Schools in Action*, p. 387.
15. Notes on the Arthurdale School 1934–1935. ERCP 21/3/6.
16. Clarence Pickett, *Far More Than Bread: An Autobiographical Account of Twenty-Two Years' Work with the American Friends Service Committee* (Boston: Little, Brown, and Co., 1953), p. 58. Federal officials discussed whether to send the Arthurdale children to local schools or to build a school in the community. See "Minimum Budget Required to Complete 125 houses—subsistence homestead project Reedsville, West Virginia." Department of the Interior. Record Group 48. 1–277 Box 503. National Archives. Washington, D.C. Pickett was instrumental in the relief efforts in the Scotts Run area and strongly supported Elsie to head the Arthurdale School.
17. "Mrs. Roosevelt's Project Defended Here," undated newspaper article 1933–1934. ERCP 21/4/2. The quote from the miner occurs in Clapp, *Community Schools in Action*, p. 116. Eleanor Roosevelt in *This I Remember* (New York: Harper Brothers, 1949), recalled a 1939 press conference when she noted the people of Scotts Run were walking around like

they were dead. "They were alive," she wrote, "but they were dead as far as any real living was concerned," p. 129.
18. Clapp, *Use of Resources*, p. 14.
19. Gugler was a member of the architectural firm of Gugler and Toombs at 101 Park Avenue in New York City. Gugler eventually left the Arthurdale project, and Steward Wagner took over the supervision and construction of the school complex. See letter from Benjamin Betts to M.L. Wilson, November 28, 1933. RG 96 Entry 9 Box 3. Records of the Department of Interior. National Archives, College Park, Maryland.
20. For biographical information on Jessie Stanton, see ERCP Misc. Fragmentary materials. 21/3/11. Joyce Antler's *Lucy Sprague Mitchell* also had some information, pp. 327–329. Cremin's *Transformation of the School* also mentions Stanton and her work with Caroline Pratt, pp. 204–205, 377. Stanton was the official director of the nursery school at Arthurdale, but she was not present for the day-to-day operation. Day-to-day operation fell to Stanton's recommendation, Mary Elizabeth Sedman.
21. Clapp, *Use of Resources*, p. 15.
22. See "Deaths," *New York Times*, 9 August 1934, p. 17 for the notice of Sarah Ripley Clapp's death.
23. O.B. Smart was the on-site director from the federal government to oversee the construction and advise on agricultural matters on the homestead community. It did not seem to be a priority for the federal planners to have adequate school facilities the first year. During Elsie's tenure at Arthurdale there were three project managers at Arthurdale; Bushrod Grimes, O.B. Smart, and G.M. Flynn. See Haid, *Arthurdale*, p. 339.
24. *Use of Resources*, p. 16.
25. Ibid., p. 17.
26. Ibid., p. 21. Impetigo is a contagious infection of the skin. Scabies is a contagious itch caused by mites or parasites.
27. Ibid., p. 27.
28. Ibid., p. 37. For a more comprehensive view of the medical care in the Scotts Run area, see Sandra Barney, "You Get What You Pay for," in *A New Deal for America*. This article discusses how poorly the residents of Scotts Run were treated by area physicians, pp. 25–44.
29. Interview Fletcher Collins. Elsie's contention supporting square dancing is supported by music and drama teacher, Fletcher Collins. One of Eleanor Roosevelt's favorite activities at Arthurdale was square dancing. She can be seen participating in the dances in *McCall's Magazine*, October 1958 issue, p. 58.
30. *Use of Resources*, p. 29.
31. More specific information about the activities of the first graders can be found in *Community Schools in Action*, pp. 132–133. Elsie used information from the semester reports of the teachers to write *Community Schools in Action* and *The Use of Resources*. I have not been able to locate any of the teachers' reports she used.
32. *Use of Resources*, p. 39.
33. Ibid.
34. Ibid., p. 40.

35. Sheffield reported in her yearly report that by February the children were now reading at grade level with two children above grade level. She used a reading test to determine her conclusion but does not list the type of instrument used. *Use of Resources*, p. 48.
36. Ibid.
37. Perlstein and Stack, "Building a New Deal Community," p. 221.
38. *Community Schools in Action*, pp. 143, 151.
39. *Use of Resources*, p. 50.
40. Ibid., p. 151. Also see *Community Schools in Action*, p. 154–156 for another description of this group.
41. Elsie compiled this information from Collins' January 1935 report, his diary record, and from an account he wrote about the homesteader's cultural resources. See Community School in Action, pp. 218–272 for this report titled, *Cultural Resources at Arthurdale*.
42. Fletcher Collins, "Cultural Resources at Arthurdale," in *Community Schools in Action*, p. 219.
43. *Use of Resources*, p. 55.
44. George Beecher's accounts of his experiences are included in *Community Schools in Action*, pp. 273–331; and in *The Use of Resources*, pp. 55–61. The upper high school was generally 9–12 grades, although due to size grades were usually combined.
45. See *Community Schools in Action*, pp. 397–399 for the complete Arthurdale staff from 1934 to 1936. Adolph Ipcar would marry Dahlov Zorach, the daughter of William Zorach.
46. George Beecher, "Arthurdale High School," in *Community Schools in Action*, p. 280.
47. Clapp, *Community Schools in Action*, p. 281.
48. *Use of Resources*, p. 62.
49. Ibid., p. 63
50. Ibid.
51. Ibid., p. 65.
52. Ibid., p. 66.
53. This form of entertainment was popular during the time Jim Crow still ruled in West Virginia. While African Americans and whites worked together in the mines of Scotts Run, there was a prejudice among white miners that blacks were strike breakers brought in from the South.
54. "Mrs. Roosevelt Earns at Rate Near Husband's," *New York Times*, 3 March 1935, p. 1. The President was reported to earn $75,000 annually.
55. The square dance was a favorite for Eleanor Roosevelt and she often participated. Evidence of her dancing can be seen in the *McCall's* October 1958 issue, p. 58.
56. *Use of Resources*, p. 80.
57. Ibid., p. 82.
58. Ibid., p. 83.
59. *Community Schools in Action*, p. 299. Due to the darkness of the coal camps and to health concerns, the architects sought to make structures accessible to air and sunlight to improve the health of the children, who often suffered from respiratory illness. The nursery school with its large porches and windows is a prime example of this.
60. See proposed budget for Reedsville Experimental Village. West Virginia Regional Collection. West Virginia University Libraries. Folder 4, 8 January 1934. This proposal contains information on the equipment to be purchased and the graded reductions in construction costs from $40, 000 to $35, 000.

61. *Community Schools in Actions*, p. 301.
62. Ibid., p. 302. Architect Steward Wagner describes the school buildings and project in "School Buildings: Arthurdale, West Virginia," *Progressive Education* 15 (April 1938), pp. 304–319. Elsie was editor of *Progressive Education* at this time.
63. *Community Schools in Action*, p. 216.
64. *Use of Resources*, p. 96.
65. *Community Schools in Action*, p. 153.
66. *Use of Resources*, p. 105.
67. *Community Schools in Action*, p. 159.
68. Elsie makes no reference to the work of Nell Rider or Susan Gross in either *Use of Resources* or *Community Schools in Action*, the best documentation of her work at Ballard and Arthurdale.
69. *Use of Resources*, p. 113.
70. *Community Schools in Action*, p. 116.
71. *Use of Resources*, p. 124.
72. The older high school students and some of the young adults were constantly plagued by the lack of job prospects following graduation. This concern led to George Beecher and Fletcher Collins writing a grant to investigate the possibility for helping the students develop or find employment. The "Proposal for Field Research Work in Rural Community High School and Adult Education at Arthurdale," written and developed by the teachers, listed several possibilities for investigation such as honey bee production, diary and milk production, raising poultry, plant physiology, and the possibility of a small glass-making operation. The idea was to link the teaching of subject matter such as chemistry, biology, botany, etc., as well as provide possible avenues for employment. See *Use of Resources*, pp. 163–164. Unfortunately these plans came to a halt when it became known by July 1936 that the school would become part of the Preston County system the following year.
73. Examples of the newspaper can be seen at the Arthurdale archives of Arthurdale Heritage Inc., in Arthurdale, West Virginia. No complete set of the papers exists. Collins donated the papers in his possession to Arthurdale.
74. *Use of Resources*, pp. 126–127.
75. John Martin Taylor, "A Study of the Graduates of Arthurdale High School to Determine the Influence of High School Training on Occupational Adjustment" (MA thesis, West Virginia University, 1941), p. 78.
76. This may have been true for many graduates of progressive secondary schools, but progressives believed the Eight-Year Study vindicated them and refuted the charges of the traditionalists. As far as the progressive were concerned, their students did just as well as those educated in traditional environments. There are problems in the methodology of the Eight-Year Study and the types of schools involved in the study. They consisted of private schools, lab schools, and a few public schools. None remotely resembled the student population at Arthurdale in class and poverty. See Cremin, *Transformation of the School*, pp. 253–256. The study was sponsored by the PEA and directed by the Commission on the Relation of School and College, p. 251.

77. John Dewey, *School and Society and The Child and the Curriculum* (Chicago: University of Chicago Press, 1990), p. 10.
78. See Eleanor Roosevelt, "My Day," 28 January 1936. Reedsville, W.Va. Eleanor Roosevelt Papers, FDRL. This column was popular and widely circulated in the press. E.E. Agger of the Resettlement Administration, Nancy Cook, and Clarence Pickett of the American Friends Service committee were among the contingent.
79. For examples of this, see Elsie Clapp to Eleanor Roosevelt, 24 August 1935 Eleanor Roosevelt Manuscripts [ERM] 4, pp. 264–265. Also see Elsie Clapp to Eleanor Roosevelt, May 1936, ERM 4: pp. 410–411.
80. Wirt's critique appears in the local Morgantown paper, *Dominion Post*, 6 April 1934. See also *Dominion Post*, 10 April 1934 for further information. Wirt's criticism shows the great diversity in the progressive education camp. Politically, Elsie was among the moderates, avoiding the extremes of Wirt's administrative progressivism and Counts' social reconstructionism and critique of the capitalism order. See Ron Cohen, *Children of the Mill*, for more information on Wirt and his work in the Gary Schools.
81. Martha Strayer, "Head of Reedsville School Taking Active Part in Discussions of Education There," ERCP. Misc. fragmented materials on Arthurdale 21/3/11. Elsie kept numerous newspaper clippings in a scrapbook but usually did not note the source of information.
82. See Stephen Haid, "Arthurdale's Greatest Failures and Successes," in Bryan Ward, *A New Deal for America*, pp. 65–98, for a description of the various economic projects considered and some implemented. Eleanor Roosevelt wanted to locate industry at Arthurdale and often escorted potential investors to the community. It was estimated at the time that the homesteaders would need $1,000.00 per year income to make ends meet. See also the Committee for Economic Recovery, "Arthurdale: A Partial Pattern for a New American Way of Life." Report prepared for President Roosevelt (1937), pp. 1–2. See also "Employment at Arthurdale," 30 July 1937. Record Group 96, National Archives.
83. Haid, "Arthurdale's Greatest Failures," p. 87.
84. *Community Schools in Action*, p. 390. Elsie's salary was provided through these contributions and her group of teachers. Elsie was making close to $6,000.00 annually. Baruch and Eleanor Roosevelt also supplemented the nursery school, which all received some Works Progress Administration funds, teaching materials, and expenses for running the school. Officially, Elsie was actually employed by the Department of the Interior and received $1.00 per year for her services. See Employment and biographical data ERCP 21/1/2. Elsie wrote, "The decision to turn the school over to the county was also discussed with the West Virginia Advisory School committee, and plans were made for carrying on the school. The Committee voted unanimously to continue the School as a community school…" p. 390.
85. See William Brooks, "Arthurdale—A New Chance," *Atlantic Monthly* (February 1935), p. 199.
86. Anna Roosevelt, *The Evolution of a Reformer* (Boston: Houghton Mifflin, 1968), p. 160.
87. Dan Anderson, "Prospective Homesteaders Put through Stiff Examination" (19 July 1934), ERCP 21/3/11. No source.
88. For a discussion of the NAACP response to this, see Daniel Perlstein, "Community and Democracy in American Schools: Arthurdale and the Fate of Progressive Education,"

Teachers College Record 97 (Summer 1996), pp. 625–650. See Du Bois' concerns in "Subsistence Homestead Colonies," *Crisis* (February 1934), p. 85.
89. Bernard Baruch to Eleanor Roosevelt, 22 June 1936. ERM Microfilm Reel 4, p. 416. FDRL.
90. Elsie Clapp to Eleanor Roosevelt, 4 October 1936, ERM Microfilm Reel1, p. 302. FDRL.
91. Haid, "Arthurdale's Greatest Failure," p. 91.
92. *Community Schools in Action*, p. 89.
93. During FDR's administration, Eleanor invited all the graduates of the Arthurdale high school to spend a day at the White House.
94. Eleanor Roosevelt, "My Day," 25 June 1936. Reedsville, W. Va. ERP. FDRL.
95. Eleanor Roosevelt, "For Release Wednesday 8 July and Thereafter," ERP. FDRL.
96. *Use of Resources*, p. 164.
97. Adolph Ipcar to Sam Stack, 9 November 1998. Elsie knew the Ipcars and rented a cottage from them in her later years. Ipcar had a good sense of Elsie's career and understood her from a more personal perspective.
98. *Use of Resources*, p. 139. Elsie never made mention of Dean Russell's contributions. Her colleague and friend William H. Kilpatrick despised Russell and found him no friend to progressive education. See John Bienke, *And There Were Giants in the Land: The Life of William Heard Kilpatrick* (New York: Peter Lang, 1998), pp. 225–256 for how Russell treated Kilpatrick. Elsie had great respect for Kilpatrick.
99. John Dewey to J.A. Rice, General file box 7 (1933–1936) Black Mountain College Papers. Special Collections, Morris Library, Southern Illinois University. I thank the staff at the Center for Dewey Studies for locating this comment from Dewey. Eleanor Roosevelt remembered the three days in April as "gray and rainy," but she also reported that the National Advisory Committee was so interested in the efforts of the school that they hardly noticed the weather. See Eleanor Roosevelt, "My Day," 7 April 1936. Reedsville, W. Va. ERP. FDRL.
100. *Use of Resources*, p. 165.

Chapter Twelve

1. Elsie Ripley Clapp, *Community School in Action* (New York: Viking Press, 1939). The book was reprinted in 1971 as part of a series of work in American Education: Its Men, Ideas and Institutions. The advisory editor for the series was Lawrence Cremin, Frederick Barnard Professor of Education at Teacher College, Columbia University. This book was reprinted from a copy of the 1939 text housed in the Newark Public Library. The ERCP are sparse in materials after Elsie's departure from Arthurdale and her memoirs stop around the time she began the Ballard School in Kentucky. The last twenty years of her life are exceedingly difficult to chronicle.
2. Elsie Clapp to Eleanor Roosevelt. December 1936. Box 1418. Eleanor Roosevelt Papers. Franklin Delano Roosevelt Library. [hereafter ERP/FDRL] This letter is in response to a Christmas remembrance Eleanor Roosevelt sent Elsie. Elsie also notes her concerns about Franklin Jr.'s recent sinus infection.

3. Eleanor Roosevelt to Elsie Clapp. 8 January 1937. Box 1418. ERP. At the time Elsie was living at 160 Claremont Avenue in New York.
4. F.L. Redefer was Executive Secretary of the Progressive Education Association at this time, Graham, *Progressive Education*, p. 116.
5. Elsie Clapp to Eleanor Roosevelt. 24 June 1937. ERP. When Elsie accepted the position the journal, often called a magazine, was published monthly, October through May. A year's subscription was $3.00 and a two-year subscription was $5.00. The editorial and professional offices for the Progressive Education Association were located at 310 West 90th Street, New York City. The files on the Progressive Education Association at the University of Illinois do not have information on Elsie during her editorship of the journal.
6. Eleanor Roosevelt, "My Day," 3 August 1937. ERP. Mrs. Roosevelt's column was syndicated nationwide and was popular. She began the column in 1936. See Blanche Cooke, *Eleanor Roosevelt (1884–1933)* (New York: Viking, 1992), p. 489.
7. This is the only reference I have located by Elsie to the death of her brother Lawrence. Elsie Clapp to Eleanor Roosevelt. 7 August 1937. ERP.
8. Graham, *Progressive Education*, p. 86. Counts represented the more radical left wing of progressive education. He articulated a position of using the school as a tool of social reform and felt it necessary to "impose" or "indoctrinate" students to the values and traits of democratic society. Elsie had expressed her concerns about Counts' views in her response to his article, "Dare the School Build a New Social Order."
9. Lois Meek, Notes, October 1937, 14, *Progressive Education*, p. 472.
10. Elsie Clapp to Eleanor Roosevelt. 16 July 1937. ERP.
11. Eleanor Roosevelt did not respond as quickly as Elsie would have liked and there were several letters detailing their correspondence on the issues. See Elsie Clapp to Eleanor Roosevelt 16 July 1937. ERP. Elsie Clapp to Eleanor Roosevelt 27 July 1937. ERP. This letter includes seven of the nine questions published in the October issue, *Progressive Education*, p. 407. Mrs. Roosevelt sent the last two questions in a later letter, 7 August 1937. ERP.
12. Elsie also wished to have responses from Secretary of Labor Sidney Hillman and a Mr. Filene, an industrial leader, but they were not included. Elsie Clapp to Eleanor Roosevelt 7 August 1937.
13. Elsie Clapp, Notes and News, *Progressive Education*, 14 p. 564. The November issue included articles on questions progressive education must answer, the education of teachers, and the school and classroom experiences. *Progressive Education*, pp. 489–576.
14. *Progressive Education*, 14, pp. 578–676.
15. See "Outlook of Youth in America: Report of Panel Discussion," *Progressive Education* 14 (December 1937), p. 595.
16. Ibid., p. 596.
17. Marni Mitchell's poem was titled *Plowing*. Dahlov Zorach wrote about forests; pp. 34–35. Both were students in Group XI at the City and Country School. Their work was also published in the book *The Printer's Pie* (1929). See also in this issue Verna Warren, "The Creative Work of a Child," *Progressive Education* 15 (January 1938), pp. 36–41. And Flora J. Arnstein, "The Growth of Poetic Criteria in Children," in the same issue.

18. Dahlov Zorach will become the wife of Adolph Ipcar, who taught at Arthurdale. Elsie will spend her later years living near the Ipcars in New Hampshire.
19. John Dewey, *My Pedagogic Creed*, EW 5: 86–87.
20. John Childs, *The Educational Frontier*. Chapter II. The Social Economic Situation and Education (New York: Century, 1933), p. 89.
21. Elsie Ripley Clapp, "Schools Socially Functioning," 15 *Progressive Education*, p. 90.
22. At the time Pickett wrote the article he was the Education Secretary of the American Friends Service Committee in Philadelphia.
23. See George Beecher, "Resources for Learning in Alamance County, North Carolina," pp. 140–142. Fletcher Collins, "Cultural Resources in America," pp. 147-151, and Carson Ryan "Science with the Eastern Cherokee Indians," *Progressive Education* 15 (January 1938), pp. 143–146. Elsie's friend from graduate school, Dorothy Brewster, contributed a book review on "Famine" by Liam O'Flaherty. At the time of publication, Beecher was a professor in the Department of Education at Elon where Collins was head of the English department. Ryan was head of the science department at Central High on the Cherokee Indian Reservation in Cherokee, North Carolina.
24. George Dykhuizen, *The Life and Mind of John Dewey*, p. 172.
25. Elsie Clapp, "Facts and Figures," *Progressive Education* 15 (April 1938), pp. 297–300. This issue also contains a book review from Elsie's nephew David Moffat Myers II, the son of Elsie's sister Marjorie and James Myers. At the time he was becoming a noted photographer and his article was titled, "Making Pictures with the Miniature Camera."
26. Ibid., p. 298.
27. Ibid., p. 300.
28. Elsie is playing with the term used by Counts and other reconstructionists drawn from his 1932 address to the PEA, "Dare the School Build a New Social Order?"
29. Steward Wagner, "School Buildings: Arthurdale, West Virginia," *Progressive Education* 15 (April 1938), pp. 304–319. Wagner was a member of the architectural firm of Fellheimer and Wagner. During the mid 1930s he was in charge of all architectural and engineering work for the Resettlement Administration. Elsie will include many of these photographs in her book *Community Schools in Action* published the following year, 1939.
30. See cover page, *Progressive Education* 15 (May 1938).
31. Robert Westbrook, *John Dewey and American Democracy*, p. 391. See also Thomas Alexander, *John Dewey's Theory of Art, Experience and Nature* (New York: SUNY Press, 1987) and Dewey's *Experience and Nature* and *Art as Experience* later works 10: 9 (1934).
32. John Dewey, *Art as Experience* (New York: Milton and Balch, 1934), p. 81.
33. William Zorach, "The Arts," *Progressive Education* 15 (May 1938), pp. 370–378.
34. Zorach was also an important founder of the Provincetown Players and saw drama as a means of creativity and imagination. See Robert Sarlos, *Jig Cook and the Provincetown Players: Theatre in Ferment* (Amherst: University of Massachusetts, 1982), p. 9.
35. See Patricia Graham, *Progressive Education*, p. 100.
36. Elsie Ripley Clapp, News and Notes, *Progressive Education* 15 (May 1938), p. 423.
37. See *Progressive Education* 15 (October 1938), p. 477 for the photograph of an Arthurdale child lying on a cot. This picture was part of an article by Grace Landgon, Developing a WPA Nursery School," pp. 472–484.

NOTES

38. Eleanor Roosevelt, "A Child's Life," *Progressive Education* 15 (October 1938), p. 451.
39. These concerns about early childhood education expressed by Eleanor Roosevelt and Elsie are not fully addressed until the passage of the Civil Rights Act of 1964, the Economic Opportunity Act, and legislation leading to meeting the health and poverty needs of children. The Head Start program is the outstanding example. This issue also included a book review by Margaret Collins, wife of Arthurdale teacher Fletcher Collins, *Progressive Education*, p. 508.
40. This issue contains reviews of Dewey's *Experience and Education* published in 1938 as well as Boyd Bode's *Education at the Crossroads*, pp. 572–573.
41. Carson Ryan, Editorial, *Progressive Education* 16 (January 1939), p. 6.
42. George Counts, "The Current Challenge and Practice of Democracy," *Progressive Education* 16 (February 1939), p. 91.
43. Alice Keliher, "Frontiers of Democracy, " *Progressive Education* 16 (February 1939), p. 131. Keliher was the Chairwoman of the Commission on Human Relations of the Progressive Education Association. This issue also contains a tribute to progressive pioneer Marietta Johnson, of the Edgewood School, but best known for work at Fairhope, Alabama, pp. 117–118.
44. John Dewey, *Experience and Education* (New York: Kappa Delta, 1938).
45. Photo of Young Girl-Ready. *Progressive Education* 16 (April 1939), p. 224.
46. Jessie Stanton, "What is Education for the Child Before He Is Six?" *Progressive Education* 16 (April 1939), pp. 234–241.
47. See also George Beecher's review of Lancelot Hogben, "Science for the Citizen," *Progressive Education* 16 (April 1939), pp. 282–283. Ellen Steele Reece, "An Interesting Age to Teach," pp. 234–241.
48. Carson Ryan, Editorial, *Progressive Education* 16 (May 1939), p. 304.
49. For articles supporting this theme see Ernest Melby, "Creative Human Relations," *Progressive Education* 16 (May 1939), pp. 305–307. Jane Welling, "The Place of the Arts in the Progressive School Program," pp. 308–313 and Freda Pepper, "Creative Expression for All Children," pp. 314–319. Leni Reifenstahl's *Triumph Of The Will* documentary film of the Nazi Nuremberg rallies was the most infamous use of art to express the National Socialist message.
50. Elsie Clapp, *Community Schools in Action*, p. v. Elsie attempted to use fictitious names of the adults and children of both Ballard and Arthurdale.
51. Ibid.
52. Ibid., p. vi.
53. Ibid., p. vii. Dewey visited Arthurdale only once, on April 6, 7, and 8, 1936.
54. Ibid. p. viii.
55. Ibid., p. x.
56. The review is from a typed copy in the ERCP, 21/2/28, titled "Review of Community Schools in Action," Samuel Everett, *Curriculum Journal* 11 March 1940, Nashville, Tennessee. The ERCP also contains a typed response from Dewey to Everett dated April 29, 1940.
57. Everett's review, *Community Schools in Action*, ERCP 21/2/28, p. 2.
58. Ibid.

59. John Dewey to Samuel Everett. 29 April 1940. ERCP 21/2/28.
60. Ibid.
61. Siegfried, *Pragmatism and Feminism*, p. 65.
62. John Dewey, *The Public and Its Problems*, LW 2: 368.
63. See John Dewey and others to Franklin D. Roosevelt, June 1942. Record Group 48. National Archives, 1-277, Box 500. This is a letter signed by Dewey and others in support of Odell Waller, an African American sentenced to die on 19 June 1942. The letter was generated through the Workers Defense League under the direction of George S. Counts. Record Group 48 contains documents from the Department of the Interior.
64. Eduard Lindeman, "Book Review of Community Schools in Action," *Progressive Education* 16 (November 1939), p. 522.
65. Ibid.
66. Eleanor Roosevelt also noted the publication of *Community Schools in Action* in her February 28, 1940 My Day Column. She wrote: "If you happened to be interested in the effect that schools can have on the growth of communities, I think you will enjoy reading Miss Elsie Clapp's book *Community Schools in Action*. She is a most interesting and unique person who did a remarkable piece of work in two different schools for the communities in which she lived." Eleanor Roosevelt, "My Day," 28 February 1940. ERP.
67. Elsie Clapp to Eleanor Roosevelt, 17 January 1940. ERP.
68. Elsie Clapp to Eleanor Roosevelt, 20 January 1940. ERP.
69. Elsie Clapp to Eleanor Roosevelt, 1 January 1942. ERP. Danilevsky and Davis were workers supported by the American Friends Service Committee at Arthurdale. They were also living in Chapel Hill at the time. Davis eventually became County Relief Administrator. She was also a specialist in childcare and nursery schools. See *Community Schools in Action*, p. 69.
70. Elsie Clapp to Eleanor Roosevelt, 20 May 1943. ERP.
71. See Eleanor Roosevelt to Edgar Kaiser, 18 June 1943; Elsie Clapp to Eleanor Roosevelt 14 June 1943, Elsie Clapp to Eleanor Roosevelt 22 June 22 1943. ERP. At the time Elsie was residing at 102 East 22nd Street, New York, and spent some time at the home of her sister Mrs. James Myers [Marjorie] at 76 Irving Place.
72. ERCP. 21/1/2 Application to Connecticut State Teachers College.
73. Eduard Lindeman to Elsie Clapp, 25 March 1947. ERCC. This was a recommendation letter from Lindeman supporting Elsie's grant request. Such as request from the Guggenheim Foundation might have secured around $2,400.00. Carson Ryan, Kenan Professor of Education at the University of North Carolina, also wrote a letter of support for Elsie to the Guggenheim Foundation. For a copy of the letter see ERCP 21/1/3. Apparently Elsie had angered Dewey in pushing him to write a letter for her to the foundation during the summer of 1946. In a note to him she apologized for her behavior and congratulated him on his marriage to Roberta Lowitz. One senses she was not confident she would receive support for writing her book on the use of resources. See Elsie Clapp to John Dewey, 18 December 1946. John Dewey Papers. 102/15/8. Special Collections, Morris Library, Southern Illinois University, Carbondale.
74. Elsie Clapp to Ernest Melby, 8 April 1947. ERCC.
75. Ibid.

NOTES 301

76. Ernest Melby to Elsie Clapp. 14 April 1947. ERCC. All Elsie's references agreed to support her grant request. See John Dewey to Elsie Clapp, 14 April 1947, Dewey was in Key West, Florida, at the time. William H. Kilpatrick to Elsie Clapp, 10 April 1947, Edmund deS Brunner to Elsie Clapp, 10 April 1947. Elsie also asked Harold Rugg to write a letter of support since he had used her book *Community Schools in Action* in some of his classes.
77. John Dewey to Elsie Clapp, 19 July 1947. ERCC.
78. John Dewey to Elsie Clapp, 6 August 1947. ERCC.
79. Elsie Clapp to John Dewey, 20 August 1947. ERCC. Elsie asked Dewey to suggest in his correspondence to the Society that she would need approximately $600 to $900 to complete the work. As far as we know Dewey requested no changes to Elsie's synopsis of the book. John Dewey to Elsie Clapp, 26 August 1947. ERCC.
80. I.N. Thut to John Dewey, 26 August 26 1947. ERCC.
81. I.N. Thut to Elsie Clapp, 13 September 1947. ERCC.
82. John Dewey to Elsie Clapp, 21 September 1947. ERCC.
83. Elsie Clapp to I.N. Thut, 1 October 1947. At this time Elsie was living in Washington, Connecticut, but would soon move to 29 Linden Street in Exeter, New Hampshire, where she spent the rest of her life.
84. The proposed book on *The Use of Resources in Education* included in correspondence to I.N. Thut, 1 October 1947. ERCC.
85. Elsie Clapp to I.N. Thut, 28 October 1947. ERCC.
86. Elsie Clapp to W.H. Kilpatrick, 28 October 1947. ERCC.
87. W.H. Kilpatrick to Elsie Clapp, 29 October 1947. ERCC.
88. I.N. Thut to Elsie Clapp, 25 November 1947. ERCC.
89. John Dewey to Elsie Clapp, 3 December 1947. ERCC.
90. I.N. Thut to Elsie Clapp, 5 January 1948. Elsie Clapp to John Dewey September 1947. ERCC.
91. I.N. Thut to Elsie Clapp. 27 February 1948. ERCC.
92. Dorothy Dunkle to Elsie Clapp, 3 September 1948. ERCC. Elsie received her final $150.00 installment from the John Dewey Society in early September 1948.
93. Elsie Clapp to W.H. Kilpatrick, 14 October 1948. ERCC.
94. John Dewey to Elsie Clapp, 15 October 1948. ERCC.
95. W.H. Kilpatrick to Elsie Clapp, 19 October 1948. ERCC. The advisory committee for the book included Kilpatrick, Dewey and deS Brunner.
96. Elsie Clapp to John Dewey, 14 December 1948. ERCC.
97. John Dewey to Elsie Clapp, 11 0ctober, 1949. Elsie Clapp to W.H. Kilpatrick 27 October 1949. ERCC. Kilpatrick was heavily involved in Dewey's nineteeth birthday celebration.
98. Elsie Clapp to John Dewey, 27 October 1949. ERCC.
99. Ibid.
100. John Dewey to Elsie Clapp, 3 November 1949. See Elsie's response to Dewey, Elsie Clapp to John Dewey, 3 November 1949. ERCC.
101. Elsie Clapp to I.N. Thut, 8 November 1949. ERCC. I.N. Thut to Elsie Clapp, 4 November 1949. At the time of this correspondence Kilpatrick was president of the John Dewey Society, Harold Alberty was vice-president, and Thut was still executive-secretary trea-

surer.
102. John Dewey to Elsie Clapp, 11 January 1950; W.H. Kilpatrick to Elsie Clapp, 27 January 1950; Elsie Clapp to W.H. Kilpatrick, 12 February 1950 and W.H. Kilpatrick to Elsie Clapp, 9 March 1950. ERCC.
103. Elsie Clapp to John Dewey, 9 March 1950. Eduard Lindeman to Elsie Clapp, 9 May 1950. ERCC. Several of Elsie's paintings are in the possession of her niece Barbara Rahn. Elsie's fondness for landscapes is clearly evident.
104. Elsie Clapp to W.H. Kilpatrick, 23 May 1950. Roberta Dewey to Elsie Clapp, 10 June 1950. ERCC.
105. Ordway Tead to Elsie Clapp, 10 July 1950. ERCC. Tead was editor for Social and Economic Books for Harpers and Brothers. Interestingly, Tead had an early relationship with the Provincetown Players, a relationship Elsie was most likely not aware of. Tead (1891–1973) was considered an educator, editor, and author. He was an alumnus of Amherst College and was a strong proponent of women's rights. He had also lectured at Columbia University on industrial relations. See Sarlos, *Jig Cook and the Provincetown Players*, p. 197.
106. Elsie Clapp to W.H. Kilpatrick, 21 July 1950. Elsie also complained to Dewey. Elsie Clapp to John Dewey, 12 December 1950. ERCC. Elsie believed Tead was offended because he had little say over the book since Dewey and Kilpatrick had already reviewed it.
107. Elsie Clapp to Roberta Dewey, 16 October 1950. ERCC. Elsie also sent a note to Dewey at the same time. ERCC.
108. Agreement between the John Dewey Society and Elsie Ripley Clapp and Harper and Brothers for the publication of *The Use of Resources in Education*. Contract signed 20 November 1951. ERCC. The contract stipulated the publisher pay a royalty of 10% on the first 2500 copies sold, 12% on the next 2500 copies sold, and 15% on all copies sold thereafter. The book was to be between 125,000 and 127,000 words. It was also agreed that the publisher sell copies of the book at 40% off retail for use by the John Dewey Society and no royalty paid. The John Dewey Society was further to receive 50% of all royalties earned for the sale of the book until the total reached $600.00. All royalties after that went to Elsie. The contract also provided for a textbook edition for educational institutions at a reduced rate. I.N. Thut signed for the John Dewey Society.
109. Elsie Clapp to John Dewey, 19 March 1951. Kilpatrick supported Elsie's writing to Dewey. W.H. Kilpatrick to Elsie Clapp 21 March 1951. Dewey was quite ill from 1949–1951 and according to a note from Roberta Dewey to Elsie, Dewey had been diagnosed with flatulence, bronchitis and had had surgery for a hernia in Los Angeles. Roberta wrote to Elsie in confidence. Dewey did feel well enough to receive an honorary degree from Yale in 1951 and this did revive Elsie's hope that he would write the introduction for her. Elsie Clapp to W. H. Kilpatrick, 5 May 1951. ERCC.
110. Roberta Dewey to Elsie Clapp, 18 July 1951. Elsie Clapp to W.H. Kilpatrick 31 March 1952. Elsie was given eight complementary copies and received a forty percent discount on other copies she personally she personally requested. See Ordway Tead to Elsie Clapp, 16 April 1952. ERCC. Members of the John Dewey Society were also to receive copies as part of their membership and because the book was a yearbook.

111. Elsie Clapp to Ordway Tead, 19 April 1952. ERCC.
112. Elsie Clapp to John Dewey, 29 April 1952. ERCC.
113. See Harper and Brothers brochure announcing the publication of *The Use of Resources in Education*. ERCC. Other publications are also listed from the Society, most fifty cents to a dollar, much cheaper than Elsie's book that sold at four dollars.
114. Elsie Clapp to W.H. Kilpatrick, 3 May 1955. W.H. Kilpatrick to Elsie Clapp, 10 May 1955. Elsie Clapp to W.H. Kilpatrick, 13 May 1955. ERCC.
115. Ibid.
116. I.N. Thut to Elsie Clapp, 10 August 1955. Thut reiterated to Elsie there was no need for her to send the society funds, but she insisted. According to Elsie's notes from June 1952 to June 1955 the book sold 1510 copies. Total royalties for the period were one hundred thirty five dollars. ERCC.
117. Elsie made no personal response to Dewey's death, but it must have touched her deeply. There is no evidence that Elsie attended the ceremonies at the University of Vermont marking Dewey's death.

Chapter Thirteen

1. See the entire issue of *Progressive Education*, 29 (January 1952). Note the articles "Meeting the Attacks on Education," pp. 65–122. See also Archibald Anderson, "The Cloak of Respectability: The Attackers and Their Methods," pp. 69–70.
2. Cremin, *The Transformation of the School*, p. 351. Cremin is using the German terms for community and society discussed by many social theorists such as Ferdinand Tönnies in *Community and Society (Gemeinshaft and Gesellshaft)* (New York: Harper and Row, 1963).
3. John Dewey, *School and Society*, p. 29.
4. Mead, *Mind, Self and Society*, p. 423.
5. Joseph Hart, *The Discovery of Intelligence* (New York: Century, 1924), p. 382. Hart held a keen interest in the Danish folk high school, which also stressed a theory of community.
6. James Campbell, "Dewey's Conception of Community," in Larry Hickman, *Reading Dewey: Interpretations for a Postmodern Generation* (Bloomington: Indiana, University Press, 1998), p. 38. See also James Campbell, *Understanding John Dewey* (Chicago: Open Court, 1995) for a discussion of Dewey's philosophy. An obscure but interesting book on Dewey and community is Feodor Cruz, *John Dewey's Theory of Community* (New York: Peter Lang, 1987). See further John Dewey MW 9: 89.
7. Charlene Siegfried, *Pragmatism and Feminism*, p. 224 for Dewey's views on social ethics and imagination. Also Dewey LW 1: 138.
8. Samuel Everett, *The Community School*, (New York: Appleton-Century, 1938), p. vii. Everett edited this collection of essays.
9. Carmelita Hinton, "A School that Attempts to be a Community," *Progressive Education* 29 (March 1952), pp. 186–188.
10. Mildred Price, Book review of *The Use of Resources in Education*, *School and Society* 75 (3 May 1952), p. 285. See *Springfield Republican*, 8 June 1952, p. 9C. A review can also be found in the *United States Quarterly Book Review*, 8 p. 277.

11. See the entire issue *Progressive Education*, 31 (January 1954).
12. H. Gordon Hullfish, "Hail and Fairwell," *Progressive Education* 34 (July 1957), p. 119.
13. Cremin, *Transformation of the School*, p. 347.
14. Elsie Clapp to Una Sait, 14 February 1959. ERCC.
15. Some of these materials are housed in Special Collections, Morris Library, Southern Illinois University, which also houses professional papers from other progressive educators including Dewey, Childs, and Counts.
16. Judy Long, *Telling Women's Lives* (Subject/Narrator/Reader) (New York: NYU Press, 1999), p. 50.
17. Charlene Siegfried, *Pragmatism and Feminism*, p. 208.
18. Ibid., p. 57.
19. See Mary Hilton and Pam Hirsch, *Practical Visionaries: Women, Education and Social Progress, 1790–1930* (New York: Pearson, 2000), p. 16.
20. Lawrence Cremin, *Transformation of the School*, p. viii.
21. See Carole Gilligan, *In a Different Voice: Psychological Theory and Women's Development* (Cambridge: Harvard University Press, 1982), p. 43. Also see Mary Hilton and Pam Hirsch, *Practical Visionaries: Women, Education and Social Progress 1790–1930* (New York: Pearson, 2000).
22. John Dewey, MW 9: 87–89. See also an essay he wrote titled, "Teaching Ethics in the High School," EW 4: 57.
23. John Dewey, LW 13: 103. See James Campbell, "Dewey's Conception of Community," p. 40 for the original discussion of this point.
24. This information comes from a variety of sources. Adolph Ipcar to Sam Stack, 10 September 1998. At the time of this correspondence, Adolph Ipcar was living in the home Elsie rented from William and Marguerite Zorach when she spent summers in Robinhood, Maine. Ipcar was the son-in-law of the Zorachs and had married Dahlov. Ipcar notes Elsie's basic home in her later years was in Exeter, New Hampshire. I also spoke with Barbara Myers Rahn, Elsie's niece, about Elsie's declining health during this time. During the later years Elsie maintained residence under Mrs. Daniel Hartwell, who helped take care of Elsie during her elderly years. Barbara Rahn described Mrs. Hartwell as "a wonderful person, very caring, and we were all lucky Elsie could stay with her." Email correspondence, 5 March 2003. According to Mrs. Rahn, Elsie had lived in Connecticut prior to her move to New Hampshire. Elsie's great niece was married to a teacher at Exeter and it was just by happenstance Elsie was in Exeter at the same time.
25. "Miss Elsie Clapp, 86, Aide of John Dewey," *New York Times*, 31 July 1965. p. 21.

Index

A

Addams, Jane, 56
Ainslie, Fay, 144, 147, 157
Ainslie, Maude, 144, 147, 157
Allen, Arthur, 149, 157, 158, 163
Allen, Jane, 149, 157, 158, 163
Alexander, Thomas, 84
Antler, Joyce, 75
Aristotle, 79
Arthurdale School, 2, 37, 78, 132, 179; American Friends Service Committee, 189–192; Arthurdale Advisory School committee, 188–189, 206, 208; architecture of school, 216, 217; building the village, 193; curriculum integration, 202; design of school plant, 199–200; health issues of community, 192; high school curriculum, 196; homesteader discontent, 199; miner union conflict, 206; Mountaineer Craftsmen's Cooperative, 190, 199; National Advisory Committee, 189, 209; Native American studies, 193, 201, 202; parental involvement, 193; pioneer studies, 194; racial concerns, 198, 207; recreation in the community, 200; role of music and drama, 196, 198–199; school newspaper, 203; textile studies, 201, 203; West Virginia studies, 195
Ashley Hall, 89, 108; race and class, 89–90
Ashley, Jessie, 92, 94; Paterson strike Committee on Children, 95
Arts Students League, 36; See Coleman, Eleanor

B

Backus, Truman, 28
Bank Street College, 131; See Mitchell, Lucy Sprague
Ballard School (Roger Clark), Louisville, Kentucky, 2, 3, 37, 78, 87, 157, 160 161, 163–186, 190, 192, 207, 221–222; as a community school, 174, 179; behavior problems, 170; curriculum, 168–169; description of community life, 165; description of the school, 166; effects of the Depression, 176, 182; gender issues, 180; grant proposal, 178; high school, 171; list of teachers, 167; health issues of school, 175; Native American studies, 185; pioneer studies, 169, 171, 180; racial issues, 186; role of teachers, 167; school newspaper, 172; University of Louisville, 179, 183; use of local resources, 186
Bar Harbor, Maine, 111, 113; Elsie's business venture, 113–114, 117
Barnard College, 53, 68, 116
Baruch, Bernard, 205, 209
Beecher, Henry Ward, 7
biography, 1; biographical stories, 4; educational biography, 5
Bligh, Stanley, 63
Bode, Boyd, 81, 214
Boyd, William, 92, 99
Brewster, Dorothy, 70, 73; role in Paterson strike, 100
Brooklyn Heights, 5, 7; description of 164 Hicks Street, 8; description of 176 Hicks Street, 15
Brooklyn Heights Seminary, 53, 55–56, 92, 106, 107; relations with Florence Greer, 106, 108, 112–115, 116–118, 120, 123, 139, 144, 152
Burns, Lucy, 40, 42; description of, 42–43; role in women's suffrage, 102
Bush, Wendel, 59
Butler, Nicholas Murray, 59

C

Campbell, Jack, 1
Campbell, James, 84; on democratic community, 87
Carpenter, Agnes, 113
Cattell, James, 60
Chickering, William 56–57, 61
child centered, 181

City and Country School, 120, 123–125, 130, 134–137, 146; description of, 126–128

Clapp, Elsie Ripley, adolescent restlessness, 34; childhood memories, 15; community, 53; community school, 51, 79, 83, 86, 102, definition of, 184; *Community Schools in Action* (1939), 3, 221, 225, 228, 232; democratic community, 87; early education, 23; early friendships, 25, 33; education for social betterment, 109; in Exeter, New Hampshire, 231; family lifestyle, 26; feelings of insecurity, 8, 20, 27, 111; love of history, 11; interest in art, 30; illnesses, 43, 106, 122, 129, 144, 229, 233; philosophy of education, 67; doctoral preliminaries, 71–76; relations with grandparents, 11; relations with father, 13; relations with mother, 14; rural education, 183; sailing, 47, 53; scholarships, 36; selling Beleekware, 49; studies at Packer Institute, 29–30; teaching English, 56; *The Use of Resources in Education* (1952), 3, 226, 228, 231–233; Vassar friends, 49–50;

Clapp, Edith, 72, 76, 114

Clapp, Carrie, 56

Clapp, George Moseley, 12–13

Clapp, Lawrence, 12, 41, 45, 47, 51, 57–58, 69–70, 91, 105, 115, 135, 211

Clapp, Marjorie (Myers), 12, 41, 45, 47, 56, 58, 69, 91, 98, 107, 115, 134–135, 144

Clapp, Sarah Louise Ripley cult of womanhood, 13; death of, 190; Elsie's relations with, 14, 41; Vassar College, 13

Clapp, William Gamwell, 12; business trips, 19; death of, 105; stock trading, 26

Coleman, Eleanor, 30, 52

community school, 3, 133, 137, 174, 184, 186, 194, 199, 204, 207, 215, 216

Columbia University, 33, 153, 56, 86–87, 129, 225–226

Cooke, Blanche, 20

Counts, George, 182, 219
  Dare the School Build a New Social Order, 181
  Elsie's response to Counts, 181

Crampton, Clara, 32, 41–42, 52

Cremin, Lawrence, 1, 144

Cubberley, Ellwood, on the rural school, 164

Curtis Fellowship, Columbia University, 70

cult of domesticity, 5, 76

D

Daniel, Lou, 116–117, 136

democratic community, 2, 187, 207

Depression of 1893, 91, affects on railroads, 27; affects on Clapp family, 46

Depression (Great), 182 183; New Deal 186–187, 205; in West Virginia, 187; National Industrial Recovery Act, 187; Division of Subsistence Homesteads, 190

Denzin, Norman, 4

deS Brunner, Edmund, 226, 230

Dewey, John, 1, 3, 20, 52, 59, 60–61, 65, 68, 70, 76, 78–79, 81, 83–85, 97, 116, 120, 129 130, 134, 143–144, 158, 161,182, 211, 215, 217, 225, 228–229, 231, 233; advice on Rosemary Junior School, 135, 151; Arthurdale, 209; Ballard School, 163; Concept of self, 20; community school, 51, 204; cover of *Progressive Education*, 219; *Cyclopedia of Education*, 82; dedication to Dewey, 221; *Democracy and Education*, 78–79; Dewey lab school, 50; Elsie's courses with, 59, 69; *Ethics*, 64; on experience, 85; *Experience and Education*, 220; *Freedom and Culture*, 223; *How We Think*, 81, 83, 125, 132; influence on Elsie, 77 88; on intelligence, 85; on interests, 128; illnesses of, 230; Jersey City High School, 91; *My Pedagogic Creed*, 50, 77, 214; philosophy as method, 82; pragmatism, 80; reflection, 132; response to Elsie's doctoral preliminaries, 74 75; *School and Society*, 77, 204; *Schools of To-morrow*, 125; traits of democracy, 80; *The Public and Its Problems*, 223 224

Dewey, Roberta, 231

DuBois, W.E.B., 206

Dykhuizen, George, 50, 59, 81, 215

E

Eastman, Anis Ford, 51–52

Eastman, Crystal, 40, 51, 60; and women's suffrage, 102

Eastman, Max, 51, 60; association with Paterson strike; description of, 60; on Dewey's teaching, 66; review of Dewey's *How We Think*, 81
Edgewood School, 133
Eight Year Study, 219
Emerson, Ralph Waldo, 1
Everett, Samuel, 223; review of *Community Schools in Action*, 222

F

Finkelstein, Barbara, 4
Flynn, Elizabeth Gurley, 92 95; Committee on Children 95; response to Paterson Pageant, 100
Francis Parker School, 119

G

Gary School (Gary, Indiana), 91
Gatch, Elizabeth, 90, 108
Germantown, Pennsylvania, 44; Elsie's recuperation in, 45
Giese, Laura, 31
Giovanniti, Arturo, 93, 99; on Paterson Pageant, 100
Golin, Steve, 92, 96; *The Fragile Bridge*, 109
Goodwin, Sara, 116, 118, 124; see also Milton Academy
Goodsell, Willystine Elsie's book review, 63 64
Goodson, Ivor, 5
Greenwich Village, 109, 125–126
Greer, Edith, 115, 122, 144
Greer, Florence, 56, 60, 92, 97, 102, 104, 111, 113, 114, 116, 120, 123, 144, 152; see also Brooklyn Heights Seminary

H

Hall, Charles Cuthbert, and First Presbyterian Church, 10, 17, 105; Union theological Seminary, 17; funeral of William Gamwell Clapp, 106
Hartman, Gertrude, 143
Hauser, Mary, 126

Haywood, William (Bill), 93–94, 95, 99; at Paterson Pageant, 100; end of Paterson strike, 101
Hickok, Lorena, 188
Hine, Lewis, 153
Hocking, Agnes, 159, 161
Hook, Sidney, on Dewey's teaching, 65
Hopkins, Edna, 119, 135
Hopkins, James, 119, 211; at Ohio State, 124
Horace Mann School, 62
House, Florence, 139 140, 147, 150, 152

I

idealism, 82; Kantian idealism, 80
International Workers of the World (IWW), 92–93, 96, 100, 109

J

James, William, 47, 50, 81; *Principles of Psychology*, 77
Jersey City High School, 90, 92
Johnson, Harriet, 132, 136, 161, 215; description of childhood, 131
Johnson, Marietta, 133, 161, 215
John Dewey Society, 226–229, 232
Johnson, Samuel, 1
Jordan, Clark, 68, 70, 73, 74
Journal of Philosophy, Psychology, and Scientific Methods, 62–63, 67, 81

K

Keyes, Florence, 39
Kilpatrick, William H., 59, 158, 182, 219 220, 226–227, 229, 232
Kirchway, Frieda, 68
Krapp, George, 66

L

Lange, Dorothea, 213, 218
Light, Gertrude, 94
Lindeman, Eduard, 224, 230
Lovejoy, Arthur, 60
Lowndes, Mary, 134, 139, 147–148, 151, 159

M

Mayhew, Katherine Camp, 154–155
Marot, Helen, 125–126
Mead, George Herbert, 1
Miller, Janet, 4
Milton Academy, Massachusetts, 116–118, 120–122, 124, 136, 152
Mitchell, Lucy Sprague, 24, 123, 130, 132, 136, 161, 209, 214–215, 223
Montague, William, 58, 67
Moyer, Diana, 2
Myers, Moffat, 42

N

Naumberg, Margaret, 143–144
Newman, Joseph, 133
New psychology, 46
Nickerson, Marjorie, 29

P

Packer Collegiate Institute, 28–30, 39, 46
Parker School District, South Carolina, 1
Parker, Francis Colonel, 214
Paterson Silk Workers, 109, 115, 130, 182; Committee on Children, 95; Committee on One Hundred, 96, description of, 92; end of strike, 101; *New York Times* response, 97; Pageant at Madison Square Garden; relation to Lawrence strike, 95; sabotage, 100;
Petrick, Barbara, 91
Pierce, Charles Sanders, 50
Plato, 79
Pratt, Caroline, 120–121, 123, 125–126, 128, 131, 132, 136, 161, 215; also see City and Country School
Pratt Institute, 56
Progressive Education (journal), 143–144, 159, 169, 172, 174, 181, 211, 213, 220, 221, 231
progressive education, 82, 119, 127, 155, 173 174, 177
Progressive Education Association, 3, 87, 154, 173, 205, 211, 213, 217, 220
Provincetown Players, 103, 121
Provincetown art colony, 120, 144

R

Ratner, Joseph, 231
Red Cross Canteen, 111–112, 116, 124
Reed, John, 94; association with Paterson Pageant, 99
Ripley, Anna, 9
Ripley, George Clinton, 7, 8, 10–11
Ripley, Hannah Bass Penniman, 7, 8, 35
Ripley, Mary Churchill, 107
Robinson, James Harvey, 60–61
Roebling, Washington, 7
Rooney, Mary, 9
Roosevelt, Eleanor, 185–186, 188, 198, 204 206, 208–209, 211–212, 218, 221, 224, 225
Roosevelt, Franklin, 187, 207
Rosemary Junior School, 37, 83, 130, 135 137, 139 161, 163, 173, 174; school bulletin, 141–142; curriculum 141; disruptive parents, 140; role of subject matter, 142; staff problems, 152; history of, 133
Rothstein, Arthur, 213, 218
Rugg, Harold, 155, 182
Russell, James Earl, 59
Ruutz-Rees, Caroline, 133, 141, 143, 147, 151, 154, 158, 159; teaching skills, 148; also see Rosemary Junior School

S

Sanger, Margaret, 92–93, 94; Committee on Children, 95; planning the Paterson Pageant, 99; the *Woman Rebel*, 103
Santayana, George, 59
Sarlos, Robert, 121
Scotts Run, West Virginia, 190, 195, 202, 204, 207
Semel, Susan, 126
Shady Hill School, Massachusetts, 119, 159, 173
Shumaker, Ann, 155, 181, 182
Siegfried, Charlene, 2, 3, 223
social reconstructionists, 181, 215
Steffens, Lincoln, 94
Stanton, Jessie, 24, 131–132, 136; Arthurdale Nursery School, planning the nursery school, 191, 200; sharing

apartment with Elsie, 211; visit to Scotts Run, 190
Steele, Ellen, 119, 121–125, 134, 136, 139 140, 143, 149, 152–154, 167, 220; head of Rosemary Junior School, 159; use of subject matter, 146, study of textiles, 153; trip to Ballard School, 157; use of art and music, 145–150
Subsistence Homesteads, 185; also see Arthurdale
Surdovel, Catherine, 2

T

Taylor, Katherine, 119, 173; also see Shady Hill School
Teachers College, 59, 66, 86, 116, 119, 128, 134, 147, 149, 158, 177, 217, 225–226
Tead, Ordway, 230
Thut, I.N., 227, 229, 232, 233; also see John Dewey Society
Tresca, Carlo, 93–94
Tripp, Anne, 100

V

vanDoren, Carol, 68
Vassar College, 36, 39–53, 57, 59, 156–157, 159, 183; colleagues at Vassar, 52; courses taken, 40, 46; Vassar library, 41; petition to the Vassar faculty, 48; student teachers, 149

Vassar, Matthew, 39
Victorian era, 20; expectations of women, 24, Elsie's challenge to, 38
Vorse, Mary Heaton, 95–96, 101, 119

W

Walden School, New York, 143
Ward, Kate Morgan, 32
Ware, Caroline, 126
Whicher, George, 31
Wirt, William, 205
Women's suffrage, 87; marching in inaugural parade, 102; National American Women's Suffragist Association, 102
Woodbridge, F.J.E., 58, 60, 62, 67–70
Wylie, Laura, 39, 52
Weiler, Kathleen, 4
Welter, Barbara, 13

Z

Zilversmit, Arthur, 136–137
Zorach, Marguerite, 152; description of, 154
Zorach, William, 36, 120, 123, 124, 131, 214, 217; Birch Walthen School, 212; Rosemary Junior School, 140, 145, 147, 149, 152–154; Walden School, 121

HISTORY OF SCHOOLS & SCHOOLING

THIS SERIES EXPLORES THE HISTORY OF SCHOOLS AND SCHOOLING in the United States and other countries. Books in this series examine the historical development of schools and educational processes, with special emphasis on issues of educational policy, curriculum and pedagogy, as well as issues relating to race, class, gender, and ethnicity. Special emphasis will be placed on the lessons to be learned from the past for contemporary educational reform and policy. Although the series will publish books related to education in the broadest societal and cultural context, it especially seeks books on the history of specific schools and on the lives of educational leaders and school founders.

For additional information about this series or for the submission of manuscripts, please contact the general editors:

Alan R. Sadovnik
Rutgers University-Newark
Education Dept.
155 Conklin Hall
175 University Avenue
Newark, NJ 07102

Susan F. Semel
The City College of New York, CUNY
138th Street and Convent Avenue
NAC 5/208
New York, NY 10031

To order other books in this series, please contact our Customer Service Department:

800-770-LANG (within the U.S.)
212-647-7706 (outside the U.S.)
212-647-7707 FAX

Or browse online by series at:

www.peterlangusa.com